to the memory of
Douglas Godfrey Christian
1923–1974

The website for this book is at <www.spub.co.uk/tgi3/>

THE GENEALOGIST'S INTERNET

THE GENEALOGIST'S INTERNET

3rd Edition

PETER CHRISTIAN

the national archives

First edition published in 2001 by
the Public Record Office (1 903365 16 3)

Third edition first published in 2005 by
The National Archives
Kew, Richmond
Surrey, TW9 4DU
UK

www.nationalarchives.gov.uk

The National Archives (TNA) was formed when the Public Record
Office (PRO) and Historical Manuscripts Commission (HMC)
combined in April 2003.

Reprinted 2003, 2004, 2006

A catalogue card for this book is available from
the British Library

ISBN 1 903365 83 X

Cover images from left to right:
Wedding guest, 1892 (TNA: PRO COPY 1/408;
photographer Arthur Thomas Dean).
George Knight at his wedding, Gullane, 1963 (courtesy of George Knight).
Romany woman, 1903 (TNA: PRO COPY 1/460; photographer Oxley Grabham).
Crimean War veteran, Brecon, 1898 (TNA: PRO COPY 1/434;
photographer David Jenkins).
Victorian matron, 1860s (courtesy of Robert Pols; photographer Newell of York).
Child on postcard, 1940s (courtesy of Robert Pols; photographer unknown).

Photograph of the author, by Catherin Priest

Typeset by
Florence Production Ltd, Stoodleigh, Devon

Printed in the UK by
TJ International Ltd, Padstow, Cornwall

CONTENTS

PREFACE

The statistics tell us that a large majority of UK genealogists have internet access at home,[1] and many others no doubt do so from work or a local library, so this book assumes a reader who has at least basic familiarity with the internet, using email and a web browser. However, I have not assumed any experience of other internet facilities, nor any technical knowledge, so even the absolute internet novice should not be unduly baffled. The book is about what you can find online rather than on the technicalities of how it gets to you. All the same, there are one or two areas where it's useful to have some understanding of how things work (and why they sometimes don't), so there is detailed discussion of search engines, mailing lists, newsgroups and web publishing in the later chapters. The professional internet user will probably want to skip some of this, but the queries and problems which are raised in online discussion forums suggest that even quite seasoned internet users do not always exploit these resources as fully as they could.

This book also does not assume you are already an expert in genealogy, but it can't pretend to be a general introduction to researching your family tree, nor provide guidance in how to organize your research. The basics of family history are covered briefly in Chapter 2, 'First Steps', along with some recommended internet resources for the beginner, and the chapters relating to records explain why you might want to look at those records. But if you are completely, or fairly, new to family history you'll need a good book on offline genealogy (see p. 12 for recommendations).

CITING INTERNET ADDRESSES

In this book URLs (Uniform Resource Locators) for internet resources have been placed between angled brackets. According to strict citation stan-

---

1 By the end of 2004, according to research from Ofcom, 57% of UK adults had internet access at home (see <www.ofcom.org.uk/research/cm/jan2005_update/update.pdf>). In the September 2003 *Genealogists' Magazine* the SoG published a survey which showed 78% of the Society's UK members with home internet access.

dards, every internet resource should begin with a specification of its type: the National Archives home page on the World Wide Web should be cited as **<http://www.nationalarchives.gov.uk/>** rather than simply as **<www. nationalarchives.gov.uk>**. However, since web browsers manage perfectly well without the **'http://'** I have allowed myself to omit these. Newsgroup names are discussed in Chapter 15: although they may look similar to web addresses, either the context or the word newsgroup in the text will identify them correctly.

Any hyphen within a URL is an essential part of the reference, not a piece of ad hoc hyphenation. Some of the longer URLs in this text have been broken over two lines for typographical reasons, but the URL should be read as an unbroken sequence of characters – there are *never* spaces or line breaks in internet addresses.

Addresses for web pages are *partially* case sensitive. Anything up to the first / is not case sensitive; anything after that usually *must* be in the correct case. URLs are mostly all lower case, but note that Genuki in particular uses upper case for county abbreviations (e.g. LAN in all the Lancashire pages) and often has the first letter after a / in upper case.

In general, titles of websites have been indicated solely by initial capitals, while individual pages are between inverted commas. However, the distinction between a site and page is not always easy to make, and I wouldn't claim to have been thoroughly consistent in this respect.

Occasionally, a URL has been so long that I have given instructions on how to get to the page rather than give the full URL. Unfortunately, this tendency for long URLs seems to be increasing, as more and more sites deliver their pages from a database or content management system. The longest URL not cited in the text is 159 characters long, for a page on the Customs and Excise site. County Record Offices seem to have a particular propensity for unwieldy URLs.

In such cases the direct link is usually available on the website for this book at **<www.spub.co.uk/tgi3/>**, except where this would bypass a page the site owner needs you to see first.

▌DISAPPEARING RESOURCES

Internet resources are in a constant state of flux. Of the 1,100 or so links for the second edition of this book, about 15% had moved within two years (some more than once!), and around 40 sites or pages had disappeared entirely. Of the 750 URLs in the first edition, at least one third are no longer at the same address four years later. There is no reason to think that the material in this edition will be more stable, I'm afraid.

Of course, it is only to be expected that personal sites will move or vanish without warning as people change internet service provider or decide they no longer have the time to maintain them. But official and commercial sites, too, are regularly being redesigned and reorganized, and the old pages do not always redirect you to the new location as good practice demands.

With these sites, admittedly, you can be reasonably sure that the material is still there somewhere, and there's usually a site search facility to help. But it can be very hard to discover what has become of valuable resources made available by individuals.

For print, all this raises insurmountable problems, and it is something all internet books have to live with. But one of the advantages of the web is that links can be kept up to date, so on the website for this book at <www.spub.co.uk/tgi3/> there are links to all the resources mentioned in the text, and the aim is to keep those links current.

▌WHAT'S NEW IN THIS EDITION

The many resources that have moved or disappeared in the two years since the last edition of this book are one good reason for revision. But there have also been some important new sites. For example, the General Register Office at long last has a site of its own, and a new National Archives site, combining the Public Record Office and Historical Manuscripts Commission, was launched in summer 2004. In particular, the explosion in the amount of data available has continued. Civil registration and census material is now accessible from many more sites than two years ago. The millions of records from family history societies at FamilyHistoryOnline and the rise of the Online Parish Clerks schemes have increased the amount of material at parish level, too.

But there have also been more general online developments which affect the genealogist – major changes in the search engines, the spread of new techniques in web publishing, the increasing prominence of 'blogs', for example.

Another important factor has been the increasing availability of broadband in the home. At least one major site is introducing higher quality images alongside its existing offering to take advantage of this (see p. 84). Although broadband has not (or not yet) revolutionized the genealogical content available on the web, in the way that it has for music and film, it has meant that sites with high quality maps and photographs can be more readily recommended.

This all means a larger book. All in all there are over 150 additional links mentioned in this edition, taking the total to around 1,275.

▌ACKNOWLEDGEMENTS

Many of the new sites covered in this edition are here because someone drew them to my attention. While I can't thank everyone who has ever mentioned a site to me, there are some online publications which have been a regular source of new material: John Fuller's announcements of new mailing lists (p. 228), Dick Eastman's online newsletter (p. 309), and the Cyndi's List mailing list (p. 23) have all been invaluable. My fellow Genuki trustees have been particularly important in alerting me to new or at least not well known resources. It is also worth noting that coverage of internet resources in the family history magazines has increased significantly in the last two years, and this has been useful in keeping up to date.

I have to thank John Dawson for suggesting a number of corrections and improvements over the previous edition, and Roland Clare for some stylistic polishing.

Finally, since things are changing at such a rapid rate, I am particularly grateful to a number of the data services mentioned in Chapters 4 to 8, who have provided information on planned future developments, some of which will already have been launched in the gap between my writing and your reading.

CHAPTER 1

INTRODUCTION

GENEALOGY AND THE INTERNET

The steady growth in the number of people interested in family history
may have its roots in greater leisure time, or it may be a reaction to social
and geographical mobility. Recent television programmes on family history
and the use of DNA testing to trace migration patterns have certainly
contributed to a surge of interest. But above all it is closely related to the
growth of the internet and the fact that the majority of the population
now have internet access. While the internet has not changed the fundamental principles of genealogical research, it has changed the way in which
some of that research is done and made a huge difference in what the individual genealogist can do with ease.

Indexes to primary records, in many cases linked to a digitized image
of the original document, are increasingly available on the World Wide
Web. Even where records themselves are not online the ability to check
the holdings of record offices and libraries via the web means that a visit
can be better prepared and more productive. Those who have previously
made little progress with their family tree for lack of time or mobility to
visit archives can pursue their researches much more conveniently, with
access to an increasing range of records from their desktop. Likewise, those
who live on the other side of the world from the repositories which hold
records of their ancestors' lives can make progress without having to
employ a researcher. Online data is a boon, too, for anyone who has difficulty reading from microfilm or original records.

Archives have realized that the internet is also a remedy for some of
their pressing concerns: lack of space on their premises, how to make their
collections available while preserving them from damage, not to mention
the pressure from government to provide wider access. In addition, there
is the obvious commercial potential: online record transcriptions can attract
distant and, particularly, overseas users in large numbers, while even those

living less far away will use a charged service which saves them time and travel costs.

Genealogists also benefit from the ease with which messages and electronic documents can be exchanged around the world at effectively no cost. It is easier than ever to contact people with similar research interests, and even to find distant cousins. It is easier than ever, away from a good genealogy library or bookshop, to find expertise or help with some genealogical problem. And if you need to buy a book, there are genealogy bookshops with online catalogues and secure ordering.

Any information stored digitally, whether text or image, can be published on the web easily and more or less free of cost to both publisher and user. This has revolutionized the publishing of pedigrees and other family history information. It has allowed individuals to publish small transcriptions from individual records, material which it would otherwise be difficult to make widely available. Individual family historians can publicize their interests and publish the fruits of their researches to millions of others.

The internet has enhanced cooperation by making it possible for widely separated people to communicate easily as a group. While collaborative genealogy projects did not start with the internet, email and the web make the coordination of vast numbers of geographically distributed volunteers, such as the 8,000 or so involved in FreeBMD (see p. 51), much easier.

▊OFFLINE GENEALOGY

Inevitably, however, the explosion of the internet and what it has made possible for family historians has given rise to unrealistic expectations in some quarters. Stories of messages posted to mailing lists or newsgroups asking, 'Where will I find my family tree online?' are not apocryphal.[2]

The fact is that if you are only beginning your family tree, you will have plenty to do offline before you can take full advantage of what is online. For a start, because of privacy concerns, you won't find much online information about any ancestors born less than a century ago. Scotland has some more recent records online for marriages and deaths (see p. 63), but for England and Wales there are only *indexes* to twentieth-century birth, marriage and death records online. This means that in tracing the most recent generations most of the work must be done offline, though for living people you may well be able to find addresses, phone numbers and perhaps websites.

---

2 See 'Internet Genealogy' at <www.cyndislist.com/internet-gen.htm> for a look at some of the common misconceptions about what the internet can do for the genealogist.

But even without all the original records you need online, you can still expect to make contact with other genealogists who share your interests. To do this effectively, however, you will need to have established a family tree for the last three or more generations. The reason for this is that if you're going to discover others on the internet who have done research into your ancestors, they are not likely to be close relations. Most people know their first cousins, and at least know of the existence of their second cousins. So on the whole any new relatives discovered via the internet will be no closer to you than third cousins. A third cousin is a descendant of your great-great-grandparents, who were born perhaps 100 or so years before you. So unless you know the names of your great-great-grandparents and where they came from, you will not be in a position to establish that you are in fact related to someone who has posted their pedigree online.

Of course, if your surname is unusual, and particularly if you know where earlier generations of your family lived, you may be able to make contact with someone researching your surname and be reasonably certain that you are related. Or you may be lucky enough to find that someone is doing a one-name study of your surname. In this case, they may already have extracted some or all of the relevant entries in the civil registration records, and indeed may have already been able to link up many of the individuals recorded.

But, in general, you will need to do work offline before you can expect to find primary source material online and before you have enough information to start establishing contact with distant relatives.

However, one thing that is useful to every family historian is the wealth of general genealogical information and the huge range of expertise embodied in the online community. For the absolute beginner, the internet is useful not so much because there is lots of data online, but because there are many places to turn to for help and advice. And this is particularly important for those who live a long way away from their family's ancestral home.

All the same, it is important to remember that, whatever and whoever you discover online, there are many other sources for family history, both in print and in manuscript, which aren't on the web. If you restrict yourself to online sources you may be able to construct a basic pedigree back to the nineteenth century, but you won't be able to get much further, and you will be seeing only the outline of your family's history. On the other hand, if you are one of those who refuses on principle to use the internet (and who is presumably reading this by accident, or to confirm their worst fears), you are just making your research into your family history much harder than it need be.

▊ HISTORY

With the rapid rate at which new developments are taking place, and the relative novelty of the World Wide Web (which has only been widely used beyond a circle of computer buffs for perhaps eight or nine years), online genealogy might seem to be a new development, but in fact it has quite a history and a number of distinct historical sources.

On the internet itself, online genealogy started in 1983 with the newsgroup net.roots and with the ROOTS-L mailing list. Net.roots became soc.roots, and eventually spawned all the genealogy newsgroups discussed in Chapter 15; ROOTS-L gave rise to RootsWeb <**www.rootsweb.com**>, the oldest online genealogy co-operative.[3]

But in that period internet access was largely confined to academics and the computer industry, so for many people online genealogy meant bulletin boards run by volunteers from their home computers and accessible via a modem and phone line. A system called FidoNet allowed messages and files to be transferred around the world, albeit slowly, as each bulletin board called up its neighbour to pass messages on. The only commercial forums were the growing online services which originally targeted computer professionals and those in business, but which gradually attracted a more disparate membership. Of these, CompuServe, with its Roots forum, was the most important. One significant feature of these commercial services was the ability to access them from all over the world, in many cases with only a local call, which we now take for granted.

These systems had the basis of what genealogists now use the internet for: conversing with other genealogists and accessing centrally stored files. But the amount of data available was tiny and discussion was the main motivation. Part of this was down to technical limitations: with modem speeds something like five hundred times slower than a modern broadband connection, transferring large amounts of data was unrealistic or at best painfully slow, except for the few with deep pockets or an internet connection at work. No government agencies or family history societies had even contemplated an online presence, though genealogical computer groups were starting to spring up by the end of the 1980s.

What changed this was the World Wide Web, created in 1991 (though it was 1995 before it started to dominate the internet), and the growth of commercial internet services. The innovation of the web made it possible for a large collection of material to remain navigable, even for the

---

3 For a history of the newsgroups, see Margaret J. Olson, 'Historical Reflections of the Genealogy Newsgroups' at <**homepages.rootsweb.com/~socgen/Newshist.htm**>. For the history of ROOTS-L and RootsWeb, see <**www.rootsweb.com/roots-l/**>.

technologically illiterate, while at the same time the explosion in public use of the internet was providing the impetus for it to become more user friendly.

The result of these developments is that the internet is now driving developments in access to genealogical information – just as computers had done in the 1980s, and microfilm before that. This in turn is drawing more people to start researching their family tree, which increases the chance of encountering distant cousins online, and motivates data holders to make their material available on the web.

The timeline at <homepages.gold.ac.uk/genuki/timeline/> identifies some of the more significant online developments for UK family historians and gives starting dates for key websites and online facilities.

CHAPTER 2

FIRST STEPS

Your first online steps in genealogy will depend on how much research you have already done on your family tree, and what your aim is. If you are just beginning your family history, you will be able to use the internet to help you get started, but you shouldn't expect to find much primary source material online, i.e. original records, until you get back to the start of the twentieth century.

The box on the next page shows a simplified outline of the process of constructing a family tree, which is the foundation on which your family history will be built. For the first two steps, you will find indexes to certificates online (see Chapter 5), but not the certificates themselves, and online materials won't help you work out which is going to be the certificate you need. This stage is mostly about interpreting information from family members and trying to verify it. It's only once you get to step 4 that you will find a significant amount of source material online. In the initial stages, the internet will probably be more important as a source of information, help and advice. The material in the 'Tutorials' and 'Getting help' sections below should help you get going.

If you are not new to family history, but have just started to use the internet, your needs will be rather different. You will already be familiar with civil registration and census records, and know what is involved in researching your family tree, so your initial questions will not be about constructing a family tree but: What's online and how do I find it? Who else is working on my family?

Chapter 3 looks at sites that provide links to genealogy resources, while the five subsequent chapters, 4 to 8, look at online records. Chapters 11–14 look at internet resources relating to particular aspects of genealogy, while Chapter 16 covers general techniques for finding websites that have specific information. For making contact with others, look at Chapters 10, 15 and 17.

Whatever stage you are at, it will be worth looking at the discussion groups in Chapter 15, and the information on archives and libraries in Chapter 9.

1   Interview your elderly relatives and collect as much first- or second-hand information as you can (and continue doing so, as you find out more in subsequent steps).

2   Get marriage and birth certificates for the most recently deceased ancestors.

3   From these, work back to the marriages and then births of the parents of those ancestors.

4   Keep repeating this process until you get back to the beginning of General Registration (1837 for England & Wales, later for Scotland and Ireland).

5   Once you have names and either places or actual addresses for a date in the nineteenth or early twentieth century, refer to the censuses to see
   (a) whole family groups
   (b) birth places
   (c) ages, from which you can calculate approximate birth years.

6   Once you have found a census entry for an adult ancestor who was born before General Registration, use the birth place and age information in the census to locate a baptism in parish registers.

7   From this, work back to the marriages, and then baptisms, of the parents of that ancestor in the parish registers.

8   Repeat for each line of your ancestry until you hit a brick wall (at which point you will need to consider other approaches and other sources).

▮ TUTORIALS

While the internet cannot match the wealth of introductory books for family historians, there is quite a range of material covering the basics of genealogical research in the British Isles.

One important source for such materials is Genuki (described more fully in Chapter 3, p. 18), which has a page devoted to 'Getting Started in Genealogy and Family History' at <www.genuki.org.uk/gs/>. There are individual pages on major topics, such as that for 'Civil Registration in England and Wales' at <www.genuki.org.uk/big/eng/civreg/>.

Roy Stockdill's concise but comprehensive 'Newbies' Guide to Genealogy and Family History' is available on Genuki at <www.genuki.org.uk/gs/Newbie.html>.

The FamilyRecords portal (see p. 16) has a guide for beginners at <www.familyrecords.gov.uk/guides/beginners.htm>, while the National

Archives has extensive introductory material on its website. Its 'In-depth learning guides' include material on family history, local history, and palaeography. The family history section is at **<www.nationalarchives.gov. uk/pathways/familyhistory/>**, and the box on the next page lists the topics covered.

The Society of Genealogists (SoG) has a number of introductory leaflets online at **<www.sog.org.uk/leaflets/>**. Though they are not designed as a coherent introduction to family history, they include 'Starting genealogy' and 'Note taking and keeping for genealogists'. The Federation of Family History Societies (FFHS) has some online leaflets at **<www.ffhs.org.uk/ General/Help/>**, including 'First Steps in Family History', 'Record Offices', and 'Strays (People who moved)'. GenDocs has a substantial page for those 'New To Family History' at **<www.gendocs.demon.co.uk/newbie.html>**.

Both the BBC and Channel 4 have areas of their websites devoted to genealogy. These started life as support materials for particular TV series, but now have an independent existence. The Channel 4 Guide to Genealogy is at **<www.channel4.com/history/microsites/U/untold/resources/geno/ genof.html>** with general information about post- and pre-1837 family history, and a particularly strong section on tracing immigrant ancestors, discussed in more detail in Chapter 11.

The BBC's Family History site will be found at **<www.bbc.co.uk/ history/familyhistory/>** and includes a wide range of material, partly but not exclusively related to 2004's *Who Do You Think You Are?* series. The 'Family History Trail' area of the site has quite full introductory material

Figure 2-1 The BBC's Family History site at **<www.bbc.co.uk/history/familyhistory/>**

Naming Names and Tracing Places
- Civil registration
- Stand up and be counted
- What about births, marriages and deaths before 1837?
- Dissenting voices
- Britons born, married or dying on board ship
- Wills and death duty registers
- Finding taxpayers
- Ancestors as investors
- Oath rolls
- Timeline

People at Work
- Apprentices
- Police
- Customs and excise
- Coastguards
- Lawyers in the family
- Other records about people at work

The Army and Navy
- Soldiers' papers
- Tracing army officers
- Regimental diaries

- War medals
- The British Army before the First World War
- The Royal Navy: officers
- Tracing ratings
- Merchant seamen
- Crew lists
- Log books
- Timeline

Migrant Ancestors
- Movements of the poor
- Britons abroad
- Children on the move
- Wartime evacuees
- Immigrants to Britain
- Refugees
- Ships' passenger lists

Ancestors and the Law
- Name changes
- Bankrupts
- Criminal courts
- Prisoners and transportation
- Licences and pardons
- Cases in Chancery
- The Court of Requests

on: getting started, the census, military records, and basic research tools. Under the heading 'Articles' is a 'Family History Overview', a brief history of surnames, and an introduction to Caribbean family history. The booklet from the series, 'Family History. The Basics and Beyond', published by the National Archives, can be downloaded free from <**www.nationalarchives. gov.uk/familyhistory/pdf/family_history_leaflet.pdf**>.

For those who have already made a start on their family tree, Else Churchill's 'Eight-part guide to advanced genealogy' at <**www.bbc.co.uk/ history/your_history/family/genealogy_guide.shtml**> (which is not linked from the main Family History page) looks beyond the most common sources and discusses how to find elusive ancestors.

For an introductory guide which focuses on web resources, see the online history magazine *History in Focus* (see p. 309) which has an introductory guide 'Family History on the Internet' in its launch issue at <**www.history.ac.uk/ihr/Focus/Victorians/family.html**>.

The Church of Jesus Christ of Latter-day Saints (LDS) has extensive introductory material on its FamilySearch website at <**www.familysearch. org/Eng/Search/RG/frameset_rg.asp**> (or go to the home page at <**www. familysearch.org**> and select **Search**, then **Research Guidance**). There are separate 'Search Strategy' pages for England, Wales, Scotland and Ireland. Each of these has links to material on looking for births, marriages and deaths in the three main periods for genealogical research: general registration, parish registers, and before parish registers (see Figure 2-2). Clicking on the 'For Beginners' tab will take you to general material on:

- Organizing your paper files
- How to find the name of the place where your ancestor lived
- How to find information about the place where your ancestor lived
- How to find maps
- How to find compiled sources.

Introductory material specific to Scottish research includes the 'Getting Started' section of ScotlandsPeople – go to <**www.scotlandspeople.gov.uk**>, select **Features**, then **Getting Started** – and the Scottish Archive Network's family history pages at <**www.scan.org.uk/familyhistory/**>. Genuki has an 'Introduction to Scottish Family History' at <**www.genuki.org.uk/big/sct/ intro.html**>.

For Ireland, the Irish Ancestors site has an excellent range of introductory material at <**scripts.ireland.com/ancestor/browse/**>, including

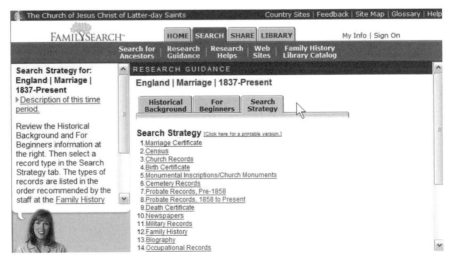

Figure 2-2 FamilySearch's Research Guidance page for English Marriages in the period since 1837 at <**www.familysearch.org**>

information on the counties and emigration (see Chapter 11) and good pages on the various Irish genealogical records. This is based largely on John Grenham's book *Tracing your Irish Ancestors*. Also by John Grenham is the 'Irish Roots' section of Moving Here (see p. 167) at <www.movinghere.org.uk/galleries/roots/irish/irish.htm>.

On Cyndi's List (see p. 23) you will find a comprehensive 'Beginners' page at <www.cyndislist.com/beginner.htm>, and a collection of links on 'Researching: Localities & Ethnic Groups' which will be useful if you need to start looking for ancestors outside the UK and Ireland. Cyndi's 'How to: tutorials and guides' page at <www.cyndislist.com/howtotut.htm> provides an outline of all the introductory materials on seven major genealogy sites. These sites are US-based, so much of the material on specific records will not be of use unless you are tracing American ancestors. However, this page should help you find some of the more general information buried in these sites.

About.com has a large collection of introductory articles at <genealogy.about.com>. The best way to find material on particular topics is to go to the list of articles by category at <genealogy.about.com/blresourceindex.htm>. Although, again, many of the articles on specific records are intended for those researching American ancestry, there is useful material on general topics, such as 'Top Ten Genealogy Mistakes to Avoid' at <genealogy.about.com/library/weekly/aa072100a.htm>, and links to articles on the British Isles will be found at <genealogy.about.com/od/british_isles/>.

The Wikipedia's Genealogy page at <en.wikipedia.org/wiki/Genealogy> has links to articles on the major types of record used in genealogy and a number of other introductory topics. The material is not specific to any one country.

50connect has a basic introduction to genealogy at <www.50connect.co.uk/50c/gene.asp> and a collection of articles at <www.50connect.co.uk/50c/genealogylibrary.asp> on topics such as the census, military records, and Irish ancestors.

If you are trying to research British or Irish ancestry from overseas, Genuki's 'Researching From Abroad' page at <www.genuki.org.uk/ab/> will be useful. The SoG has a leaflet 'Notes for Americans on tracing their British ancestry' online at <www.sog.org.uk/leaflets/americans.html>. Mark Howells's 'Guide to Researching Ancestors from the United Kingdom using the LDS Family History Center Resources' at <www.oz.net/~markhow/uksearch.htm> is also recommended.

If you are unfamiliar with the administrative subdivision of Britain into counties and parishes, you should consult Jim Fisher's page 'British Counties, Parishes, etc. for Genealogists' at <homepages.nildram.co.uk/~jimella/counties.htm>. This also explains the meaning of names for regions such as the Peak District or the Wirral, which are not those of administrative divisions and are not necessarily well defined. Genuki's pages on 'Administrative Regions of the British Isles' at <**www.genuki.org. uk/big/Regions/index.html**> is worth consulting. See also the section on 'The counties' on p. 186.

GETTING HELP

Even with these tutorial materials, you may still have a question you can't find an answer to. One solution is to use a search engine to find pages devoted to a particular topic (see Chapter 16). However, this can be a time-consuming task, since you may end up following quite a few links that turn out to be useless before you find what you are looking for. Also, it may not be easy to establish how authoritative the material is.

The various discussion forums discussed in Chapter 15 are ideal places for getting help and advice. Before posting a query to one of these, though, make sure you read the FAQ (Frequently Asked Questions) – see p. 247. This will give the answers to the most common questions. There are a number of mailing lists for beginners, notably GEN-NEWBIE-L 'where people who are new to computers and genealogy may interact'. Information on how to join this list will be found at <**www.rootsweb.com/~newbie/**>, and past messages are archived at <**archiver.rootsweb.com/th/index/ GEN-NEWBIE**>. UK-GENEALOGY-NEWBIES is a similar list with a specifically UK focus – details at <**lists.rootsweb.com/index/intl/UK/ UK-GENEALOGY-NEWBIES.html**> – but it seems rather quiet, so may not be very helpful. If you are already a member of a family history society, it may have a mailing list where you can turn to other members for assistance. Another place to look is the archive of newsgroup messages (see p. 243) on Google Groups at <**groups.google.com**>.

Ask a Librarian is an 'online reference service' run by CoEast, a public library consortium, at <**www.ask-a-librarian.org.uk**>. You can email a question and you will get a reply within two working days. Before asking a family history question, consult the 'tips on asking your question' page at <**www.ask-a-librarian.org.uk/tips.html**>, and don't expect them to search original records on your behalf to find your great-grandparents' wedding.

However, there is one really important step that will save you a lot of this trouble: get a good book on family history. If you are a relative beginner, you might start with Anthony Adolph's *Collins Tracing Your Family History*, David Hey's *Journeys in Family History: The National Archives' Guide to Exploring your Past, Finding your Ancestors* or Jean Cole and John Titford's *Tracing your Family Tree*. If you have already made some progress, Mark Herber's *Ancestral Trails* should be on your bookshelf. Contrary to the hype, the internet has not made such publications redundant. There is a lot of good reference material on the internet, and an increasing amount of primary data, but tutorial material is still a relatively underdeveloped area despite all the sites listed in this chapter.

▌ GENEALOGICAL TERMS AND ABBREVIATIONS

Whatever your level of experience in family history, you're very likely at some point to come across unfamiliar terms and, especially, abbreviations. Internet resources for legal terms are covered in Chapter 13 (p. 214) while words for obsolete occupations are covered in Chapter 11 (p. 156). But genealogy as a discipline has its own specialist terms, which may baffle at first.

GenealogyPro has a Glossary of Genealogy Terms at <**genealogypro. com/details/glossary.html**> with around 130 entries, while Sam Behling has a page of about 400 terms at <**homepages.rootsweb.com/~sam/terms. html**>. Gareth Hicks's page on Technical Words/Expressions at <**home. clara.net/tirbach/hicks3.html**> is arranged under a number of key topic headings, which is useful if you're not sure of the distinction between a vicar, rector and parson, for example. This provides quite detailed explanations of historical terms, and is more or less an encyclopedia. Dr Ashton Emery's 'A–Z Of British Genealogical Research' at <**www.genuki.org. uk/big/EmeryPaper.html**> covers about 100 important terms presented as a dictionary rather than a connected account.

In the long run, the most comprehensive online reference work of this type will probably be the collaborative online Encyclopedia of Genealogy at <**www.eogen.com**>, started by Dick Eastman in 2004, which has articles on a wide range of topics, entries for abbreviations, and acronyms for genealogy organizations. The advantage of this project is that it allows users to comment on and correct the entries, as well as submitting new entries of their own.

If you have to read documents written in a language other than English then FamilySearch has wordlists of key genealogical words in 15 European languages at <**www.familysearch.org/Eng/Search/rg/research/type/ Word_List.asp**>. These lists are not comprehensive but should at least help you identify key words like 'husband', 'parish' and 'baptism'. Web resources for Latin are discussed in more detail on p. 212.

One frequent question from those getting started is about the meaning of phrases like 'second cousin once removed'. To help you with this, About.com has a Genealogy Relationship Chart at <**genealogy.about.com/ library/nrelationshipchart.htm**>. Genealogy.com's article 'What is a First Cousin, Twice Removed?' at <**www.genealogy.com/genealogy/16_cousn. html**> explains all.

For making sense of abbreviations and acronyms, there are a number of sites to help you. Most of the glossaries mentioned earlier include many abbreviations. Mark Howells has a page devoted to 'Common Acronyms & Jargon' found in UK genealogy at <**www.oz.net/~markhow/ acronym-uk.htm**>, and RootsWeb has a more general list of abbreviations used in genealogy at <**www.rootsweb.com/roots-l/abbrevs.html**>. But by far the most comprehensive is GenDocs' 'Genealogical Abbreviations and Acronyms' page at <**www.gendocs.demon.co.uk/abbr.html**> with over 2,000 entries.

For links to other online dictionaries and lists of abbreviations, look at the page on Cyndi's List devoted to 'Dictionaries & Glossaries' at <**www.cyndislist.com/diction.htm**>.

ONLINE STARTING POINTS

Subsequent chapters in this book are devoted to particular types of genealogical resource or internet tools. This one looks at some of the online starting points for genealogy on the web, sites which provide links to other resources. These go under various names: directory, gateway or portal:

- An internet **directory** is the electronic equivalent of the Yellow Pages, a list of resources categorized under a number of subject headings.
- A **gateway** is a directory devoted to a single subject area, and may also offer knowledgeable annotation of the links provided as well as additional background information. A gateway is not just a directory; it can be more like a handbook.
- A **portal** is a site which aims to provide a single jumping-off point on the internet for a particular audience, bringing together all the resources they might be interested in. Like a gateway, a portal may provide information as well as links.

In genealogy, since the audience is defined by its interest in a particular subject, it is not always possible to maintain a clear distinction between gateways and portals. 'Portal' tends to be the preferred term in the case of a site which has some official status or which aims to be definitive. Both gateways and portals are selective and only include links to recommended resources, whereas directories tend to be less scrupulous. (The term 'gateway' is also used in a quite different sense; see p. 243.)

Directories, gateways and portals are not the only way to find information on the internet: general-purpose search engines such as Google <www.google.com>, discussed in Chapter 16, can also be used to find genealogical material online. The differences between directories, gateways and portals on the one hand and search engines on the other are summarized in Table 16-1 on p. 255. The most important is that directories, etc. provide lists of web*sites* while search engines locate individual web *pages*, so the former are better for locating significant resources on a particular topic rather than mere mentions of a subject. This makes them preferable for initial exploration. The fact that the entries are selected, and perhaps helpfully annotated, makes them even more useful. However, there are certain things they are poor for, notably information published on the personal websites of individual family historians, and material relating to individual surnames.

THE BRITISH ISLES

There are two online starting points which are essential for British genealogy: the FamilyRecords portal, which is the government's gateway to official websites of use to family historians; and Genuki, which aims to be comprehensive in its coverage of sites relating to genealogy in the British Isles. In addition, there are a number of other official and unofficial sites which provide starting points for exploring specifically British and Irish internet material. Sites linking to more general resources are discussed later in this chapter (p. 23ff.).

FAMILYRECORDS

The FamilyRecords portal at <**www.familyrecords.gov.uk**> (Figure 3-1) is run by a consortium made up of the National Archives, Public Record Office of Northern Ireland, National Archives of Scotland, the National Library of Wales, the General Register Office, the General Register Office

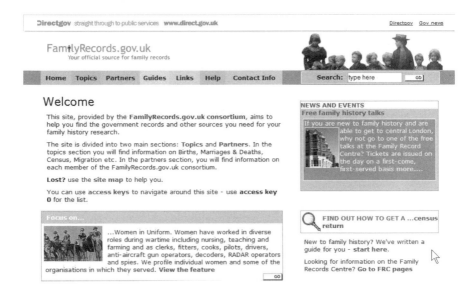

Figure 3-1 The FamilyRecords portal at <**www.familyrecords.gov.uk**>

for Scotland and the British Library India Office. FamilyRecords provides basic information about the major national repositories, including contact details and links to their websites – this is in the 'Partners' area of the site at <www.familyrecords.gov.uk/partners.htm>. In the 'Topics' area at <www.familyrecords.gov.uk/topics.htm> are brief descriptions of the main types of public record, with links to the bodies that hold them. Although deliberately limited in scope, it provides a good way of locating specific material on the official websites. The websites of the individual bodies linked to the FamilyRecords portal are discussed in Chapter 5, 'Civil registration' and under 'National archives' in Chapter 9 (p. 117ff.).

DIRECTGOV

While the FamilyRecords portal is restricted to genealogical coverage, there is also a general-purpose government gateway called Directgov at <www.direct.gov.uk>. This site provides access to *all* official information online, with links to all branches of local and national government. It therefore covers local authorities, county record offices and the like, which are not linked from FamilyRecords – the easiest way to find these is via the 'A-Z of local councils' link from the home page. There is a search facility as well as alphabetical indexes of national and local government services. On the home page is a link to a directory for 'Public records and genealogy', though this offers nothing more than what is available from FamilyRecords.

IRELAND

Obviously, there is no link from FamilyRecords to official bodies in the Republic of Ireland, but the official website of the Irish government will be found at <www.irlgov.ie>, and this has links to sites of government departments and state organizations.

The National Archives of Ireland at <www.nationalarchives.ie> have several pages of genealogy links covering

- Related Irish resources
- National archives worldwide
- National and international associations and professional bodies
- Research sources in Ireland and the UK
- Electronic records and archives
- Other sites of archival interest.

These are accessed from the 'Links' drop-down menu on the home page, but on some browsers (Netscape, Firefox) you will need to choose the 'text only' option to access these pages. Alternatively, go to <www.nationalarchives.ie/text/links/IRLarchives.htm>.

Genuki, described in the next section, has a comprehensive collection of links to Irish material online at <**www.genuki.org.uk/big/irl/**>. The Irish Ancestors site has links to the major Irish bodies with genealogical material at <**scripts.ireland.com/ancestor/browse/links/**>, with sub-pages devoted to libraries, societies and individual counties, as well as passenger lists and emigration resources. Irish libraries and archives are covered in Chapter 9, while Irish civil registration is covered in Chapter 5.

GENUKI

The most comprehensive collection of online information about family history for the British Isles, with an unrivalled collection of links, is Genuki, the 'UK & Ireland Genealogical Service' at <**www.genuki.org.uk**>. Genuki describes itself as 'a virtual reference library of genealogical information that is of particular relevance to the UK & Ireland'. As a reference source, the material it contains 'relates to primary historical material, rather than material resulting from genealogists' ongoing research'. This means it is effectively a handbook of British and Irish genealogy online. But Genuki also functions as a gateway, simply because it has links to an enormous number of online resources for the UK and Ireland, including every genealogical organization with a website.

Genuki has its origins in the efforts of a group of volunteers, centred on Brian Randell at the University of Newcastle and Phil Stringer at the University of Manchester, to set up a website for genealogical information in 1995, when the World Wide Web was still very young. Genuki has always been an entirely non-commercial and volunteer-run organization.

Figure 3-2 The Genuki home page <**www.genuki.org.uk**>

All the pages are maintained by a group of about 50 volunteers on many different websites, mostly at UK universities or on the personal sites of the volunteers. Many other individuals have provided information and transcripts of primary data. Genuki started as an entirely informal group, but is now a charitable trust.

There are two distinct parts to Genuki.

First, there are a number of pages devoted to general information about family history in the British Isles:

- Frequently Asked Questions (FAQs) – typical queries asked by Genuki users.
- Getting started in genealogy – a range of beginners' guides (or links to them). See 'Tutorials' on p. 7.
- Pages devoted to individual general topics, such as 'Military Records' or 'Immigration and Emigration', all linked from <**www.genuki.org. uk/big/**> (many of these are mentioned in later chapters).
- Researching from abroad – useful links for those who dwell outside the UK, especially in North America.
- World genealogy – a small collection of links for those researching non-British ancestry.
- Genealogical events relating to UK and Ireland ancestry (see p. 307).
- Information on Genuki itself – how it is run, the principles on which it is structured.

Second, it provides information on and links to online resources for all the constituent parts of the British Isles, with pages for:

- England, Wales, Scotland, Ireland, the Isle of Man, and the Channel Islands
- Every individual county in these areas
- Many individual towns and parishes.

The county pages (see Figure 3-3) in turn provide links to the websites of:

- County record offices and other repositories of interest to family historians (see Chapter 9)
- Local family history societies (see Chapter 18)
- County and other local mailing lists (see Chapter 15)
- County surname lists (see Chapter 10)
- Any online data collections for the county
- Other online resources relating to genealogy in the county.

Each county page has a link to a list of individual towns and parishes, and many of these have their own pages with local information and links.

Most material on Genuki will be found on these geographical pages, which are organized hierarchically. Figure 3-4 shows a diagram of the hierarchy.

STAFFORDSHIRE

"A county of England, bounded by, Shropshire Cheshire, Derbyshire, Warwickshire, and Worcestershire. It is in length about 54 miles, and varies in breadth from 18 to 36. It is divided into 5 hundreds, which contain 1 city, 21 towns, 181 parishes, and 670 villages. The principal rivers are the Trent, Dove, Sow, Churnet, Stour, Penk, and Manifold. The air is reckoned pleasant, mild, and wholesome. The middle and southern parts are level and plain, and the soil is good and rich; the north is hilly, and full of heaths and moors. Staffordshire is famous for its potteries, its inland navigations, and its founderies, blast furnaces, slitting mills, and various other branches of the iron trade. The mines of coals, copper, lead, and iron ore are rich and extensive; and there are also numerous quarries of stone, alabaster, and limestone. Stafford is the county town. Population, 510,504. It sends 17 members to parliament."
[Barclays Complete & Universal English Dictionary, 1842-1852]

INFORMATION RELATED TO ALL OF STAFFORDSHIRE

* Archives and Libraries
* Bibliography
* Business Records
* Cemeteries
* Census
* Church History
* Church Records
* Civil Registration
* Correctional Institutions
* Court Records
* Description and Travel
* Directories
* Genealogy
* Historical Geography
* Maps

* Medical Records
* Military History
* Military Records
* Names, Geographical
* Names, Personal
* Newspapers
* Occupations
* Orphans and Orphanages
* Periodicals
* Poorhouses, Poor Law, etc
* Probate Records
* Societies
* Taxation
* Voting Registers

Figure 3-3 A Genuki County page

Genuki also has central listings of:

* National genealogical organizations and local family history societies at <www.genuki.org.uk/Societies/>
* All mailing lists relevant to British and Irish genealogy at <www.genuki.org.uk/indexes/MailingLists.html>
* All county and other surname lists at <www.genuki.org.uk/indexes/SurnamesLists.html>.

Because of the enormous amount of material on Genuki – there are almost 60,000 pages – it is well worth taking the time to look at the 'Guidance for First-Time Users of These Pages' at <www.genuki.org.uk/org/>, which gives an outline of what Genuki is. There is a more detailed online user guide, 'How the information on this server is presented to the user' at <www.genuki.org.uk/org/user.html>.

A particular virtue of Genuki is that it uses well-defined subject categories, which are based on those used in the LDS Church's library catalogue and have therefore been designed by genealogically literate librarians. Its coherent coverage of every county, with a long-term aim of covering every parish, is the other feature which makes it useful.

The list of categories used on Genuki is shown in Table 3-1.

Some of these categories (for example Handwriting, Politics and Government) will be relevant only at the top, national levels, but topics such as church records, local records and maps should be represented on every county page. Since the list of subject headings pre-dates the internet, there are no specific categories for internet-related subjects such as surname lists and mailing lists, so Genuki places these under the Genealogy heading.

For a detailed guide to Genuki there is a book, simply called *Genuki*, by David Hawgood, one of the Genuki trustees, published by the FFHS. The complete text is available online at <**www.hawgood.co.uk/genuki/**>.

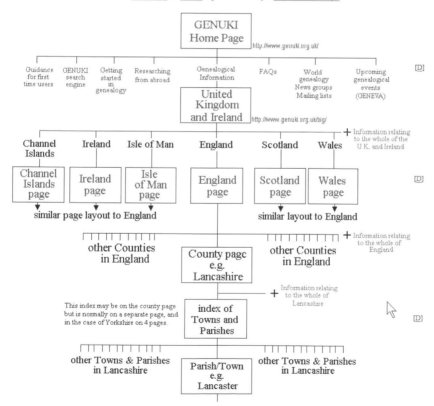

Figure 3-4 How Genuki is organized <**www.genuki.org.uk/org/Structure.html**>

Table 3-1 Genuki subject headings

Almanacs	Medical Records
Archives and Libraries	Merchant Marine
Bibliography	Migration, Internal
Biography	Military History
Business and Commerce Records	Military Records
Cemeteries	Minorities
Census	*(Monumental Inscriptions – see Cemeteries)*
Chronology	Names, Geographical
Church Directories	Names, Personal
Church History	Naturalization and Citizenship
Church Records	Newspapers
Civil Registration	Nobility
Colonization	Obituaries
Correctional Institutions	Occupations
Court Records	Officials and Employees
Description and Travel	Orphans and Orphanages
Directories	*(Parish Registers – see Church Records)*
Dwellings	Pensions
Emigration and Immigration	Periodicals
Encyclopedias and Dictionaries	Politics and Government
Ethnology	Poorhouses, Poor Law, etc.
Folklore	Population
Gazetteers	Postal and Shipping Guides
Genealogy	Probate Records
Guardianship	Public Records
Handwriting	Religion and Religious Life
Heraldry	Schools
Historical Geography	Social Life and Customs
History	Societies
Inventories, Registers, Catalogues	Statistics
Jewish History	Taxation
Jewish Records	Town Records
Land and Property	Visitations, Heraldic
Language and Languages	*(Vital Records – see Civil Registration)*
Law and Legislation	Voting Registers
Manors	Yearbooks
Maps	

Genuki also has a search facility at <**www.genuki.org.uk/search/**>, discussed on p. 275.

Because Genuki is very comprehensive, it can be easy to overlook the fact that there are things it does not do. First, it has deliberate restrictions in its linking policy: it does not link to sites which provide information only on an individual family, pedigree or surname; its links are strictly confined to sites which are relevant to UK and Ireland genealogy. However, as long as what you are looking for is available online and falls within Genuki's scope you should expect to find it listed.

Another service Genuki does not provide is answering genealogical queries from individuals. There is a Genuki email address, but this is intended only for reporting errors on the site or drawing attention to new resources not listed on Genuki. See 'Getting help' on p. 12 and Chapter 15 for places to post genealogical queries.

▌GENERAL GENEALOGY GATEWAYS

If you have ancestors who lived outside the British Isles you will need to look at some of the general genealogy directories and gateways. And even if all your ancestors were British or Irish, there are good reasons to use other gateways and directories. Since FamilyRecords and Genuki take a strictly geographical approach, you need to look elsewhere for genealogical resources, such as computer software, which are not tied to a particular country or region.

CYNDI'S LIST

The most comprehensive genealogy gateway is Cyndi's List at <**www. cyndislist.com**>, maintained by Cyndi Howells. You can get an idea of the scope of the list, which has over 240,000 links, from the 160 or so main categories on the home page.

Unlike Genuki (p. 18) or Yahoo (p. 28), Cyndi's List has a fairly flat structure: most subject headings lead to a single page, while a few act as indexes to a whole group of pages on their subject (these have the word 'index' in their title). So, for example, the main UK page at <**www. cyndislist.com/uksites.htm**> acts simply as an index to the sub-pages devoted to the various parts of the British Isles, to general UK sites, and to British military sites. The advantage of this flat structure is that you don't have to go deep into a hierarchy to find what you're looking for; the disadvantage is that the individual pages tend to be quite large and can take a while to download.

However, alongside the main home page, Cyndi provides other, quicker ways to get to where you want once you are familiar with the site. There are four other 'home pages':

- The 'No Frills' index at <www.cyndislist.com/nofrills.htm> is essentially the home page, but with just the headings – no descriptions or update information, and no cross-references.
- The 'Alphabetical Category' index at <www.cyndislist.com/alpha.htm> is a complete list of all pages and sub-pages in alphabetical order, with cross-references.
- The 'Topical Category' index at <www.cyndislist.com/topical.htm> lists all categories under 11 main headings (Localities, Ethnic Groups and People, Religions, Records, Research Tools and Reference Materials, Help from Others, Marketplace, History, Military, Internet Tools for Genealogy, Miscellaneous).
- The 'Text Only Category' index at <www.cyndislist.com/textonly.htm>.

Once you are familiar with the List, it may be quicker to use these alternative entry points if you are using a dialup connection – the main home page is over 160k, while these are under half that. The smallest is the text-only page at about 32k.

Another way to speed up access to Cyndi's List is to save a copy of the home page to your own hard disk. You will find that clicking on the links from this copy (assuming you are online!) will take you to the sub-page without having to wait while the main page loads over the web. Obviously, you will need to check periodically that no new categories have been added to this top-level page. It is also worth bookmarking any part of the site that you regularly refer to.

Even if your genealogical interests are confined to the British Isles, a number of categories and topics on Cyndi's List are worth noting. The pages devoted to individual religious groups will be useful if you have Catholic, nonconformist or Jewish ancestors (covered in Chapter 11). The 'Software & Computers' page <www.cyndislist.com/software.htm> has a very useful collection of links for genealogy software. The Personal Home Pages section <www.cyndislist.com/personal.htm> lists several thousand websites of individuals, while the Surnames page <www.cyndislist.com/surnames.htm> has over 5,000 sites for individual surnames.

Cyndi's List also has a very comprehensive page of 'Handy Online Starting Points' at <www.cyndislist.com/handy.htm>, with about a hundred sites which provide general genealogy links.

GENWEB

For ancestors from outside the British Isles, you will find a wide coverage of countries and regions on Cyndi's List. But there is also a purely geographical gateway with worldwide coverage in the GenWeb projects. In GenWeb, the world is split into a number of regional projects, each of which has its own website, and a separate volunteer is responsible for each

individual country or island in the region. Apart from USGenWeb at
<**www.usgenweb.org**> and CanadaGenWeb at <**www.rootsweb.com/
~canwgw/**>, which are independent, the remainder are coordinated under
the WorldGenWeb project at <**worldgenweb.org**>.

In all, there are around 100 countries, islands or island groups for which
there are actively maintained websites, grouped as follows:

- Africa (7 countries active)
- Asia (16 countries active)
- British Isles (including the Falkland Islands, Gibraltar, St Helena)
- Canada
- Central Europe (all but Lithuania active) – actually Northern Europe
  would be a more accurate description
- Caribbean (24 islands/island groups active)
- Eastern Europe (12 countries active)
- Mediterranean (7 countries active) – actually more like Southern Europe,
  since it excludes African and Middle Eastern states, though it includes
  Turkey
- Middle East (9 countries active)
- North America (all but Nicaragua active) – actually Central America,
  since it excludes Canada and the USA
- Pacific (4 'areas' active – Australia and 3 groups of islands – though
  not every individual island has an active page)
- South America (7 countries active)
- United States.

Most of the links to UK and Irish material at <**www.britishislesgenweb.
org**> will in fact be found on Genuki, whose county pages are generally
more comprehensive. So the real strength of the GenWeb sites, from the
point of view of British and Irish family historians, lies in the material
relating to former British colonies and those countries from which immigrants came to the UK (see Chapter 11). The Caribbean GenWeb at
<**www.rootsweb.com/~caribgw/**>, for example, is an essential starting
point for West Indian ancestry.

There is huge variation in the amount of material available: for some
countries there is a single page, while for others there are individual pages
for administrative subdivisions, for example French *départements*. In
general, the level of detail does not go down to the equivalent of individual parishes, though for each US state there are pages for the constituent
counties.

While most of the pages are in English, quite a few are maintained by
natives of the countries concerned and are in the local language. Some,
notably the Caribbean and South American pages, are available in more
than one language.

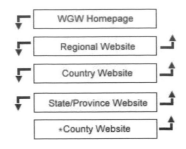

WGW Homepage

Regional Website

Country Website

State/Province Website

*County Website

* Not all countries have counties.
The term county is used here in the general sense and
refers to the most common political or administrative district
in a country. Other names include shires, parish, townlands,
states, prefects, rajones, etc.

Figure 3-5 How WorldGenWeb is organized <**worldgenweb.org/policy.html**>

On the WorldGenWeb projects, the topics on each page are sorted under the following headings:

- History
- Resource Addresses (libraries, archives)
- Society Addresses
- Maps
- Geography
- Culture and Religious History
- Query Board
- Mail List
- Reference Materials (census, deeds, biographies).

Beyond this, the pages do not necessarily have the same layout or look. A useful feature to note is that every GenWeb page has a Query Board where readers can post queries. Such a board is often available for countries which have no maintained web page.

GENEALOGY RESOURCES ON THE INTERNET

One of the longest established genealogy directories on the internet is Chris Gaunt and John Fuller's Genealogy Resources on the internet site at <www.rootsweb.com/~jfuller/internet.html>. This differs from Genuki, GenWeb and Cyndi's List in that its main division of material is not by subject or by area but by type of access – web, email, etc. This reflects its origins at a time before web browsers provided a way of integrating all types of internet resources into a single interface – it was originally sent out by email – and when different software was required for each type of resource. This may be the only place where you'll still see references to Gopher and Telnet sites. One of the great virtues of this site is that the pages are designed for very fast downloading, with very simple layouts and few graphics.

The sections devoted to newsgroups and the web provide excellent starting points and, in particular, the pages on mailing lists (main page at <www.rootsweb.com/~jfuller/gen_mail.html>) are one of the essential genealogy resources on the web. Mailing lists are discussed further in Chapter 15.

Another interesting collection of resources listed here is those accessible by email rather than the web, at <www.rootsweb.com/~jfuller/gen_email. html>. Although many of these started off as services for people with email but without web access (which is nowadays almost no one), there are still some interesting things on this page you are unlikely to see mentioned elsewhere.

OTHER GENEALOGY GATEWAYS

While Cyndi's List may be the most widely used general genealogy directory, and Genuki is certainly the pre-eminent gateway for UK material, there are many others. Each has its own particular strengths, though many are US-based and are therefore naturally stronger in US resources. There is not enough space here to list them all, let alone describe them in detail. The following represent a small selection:

• The Genealogy Gateway at <www.gengateway.com>
• Genealogy Links at <www.genealogylinks.net>
• The Genealogy SiteFinder at <www.genealogy.com/genealogy/links/>
• I Found It! at <www.gensource.com/ifoundit/>.

SPECIALIST GATEWAYS

There are also a number of gateways that are not specifically devoted to genealogy but which have links to sites of interest to genealogists. The National Maritime Museum's Port site at <www.port.nmm.ac.uk>, for example, has links to naval resources on the web, which may be of interest to those with maritime ancestors. The same is true for several of the military sites mentioned in Chapter 11 – even those with no genealogical information may provide links to other military genealogy sites.

GENERAL DIRECTORIES

In addition to the specifically genealogical gateways discussed so far, the general directories of the web also provide genealogical links. On the whole, anyone who is sufficiently interested in genealogy to be reading this book will probably find them less useful than the dedicated sites already mentioned, not least since they are not edited and maintained by people with expertise in the subject, and cannot aim to be comprehensive. For example, neither of the two general directories discussed below has links to a single UK county record office in their genealogy sections.

YAHOO

The best known and most widely used directory is Yahoo <dir.yahoo.com>. This organizes subjects in a hierarchical structure, and the main Genealogy area comes under History, itself a subsection of Humanities. However, companies that sell genealogy products will be found under the Business heading, and genealogy resources for individual countries will be found under the relevant country heading. The main general page for genealogy is <dir.yahoo.com/arts/humanities/history/genealogy/>, and there is UK-specific material at <uk.dir.yahoo.com/Regional/Countries/United_ Kingdom/Arts_and_Humanities/Humanities/History/Genealogy/>. You can get a complete list of relevant Yahoo subject pages by doing a search on *genealogy*, as there are many other areas of Yahoo which will have material of interest to a family historian.

Although Yahoo, like other directories and gateways, is selective, its basis of selection is not entirely satisfactory since it depends in part on submissions from websites that want to be listed. For example, some UK family history societies are listed, but only a small number.

THE OPEN DIRECTORY PROJECT

The Open Directory Project at <dmoz.org> is a non-commercial web directory, entirely maintained by volunteers. (Yahoo does not, of course, charge users, but it does carry advertising and give prominence on some pages to sponsored links.) Genealogy comes under the heading of 'Society' at <dmoz.org/Society/Genealogy/>.

There is no UK version, and so the links for some of the categories have a US bias – 'immigration', for example, means immigration into the USA – but many of the other topics such as Heraldry or Software (under Products and Services) are of general relevance. Specifically UK material will be found at <dmoz.org/Regional/Europe/United_Kingdom/>.

CHAPTER 4

USING ONLINE SOURCES

The aim of the four following chapters is to look at what the internet holds in the way of primary source material, while Chapter 11 will look at topics of relevance for tracing particular ancestors – for example, military and emigration – and Chapters 12 to 14 examine non-genealogical material of interest to the family historian. This chapter discusses some of the general issues of using the internet for genealogical sources, and looks at the payment systems on the major commercial data services.

The core of any family history research in the British Isles is the information drawn from the registrations of births, marriages and deaths over the last 170 years, and from the records of christenings, marriages and burials in parish registers starting in the sixteenth century. Linking these two sources are the census records, which enable an address from the period of civil registration to lead to a place and approximate year of birth in the time before registration. In addition, wills and memorial inscriptions, quite apart from providing additional information, can substitute for missing or untraceable death and burial records.

While the internet is the ideal way of making all this material widely available, particularly to those who are distant from the relevant repositories and major genealogical libraries, the fact is that a huge amount of work is involved in publishing such material on the web. For example, there may have been as many as 100 million births, marriages and deaths registered between 1837 and 1900; and each census includes a record for every member of the population. Nonetheless, there has been enormous progress over the last two or three years in putting genealogical data online, described in the following chapters.

There are a number of ways in which genealogical data projects can be funded. Volunteer-run projects tend to rely entirely on goodwill and occasional sponsorship, while a number of projects have public funding, usually from the Heritage Lottery Fund. In such cases, access to the data is normally free. Other data holders have taken three main routes to making material available online commercially:

- Setting up an in-house data service (e.g. the FFHS's FamilyHistoryOnline site)
- Partnership with a commercial firm for a combined data service (e.g. ScotlandsPeople)
- Licensing of data to third parties (e.g. the 1891 census on Ancestry.com, licensed from the National Archives).

Prior to the release of the 1901 census in January 2002, there was considerable debate within the online genealogical community about the appropriateness of government agencies already funded by the taxpayer seeking income by charging for online access to public records. There was a feeling that the limited offline availability of the 1901 census on microfiche, which cynics viewed simply as a move to safeguard online income, took insufficient account of the many people who were not computer-literate or had no internet access.

Leaving aside the matter of principle, however, the fact is that progress on digitizing the nation's historical records will be very much slower if it has to be done from existing funds or rely on the lottery. In fact, for most people the costs of using an online service will be very significantly less than the costs in time and travel of visiting a repository, not to mention the fact that the money goes to the data providers rather than to train or oil companies.

In fact, now that so many homes have internet access and it is so widely available in public places, providing a service primarily online is not the contentious issue it once was. Indeed, with the government promoting the use of the internet for the delivery of all sorts of services, it is now very hard for a public body to publish *any* material without being obliged to make it available on the web.

In any case, it shouldn't be forgotten that traditional modes of access to records are also heavily biased against quite large groups of people: anyone who is not mobile, lives far from repositories they need to consult, or has no free time during the day has always found it hard to make progress with their family history.

IMAGES, TRANSCRIPTIONS AND INDEXES

There are three main ways in which any historical textual source can be represented digitally:

- As an image – the original document is scanned
- In a transcription – the full text of a document is held in a file

- As an index – a list of names, with or without other details, directs you to the relevant place in a transcription or to the relevant scanned image, or provides you with the full reference to an original document.

Ideally, an online index would lead to a full transcription of the relevant document, which could then be compared to an image of the original. But for material of any size this represents a very substantial investment in time and resources, and to date very little of the primary genealogical data is so well served.

The reason for this is the very great disparity between the amount of data involved in making text and images available online. In spite of advances in information technology, images require significantly more resources from the website which hosts them, both in terms of disk space to store them and the bandwidth to download them to the user. Even disregarding any costs for creating the digital images of source documents, for a large project this can mean enormous differences in financial practicability between a text-only data collection and one which includes digitized documents.

Images can be supplied economically for census records because they are central to family history and are universally needed, which means that costs can be covered. This has also been done in a number of lottery-funded projects for less widely used material (such as the Old Bailey Proceedings, see p. 157), where costs do not have to be recouped at all. It has been done for wills, where a transcription of the entire document would be commercially impracticable, but where a higher charge can be made for a complete digitized document. But otherwise, there are relatively few images of original sources online.

However, there are many more images than transcriptions. For a document containing running text, a transcription takes much more time to prepare than an index, and except for particularly difficult documents (e.g. a seventeenth-century will) is not really necessary, as long as there is good indexing. A project like the Old Bailey Proceedings, which has document images with an indexed transcription, is in fact very exceptional. On the other hand, it is certainly true that with some sources, such as the censuses, comprehensive indexing can sometimes approach a full transcription.

Most online data, then, comes in the form of indexes linked to images, or, more often, just plain indexes. And this has important implications for how you use the internet for your research: you simply cannot do it all online. Except where you have access to scans of the original documents, all information derived from indexes or transcriptions will have to be checked against the original source. This might not be apparent to you if you are just starting out, since the first online sources you use, the GRO indexes and census records, are available as images, but you will find a very different story once you get back beyond 1837 – the only online images of parish registers even *promised* at this stage are those for the Scottish registers.

INDEX PROBLEMS

The perfect index would be made by trained palaeographers, familiar with the names and places referred to and thoroughly at home with the handwriting of the period, working with original documents. Their work would be independently checked against the original, and where there was uncertainty as to the correct reading this would be clearly indicated.

Needless to day, very little of the genealogical material on the web has been transcribed in this way. The material online has been created either in large-scale projects or by individual genealogists, and often working from microfilms, or digitized images of them, not original records. On large-scale projects the data are input at best by knowledgeable amateurs such as family history society members, but more often by clerical workers. In the latter case, there will always be a question about the quality of data entry. It is self-evident that adequate levels of accuracy can only be achieved where there are good palaeographical skills, and knowledge of local place names and surnames.

The only area where one can expect a lower error rate is in the transcription of printed sources such as trade directories, where problems of identifying names or individual letters are less great.

A particularly troubling issue is the question of data validation. 'Validation' is an essential component of any data entry project – it means checking that everything entered is, if not demonstrably correct, at least plausible. Of course, it's one thing to do this with, say a modern postcode, where it's a simple matter to check that it is present in a list of valid postcodes or that it at least has the correct structure for a postcode. It is much harder to do the same with handwritten historical sources, particularly where surnames are involved. Even so there have been some notable and entirely avoidable failures in major genealogical projects, which have reduced their reliability and usefulness.

How is it possible, for example, that some names in the 1881 census index at FamilySearch have numbers in the middle of them, e.g. *Bart0n*, or *S1mmons*, or *Co0ley*? How was it possible that in the original release of the 1901 census there were individuals with biologically implausible ages over 200? It's not clear whether these are misreadings or miskeyings, but either way, given that data entry errors are inevitable, why did those planning such projects not put mechanisms in place to spot them?

In other cases, there are things that *might* be right, but are statistically so anomalous that they need manual checking. For example, both Ancestry and TNA have significant numbers of people indexed with the wrong gender in their 1901 census indexes – Ancestry has over 3,000 female Johns. One or two are genuine (I noticed a *Marion St John Adcock*), but almost all the ones I have checked are very clearly transcription errors, usually a misreading of a female forename. It's easy to get a name wrong in a census transcription, but many of the errors will be self-evident, because of gender differences in naming – it is a trivial matter to query a database for gender errors with common forenames, to flag entries that need manual checking.

Sometimes a lookup table will suffice to trap errors: there are some strange misspellings of place names in the census indexes (e.g. *Harimersmith* for *Hammersmith*). Why haven't these been checked against a gazetteer, with manual checking for those not found?

Another problematic issue is how hard-to-read entries are treated. Techniques for editing manuscript documents to indicate uncertainties of reading were available long before the advent of computers and much work has been done on ways of indicating variants and unreadable text in electronic editions. So why do genealogical projects not take account of this? As far as I can see, no major electronic transcription used by genealogists has any mechanism for indicating that an individual character or a word is not unambiguously decipherable, in spite of the fact that it is a common enough experience for every genealogist. The transcriber simply puts their best guess, a solution which is utterly inadequate and entirely unhelpful to the user. For example, the barely legible surname in the middle line of Figure 6-10 (p. 83) is transcribed by Ancestry as *Boucha* and by Origins as *Bnecker*, and both seem reasonable attempts in the circumstances. But surely neither of the transcribers in this instance can have been quite certain that their reading was correct. It would be much more helpful for a data provider to admit that there cannot be a definitive reading here and recognize that someone looking for *Bnecker* or *Boucha*, or a range of similar names, should be shown this entry as a possible match.

This points to another issue which underlies much of the difficulty of finding people in online genealogical databases – they do not distinguish clearly between a transcription and an index. The job of a transcriber is to reproduce exactly the letters that can be identified on the original page, that of the indexer to make things findable. Many of the so-called indexes are actually searchable transcriptions, not true indexes, and this is most noticeable in the representation of place names.

For example, the 1871 census has a John Baker living at 20 Gibraltar Walk, Bethnal Green. The enumeration book (RG10/477 folio 58, page 10) gives his birthplace as 'Surry, Lambeth.' Ancestry have quite correctly *transcribed* this as *Surry*, but they have also *indexed* it as *Surry*, so you won't find this John Baker if you enter *Surrey* in the birthplace field – you have to guess the non-standard spelling used by the enumerator! Origins, on the other hand, offers you a drop-down list of possible birth counties – choosing John Baker, born *Surrey*, finds this individual, as you would hope, even though that is not the spelling in the original. Of course, it can't be denied that there are limits to what can be done for some items of data – surnames are the obvious example – but should we really have to search for birthplaces using all possible misspellings and abbreviations?

On a more positive note, though, it is worth remembering that although all indexes are subject to error, the great virtue of online indexes is that mistakes can be corrected – most of the systematic errors in the 1901 census have now been dealt with, for example. In printed or CD-ROM publications this can only be done if and when a subsequent edition is produced.

Of course, as long as an error does not prevent you actually locating an individual, then checking against the digitized image or the original record will provide the correct information. That means errors in gender may not be very significant – as long as you don't specify gender in your search, that is. On the other hand, large errors in ages and misspellings of place names may well make someone effectively unfindable. As with any transcription or index, a failure to locate an individual in an online index does not permit you to draw negative inferences.

▌ PAYMENT SYSTEMS

There are major data collections such as FreeBMD (see p. 51) and FamilySearch (p. 89) which do not charge for access to their material, and there are smaller free collections which are maintained by volunteer efforts or have some source of public funding. But generally there is a charge for access to larger datasets. There are three basic methods that sites use to levy their charges: subscription, pay-per-view, and online shop.

The subscription model is in fact not widely used. The reason for this is that it requires people to pay a flat fee up front regardless of how much data they end up using. The only major data services to use this are Ancestry at <**www.ancestry.co.uk**> and Origins at <**www.origins.net**>, which can do so because they have a wide range of datasets, which no genealogist is likely to exhaust quickly. Another subscription-based service is Otherdays at <**www.otherdays.com**> which has a very diverse collection of Irish sources.

In pay-per-view systems you pay, in principle, for each item of data viewed. However, it is problematic to collect small amounts of money via credit and debit cards, not to mention tedious for users to complete a new financial transaction for each individual record they want to view. Therefore, all such systems require you to purchase a block of 'units' or 'credits' in advance, which are then used up as you view data. Sometimes these are only available in discrete amounts, and work with either real or virtual vouchers for round sums of money; sometimes you must pay a minimum charge up front, and at the end of your session a higher charge is made if you have viewed more data than is covered by the minimum. There is usually a time limit, which means you could have units unused at the end of your session. You won't be able to claim a refund, but in some cases you can carry forward unused portions of a payment to a subsequent session.

In an online shop, whether it's for genealogical data or for physical products, you add items to a virtual 'shopping basket' until you have everything you want, and pay for all of them in a single transaction at a virtual 'checkout'. Only then can you download the data you have paid for. Such a procedure would make little sense for individual data entries, but is a good way of delivering entire electronic documents, so it is ideal for the wills available from DocumentsOnline or ScotlandsPeople (see Chapter 8). It also allows items to be priced individually, though these two services in fact charge at a flat rate.

An overview of the current charging systems for the major commercial data services in the UK is shown in Table 4-1.

MAJOR COMMERCIAL DATA SERVICES

The following chapters cover the various types of record and look at sites relevant for each. But there are a number of commercial sites which have datasets drawn from a variety of different records, and these are discussed here for convenience. All the sites mentioned are constantly adding to their data, sometimes on a monthly basis, so you will almost certainly find there is a wider range of data than mentioned here. Prices, on the other hand, have tended to be very stable, and are not likely to be much different from the details quoted.

ORIGINS

Origins at <www.origins.net> comprises four sub-sites: British Origins, Irish Origins, Scots Origins and Origins Search. The first two of these are online data services.

British Origins at <www.britishorigins.com> went live at the end of 2000 (under the name English Origins) with data from the collections of the SoG, and has recently started to include data from other sources and to create its own census indexes. The complete list of datasets available is:

- Marriage Licence Allegations Index 1694–1850 (670,000 names)
- Bank of England Will Extracts Index 1717–1845 (61,000 names)

Table 4-1 Commercial online genealogy data services in the UK (prices and facilities as of summer 2005)

Service	Type of System	Min. Charge	Index Cost	Transcription	Doc. Image	Duration
1837online	pay-per-view	£5 for 50 units	free	–	BMD 1 unit census 3 units	min. 90 days
1901 census	pay-per-view	£5	free	50p	75p per page	48 hours
Ancestry	subscription	£24.95	free	free	free	3 months
	pay-per-view	£6 for 20 credits	free	1 unit	1 unit	7 days
DocumentsOnline	shop	none	free	–	£3.50 per document	–
FamilyHistoryOnline	pay-per-view	£5 voucher	free	<10p	–	6 months
FamilyRelatives	pay-per-view	£6 for 60 units			2–4 units	
National Archivist	pay-per-view	£7 for 35 credits	free	–	1–4 units per page	min. 45 days
Origins	subscription	£6 for 150 units	1 unit per entry	–	£10 per document (post)	7 days
The Genealogist and BMDindex	subscription	£4.66	free	free	free	1 month
		£5 per dataset	free	free	free	90 days
	pay-per-view	£5 for 50 units	free	–	1 unit	90 days
Otherdays	subscription	$8	free	free	free	72 hours
ScotlandsPeople	pay-per-view	£6 for 30 units	1 unit per 25 entries	–	5 units per page £10 per document (post)	7 days
	shop	none	free	–	£5 per document	–

- Archdeaconry Court of London Wills Index 1750–1800 (5,000 names)
- London Consistory Court Depositions Index 1700–1717 (3,200 names)
- London City Apprenticeship Abstracts 1442–1850 (300,000 names)
- Prerogative Court of Canterbury Wills 1750–1800 (208,000 records)
- Boyd's Marriage Index 1538–1837 (over seven million records)
- Apprentices of Great Britain: 1710–74 (over 600,000 records)
- Boyd's Inhabitants of London: fourteenth to nineteenth centuries (60,000 families)
- Boyd's London Burials (over 300,000 names)
- York Medieval Probate Index 1267–1500 (over 10,000 wills)
- York Peculiars Probate Index 1383–1883 (over 25,000 wills)
- Inheritance Disputes Index 1574–1714 (over 26,000 lawsuits)
- Militia Attestations Index 1886–1910 (29,000 names)
- 1841 Census Index (in progress)
- 1871 Census Index (in progress).

The datasets on British Origins will mostly be of use to those who have already got some way with their pedigree, as apart from the 1871 census the records only go up to the mid-nineteenth century. The range of London records makes this site invaluable to those with ancestors from the city.

Irish Origins at <**www.irishorigins.com**> currently includes the following datasets:

- Griffith's Valuation 1847–1864
- Dublin City Census 1851
- Index of Irish Wills 1484–1858
- Militia Attestations Index 1872–1915
- Passenger Lists: Irish ports to USA 1890.

There are also collections of maps, plans and photographs.

Origins was originally a pay-per-view service but it moved to a subscription system in July 2004. There are a number of subscription options: you can sign up for 72 hours, one month, one quarter or a year; there are separate subscriptions for British Origins, Irish Origins, and Origin Search Pro, or the Origins Total Access subscription covers all services. The 72-hour subscription is £5.95 for British Origins and £3.95 for Irish Origins, while the annual charge is £22.50 for each. Members of the SoG have one free session on British Origins per quarter. Before paying, however, you can do initial searches on surname and year range to see how many records there are in each database which contain the surname. Full details and prices are given at <**www.originsnetwork.com/signup-info.aspx**>.

Once you have purchased credits, you can search in individual datasets or across the entire collection. If you do the latter, you will get a screen like that in Figure 4-1, which indicates how many records were found in each dataset. You can then view the results for a single dataset, or refine your search. Figure 4-2 shows the results of a search in the Bank of England Wills. In this case, since a will is a substantial document, you cannot read the will itself online but must order a hard copy from the SoG, so the search results give you only the basic details. In other cases, such as the

the**Origins**network   User details   **British Origins**   Irish Origins | Scots Origins | Origin Search Pro | 🛒 logout

▸ Search by Name   ▸ Search by Place   ▸ Saved Searches   ▸ Gallery   ▸ Origins Store   ▸ Discussion   ▸ Articles   ▸ Help   ▸ About

Records found

Search criteria: Last name:BISHOP
First name: JOSEPH + All variants
Year range: 1750 to 1820

Dataset	No. of records	View	Search
England and Wales Census 1871	0		Refine search
England and Wales Census 1841	0		Refine search
Boyd's Marriage Index (1538-1840)	31	View Records	Refine search
Marriage Licence Allegations Index - Vicar-General (1694-1850)	119	View Records	Refine search
Marriage Licence Allegations Index - Faculty Office (1701-1850)	1	View Records	Refine search
Bank of England Will Extracts Index (1717-1845)	4	View Records	Refine search
Prerogative Court of Canterbury Wills Index (1750-1800)	8	View Records	Refine search
Archdeaconry Court of London Wills Index (1700-1807)	0		Refine search
York Medieval Probate Index (1267-1501)	0		Refine search
York Peculiars Probate Index (1383-1883)	0		Refine search
London Apprenticeship Abstracts (1442-1850)	6	View Records	Refine search
London Consistory Court Depositions Index (1700-1713)	0		Refine search
Inheritance Disputes Index (1574-1714)	0		Refine search
Boyd's London Burials Index (1538-1840)	1	View Records	Refine search
Militia Attestations Index (1886-1910)	0		Refine search
Trinity House Calendars (1787 - 1854)	2	View Records	Refine search

Save search ▸

Figure 4-1 General search in BritishOrigins

the**Origins**network   User details   **British Origins**   Irish Origins | Scots Origins | Origin Search Pro | 🛒 logout

▸ Search by Name   ▸ Search by Place   ▸ Saved Searches   ▸ Gallery   ▸ Origins Store   ▸ Discussion   ▸ Articles   ▸ Help   ▸ About

View records - Bank of England Will Extracts Index 1717-1845

Search criteria: Last Name: WOODHAM + Close variants
Year range: 1717 to 1845

Click column heading links to change order of results ?

Personal Details	Year	Book	Reg. No.	Film	Order Original
WOODHAM David Gent. of Duke Street Grosvenor Square	1766-79	23	1149	57/2	🛒 Add to cart
WOODHAM Elizabeth Widow of Deptford Kent (in the will is Elizabeth WOODHAMS)	1770-3	25	2209	58/1	🛒 Add to cart
WOODHAM John Baker of Greenwich Kent	1770-3	25	2032	58/1	🛒 Add to cart
WOODHAMS Eleanor Wife later Widow of Richard Woodhams Gent. of Peasmark Sussex	1805-7	37	2139	61/1	🛒 Add to cart

Figure 4-2 Search results in the Bank of England wills at BritishOrigins

theOriginsnetwork   User details   **British Origins**   Irish Origins   Scots Origins   Origin Search Pro   ⊞ logout

▶ Search by Name   ▶ Search by Place   ▶ Saved Searches   ▶ Gallery   ▶ Origins Store   ▶ Discussion   ▶ Articles   ▶ Help   ▶ About

View records - London Apprenticeship Abstracts 1442-1850

Search criteria:
Surname: WOODHAM + Close variants
Year range:*1442 to 1850*

Click column heading links to change order of results ?

Year	Description
1740	Woodham John, son of Christopher, Enfield, Middlesex, farmer, to Solomon Baker, 14 Oct 1740, Distillers' Company
1749	Woodham Webb, son of Thomas, Sandy, Bedfordshire, husbandman (deceased), to William Harris, 20 Jun 1749, Carmens' Company
1750	Woodham Christopher, son of Christopher, Enfield, Middlesex, farmer, to Thomas Wakeling, 10 Apr 1750 [9 Jan 1753 turned over with consent of James Read, citizen and broderer, exec. of master to said James Read], Distillers' Company
1757	Woodham John, son of Benning, Southill, Bedfordshire, yeoman, to William Ringsted, 8 Dec 1757, Coachmakers' and Coach Harness Makers' Company
1782	Woodham Samuel, son of John, Shambrook, Bedfordshire, victualler, to George Summerlin, 4 Jan 1782, Pavoiurs' Company

Figure 4-3 Search results in the apprenticeship records at BritishOrigins

City of London Apprentices, all the genealogically significant information is given in the results (Figure 4-3) and there is nothing further to view.

FAMILYHISTORYONLINE

FamilyHistoryOnline at <www.familyhistoryonline.net> is the data service of the Federation of Family History Societies, which went live at the beginning of 2003. It offers data transcribed by FFHS member societies. The main types of record indexed are:

• marriages
• burials (data from the National Burial Index on CD-ROM)
• monumental inscriptions
• census records.

There are a few datasets for other types of record, and the 1881 census index for England and Wales is accessible free of charge. A full list of datasets is available on the site at <www.familyhistoryonline.net/database/>. Disregarding the 1881 census index, there are around 30 million records in all.

A search of the indexes is free of charge, though you need to log in with a username and password (free) to access the search facility. When you do a search, this provides you with a list of matching entries with details of the dataset in which the match was found and the year of the event (see Figure 4-4). In order to view full entries, you need either to have bought a physical pre-payment voucher (£5 or £10), available from

Figure 4-4 Search results in FamilyHistoryOnline

GENfair (see p. 314) and a number of family history societies, or you can buy a virtual voucher online (£5, £10, £20 or £50). Both types of voucher are valid for six months – in the case of the physical vouchers this means six months from first use.

The charge made for each individual item retrieved depends on the nature of the data, as shown in Table 4-2. As you can see from Figure 4-4, on the search results pages the cost of every item is indicated individually. Where there are several results for a particular county dataset, you also have the option to pay 1p each to see a list of the places for these events (subject to a minimum charge of 10p). Entries from the 1881 census index are free of charge.

At some point FamilyHistoryOnline will be introducing a facility for images of records to be added to datasets. This would allow photographs of monumental inscriptions to be linked to MI indexes, for example. However, it will be up to the contributing societies whether they take advantage of this.

Table 4-2 FamilyHistoryOnline Charges (summer 2005)

Indexes	Surname only	3p
Transcriptions	Other	5p
	General	7p
	Census from 1851 onwards Marriages from July 1837 onwards	9p

Any records not yet checked by the database provider cost 1p less in each case.

SCOTLANDSPEOPLE

The Scottish civil registration indexes were the first genealogical records in the UK to be put online by a government agency, when Scots Origins opened its electronic doors in 1998 to provide the data on behalf of GROS. In 2002, the contract for online service was awarded to Scotland On Line, who now provide it on the ScotlandsPeople site at <**www.scotlandspeople.gov.uk**>. The site makes the following data available:

- Old parish registers from 1553
- Birth, marriages and deaths from 1855 to 1904 or later
- Census records from 1871 to 1901
- Wills and testaments from 1513 to 1901.

A more detailed description of what material is available for each of these classes of record will be found in the sections on civil registration (p. 63), census (p. 79), parish registers (p. 93), and wills (p. 98). Work on these data collections is ongoing. Civil registration material is complete, with indexes and images. For the parish registers, indexes are available and images are due to be added during 2005. The remaining censuses are also due in 2005.

This is a pay-per-view system and you purchase access in blocks of 30 credits for £6. An initial search is free of charge, but this only tells you

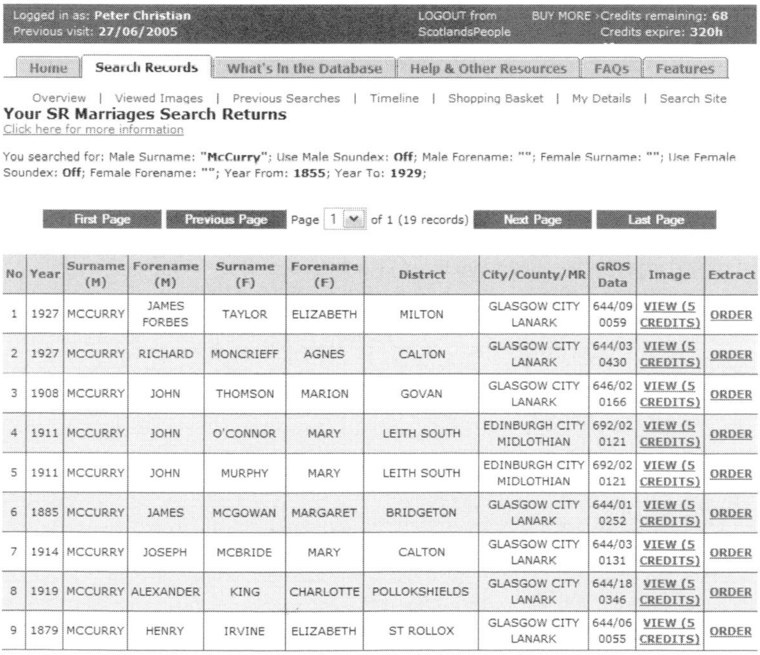
Logged in as: **Peter Christian**
Previous visit: **27/06/2005**
LOGOUT from ScotlandsPeople
BUY MORE › Credits remaining: **68**
Credits expire: **320h**

Home | Search Records | What's In the Database | Help & Other Resources | FAQs | Features

Overview | Viewed Images | Previous Searches | Timeline | Shopping Basket | My Details | Search Site

Your SR Marriages Search Returns

Click here for more information

You searched for: Male Surname: **"McCurry"**; Use Male Soundex: **Off**; Male Forename: ""; Female Surname: ""; Use Female Soundex: **Off**; Female Forename: ""; Year From: **1855**; Year To: **1929**;

First Page | Previous Page | Page 1 of 1 (19 records) | Next Page | Last Page

No	Year	Surname (M)	Forename (M)	Surname (F)	Forename (F)	District	City/County/MR	GROS Data	Image	Extract
1	1927	MCCURRY	JAMES FORBES	TAYLOR	ELIZABETH	MILTON	GLASGOW CITY LANARK	644/09 0059	VIEW (5 CREDITS)	ORDER
2	1927	MCCURRY	RICHARD	MONCRIEFF	AGNES	CALTON	GLASGOW CITY LANARK	644/03 0430	VIEW (5 CREDITS)	ORDER
3	1908	MCCURRY	JOHN	THOMSON	MARION	GOVAN	GLASGOW CITY LANARK	646/02 0166	VIEW (5 CREDITS)	ORDER
4	1911	MCCURRY	JOHN	O'CONNOR	MARY	LEITH SOUTH	EDINBURGH CITY MIDLOTHIAN	692/02 0121	VIEW (5 CREDITS)	ORDER
5	1911	MCCURRY	JOHN	MURPHY	MARY	LEITH SOUTH	EDINBURGH CITY MIDLOTHIAN	692/02 0121	VIEW (5 CREDITS)	ORDER
6	1885	MCCURRY	JAMES	MCGOWAN	MARGARET	BRIDGETON	GLASGOW CITY LANARK	644/01 0252	VIEW (5 CREDITS)	ORDER
7	1914	MCCURRY	JOSEPH	MCBRIDE	MARY	CALTON	GLASGOW CITY LANARK	644/03 0131	VIEW (5 CREDITS)	ORDER
8	1919	MCCURRY	ALEXANDER	KING	CHARLOTTE	POLLOKSHIELDS	GLASGOW CITY LANARK	644/18 0346	VIEW (5 CREDITS)	ORDER
9	1879	MCCURRY	HENRY	IRVINE	ELIZABETH	ST ROLLOX	GLASGOW CITY LANARK	644/06 0055	VIEW (5 CREDITS)	ORDER

Figure 4-5 Search results in ScotlandsPeople

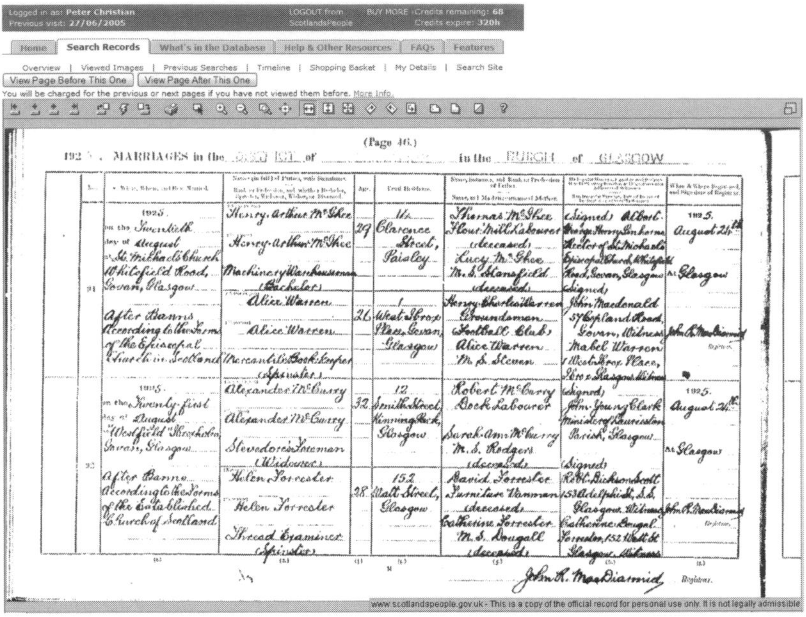

Figure 4-6 An original document in ScotlandsPeople's viewer

how many hits your search produces. Each page of search results costs you one unit and includes a maximum of 25 entries. For the births and deaths, there is then an option to view an image of the original register page at a cost of five credits. For all events you can order a copy of the relevant certificate for £10. This is paid for separately and does not come out of your pre-paid units. A session lasts 168 hours (i.e. seven days), timed from when you last bought credits, and any unused units bought are automatically carried forward to a subsequent session.

The site keeps a record of all search result pages and certificates that you have paid to view and these can be retrieved at any time, not just during the session in which they were first accessed. You therefore don't need to pay to return to the site to review material you have already paid for.

The images are delivered as TIFF format files. These are displayed in a special viewer plug-in, which requires Java to be installed on your computer (see p. 47). Images can be enlarged or printed direct from the viewer, and you can save them to your hard disk. TIFF is a standard graphics format, so you should be able to display, manipulate and print the files with any graphics program. Note that the images are black and white, not greyscale like photographs, and some of the poorer quality originals can be hard to read, particularly as they are scanned at only 200 dots per inch.

The site's menu appears to offer a discussion group, but this facility has in fact been withdrawn. The Help & Other Resources option links to material to help you get the most from the site, and includes glossaries of occupations and other terms.

On its launch, ScotlandsPeople faced a number of problems and met with a great deal of criticism from users. Apart from technical teething problems such as might be expected for any new system, users reported inconsistent search results, missing images, and concern about image quality. Improvements have been made since the launch and a user group was set up to offer feedback from users and advise on future developments. Unfortunately, the closure of the discussion group makes it difficult to tell whether the problems have been resolved to the satisfaction of users.

In 2004, plans were announced for a unified Scottish Family History Service. There have already been some changes in ScotlandsPeople, including a redesign of the site in summer 2005, and the move of Scottish wills from ScottishDocuments. There may well be further developments in the site as part of the creation of this new service.

ANCESTRY

The Ancestry.com website <**www.ancestry.com**> is the largest commercial collection of genealogical data. It holds over 2,000 separate datasets, many of them derived from printed materials which may be more or less difficult to find outside a major genealogical library. For genealogists in the British Isles, however, the UK version of Ancestry at <**www.ancestry.co.uk**> is more convenient as it contains only those records relating to the British Isles or emigrants from them, such as the Australian Convicts Index. For Americans with UK ancestors, there is a subscription option at the main site which includes both US and UK records.

Among the records for the British Isles are:

- Census indexes linked to images for 1861–1901, with the earlier censuses to follow
- GRO indexes for marriages and deaths, 1984–2002
- Parish and/or probate register extracts for all counties
- Pallot's Baptism and Marriage Indexes
- a number of historic books and newspapers.

Ancestry has traditionally been a subscription service, and a quarterly or annual payment provides access to *all* paid databases. The subscriptions for UK material as of summer 2005 are £29.95 for a quarter, or £69.95 for a year. However, with the introduction of the UK censuses in partnership with the National Archives, a pay-per-view option was introduced, with a payment of £6.99 permitting 20 page views within a seven-day period. This covers not just the census, but all datasets on the site. If you use the pay-per-view option, you can extend it to a quarterly or annual subscription by paying the difference. The main Ancestry site at

<www.ancestry.com> has a seven-day free trial offer, but this has been the subject of some criticism in mailing lists, since you have to provide credit card details and if you fail to cancel before the trial expires a subscription is automatically charged to your credit card. If you are going to subscribe, you may prefer to subscribe to the UK & Ireland Collection from the main Ancestry site rather than subscribing via <www.ancestry.co.uk> – at current exchange rates its $99.95 annual subscription works out about £15 cheaper than the £69.95 available from the UK site.

Although Ancestry is a commercial service, some of the material is free of charge. For example, FreeBMD's GRO index data is available here as well as on FreeBMD's own website.

A full list of databases available on Ancestry can be found at <**www. ancestry.com/search/rectype/alldblist.asp**>, while <**www.ancestry.co.uk/ search/rectype/alldblist.asp**> lists only those for the British Isles.

A useful site is Hugh Watkins's Exploring Ancestry blog at <**ancestry. blogspot.com**>. This notes new developments, provides hints and tips, and discusses problems and issues in using Ancestry. Ancestry's own message board for UK and Ireland records at <**boards.ancestry.com/mbexec?htx= board&r=rw&p=topics.ancestry.uk-ire**> can also be useful.

NATIONAL ARCHIVIST

The National Archivist at <**www.nationalarchivist.com**> is a pay-per-view site with a wide variety of records. They represent classes of material not well covered elsewhere, often licensed from the National Archives (there is no other connection between this site and TNA).

The material on the site falls into six categories:

- Births, Marriages and Deaths – Births, Marriages and Deaths at Sea, Divorces
- Military Records – Army Lists and Medal Rolls, the Waterloo Roll Call
- Emigration and Passports – Passport Applications, Emigration Shipping
- Wills, Administrations and Taxes – Death Duty Registers
- British Colonies – records for India and the East India Company
- Directories and Professionals – medical and clergy.

You need to register (free of charge) to use the site. There is some free data, including a list of Officers of the Grenadier Guards, and initial searches are free. For access to the charged records the minimum payment is £7.00, which gives you 35 credits valid for 45 days. Depending on the dataset, each viewed page from an original source costs between one and four credits, i.e. between 20p and 80p. A viewing history keeps a list of all images viewed in the last 30 days and these can be viewed again without further charge.

Images are provided in the DjVu format, so to view them, your browser will need to have the DjVu viewer plug-in installed. The images themselves

Figure 4-7
The National
Archivist

are greyscale and at quite respectable resolutions. The site also has an online shop with data on CD-ROM and genealogy software.

OTHERDAYS

Otherdays is a subscription site devoted to Irish records at <**www.otherdays. com**>. The most important dataset on the site is Griffith's Valuation (see p. 104), indexed with images of the original. Other smaller datasets include directories, newspaper indexes, and Dublin wills and marriage licences. Landowners of Ireland and more directories are promised in the near future. There are a number of free resources including many maps, prints and photographs. Rather oddly, the only way to get a complete list of the datasets is to download the PDF brochure at <**www.otherdays.com/MiniHP/ downloads/consumer_brochure.pdf**>. Subscriptions range from $8.00 for 72 hours up to $44 for a year.

THE GENEALOGIST

The Genealogist at <**www.thegenealogist.co.uk**> is a data service run by well-known software retailer S&N Genealogy Supplies. It provides indexes to census and civil registration records on a subscription basis, with a variety of options. A £4.66 per month 'all-inclusive' subscription gives complete access to all datasets with unlimited viewing. Alternatively it is possible to buy a three-month or one-year subscription to an individual dataset (i.e. one census for one county) – each dataset is priced individually, and in some cases there is a limit to the number of searches or page views.

The civil registration records are made available on the BMDindex site at <**www.bmdindex.co.uk**>, which is discussed on p. 55. The census indexes on The Genealogist are discussed with other census indexes on p. 85.

▌COMMON PROBLEMS

It is not uncommon for users to experience problems with commercial genealogy sites, as indeed with all e-commerce sites. This is nothing to do with the security concerns people have about online payments (these are addressed in Chapter 18), but relate to the web browser and how it is configured. While it is not possible here to cover every eventuality, most of these problems arise from a readily identifiable set of facilities used by commercial websites, and are more or less straightforward to solve. Sites that use such facilities usually provide information on what is required – see, for example, the National Archives' 'Technical Information' page for DocumentsOnline at <**www.nationalarchives.gov.uk/documentsonline/ help/help-technical.asp**> – and you should normally see a warning if some required facility is absent from your configuration (see Figure 4-8).

The main features which cause problems are:

Cookies

A 'cookie' is a piece of information a website stores on your hard disk for its own future use. This is how a site can 'remember' who you are from one visit to the next – even if you are using a different ISP – or even during a single session.[4] However, browsers can be configured to reject cookies, and some people do this to preserve their internet privacy. This will make pay-per-view sites and online

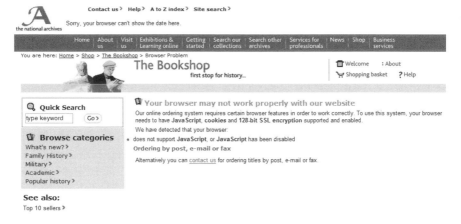

Figure 4-8 A typical browser warning. This one is from the National Archives' online shop

---

4 It may appear to you to be a single session, but it is not like a phone call where a line is allocated exclusively to you for the duration of your call. On the web, each page requested from the server is a completely separate transaction, and cookies are the main way of identifying continuity.

shops unusable – in fact any site that requires some sort of login will only work with cookies enabled. See <**www.nationalarchives. gov.uk/documentsonline/help/help-technical.asp#cookies**> for information on how to enable cookies.

JavaScript

This is a scripting language which, among other things, makes it possible for a web page to validate what the user enters in an online form (checking, for example, that you haven't left some crucial field blank) before the information is submitted to the server. You will be unable to use sites that require this if JavaScript is disabled. The online help for your browser should tell you how to check whether JavaScript is enabled, and how to ensure it is. Most sites that require it will also give instructions.

Java

Java is a programming language which allows programs (called 'applets', i.e. small applications) to run on any type of computer as long as it has software installed which can understand the language. This allows for programmable websites. Java facilities (referred to as a 'Java virtual machine') are normally installed and enabled automatically when you install a new browser, but can be disabled. Individual websites download their own applets to your machine – you will often see a grey box saying 'loading' in the browser window while an applet is being downloaded. The online help for your browser should tell you how to check whether Java is enabled, and how to ensure it is.

Plug-ins

A 'plug-in' is a small utility program which a web browser uses to display material which it can't handle with its own built-in facilities. A number of plug-ins are fairly standard (for example, Flash, QuickTime, and Shockwave) and may well be on your machine already. But some pay-per-view sites have their own plug-ins for viewing images of documents – this is the case for the 1901 census, ScotlandsPeople and 1837online sites. A plug-in needs to be downloaded before it can be run. This will usually take significantly longer than a normal web page to download. Plug-ins sometimes also require Java, as on the 1901 census site. The National Archives site has a useful page on plug-ins at <**www.nationalarchives.gov.uk/help/ plugins.htm**>, with links so you can download some of the most common.

Compatibility

Although the web is based on open standards, browsers do not all implement these as fully and consistently as they might. Also, some website designers insist on using features that only work properly on a particular browser (usually Internet Explorer, as that is the most popular). The only way around problems from this source is to have a recent version of your preferred browser and, if that is not Internet Explorer, a copy of that too. Since all the main browsers can be downloaded free, there's no real reason not to have the latest version, unless your computer is running an old operating system or has limited memory or disk space.

If you have any difficulties with online data services, there will always be a variety of help available. Sites selling data should always have a help page, and perhaps a separate technical help page which spells out hardware and/or software requirements. You are very likely to find an FAQ ('Frequently Asked Questions') page. As a last resort there should always be an email address to contact for assistance and there may also be a telephone helpline.

Incidentally, for a commercial, official or major volunteer-run site, it is a good idea to mail the webmaster if you find that it doesn't display properly in your browser. All government sites should conform to the government's own browser compatibility standards (see 'Guidelines for UK government websites', available in various formats from <**www.cabinetoffice.gov.uk/e-government/resources/handbook/introduction.asp**>).

CHAPTER 5

ONLINE SOURCES: CIVIL REGISTRATION

Birth, marriage and death certificates are generally the first official documents the family historian encounters. In an ideal world – for the genealogist at least – all of them would be online. But privacy concerns make it unlikely that full certificate details for 'recent' events will be easily accessible on the web, and so far only a small percentage of the 'historical' certificates, those from Scotland, have been digitized.

But even where certificates are not online, there is much information about birth, death and marriage records on the web to help you identify and order paper certificates, including a wide range of sites with civil registration indexes.

ENGLAND AND WALES

Civil registration of births, marriages and deaths started in England and Wales on 1 July 1837, and the original certificates are held in duplicate by the original local register office and by the General Register Office (GRO), which is part of the Office of National Statistics (ONS). The original certificates cannot be seen (for reasons which have been questioned, though not yet legally challenged), but copies can be ordered from the Family Records Centre (FRC). Indexes to the certificates can be consulted at the FRC and on microfiche in county record offices and other genealogical libraries.

The FamilyRecords portal has basic information on birth, marriage and death certificates at <**www.familyrecords.gov.uk/topics/bmd.htm**>: it explains how to get certificates and what information is on each of them. FamilyRecords also hosts the website of the FRC at <**www.familyrecords. gov.uk/frc/**>, which provides details of its location and opening hours, as well as the records and indexes the FRC holds. The GRO website at <**www. gro.gov.uk**> has comprehensive information about ordering certificates. There is also information about adoptions and overseas records.

Neither the FRC nor the GRO has a data service, and they do not provide online access to birth, marriage and death indexes or certificates. However, the GRO has an online service for ordering certificates at <**www. gro.gov.uk/gro/content/certificates/**> (covering England and Wales). In order to use the online ordering system you need to log in, and if you register (rather than using a one-off guest login) your details will be stored for future use and will not have to be re-entered for subsequent orders.

Beyond these sites, there are a number of unofficial sources of information on general registration which will be helpful for initial orientation. Genuki has a page devoted to civil registration in England and Wales at <**www.genuki.org.uk/big/eng/civreg/**>. Barbara Dixon's Registration Certificate Tutorials site at <**home.clara.net/dixons/Certificates/indexbd. htm**> describes how to order certificates and gives a detailed description of the fields on the three types of certificate. Other useful guides include Mark Howells's article 'Ordering Birth Registration Certificates from England and Wales. Using the LDS Family History Center's Resources' at <**www.oz.net/~markhow/ukbirths.htm**> and Kimberley Powell's 'Civil Registration in England and Wales. A Guide to Birth, Marriage and Death Records' at <**genealogy.about.com/library/weekly/aa062100a.htm**>.

GRO INDEXES

In 1999, in the absence of any official programme to digitize either the original certificates or the GRO indexes, a volunteer project called FreeBMD secured permission from the ONS to transcribe the indexes over 100 years old for free online access. In 2003, the GRO announced a completely open policy – any organization which has purchased the microfiche indexes is now free to transcribe or digitize the original pages and make them available online, free or charged, with no cut-off in years of coverage.[5] This has provided impetus for a number of online services offering digitized images of the original indexes.

While the older indexes are contained in the hefty physical books in the FRC, the material from 1984 onwards is rather different: the GRO has electronic records from this date, held in a number of databases. It has permitted these, too, to be made available online. The advantage of the databases over the older material is that entries can be searched for individually – rather than having to look at a series of pages in the hope of identifying the correct entry (whether online or at the FRC), you can search the whole range of years at once.

---

5 The announcement was posted (unofficially) to the soc.genealogy.britain newsgroup on 13 February 2003 under the heading 'GRO Indexes – England & Wales' and can be found in the archive of the GENBRIT mailing list at <**archiver.rootsweb.com/th/index/GENBRIT/ 2003–02**> or on Google groups at <**groups.google.com**>.

FREEBMD

FreeBMD has a large group of volunteers, currently almost 8,000, who either transcribe the indexes from microfiche in planned extractions or simply submit entries from their own extractions along with the surrounding entries. It has two sites: <www.freebmd.org.uk> is the home site and there is also a mirror on RootsWeb at <freebmd.rootsweb.com>, which can be useful in periods when the main site is busy and therefore slow to respond to searches.

By summer 2005, the project's database had reached over 100 million distinct records. The pattern of extractions has concentrated on marriages, with smaller percentages of births and deaths, and for many years the extraction of marriages is already complete. Since the relaxation of the 100-year restriction is relatively recent, FreeBMD's material is over-whelmingly for the period before 1910, though it will be extended to 1983 in due course.

Up-to-date information on the percentage of coverage for each year and each type of event will be found at <www.freebmd.org.uk/progress.shtml>. At the current rate of work, it looks as if the nineteenth century part of the project could well be complete by the end of 2006.

The material so far collected can be searched online. A comprehensive search page (Figure 5-1) allows you to search for a specific person in a chosen place and date range, or to extract all the entries for a particular

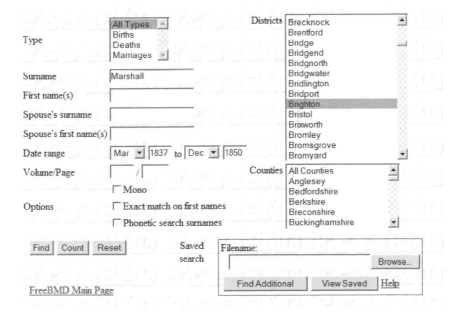

Figure 5-1 Searching FreeBMD

Search for *Type:* All Types *Surname:* Marshall *Start date:* Mar 1837
  End date: Dec 1850 *District:* Brighton

Whilst FreeBMD makes every effort to ensure accurate transcription, errors exist in both the original index and the transcription. You are advised to verify the reference given from a copy of the index before ordering a certificate.

Surname	First name(s)	Age	District	Vol	Page	
Deaths Sep 1837						
Marshall	Eliza		Brighton	7	170	Info
Marshall	John		Brighton	7	172	Info
Deaths Dec 1837						
Marshall	Elizabeth		Brighton	7	185	Info
Deaths Jun 1838						

Figure 5-2 FreeBMD search results

surname. Figure 5-1 shows a search for all events for the surname Marshall in the Brighton registration district between 1837 and 1850. Figure 5-2 shows the results of this search. Clicking on the links in the district column will take you to information on the registration district, while following the link in the page column brings up a list of all the events on that page in the original register (*not* the index). Note that the contributor's contact details are provided only for error reporting, and you cannot expect to contact the contributor for full details of the event, since he or she has only looked at the index, not the original certificates. You will need to order any certificate yourself.

A very useful feature is the ability to save a search and re-run it at any time. When you repeat a saved search, you see only new records that have been added since you saved.

Although the main focus of the project is the transcription of indexes, FreeBMD also makes digitized images of the original index pages free of charge. There is no search facility for this – once you have selected the type of event, the year and quarter, and the initial letter of the surname, it is up to you to judge where in the pages for that letter your surname occurs, so you may need to view several images to get the right one. The site gives you several image formats to choose from: PDF, GIF, JPG and TIFF. Of these, the JPG is one to avoid unless you have a broadband connection as the files are around 3MB in size, while the GIFs are around 450MB and the other formats around half that. At present only the index pages up to 1910 are available on the site.

FreeBMD is always looking for new volunteers, and details of what is involved can be found on the website. You can keep up to date with the progress of the project by joining the FreeBMD-News-L mailing list – subscription information will be found at **<lists.rootsweb.com/index/intl/ UK/FreeBMD-News.html>**.

1837ONLINE

1837online is a commercial site which went live in April 2003 at **<www.1837.online.com>** offering *all* the GRO indexes apart from the most recent 18 months. The material is provided simply as images of the original paper indexes – they are taken from the microfiche – and there is no index of individual entries. You use the index to locate the page on which a given name, alphabetically, should occur. In the original physical indexes, pages are indexed only by the first three letters of a surname. But 1837online supplies the first surname and forename on each page in full (see Figure 5-3), so you should be able to locate precisely the right page without too much trouble. Occasionally, the name you are looking for will be the first or last one on the page and you may need to check that there is not another entry for the same name at the bottom of the previous page or the top of the next one.

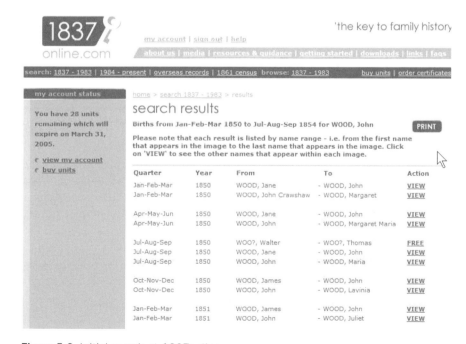

Figure 5-3 Initial search at 1837online

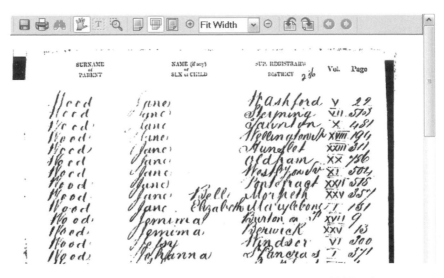

Figure 5-4 A page from the GRO indexes in the DjVu viewer at 1837online

The site operates a pay-per-view system. There are various rates depending on how many units you buy at a time. The basic rate is £5 for 50 units, each of which gives you one page view, but heavier users get discounted rates of £60 for 800 and £120 for 2,400 page views. The basic block of 50 units is valid for 90 days, but this increases for the larger blocks of units, up to a year if you spend £60 or more.

A special plug-in, DjVu, needs to be downloaded and installed before any images can be viewed. This allows you to zoom in and out, print, and save the images to hard disk (see Figure 5-4). Indeed, the viewer also allows you to select portions of text on the page, though the level of accuracy in recognizing characters is very poor. If you want to save the page images for later viewing and perhaps editing, you may find that the DjVu image format is not supported by your graphics software. In this case, check the website for your graphics software and see if they offer a DjVu plug-in.[6] For users who have problems installing the DjVu plug-in, there is a viewer with more limited facilities, DjVu Express, which allows images to be viewed without any software installation.

---

6 Alternatively, if you use Windows, download the IrfanView graphics viewer and its DjVu plug-in free from <**www.irfanview.com**>.

1837online offers the post-1983 indexes in a searchable database, and you use a search form to locate an individual entry rather than an index page. However, the search results indicate only how many records match your search criteria, with no further details, and you either have to pay to view all of them (one unit each) or narrow down your search.

1837online also offers some overseas records (see p. 67) and an 1861 census index (see p. 78).

BMDINDEX

BMDindex is an offshoot of S&N Genealogy Supplies with a website at **<www.bmdindex.co.uk>**. The site aims to offer a complete set of digitized images of the GRO indexes to births, marriages and deaths from 1837 to the present day. A pay-per-view option gives you 50 page views in a 90-day period for £5, or 200 page views in a year for £14.95. The BMD data is included in The Genealogist's 'all-inclusive' subscription for £4.66 per month – see p. 45.

A search for a name brings a link to the index image for the relevant page in each quarter. The search itself is not charged, but each image you look at costs one credit. Images are provided in Adobe Acrobat format (PDF). As long as you already have the PDF viewer installed in your browser, you will not need to download any plug-in, and this viewer has built in zoom, save and print facilities.

As with 1837online, the post-1983 material is presented in a searchable database. In addition to the straightforward birth, marriage and death

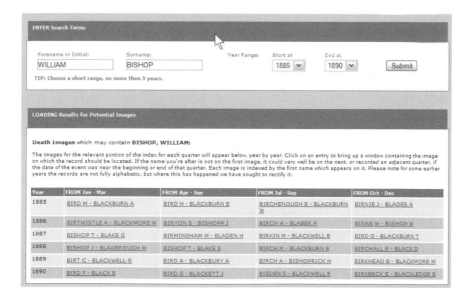

Figure 5-5 Search results in BMDindex

searches you would expect, there is an option to search for a death by the birth date of the deceased. Births can be searched by the surname of the father and maiden surname of the mother, without giving a forename for the child, making it possible to identify all the children of an individual couple. Advanced search options allow you to include additional information, such as registration district, to narrow down your search.

FAMILYRELATIVES

FamilyRelatives is a fairly new site, launched at the end of 2004 at <www.familyrelatives.org>. This is another pay-per-view system, and it offers not just images but transcription of the indexes. So far only the period 1866–1920 has been transcribed, with the earlier records promised soon. For the period 1921–1983, just the images of the original index pages are offered. 60 units costs £6.00 (discounted for larger amounts), and costs vary according to the material available. Where there's a full transcription, each page of search results costs two units (i.e. 20p) and it then costs four units (i.e. 40p) to view the index page. For the post-1921 period, searches are free and each index page image costs two units to view.

It looks as if the database has been created by optical character recognition, and without conducting some tests, it is impossible to say how

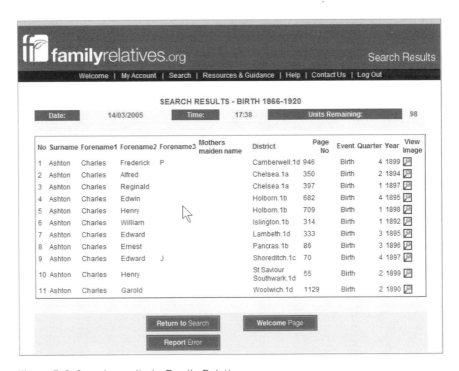

Figure 5-6 Search results in Family Relatives

accurately this has been done. Looked at per entry, this is a more expensive service than the others, but the ability to search a database of individual entries means you should be able to identify the relevant record with much less trial and error, so overall the costs may well not be any greater. Like 1837online, this site requires your browser to have the DjVu plug-in installed.

LOCAL BMD PROJECTS

While all the sites mentioned so far are national in coverage, there are a growing number of projects centred on local register offices. These go under the generic name UKBMD and links to all local BMD projects will be found on Ian Hartas's UKBMD site at <www.ukbmd.org.uk>.

It's not just that these sites supplement the national datasets. An important difference between these and all the national sites mentioned above is that they work from the original local registration records and so will be largely free of the errors that dog the GRO indexes, which were made from copies of the original registrations, putting them at two removes from the originals. If your family comes from one of the parts of the country covered, these should be used in preference to the services mentioned in the previous sections.

The first of these projects was CheshireBMD at <cheshirebmd.org.uk>, a collaboration between Cheshire County Council, Wirral Metropolitan Borough, the Family History Society of Cheshire and South Cheshire Family History Society.

Cheshire aims to have all index entries for births, marriages and deaths online for the period 1837–1950. The site has detailed information on the coverage so far for each registration district, and makes the ordering of certificates very straightforward – a link from each search result brings up a form for printing off, with the certificate reference (though not the other details) already filled in. The site already has around four million entries available for searching.

So far seven similar projects have taken a lead from the example of Cheshire, and use the same website design and software:

- BathBMD at <www.bathbmd.org.uk> has around 175,000 entries
- LancashireBMD at <www.lancashirebmd.org.uk> contains just over 2.5 million records, the majority of which are marriages
- NorthWalesBMD at <www.northwalesbmd.org.uk> has around 900,000 records, mainly births
- StaffordshireBMD at <www.staffordshirebmd.org.uk> has around 900,000 records, concentrating on births and marriages
- WestMidlandsBMD at <www.westmidlandsbmd.org.uk> has around 525,000 records, mainly births

- WiltshireBMD at <www.wiltshirebmd.org.uk> is a fairly new project with around 50,000 marriages
- YorkshireBMD at <www.YorkshireBMD.org.uk> has around three million entries to date, two thirds of which are births.

Some other local authorities are developing indexes on similar lines, sometimes with the help of local family history societies:

- Cambridgeshire County Council's CAMDEX project at <www. cambridgeshire.gov.uk/community/BMD/camdex> has over 1.2 million records, mainly births and marriages.
- Darlington Borough Council BMDs at <www.darlington.gov.uk/Living/ Register+Office/RegOfficeSearch.htm>. There is no indication on the site that coverage is not complete.
- Durham County Council has an online certificate ordering system at <www.durham.gov.uk/gro/newgro.nsf/enter> covering all marriage and many birth indexes, but death indexes only after 1981.
- Kent County Council has online ordering of certificates at <extranet3. kent.gov.uk/sp/rois/home.html>, with an index of all marriages, and of births and deaths since 1992.
- Tees Valley Indexes at <www.teesvalley-indexes.co.uk> covers the former county of Cleveland (now replaced by Middlesbrough, Hartlepool, Stockton-on-Tees, Redcar & Cleveland). Births are best represented, but Hartlepool has complete coverage of all events.
- Warwickshire has around 250,000 records in its online indexes. The URL for this site is truly horrific – 90 characters long with the last 30

Births, Marriages and Deaths on the Internet

Cheshire Birth indexes for the years: 1837 to 1839				
Surname	Forename(s)	Sub-District	Registers At	Reference
BISHOP	William	Stockport First	Stockport	ST1/2/94

Cheshire Birth indexes for the years: 1855				
Surname	Forename(s)	Sub-District	Registers At	Reference
BISHOP	William	Hyde	Tameside	HYD/24/100

Cheshire Birth indexes for the years: 1864				
Surname	Forename(s)	Sub-District	Registers At	Reference
BISHOP	William Harrie	Tranmere	Wirral	TRA/4/91

Cheshire Birth indexes for the years: 1865				
Surname	Forename(s)	Sub-District	Registers At	Reference
BISHOP	William Herbert	Knott Lanes	Tameside	KNO/14/2

Figure 5-7 CheshireBMD

or so a random assortment of characters. Follow the link from UKBMD or from the website for this book.

- Wrexham has a marriage index for 1837–1997 at <www.wrexham.gov. uk/english/community/genealogy/MarriageIndexSearchForm.cfm>.

In three cases, indexes have been prepared entirely by family history societies:

- For the Isle of Wight, the Isle of Wight FHS has a BMD index on its website at <www.isle-of-wight-fhs.co.uk/bmd/start.htm> covering, so far, all marriages, and births and deaths for most of the nineteenth century, and the period since 1990.
- The Northumberland and Durham FHS has the Newcastle Register Office Indexes online at <www.ndfhs.fsnet.co.uk/RegIndex.html>. So far births are covered for 1837–1870 and marriages to 1900.
- Derbyshire FHS offers the Derbyshire Registrar's Marriage Index, with around 325,000 records up to 1950, on the FamilyHistoryOnline site at <www.familyhistoryonline.net> (see p. 39).

NortheastBMD at <www.northeastbmd.org.uk> provides a gateway to all projects covering the north east of England.

REGISTER OFFICES AND REGISTRATION DISTRICTS

While the LocalBMD projects are very useful, they will not be much help if you do not know where an event was registered. Also, if you want to order a certificate from a local registrar, you will need to know which office to approach. For both these reasons knowledge of registration districts is valuable, and there is extensive information available online.

For historical information about registration districts (up to 1930), Genuki has a set of pages prepared by Brett Langston at <www.fhsc.org.uk/ genuki/REG/> which provide comprehensive details about registration districts in England and Wales, giving:

- Name of the district.
- Date of creation.
- Date of abolition (if before 1930).
- Names of the sub-districts.
- The GRO volume number used for the district in the national indexes of births, marriages and deaths.
- An alphabetical listing of the parishes, townships and hamlets included within its boundaries. If a district covered parts of two or more counties, the areas in each county are listed separately.
- The name(s) of the district(s) which currently hold the records. If two or more offices are listed, the one which holds most records is named first, and the one with least is given last.

There is an alphabetical list of districts at <**www.fhsc.org.uk/genuki/ REG/district.htm**>, with links to lists for individual counties, and if you are not sure what registration district a particular place is in, consult <**www. genuki.org.uk/big/eng/civreg/places/**>.

Genuki also has tables matching the GRO volume numbers to registration districts at <**www.genuki.org.uk/big/eng/civreg/GROIndexes.html**>.

The names and current contact details of individual register offices will also be found on Genuki, at <**www.fhsc.org.uk/genuki/REG/regoff.html**>. This list does not link to the websites of register offices which have an online presence, but it does provide email addresses and links to any LocalBMD site which includes that registration district.

The GRO's home page at <**www.gro.gov.uk**> has a search box to find local register offices for a particular postcode or place. The search results provide a link to the relevant local authority web page.

FUTURE DEVELOPMENTS

While the GRO has relaxed controls over putting the registration indexes on the web, an obvious question is whether England and Wales will be following Scotland (see p. 62) in putting the primary data online. The answer would seem to be yes and no: there are no firm plans for an official data service for older civil registration records in England and Wales, but other organizations will be permitted to digitize the 'historical records'. However, the registration process itself is to go electronic, and the more recent records will be digitized.

This was the proposal in a Government white paper, *Civil Registration: Vital Change*, published in January 2002, which is online at <**www. statistics.gov.uk/registration/whitepaper/**>. It was followed up in 2004 by an invitation to tender for a project called DOVE ('digitisation of vital events'), 'a central computerized database of civil registration records. This will be able to be accessed directly by citizens, other government departments and provide legitimate access for certain private enterprises to check information.' However, the access for citizens mentioned here is for new registrations and not for access to historical records.

By the end of 2004, however, it was clear that the proposed legislation which grew out of the white paper and the subsequent consultation process would not be enacted, at least in its initial form. The GRO had attempted to introduce the changes by means not of a normal Act of Parliament but through a Regulatory Reform Order (RRO), which requires scrutiny by parliamentary committees but no parliamentary debate. But the committees which scrutinize draft RROs rejected the GRO's proposals.

Reasons for the rejection include the widespread dissatisfaction expressed by the genealogical community on a number of issues: some of the information that would be withheld relating to recent events; the low quality standards proposed for the digitization of historical certificates;

and the absence of any plans for proper archiving of the original records. In view of the number of contentious issues, the committees concluded that the RRO was an inappropriate form of legislation for these changes.

Of course genealogists welcomed the freeing up of older records for digitization but were inevitably dismayed that the GRO wanted to restrict some information. The argument from the GRO has been that privacy concerns must override the interests of genealogists, but even so it is difficult to see what sense there is in some of the proposals. Who would regard a fifty-year-old address as sensitive? Can someone who has died have a right to (or even a need for) privacy? Why would anyone need their occupation kept confidential, especially since they are the ones who tell the registrar what to record? Adoptees wishing to trace their birth parents, too, would have had their legitimate expectations thwarted by some of the suggested restrictions.

There is extensive material online relating to the proposals. In addition to the original white paper, related documents from the GRO, including the text of the RRO, will be found in the 'Looking Ahead' area of its website at <www.gro.gov.uk/gro/content/aboutus/lookingahead/>. A summary of the proposals has been published by the Federation of Family History Societies on its website at <www.ffhs.org.uk/Societies/Liaison/WhitePaper.htm>, and details of which items of information were to become restricted are at <www.ffhs.org.uk/Societies/Liaison/AnnexC.htm>. Responses to the white paper from the SoG and FFHS can be found at <www.sog.org.uk/files/crr-sogresponse.html> and <www.ffhs.org.uk/registrationresp.htm> respectively.

On 26 October 2004 representatives from the Federation of Family History Societies were among those giving evidence to the House of Commons Regulatory Reform Committee on the proposed RRO. A transcript of the proceedings can be found on the UK Parliament website at <www.publications.parliament.uk/pa/cm200304/cmselect/cmdereg/uc1201-i/uc120102.htm>. The prior written submission from the FFHS is at <www.publications.parliament.uk/pa/cm200304/cmselect/cmdereg/uc1201-i/1201m3.pdf>.

The reports of the Regulatory Reform Committees will be found at <www.publications.parliament.uk/pa/ld200405/ldselect/lddelreg/14/14.pdf> for the Lords and <www.publications.parliament.uk/pa/cm200405/cmselect/cmdereg/118/118.pdf> for the Commons. These are both quite substantial reports, and those aspects most relevant for family historians have been extracted by the Federation at <www.ffhs.org.uk/Societies/Liaison/Lords.htm> and <www.ffhs.org.uk/Societies/Liaison/Commons.htm>.

The text of the DOVE tender will be found at <www.publictechnology.net/modules.php?op=modload&name=News&file=article&sid=1491>.

Clearly, full historical registration records for England and Wales will be available online in due course, and at least *some* information for more recent events. But the exact details, and how they differ from the original proposals, remain to be seen. While the defeat of the RRO may be seen as a victory for the genealogical community, there's no guarantee that the full House of Commons won't give privacy concerns a much higher priority than access to information, so it will be up to family historians to ensure that their concerns continue to be taken into account.

SCOTLAND

In Scotland, general registration dates from 1 January 1855. The website of the General Register Office for Scotland (GROS) at <**www.gro-scotland. gov.uk**> is the official online source of information about these records.

Genuki's 'Introduction to Scottish Family History' at <**www.genuki. org.uk/big/sct/intro.html**> has information on civil registration in Scotland, and GROS has a page 'How can GROS help me research my Scottish ancestors?' at <**www.gro-scotland.gov.uk/famrec/hlpsrch/**>. GROS also has a list of local register offices with contact details at <**www.gro-scotland.gov. uk/grosweb/grosweb.nsf/pages/file1/$file/reglist.pdf**>. Links to websites

Figure 5-8 The General Register Office for Scotland home page at <**www.gro-scotland.gov.uk**>

are not provided in this listing, but the domain name given in the email address (the part after the @) prefixed with *www.* will probably get you to the local authority website which hosts the pages for the local registration service.

The situation with the Scottish general registration records is much better than that for England and Wales. Currently the older indexes to births, marriages and deaths are available, along with images of the birth and death certificates, via the pay-per-view system at ScotlandsPeople described in the following section.

Not all certificates can be viewed or ordered online, and for those that cannot, the GROS website provides ordering information at <**www. gro-scotland.gov.uk/famrec/bdm/**>. Alternatively, Scots Origins (see below) allows you to order transcriptions of more recent certificates electronically. However, no index information is available online for more recent certificates, and you will need to establish the correct entry by referring to the microfilm indexes held in genealogy libraries. But the LDS church has also microfilmed the original registers, and David Wills's guide to the relevant Family History Library microfilm numbers will be useful if you want to refer to these films. The main page is at <**www.ktb.net/~dwills/ scotref/13300-scottishreference.htm**>.

GROS has a list of registration districts at <**www.gro-scotland.gov.uk/ grosweb/grosweb.nsf/pages/files/$file/old_opr.pdf**>.

SCOTLANDSPEOPLE

ScotlandsPeople at <**www.scotlandspeople.gov.uk**> is the sole and official online source for Scottish General Registration records and is described in detail on p. 41. This site offers the following registration records:

- Birth indexes and images of certificates 1855–1904
- Marriage indexes 1855–1929
- Death indexes and images of certificates 1855–1954.

Each year will see the extension of the period covered by one year. Images of all certificates are available on the site.

SCOTS ORIGINS

While Scots Origins at <**www.scotsorigins.com**> ceased to host the GROS's own pay-per-view service in September 2002, it now offers instead the 'Scots Origins Experts Research' service. This allows you to request a transcription of a number of different types of record, including the Statutory Registers of births, deaths and marriages. A search in the Statutory Registers costs £8, and the results are emailed to you within 10 days.

One reason why you might sometimes want to use this service rather than ScotlandsPeople is that it covers events up to 1990, and therefore allows online access to more recent certificates (online ordering of certificates direct from the GROS is possible only for the period covered by ScotlandsPeople). At present this is the only way to get access to information from Scottish certificates not included on ScotlandsPeople – Scotland has not made the microfilm indexes available for digitization. The transcription service, however, requires reasonably accurate information, including the registration district and the year (±2, so will only be useful where you already know approximate date and place).

▌IRELAND

In Ireland, registration of Protestant marriages dates from 1 April 1845, while full registration began on 1 January 1864. The records for the whole of Ireland up to 31 December 1921 are held by the Registrar General in Dublin, who also holds those for the Republic of Ireland from that date. The equivalent records for Northern Ireland are held by the General Register Office (Northern Ireland), GRONI. The relevant websites are at <**www.groireland.ie**> and <**www.groni.gov.uk**> respectively. The National Archives of Ireland have information on records of births, marriages and deaths at <**www.nationalarchives.ie/genealogy/birthsmarrdeaths.html**>.

While Scotland had already solved the issues of online access to historical civil registration records by 2002, it seems as if the Irish authorities, North and South, are a long way behind. For Ireland, no civil registration records, and only a tiny proportion of the indexes to them, are currently available on the web.

A consultation document, *Bringing Civil Registration into the 21st Century* at <**www.groireland.ie/images/consultation.pdf**>), was published by the Irish government in May 2001. In October 2003 they announced the official launch of the 'government approved modernisation of the civil registration service', with the promise that 'Further developments within the modernized Civil Registration Service will include the introduction of automated genealogy/family research facilities and the provision of a range of services over the Internet.' But there have been few outward signs of progress and we do not seem to be any closer to online civil registration records for the Republic than we were at the time of the first edition of this book back in 2001. Ireland's Civil Registration Bill 2003 (<**www.irlgov.ie/bills28/bills/2003/3503/b35c03d.pdf**>) makes no mention of online access to historical records in its 68 pages; it merely empowers the Registrar to consider the use of 'electronic or other information technology' where appropriate.

Sean Murphy's very useful 'Guide to the General Register Office of Ireland' at <**homepage.tinet.ie/~seanjmurphy/gro/**> covers all aspects of civil registration in Ireland. The introduction at <**homepage.tinet.ie/~seanjmurphy/gro/intro.htm**> discusses what little he has been able to discover from officials about the progress of digitization, and another page on the site discusses the 2001 consultation document. The Genealogical Society of Ireland's page (on its old website) devoted to the consultation document at **<www.dun-laoghaire.com/genealogy/civreg.html>** provides a highly critical account, both of the detail of the proposals and of the failure to make progress.

No firm plans to place records or indexes online have been announced by GRONI either. However, a consultation document, *Civil Registration in the 21st century*, published in October 2003 and available at **<www. groni.gov.uk/Publication/187200393137.pdf>**, reveals that all the indexes have been electronically indexed. Digitization is envisaged as being complete 'several years from now' and the paper offers no firm view on what material should be available online. At the time of writing, the results of the consultation were not yet available, but it will be worth checking the GRONI site for news of further progress.

All in all, it is difficult to see how any civil registration records for Ireland could be available on the web, officially, for some years. However, at least in the case of GRONI there seems to be no reason to doubt that it will happen, even if the timescale is uncertain. In fact GRONI has already taken the first step in that certificates can be ordered online via a secure e-commerce system, or you can print off blank forms in PDF format.

The only Ireland-wide material online will be found at FamilySearch **<www.familysearch.org>**, where the IGI (see p. 89) includes the births for the first five years of registration in Ireland, 1864–1868, and some early Protestant marriage registrations. Details of IGI coverage will be found in Colin Ferguson's 'Civil Registration – IGI and BVRI' page at **<www.sierratel.com/colinf/genuki/CAV/IGIBVRI.html>**. Hugh Wallis has a list of FHL batch numbers (see p. 90) relating to Irish civil registration indexes, mainly for births, at **<freepages.genealogy.rootsweb.com/ ~hughwallis/IGIBatchNumbers/CountyMisc.htm>**.

A list of Irish registration districts, which are based on Poor Law Unions, is provided by Sean Murphy at **<homepage.eircom.net/~seanjmurphy/ gro/plus.htm>** and by ConnorsGenealogy **<www.connorsgenealogy.com/ districts.htm>**, which includes the volume numbers and links to a map of registration districts at **<www.connorsgenealogy.com/RegDist.htm>**.

From-Ireland has a page devoted to Civil Registration at **<www. from-ireland.net/gene/civilregistration.htm>**, which links to some small extracts for a wide range of registration districts at **<www.from-ireland. net/gene/district.htm>**.

LOCAL TRANSCRIPTS

In the absence of any national programme of digitization for Irish registration records, there are nonetheless a few local and partial transcription projects.

The only coherent project I am aware of is Waterford County Library's online index to local death registrations 1864–1901, with full transcriptions of the original certificates, at <**83.220.200.136/ipac20/ipac.jsp? profile=death**> as part of its electronic catalogue.

Otherwise there are a number of sites which have small collections of registration data transcribed:

- Among its User Submitted Databases, RootsWeb includes some death records for County Tipperary at <**userdb.rootsweb.com/regional.html #Irl**>. There is no indication of the dates covered, and this database cannot be selected for searching, though its records will be included when you specify 'Ireland' and 'deaths' as the country and type of record to be searched.
- Margaret Grogan has a range of transcriptions for County Cork, mostly for individual places, at <**www.sci.net.au/userpages/mgrogan/cork/ a_civil.htm**>, compiled from submissions to the Cork mailing list. You need to check each one as there is no overall search facility.
- The Ireland CMC Genealogy Record Project at <**www.cmcrp.net**> has user-submitted data which includes some civil registration records, though these are mostly individual entries rather than systematic extractions. There are separate pages for Clare, Cork, Dublin, Kerry, Limerick, Mayo, Tipperary, Waterford, Wicklow, and a single page for all other counties. Once on a county page, there are links at the top of the page to the various groups of records.

OFFSHORE

The Isle of Man, and the individual Channel Islands (Jersey, Guernsey, Alderney and Sark) have their own civil registration starting from various dates.

The Isle of Man Civil Registry has a website at <**www.gov.im/registries/ general/civilregistry/**>, mainly devoted to new registrations. However, the 'Contacts' button at the top of the page will lead you to contact details, including an email address.

Alex Glendinning has a 'Research in the Channel Islands FAQ' at <**user.itl.net/~glen/genukici.html**> with information on civil registration (on the pages for the individual islands), but I am not aware of any registration data online for these islands. The relevant authorities for the individual islands do not seem to have websites. However, John Fuller's 'Channel Islands Genealogy' page at <**www.rootsweb.com/~jfuller/ ci/volunteers.html**> mentions some volunteers prepared to do look-ups in the Guernsey death registers.

CERTIFICATE EXCHANGES

Although current GRO rules specifically forbid family historians from putting scanned certificates online,[7] the UK BDM Exchange at <**www.ukbdm.org.uk**> has a service allowing people to exchange information on certificates. The site has an index of some 90,000 certificates and gives an email address so that you can contact the certificate holder for more details. The listing also indicates those cases where a certificate is no longer needed by the owner. There are also some baptisms, marriages and burials from parish registers. Search results include full names as well as date and place. Clicking on the small number in the left-hand column brings up a screen with contact details for the owner of the certificate.

The site requires registration and payment of £5 per year, though you can start with a one-month free trial, which can be extended by entering information from your own certificates.

Note that if you are not using Internet Explorer you may need to use the address <**ukbdm.corpex.com**> for the site to work correctly.

For Scotland, there is the Scotland BDM Exchange at <**www.sctbdm.com**>, which has almost 40,000 entries, though this includes some entries from parish registers. The site is free. A much more limited facility for Ireland, with under 1,000 certificates, will be found at <**www.thauvin.net/chance/ireland/bmd/**>.

OVERSEAS

Some events registered overseas form part of the UK's records, notably consular and certain army records. The indexes to these are available in the FRC, and 1837online has the following available on its pay-per-view site at <**www.1837online.com**>:

- Natal and South African Forces deaths 1899–1902
- WW1 marriages (behind British Lines) and deaths
- WW2 deaths
- WW2 deaths Indian Services
- Consular & UK High Commission births, marriages and deaths
- Army births, marriages and deaths
- Service Department marriages and deaths
- Regimental Birth Indexes
- Chaplains births, marriages and deaths
- Air births

---

7 'Guidance on the Copying of Birth, Death and Marriage Certificates', HMSO Guidance Note No. 7, online at <**www.hmso.gov.uk/copyright/guidance/gn_07.htm**>.

- Air deaths and missing persons
- Marine births and deaths
- Ionian Islands births, marriages and deaths.

If you have ancestors who were immigrants or emigrants, you may need access to other countries' civil registration services. There is no single way of getting this information for every country, but the most likely to succeed are:

- See if there is a GenWeb page for it – the index of countries at <www.worldgenweb.org/countryindex.html> will take you to the relevant regional GenWeb site, which may have the information, and should at least point you to a message board where you can ask. (See p. 24 for more information on GenWeb.)
- Check the relevant country or regional page on Cyndi's List at <www.cyndislist.com>. Sections devoted to individual countries will also be found on the pages for:
  - Births & Baptisms <www.cyndislist.com/births.htm>
  - Deaths <www.cyndislist.com/deaths.htm>
  - Marriages <www.cyndislist.com/marriage.htm>.

Don't expect other countries to be as far on the road to complete digital records as Scotland is, but you may be lucky. Some states in English-speaking parts of the world have indexes online. For example, New South Wales has an online index to historical registration records at <www.bdm.nsw.gov.au/familyHistory/searchHistoricalRecords.htm>, and British Columbia has a similar service at <www.bcarchives.gov.bc.ca/textual/governmt/vstats/v_events.htm>. For births, both of these sites list only events over 100 years ago, but more recent marriages and deaths are included. For the USA, Cyndi's List has detailed information for each state (under the heading Records), at <www.cyndislist.com/usvital.htm#States>.

CHAPTER 6

ONLINE SOURCES: CENSUS

A census has been taken every 10 years since 1801, except for 1941, and names of individuals are recorded from the 1841 census onwards. The significance of these records for genealogists is that they provide snapshots of family groups at 10-year intervals. More importantly, from 1851 onwards they give a place of birth, which is essential information for individuals born before the start of general registration. Since an approximate date of birth can be calculated from the person's age, this makes it possible to trace the line back to the parish registers.

GENERAL INFORMATION

There are two starting points for official information on the census. The FamilyRecords Portal 'Census' page at <**www.familyrecords.gov.uk/topics/census.htm**> has basic details and links to other official websites with census information and data. The FRC's site has a number of fact sheets on the census in PDF format at <**www.familyrecords.gov.uk/frc/research/censusmain.htm**>.

If you are not familiar with census records and the way they are referred to, the British-Genealogy site explains piece numbers, folio numbers, and schedules at <**www.british-genealogy.com/resources/census/**>.

Genuki has pages on the census for:

- England and Wales: <**www.genuki.org.uk/big/eng/CensusR.html**>
- Scotland: <**www.genuki.org.uk/big/sct/Census.html**>
- Ireland: <**www.genuki.org.uk/big/irl/#Census**>.

It also has a searchable database of places in the 1891 census at <**www.genuki.org.uk/big/census_place.html**>, which gives the county, registration district, registration sub-district, National Archives piece number and LDS film number (see p. 126) for any place in England, Wales and the Isle of Man.

The GenDocs site shows exactly what information was recorded for each census from 1841 to 1901 at <**www.gendocs.demon.co.uk/census. html**>, and gives the date on which each census was taken. Talking Scot's pages devoted to the Scottish census at <**www.talkingscot.com/censuses/ census-intro.htm**> do the same for Scotland.

Another useful resource for Scotland is the online index of census microfilms at <**www.ktb.net/~dwills/scotref/13311-censusfilms.htm**>, which gives the relevant enumeration district(s) and LDS microfilm number for each parish.

All census records for England and Wales are catalogued in the National Archives' catalogue at <**www.catalogue.nationalarchives.gov.uk**>. Even if you are using an online census index this may be useful, as it provides a way of establishing the piece number(s) for a particular place in each census.

▌CENSUS DATA ONLINE

While we seem doomed to an interminable wait for civil registration records to go online, there has been enormous progress in digitizing census records in the last couple of years. For Scotland all census records are due to be available by the end of 2005, while for England and Wales only the 1841 and 1851 censuses will not be complete by that date. Several censuses are available on more than one site.

The major census datasets available online are:

- England & Wales
  - 1841 available at British Origins (subscription)
  - 1861 available at 1837online (pay-per-view) and at Ancestry (pay-per-view or subscription)
  - 1871 available at Ancestry (pay-per-view or subscription) and British Origins (subscription)
  - 1881 index only at FamilySearch and FamilyHistoryOnline (free); with images at Ancestry (pay-per-view or subscription)
  - 1891 at Ancestry (pay-per-view or subscription) and, by the end of 2005, at 1837online (pay-per-view)
  - 1901 at the National Archives (pay-per-view) and Ancestry (pay-per-view or subscription)
  - Local census indexes and transcriptions made by family history societies on the FamilyHistoryOnline site (pay-per-view)
- Scotland
  - The 1871, 1881, 1891 and 1901 censuses at ScotlandsPeople (pay-per-view).

Where a census is available at more than one site, each has its own index, with the exception of the 1881 census, where all sites use the original index created by the GSU and FFHS. The two censuses available at British Origins are not yet complete.

The situation with Ireland is quite different, and this is discussed on p. 86.

▌CENSUS IMAGES

The main commercial census sites offer images of the original pages from the census enumeration books, digitized from microfilm, together with an index.

TNA'S 1901 CENSUS

The National Archives unveiled the 1901 census for England and Wales in January 2002, on a pay-per-view basis. The digitization was carried out by Qinetiq, which is also responsible for running the service. The site is now at <www.1901census.nationalarchives.gov.uk>.

Access to the data is initially via a free search facility, and there are a number of different things you can search for: a person, an address, a place, a vessel or an institution. There is also an advanced person search which allows you to specify additional data items such as occupation and marital status, while the Direct Access search allows you to retrieve a page by entering its census reference. The person search form is shown in Figure 6-1.

This is a pay-per-view site. You pay for access to the data by purchasing physical vouchers or by making a credit card payment online (the minimum is £5). This covers an account session of seven days. However, if you are using a voucher, you can use remaining time left at the end of a session on a subsequent session. If you pay by credit card, any unused units at the end of the session are lost. Vouchers can be bought online and from many genealogy suppliers, and are valid for six months from first use.

The initial person search lists matching individuals with age, birthplace, residence (county and parish), and occupation (Figure 6-2). At this point you can either view the full census entry for the person found for 50p (Figure 6-3); or the relevant page in the original enumeration book for 75p (Figure 6-4). From the full entry for a person, you have an option to view the details of other people in the same household (50p) or, again, go to the page image. Once you have viewed a particular page during a session, you can return to it without further payment.

The page image is offered in three different formats: PDF (Adobe Acrobat), Applet or TIFF. The latter is the best if you want to try editing or enhancing the image with graphics software. Choosing the Applet option opens a graphics viewer in a separate window, providing controls to resize or print the image. From here you can also save the image in TIFF format. Helpfully, the default filename provided when you save indicates the full page reference. Rather irritatingly, the image is saved in

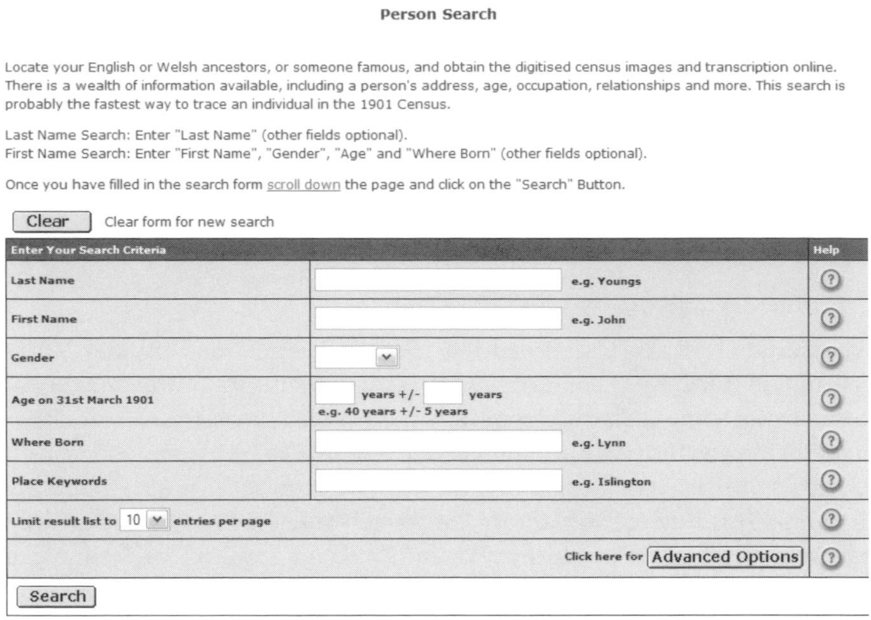

Person Search

Locate your English or Welsh ancestors, or someone famous, and obtain the digitised census images and transcription online. There is a wealth of information available, including a person's address, age, occupation, relationships and more. This search is probably the fastest way to trace an individual in the 1901 Census.

Last Name Search: Enter "Last Name" (other fields optional).
First Name Search: Enter "First Name", "Gender", "Age" and "Where Born" (other fields optional).

Once you have filled in the search form scroll down the page and click on the "Search" Button.

| Clear | Clear form for new search |

Enter Your Search Criteria		Help
Last Name		e.g. Youngs	?
First Name		e.g. John	?
Gender	▾		?
Age on 31st March 1901	years +/- years e.g. 40 years +/- 5 years		?
Where Born		e.g. Lynn	?
Place Keywords		e.g. Islington	?
Limit result list to 10 ▾ entries per page			?
	Click here for Advanced Options		?

| Search |

Figure 6-1 TNA 1901 census: person search

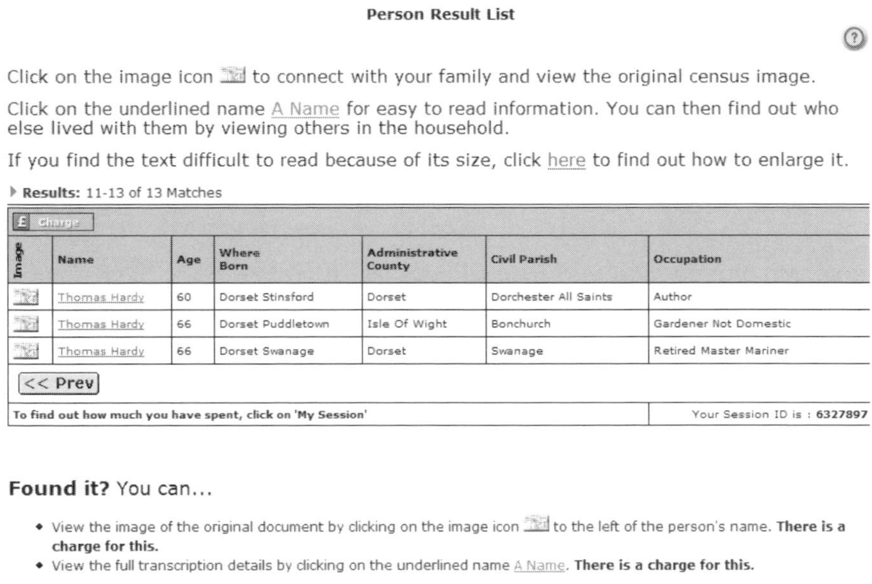

Person Result List

(?)

Click on the image icon 📷 to connect with your family and view the original census image.

Click on the underlined name A Name for easy to read information. You can then find out who else lived with them by viewing others in the household.

If you find the text difficult to read because of its size, click here to find out how to enlarge it.

▶ **Results:** 11-13 of 13 Matches

£ Charge

Image	Name	Age	Where Born	Administrative County	Civil Parish	Occupation
📷	Thomas Hardy	60	Dorset Stinsford	Dorset	Dorchester All Saints	Author
📷	Thomas Hardy	66	Dorset Puddletown	Isle Of Wight	Bonchurch	Gardener Not Domestic
📷	Thomas Hardy	66	Dorset Swanage	Dorset	Swanage	Retired Master Mariner

| << Prev |

| To find out how much you have spent, click on 'My Session' | Your Session ID is : 6327897 |

Found it? You can...

- View the image of the original document by clicking on the image icon 📷 to the left of the person's name. **There is a charge for this.**
- View the full transcription details by clicking on the underlined name A Name. **There is a charge for this.**

Figure 6-2 TNA 1901 census: search results

Person Details

Full Transcription Details for **Thomas Hardy**   View Image/Other Household members   [Back to Search Results]

National Archives Reference				
RG Number, Series	Piece	Folio	Page	Schedule Number
RG13	2001	54	28	184

Name		Language
Thomas Hardy		

Relation to Head of Family	Condition as to Marriage	Age Last Birthday	Sex
Head	M	60	M

Profession or Occupation	Employment Status	Infirmity
Author	Undefined	

Where Born	Address	
Dorset Stinsford	Maxs House Alington Avenue	

Civil Parish	Rural District	
Dorchester All Saints		

Town or Village or Hamlet	Parliamentary Borough or Division	
	Southern Dorset	

Ecclesiastical Parish	Administrative County	
East Fordington St George	Dorset	

County Borough, Municipal Borough or Urban District	Ward of Municipal Borough or Urban District	

To find out how much you have spent, click on 'My Session'	Your Session ID is : 6327897

Figure 6-3 TNA 1901 census: person details

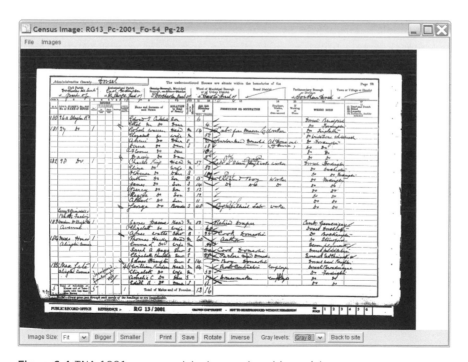

Figure 6-4 TNA 1901 census: original page viewed in applet

the wrong orientation and needs to be rotated 90 degrees anticlockwise to be read on screen after downloading.

It is always a good idea to view the page image, as this allows you to see fuller details than are included on the transcription (where some long entries are truncated). You will also need to check that the transcription is correct. The image will normally include the remainder of the house-hold, so you will probably not often want to pay for the separate household transcription.

The address search allows you to search on two fields, the house or street name, and the place name. For more advanced address searching, there is an option to specify a whole range of place fields – county, civil parish, parliamentary borough, etc. This will be particularly useful with common place names, though you may need good knowledge of 1901 administrative geography to exploit it fully. Unlike the other searches, the address search links only to a page image, not to a transcription.

There is an online form to notify transcription errors, and a list of corrections at <**www.1901census.nationalarchives.gov.uk/changes_index.html**>.

Some basic search tips are provided on the 1901 site itself (from a link on the home page), but if you are looking for a wider range of advice on making the most of the 1901 census online, the UK-1901-CENSUS mailing list is a useful unofficial resource. The list archives can be searched or browsed from <**lists.rootsweb.com/index/intl/UK/UK-1901-CENSUS. html**>.

There can be problems where an ancestor is in an institution or on-board ship, because the page on which he or she is listed may not name the ship or institution. To assist you in identifying these, there are two helpful lists compiled by Jeffery Knaggs. The page at <**homepage.ntlworld. com/jeffery.knaggs/RNShips.html**> lists Royal Navy ships that were at sea or in ports abroad on census night, while the page at <**homepage.ntlworld. com/jeffery.knaggs/Instuts.html**> does the same for all institutions. The piece, folio and page numbers given here should enable you to work out where your ancestor was living.

Some of the issues relating to the 1901 census's troubled launch are discussed in Chapter 19, p. 325.

ANCESTRY

Ancestry's UK Records Collection at <**www.ancestry.co.uk**> has the largest set of indexed census images online, with a complete run from 1861 to 1901. No doubt the two earlier censuses will be added before very long. There is also a 10% sample of the 1851 census. Ancestry has tradition-ally been a subscription site, but a pay-per-view option was introduced when the 1881 and 1891 censuses were licensed from TNA.

Ancestry separates the censuses by year and country, which means that England, Wales, the Channel Islands and the Isle of Man need to be searched separately. Alternatively there is an option to search the whole census collection.

There is a wide range of search options (though these are slightly different for the 1881 census) – see Figure 6-5. Once you get a list of individuals, you can view a detailed record for an individual or go to a page image. The image opens in a special viewer. In fact Ancestry has two image viewers. The older one, which works in all browsers, has an important limitation: while you might think you can simply right click with your mouse to save the image, this will *not* save the whole page. Instead you need to click on the **Save** icon which brings up a new window from which you *can* save by right clicking. The new image viewer, introduced in summer 2005, only works with Internet Explorer and if you access a census image using this browser you will be automatically prompted to install the new viewer. It has better navigation and viewing tools, including mouse-operated magnification of individual parts of the page. It also offers a choice between two image qualities, with the option of additional

1901 England Census
Viewing records **1-8** of **8** matches for:

Thomas Hardy

« Global Search Results

Name	Estimated Birth Year	Birthplace	Relationship	Civil Parish	County/Island	View Image
Charles Thomas Hardy	abt 1876	Hammersmith, Middlesex, England	Members Of Crew	Vessels	Dorset	🔍
Thomas Hardy	abt 1841	Stinsford, Dorset, England	Head	Dorchester All Saints	Dorset	🔍
Thomas Hardy	abt 1864	Wynford Eagle, Dorset, England	Head	Maiden Newton	Dorset	🔍
Thomas Hardy	abt 1858	Bere Regis, Dorset, England	Head	Puddletown	Dorset	🔍
Thomas Hardy	abt 1840	Swanage, Dorset, England	Head	Swanage	Dorset	🔍
Thomas B Hardy	abt 1871	Broadwinsor, Dorset, England	Head	Broadwinsor	Dorset	🔍
Thomas H Hardy	abt 1873	Purbeck, Dorset, England	Head	Portland	Dorset	🔍
Thomas Masters Hardy	abt 1888	Swanage, Dorset, England	Son	Swanage	Dorset	🔍

🖨 View printer-friendly

Refine your search of the 1901 England Census

Your search will only show records that match **all** of these fields:

thomas	hardy	Exact ▾
First name	Last name	Spelling

Residence

Dorset ▾		
County or island	Civil parish	Town

Personal Information

Any ▾		+/- 0 ▾
Gender	Relationship to head of household	Birth Year

Birthplace

Country	County or island	Parish or place

Census Information

RG13/

Piece	Folio	Page #	Keyword(s)

▲ Hide Advanced Search Options   [Search]

Figure 6-5
Ancestry 1901 census: search results and search form

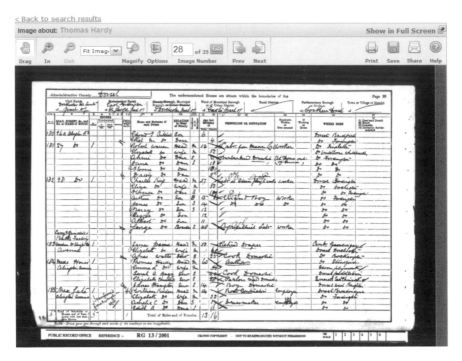

Figure 6-6 Ancestry 1901 census: image viewer

enhancement (Figure 6-6). In this viewer, saving is more straightforward – clicking on the **Save** icon immediately opens a file-saving dialog.

Unfortunately none of the image views gives the full reference for the census page unless you can read it off the image itself, so you may need to look at the individual details for this information.

There is no address search, but you can browse enumeration districts (EDs) by clicking on the name of a county below the search form – this will take you to a list of civil parishes, and then to the EDs within them. From here you can either look at the description of the ED, which will give you an idea of what streets or areas are covered, or go straight to the first enumeration page. This will be prohibitively expensive if you are using the pay-per-view option, but merely time-consuming if you have a subscription.

Hints and tips for using the census records on Ancestry will be found on the Ancestry message board for UK and Ireland records at <**boards. ancestry.com/mbexec?htx=board&r=rw&p=topics.ancestry.uk-ire**> and on Hugh Watkins's Exploring Ancestry blog at <**ancestry.blogspot.com**>.

ORIGINS

In 2004, Origins started to digitize the 1871 census on its British Origins subscription service at **<www.britishorigins.com>**, and the 1841 census was started in Spring 2005. At the time of writing, the following counties were available:

- 1841: Cambridgeshire, Derbyshire, Devon, Dorset, Essex, Gloucestershire, Lincolnshire, Norfolk, Somerset and Suffolk
- 1871: Glamorgan, London-Kent, London-Middlesex, Middlesex (ex Metro), London-Surrey, Surrey (ex Metro) and Wiltshire.

The person search results – the search form is shown in Figure 6-7 – give name, age, birthplace, relationship to head of household, and residence (county and parish). For names, you specify exact matches or various levels of fuzzy matching using a system called NameX, which is considerably superior to the Soundex matching used by Ancestry and more flexible than the wild cards used in the TNA 1901 census. (For more information on NameX, see p. 207.)

From the list of persons, you can view either the details for the individual or the page image. The initial results page just lists the number of matches with the option to view the records or refine the search. The list of matching entries shows all the information from the census page except occupation and the census reference. A very useful feature is that you can sort the results on any column – sorting on address, for example, groups households together and effectively allows you to identify families (see Figure 6-8).

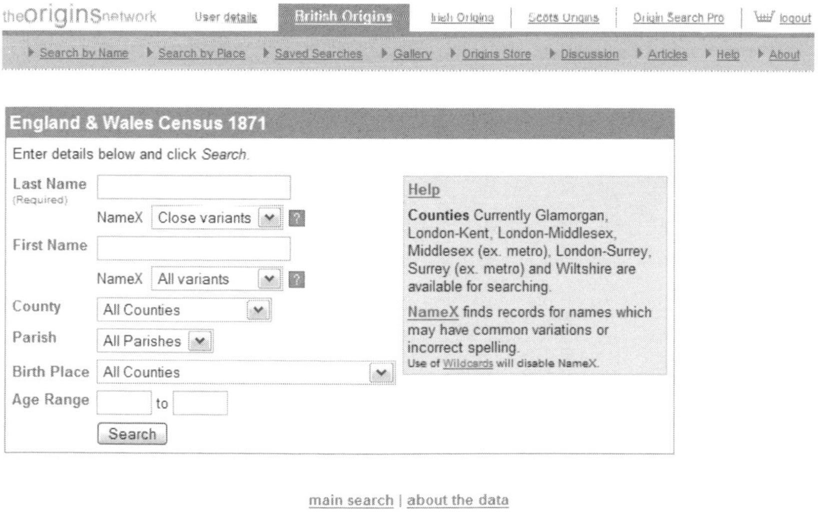

Figure 6-7 Origins: 1871 census search form

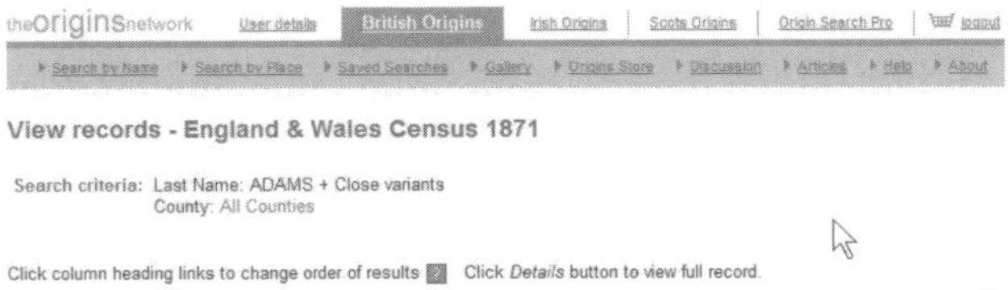

Last Name	First Name	Relation	Sex	Age	Birth County	Street	Village	Town	Parish	County	Image	Details
ADAMS	HENRY	Son	M	24	Wiltshire	17 NEWPORT ST		SWINDON	SWINDON	Wiltshire	Image	Details
ADAMS	EDWARD	Son	M	21	Wiltshire	17 NEWPORT ST		SWINDON	SWINDON	Wiltshire	Image	Details
ADAMS	WILLIAM	Son	M	17	Wiltshire	17 NEWPORT ST		SWINDON	SWINDON	Wiltshire	Image	Details
ADAMS	JOHN	Son	M	15	Wiltshire	17 NEWPORT ST		SWINDON	SWINDON	Wiltshire	Image	Details
ADAMS	THOMAS	Son	M	1	Wiltshire	17 NEWPORT ST		SWINDON	SWINDON	Wiltshire	Image	Details
ADAMS	ROBERT	Head	M	48	Wiltshire	19 BACK LANE		SWINDON	SWINDON	Wiltshire	Image	Details
ADAMS	ELIZA	Wife	F	51	Wiltshire	19 BACK LANE		SWINDON	SWINDON	Wiltshire	Image	Details
ADAMS	BERTHA	Daughter	F	27	Wiltshire	19 BACK LANE		SWINDON	SWINDON	Wiltshire	Image	Details
ADAMS	EMMA	Daughter	F	25	Wiltshire	19 BACK LANE		SWINDON	SWINDON	Wiltshire	Image	Details
ADAMS	CLARA	Daughter	F	19	Wiltshire	19 BACK LANE		SWINDON	SWINDON	Wiltshire	Image	Details
ADAMS	WILLIAM	Son	M	14	Wiltshire	19 BACK LANE		SWINDON	SWINDON	Wiltshire	Image	Details
ADAMS	GEORGE	Head	M	51	Gloucestershire	19 FLEET ST		SWINDON, NEW	SWINDON	Wiltshire	Image	Details
ADAMS	LUCINA	Wife	F	51	Gloucestershire	19 FLEET ST		SWINDON, NEW	SWINDON	Wiltshire	Image	Details
ADAMS	KATE	Daughter	F	17	Wiltshire	19 FLEET ST		SWINDON, NEW	SWINDON	Wiltshire	Image	Details
ADAMS	HERBERT	Son	M	15	Wiltshire	19 FLEET ST		SWINDON, NEW	SWINDON	Wiltshire	Image	Details
ADAMS	CHARLES	Son	M	12	Wiltshire	19 FLEET ST		SWINDON, NEW	SWINDON	Wiltshire	Image	Details
ADAMS	DANIEL	Head	M	59	Wiltshire	2 COTTAGGES	SOUTH WRAXHALL		BRADFORD	Wiltshire	Image	Details

Figure 6-8 Origins: 1871 census search results sorted by address

From here you can choose either to view the page image or see the full details, but irritatingly the latter do not include the full reference, only the folio and page number, so you actually need to see the image to get the piece number, and even there it is not always legible. As with Ancestry, the page viewer allows you to browse backwards or forwards to check neighbouring pages.

The page images are in TIFF format and you will need to download and install a viewer for your browser. From the viewer you can save pages in TIFF or BMP formats. For screenshots of Origins, see Chapter 4, pp. 38–9.

1837ONLINE

1837online at **<www.1837online.com>** (see p. 53) launched the 1861 census at the start of 2005 and it should be complete by the time you read this. The 1891 census is to follow and completion is planned for December 2005. Obviously, it is likely that further censuses will follow.

There is both a person and an address search, and initial searches are free. There is also an extremely comprehensive advanced search – this allows you to specify almost any field in the census record. A unique feature is the ability to specify the name of an additional member of the household, making it possible to look for a married couple or parent and child.

This will be particularly useful for common surnames, or where the normal spelling produces no results.

The person search results list only name, age, sex and registration district. The lack of birthplace or occupation (even though you can specify these on the search page) means it can be difficult to spot the correct individual in the search results. From the list of search results, you can select to view a transcription of the whole household or view the census image, each of which costs three units (i.e. about 30p). A useful feature is that the search results can be sorted by name, age, or sex. Screenshots from 1837online will be found on p. 53.

SCOTLANDSPEOPLE

The ScotlandsPeople site at <www.scotlandspeople.gov.uk>, discussed in Chapter 4, p. 41, has the censuses for 1871–1901 for Scotland. The earlier censuses are promised for winter 2005, though the site's published deadlines have had a tendency to be optimistic. As with the civil registration data on ScotlandsPeople, an initial search indicates how many hits your search produces, and you then need to spend one of your pre-purchased credits to see each page of the full search results. At that point, you can choose to view a census image at a cost of five units. The 1881 data is an online version of the index created by the GSU (Genealogical Society of Utah); there are no images of the original enumeration books, but one credit gets a printout of the full entry from the index.

An important difference between ScotlandsPeople and other sites is that it does not include a transcription – from the list of search results, you can only choose to see an image. There is no option to view an entire household other than by looking at the page images, and if a household is split over a page break, you may not realize it is incomplete.

TalkingScot provides a forum relating to Scottish census records at <www.talkingscot.com/forum/viewforum.php?f=6>, and much of the discussion relates to ScotlandsPeople, so this is a good place look for help with searching and other tips for using the site.

STEPPING STONES

A completely different approach is taken by Stepping Stones at <www.stepping-stones.co.uk>. This site simply provides scans of the census pages, unindexed, and you pay to look at the scans from an individual microfilm: £5 buys you 10 units, and each unit gives you access to every frame on a single microfilm for 14 days. There is an index showing the towns and villages covered by each film. Coverage so far includes a small number of counties for each of the 1841, 1851 and 1861 censuses. Since Stepping Stones also sell the 1871 census on CD-ROM, no doubt material from that census will be available on the site in due course.

Like 1837online, the site uses the DjVu viewer. Browsing the pages, even with a broadband connection, is a rather tedious process, but if you already have a page reference you should be able to find the relevant image reasonably quickly. An obvious use of the site is to see the original pages after using an index-only resource, such as the census indexes at Family HistoryOnline. Also, for anyone with an interest in a place, rather than a single family, this is very much cheaper than the pay-per-view sites for looking at, say, a whole village.

▮COMPARISON

With so many different places to turn for census indexes and images, for England and Wales at least, the obvious question is which to use. There are five main criteria which could be used to make this decision: coverage, cost, search facilities, image quality and index quality.

On coverage, Ancestry clearly wins for the moment, and if you subscribe to Ancestry (rather than using the pay-per-view option), you will probably not feel like paying for any of the other sites. If, however, you prefer pay-per-view, then the ability to access all the censuses on one site may be convenient but is not crucial, and certainly less important than quality. Also, it seems likely that both Origins and 1837online will expand their offerings to further censuses in due course.

SEARCHING

Table 6-1 provides a comparison of the search facilities of the sites discussed. The advanced searches of TNA and 1837online are the most sophisticated, and both offer a good range of different searches. But the more fields you specify in your search, the more likely your search is to fail because of an indexing error, so you won't necessarily get better results simply because you fill in more details. However, where an initial name search doesn't find the person you are looking for, or finds too many entries to be manageable, the ability to specify other fields will undoubtedly be of help.

IMAGE QUALITY

It is hard to state any categorical preference in terms of image quality, since the individual microfilm frames which have been digitized vary quite significantly. However, there are two main ways to evaluate it. The first is resolution. The 'resolution' column in Table 6-2 shows the number of pixels in a sample page image from each site. The figures are based not on the downloaded image file, but on the area occupied by the page of the enumeration book, which is what matters. Other things being equal, the greater the resolution, the clearer the image, though of course it will also take longer to download. Lower resolution will tend to make the handwriting look blockier, and fine lines may be lost.

Table 6-1 Census search options

Search option	TNA Person	TNA Adv.	TNA Direct	Ancestry General	Ancestry 1881	Origins	1837online Basic	1837online Adv.	FamilySearch
Year(s)	1901			1861–1901		1841,1871	1861		1881
Name	✓	+other name		✓	✓	✓	✓	+middle name	first/last
Name variants	wild cards	wild cards		exact/Soundex		exact/close/all	include variants		exact/Soundex
Relationship		✓		✓	✓		✓	✓	
Marital status		✓					✓	✓	
Age	✓	✓		✓	est. birth				birth year
Age range	✓	✓				✓	accuracy		accuracy
Gender	✓	✓		✓	✓		✓	✓	
Occupation		✓			✓		✓		
Birthplace	✓	✓		country/county/place	country/county/place	county			country/county
Census place	place keyword	place keyword		county/parish/town	county/parish	county/parish	county/place keywords	all fields from original	country/county city/town
Piece			✓	✓	✓				
Fol/page			✓	✓	✓				
Other						drop down lists for places	sort order	other persons in household	head of household / drop down lists for places

Table 6-2 Census image quality

	Approx. file size	Typical resolution (megapixels)	Save format	Colour depth
1837online	90k	6.8	DjVu	Greyscale
1837online photo quality	400k	6.9	DjVu	Greyscale
Ancestry (old viewer)	800k	3.8	GIF	Greyscale
Ancestry (new viewer)	500k	5.1	JPG	Greyscale
Origins	300k	12.5	TIFF/BMP	Monochrome
TNA	200k	18.1	TIFF/PDF	Monochrome
ScotlandsPeople	100k	8.1	TIFF	Monochrome
Stepping Stones	200k	8.0	DjVu	Greyscale

Another issue is colour depth: since the enumeration books were not microfilmed in colour, the only options are greyscale (as in a 'black and white' photograph, or the screenshots in this book), or monochrome (true black and white, as in the printed text in this book). Other things being equal, greyscale is preferable because it shows more detail. With monochrome every spot on the image becomes either black or white, with no intermediate shades. Monochrome *can* have the benefit of enhancing detail, especially where contrast is low, but some detail will be lost entirely – any mark on the paper lighter than some threshold value will end up white.

However, higher resolution can compensate for lack of colour depth, and the difference between high resolution monochrome and low resolution greyscale may not be significant. Figure 6-9 shows a comparison of the good quality entry for Thomas Hardy in the 1901 census, with the higher resolution monochrome image from TNA at the top and the lower resolution greyscale image of Ancestry at the bottom. Figure 6-10 shows a fairly illegible page, with a monochrome scan from Origins and greyscale scan from Ancestry. The benefits of greyscale can be seen clearly here – the monochrome scan loses some of the marks on the paper; but on the other hand higher resolution and lack of gradations make some letters easier to distinguish. Monochrome images can also be hard to read where a page has been heavily marked with pencil during analysis.

Most of the greyscale images on these sites use only a limited range of shades – 16 rather than the maximum possible 256. This is understandable in that it reduces file sizes and therefore download times, but once broadband is universal, this will seem an unwelcome limitation.

A final issue in image quality is compression. This is a technique to improve download speeds by making image files smaller. Some compression techniques, such as the GIF format used by Ancestry, do not affect image quality, but the DjVu format, used by 1837online and Stepping Stones, offers a range of compression levels, and smaller file sizes can be

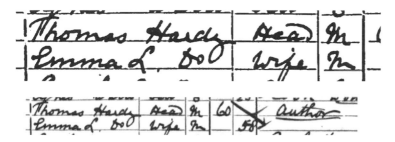

Figure 6-9 Census images from the 1901 census: TNS (top), Ancestry (bottom)

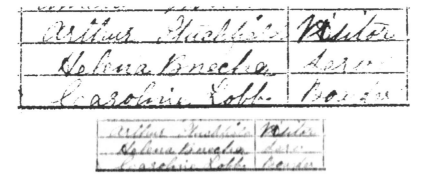

Figure 6-10 Census images from the 1871 census: Origins (top), Ancestry (bottom)

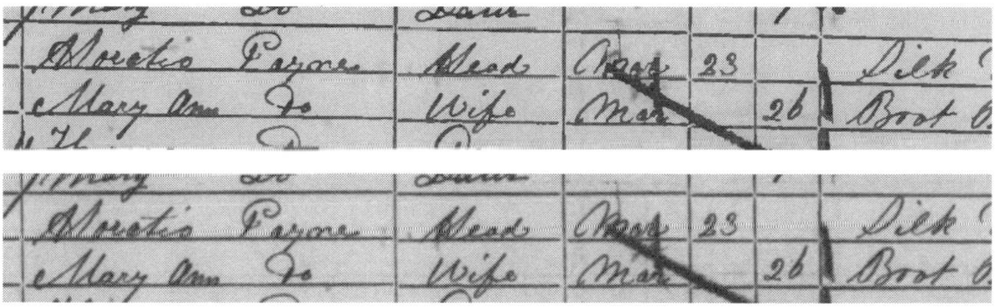

Figure 6-11 1837online: standard and photographic quality images

achieved at the cost of poorer image quality. This is why the standard quality image files from 1837online are very much smaller than Ancestry's GIFs and less clear, in spite of their higher resolution. The high quality option in Ancestry's JPG images also uses lower compression at the cost of larger file sizes than the standard quality. An odd feature of the DjVu format is that it combines a monochrome foreground with a greyscale background. This means that the handwriting comes out as more or less monochrome for some pages, and doesn't really exploit the advantages of greyscale. However 1837online has recently introduced the option of a 'photographic quality' image for the same cost in units as the standard quality, and this gives clearly the best quality images of any site at present. The difference in file size shown in Table 6-2 comes from a much lower level of compression, which gives higher quality for the same resolution. Figure 6-11 compares the standard and photographic quality – the fine lines are much clearer in the latter and the heavy mark across 'Mar' no longer obliterates the text underneath.

If you are going to use a site with DjVu images you will need to find a graphics program that can deal with them, as it is not a widely supported format (see p. 54).

INDEX QUALITY

Probably the most important issue is the accuracy of the indexing. Some of the issues with online indexes and transcriptions have been mentioned in Chapter 4 (see p. 32), and 100% accuracy is certainly unachievable in datasets with as many as 30 million entries created from handwritten records. However, an equitable comparison of the sites would be a mammoth undertaking, and all that can be done here is comment on some of the most obvious types of error you need to take into account when searching.

The most serious are what one might call systematic errors, where there has been inadequate data validation (see p. 32). The original release of the 1901 census had large numbers of people with Ditto or Do as a surname, though these have now been corrected. At its launch in March 2005, Ancestry's 1861 census showed some extraordinary geographical errors – a whole swathe of Surrey was indexed as being in Kent, and a number of places in Middlesex had been relocated to Mexico. These are particularly troublesome, for while you have some chance of guessing how a surname has been (mis)transcribed, it probably wouldn't occur to you to enter Mexico in the county field!

Errors in reading handwriting can be extremely difficult to spot, but you can get some idea from looking at mismatches between forename and gender. As mentioned in Chapter 4, there are many female Johns in the censuses. There are also female Williams, and males called Sarah or Hannah. Most are simply misreadings of the forename, e.g. Joan or Jane read as John, while the correct gender is clearly indicated on the original census page. This means you should never search on gender if you can avoid it, though unfortunately TNA's 1901 census insists on it (for no obvious reason) for some types of search.

Another problem with forenames is that some sites index variants together, but others don't. It is well worth trying a few tests to see whether a search for Elizabeth also finds Elisabeth, whether William also retrieves Wm.

Errors in surnames are the most troublesome. For a start, they may not be errors at all, since there was plenty of variation in surname spelling in the nineteenth century. All of the sites have some way of allowing fuzzy matching on surnames. Wild cards, used on the 1901 site, are useful, but it's up to you to decide which variations to cover. Soundex, as used on Ancestry and the 1881 census, is pretty poor, especially for longer names, though better than nothing. The NameX system used by Origins and 1837online is more useful, especially since you can choose how accurate you want matches to be.

What all this means is: always search on as few fields as possible. These sites don't find the *closest* matches to your search, they find only *exact* matches. And be prepared to use your imagination.

If you want to get a broader idea of the sorts of error you have to allow for, look at the 1901-CENSUS mailing list and the Ancestry message board (see p. 76). It is also instructive to look at the list of corrections made to TNA's 1901 census at <**www.1901census.nationalarchives.gov. uk/changes_index.html**>.

CENSUS INDEXES

While the commercial sites that provide images may be preferable because they allow immediate confirmation of an entry from a scan of the original record, there are some important sites that provide just census indexes.

The 1881 census index for England and Wales was a joint indexing project between the Genealogical Society of Utah (GSU) and the FFHS, which gave rise first to an index on microfiche and then, with Scotland, on CD-ROM. (There is a history of the project on the FFHS site at <**www. ffhs.org.uk/General/Projects/1881.htm**>.) In October 2002, the data for England and Wales was made available on the FamilySearch site at <**www.familysearch.org**>. It is automatically included in any search on 'All Resources', but there is also the possibility of searching only this dataset, by selecting 'Census' instead. Those who have access to the CD-ROM edition of this data should note that this remains more comprehensive both in its data and its search facilities than the online version. The version at FamilySearch does not include the data for Scotland, which is available online only on the ScotlandsPeople site.

A wide range of census indexes is provided by the FamilyHistoryOnline pay-per-view site at <**www.familyhistoryonline.net**> (see p. 39), which currently has around 10 million census records in addition to the 1881. The best represented censuses are the 1851 and 1891 with 2.5 and 3.5 millions records respectively. There is great variation in counties covered: every census is almost complete for Cornwall, while for Berkshire only the 1871 for Newbury is available. There is also variation in the information provided. Some indexes have name, age and birthplace only, while others have transcriptions of the entire record. For each dataset there is a list of the places covered and the number of records. It might seem that these records will decline in usefulness as more and more census images go online, but there's good reason to believe that these indexes are more accurate than those contracted out by the other commercial data providers – the indexes here have been produced by family history societies with local knowledge, and many have been in use for some years, giving plenty of time to correct the most obvious errors.

There is a great deal of census material being published on CD-ROM. While that falls outside the scope of this book, S&N Genealogy (see p. 313) are developing online indexes at <**www.thegenealogist.co.uk**> to the census images on their CDs. You can take out a 90-day or one-year subscription for an individual census and county; alternatively the monthly 'all-inclusive' subscription covers all the datasets (see p. 45). Searches can be made only on name and age, and the results give only the National Archives piece number and a reference to the page on the CDs. This site is probably of limited usefulness unless you have the relevant CD set – certainly, if the year and county you are interested in is on FamilyHistoryOnline that will be more useful.

FreeCEN at <**freecen.rootsweb.com**> is a comprehensive volunteer project which aims to provide a free index to all English and Welsh censuses from 1841 to 1891. Work so far has concentrated on the 1891 census, and there is still a very long way to go. However, some counties are complete or nearly complete for individual census years: Aberdeenshire, Banff for 1841, East Lothian for 1841 and 1851; Bedfordshire, Cornwall, Devon for 1891. Usefully, the site gives details of exactly which piece numbers are covered. The site has a status page for each county currently being transcribed, linked from <**freecen.rootsweb.com/project.htm**>.

There are countless other small indexes to census material on the web. You will find much census material on sites for individual villages or parishes, and even on some FHS sites. The Workhouses site at <**www.workhouses.org.uk**> has census extracts for many workhouses.

Census Finder has probably the most comprehensive set of links to local transcriptions on its UK page at <**www.censusfinder.com/united_kingdom.htm**>, organized by county. The Genuki county and parish pages will also have links to local census indexes.

IRELAND

Unlike England, Wales and Scotland, there are no national datasets online for the Irish census. One of the reasons for this is that almost all nineteenth-century census returns for Ireland have been destroyed. However, there seem to be no plans to digitize the 1901 census, the earliest one to survive in its entirety, even though it has been publicly available for over 20 years. In Ireland the 1911 census has also been available for many years, but there is no sign of any project to make it available online.

The National Archives of Ireland have a brief page of information at <www.nationalarchives.ie/genealogy/censusrtns.html>, as has the PRONI at <www.proni.gov.uk/records/census19.htm>. A good guide to the Irish censuses, detailing what is missing and what has survived, is available on the Fianna site at <www.rootsweb.com/~fianna/guide/census.html>.

There are a number of sites with census data for individual counties. In the Republic of Ireland some data from the 1901 census is online at <www.leitrim-roscommon.com/1901census/>. Available data covers all or part of the following six counties: Roscommon, Leitrim, Mayo, Sligo, Westmeath and Galway. Data for Leitrim and Roscommon is essentially complete, but for the others, only small amounts of material are present. A table gives detailed information about which individual parishes are wholly or partly covered.

Census Finder has links to many local transcriptions for Ireland at <www.censusfinder.com/ireland.htm>. These include some surviving fragments of nineteenth-century censuses, but are mainly for the 1901 census, with some material for 1911.

Because of the amount of Irish census material destroyed, the so-called 'census substitutes' are important. Fianna has a useful guide to these at <www.rootsweb.com/~fianna/guide/cen2.html>, while the National Archives of Ireland has a briefer description at <www.nationalarchives.ie/genealogy/titheapplprimvalu.html>. The PRONI has similar information at <www.proni.gov.uk/records/census18.htm>. One of the most important census substitutes, Griffith's Valuation, is discussed in Chapter 8, p. 104.

OVERSEAS

It is not possible to deal here with census data for countries outside the British Isles, but Cyndi's List provides links to census sites around the world at <www.cyndislist.com/census2.htm>.

The census data on FamilySearch includes the 1880 US census and the 1881 Canadian census, and there is a large amount of US census data online at Ancestry.com <www.ancestry.com>, which requires a special subscription.

Census Links at <www.censuslinks.com> has links to census transcriptions for a number of countries.

CHAPTER 7

ONLINE SOURCES: PARISH REGISTERS

Before the introduction of General Registration in 1837, church records of baptisms, marriages and burials are the primary source for the major events in our ancestors' lives. Unfortunately, there is very much less data online for parish registers than for the civil registration and census records covered in the previous chapters, and there are good reasons why this should be so.

The national records are centrally held and recorded on forms which ensure that the structure of the data is consistent and very obvious; they all date at the earliest from the 1830s; and they have generally been kept in fairly good conditions. All this makes digitizing and indexing them a manageable, if mammoth, task.

But for parish registers, there is much more variety. First, in England and Wales at least, they are not held centrally, so no one body can be approached to put them online. Second, there is a huge variation in their format and preservation, the more so since they usually cover the whole period since the sixteenth century. And, third, while most genealogists can become accurate readers of nineteenth-century handwriting, the same cannot be said when it comes to the writing in some of the eighteenth-century registers, never mind those from the sixteenth century. Although many parish registers have been transcribed and published in print or type-script, getting the requisite permissions simply to digitize and index these from the hundreds of individuals and groups concerned would be a substantial task. Indeed, the right to transcribe and publish parish register material seems to be legally unclear, with some dioceses refusing to allow transcription. All this conspires to make the prospect of a comprehensive collection of online parish registers for England and Wales much more distant than it is for civil registration and census records. Nevertheless, a considerable amount of data is available in online indexes, as well as information that will help you to identify what parish registers remain.

However, there are as yet no digital images of parish registers available, so recourse to the originals, or microfilms of them, in record offices remains essential.

If you are unfamiliar with parish register material, Rod Neep has some useful pages on English Parish Registers at <**www.british-genealogy.com/ resources/registers/indexf.htm**>. These describe the information given for baptism, marriage and burial entries at different periods and has some examples of original documents. The tutorials discussed in Chapter 2 will also have information on using parish registers. For help with the hand-writing found in registers, refer to the material on p. 210ff.

For parish maps, maps of counties showing the parishes, and resources to help you locate parishes see Chapter 12.

The material in this chapter refers mainly to the records of the estab-lished Church (i.e. of England, Wales, Scotland and Ireland). Other religious denominations are discussed in Chapter 11.

FAMILYSEARCH

The major online resource for all parish records is the LDS Church's FamilySearch site at <**www.familysearch.org**>. The material on this site is drawn from a number of sources, and it is important to note that not all of it is from transcriptions of parish registers ('controlled extractions', as the LDS calls them). Two of the data collections on the site, Ancestral File and Pedigree Resource File, consist of unverified material submitted by individual genealogists, which is therefore secondary material and of variable reliability – these datasets are discussed in Chapter 10. The collec-tion that contains British parish register extractions is the International Genealogical Index (IGI), originally published on microfiche and then on CD-ROM. A further collection, the Vital Records Index (VRI), has been published on CD-ROM but so far no data for the British Isles has been put online, though no doubt it will be due course. (If you are thinking of buying the VRI CD-ROM, there is a useful listing of the parishes covered at <**www.genoot.com/downloads/BVRI2/**> – the site has two PDF files for each county, detailing marriage and birth coverage.)

The IGI is a substantial collection of parish register records for England and Wales online, with many millions of entries, and as such is one of the essential tools for UK genealogy on the web. There is also much material for other countries. The majority of the IGI material is for baptisms and marriages, though with some births and a few deaths and burials. It is accessible by clicking on the Search tab on the home page.

The exact nature of the search options on FamilySearch depends on whether you choose to search in 'All Resources' or in one of the individual data collections. A good reason for choosing the IGI search (see Figure 7-1), apart from the quality of the data, is that it allows you to select not only a country, but also a UK county. You can also choose to look for all events or for just, say, marriages; you can leave the year blank, give a precise year or a range of years. If you are looking for a specific individual, you can also enter the name of the father and/or mother.

When the search has been completed, you are presented with a list of search results (see Figure 7-2), with sufficient detail to identify the most plausible matches, and you can then click on the name to get the full details of the record (Figure 7-3).

You can select an individual record or a group of records to download in GEDCOM format (see p. 279), ready to be imported into your genealogy database. Of course, you can also simply save the web page for individual records or the list of search results, though these will have to be saved in text or HTML formats and the data will have to be added to your database manually.

If you are not just looking for a single individual but want to look at a surname in a whole parish, then the information at the bottom of the screen in Figure 7-3 will be useful. This identifies the particular transcription from which this record comes. You can take the batch number, and enter it in the batch number field on the search form (Figure 7-1) to restrict the search to a particular source document – in the example in Figure 7-3 'C042501' indicates the parish registers for Pevensey in Sussex (the link from the 'Source Call No.' takes you to this information). The batch number is also important because it indicates whether a record comes from

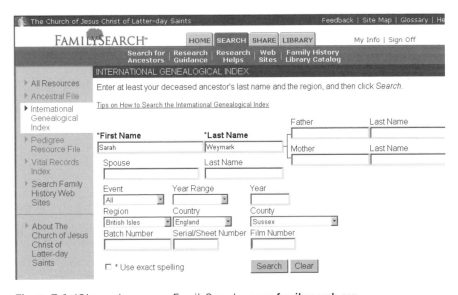

Figure 7-1 IGI search page on FamilySearch <**www.familysearch.org**>

You searched for: Sarah Weymark, Sussex, England, British Isles
Exact Spelling: Off
Results: International Genealogical Index/British Isles (30 matches)
Select records to download - (50 maximum)

☐ **1.** sarah WYMARK - International Genealogical Index
Gender: F Birth: Abt. 1678 <Of Brightling>, Sussex, England

☐ **2.** Sarah WYMARK - International Genealogical Index
Gender: F Birth: Abt. 1700 <Of Brightling>, Sussex, England

☐ **3.** Sarah WYMARK - International Genealogical Index
Gender: F Birth: Abt. 1678 <Of Brightling>, Sussex, England

☑ **4.** Sara WEIMARK - International Genealogical Index
Gender: F Christening: 30 Mar 1739 Pevensey, Sussex, England

☐ **5.** Sarah WYMARK - International Genealogical Index
Gender: F Birth: Abt. 1678 Brightling, Sussex, England

Figure 7-2 Initial search results for the search

Individual Record   FamilySearch™ International Genealogical Index v4.01

British Isles
Select record to download - (50 maximum)

☐ **Sara WEIMARK**
  Sex: F

Event(s):
Christening: 30 Mar 1739
Pevensey, Sussex, England

Parents:
Father: Edward WEIMARK
Mother: Jude_

Source Information:

Batch number:	Dates	Source Call No.	Type	Printout Call No.	Type
C042501	1569-1837	0504417	Film	0933425	Film
Sheet:					

Figure 7-3 An individual record in FamilySearch

controlled extractions – in general, batches that start with a digit are from submissions by Church members, while those starting with a letter are from controlled extractions.

Of course, it would be useful to be able to select the parish straight off without having to run a preliminary search and decode an individual record. You can do this by doing a 'Place Search' in the Family History Library Catalogue, as explained on p. 126. Genuki has detailed instructions on how to find out batch numbers by this method at <**www.genuki.org. uk/big/FindingBatchNos.html**>. The Global Gazette has a detailed article by Fawne Stratford-Devai, 'The LDS FamilySearch Website: Using The Batch Numbers', at <globalgenealogy.com/globalgazette/gazfd/gazfd36.htm>, which explains what the batch numbers are and how to use them.

Also, there are a number of sites that list batch numbers for particular counties. The most extensive, at <freepages.genealogy.rootsweb.com/~hughwallis/IGIBatchNumbers.htm>, has a comprehensive listing based on trying out each possible number. Others can be found by looking under the 'Church records' heading on the Genuki county pages. The Global Gazette page, mentioned above, has links to batch number information for a number of counties.

Bear in mind that all these listings are unofficial, and should not be regarded as authoritative. Also note that for many parishes there will be more than one batch number.

The facilities on the FamilySearch site can be quite complex to use, but because of the importance of the data it is well worth spending time experimenting and trying out different types of search. You can find more detailed guidance in David Hawgood's *FamilySearch on the Internet* (details at <www.hawgood.co.uk/fs.htm>).

It is rumoured that the FamilySearch site will at some point add page images from parish registers, but there has been no official announcement to this effect. Given the size of the task, and the complexity of matching images to record entries, any such project will take some time to reach fruition.

FAMILYHISTORYONLINE

The FamilyHistoryOnline site at <www.familyhistoryonline.net>, which is described in detail on p. 39, has something like 20 million entries transcribed from parish registers by local family history societies, and will no doubt eventually rival FamilySearch for this material. A fuller list of the datasets available is provided at <www.familyhistoryonline.net/database/>.

In particular, entries from the National Burial Index for England and Wales, which was published by the FFHS on CD-ROM, have been added for many counties. Details of the counties and parishes covered in the NBI will be found at <www.ffhs.org.uk/General/Projects/NBIcounties.htm>.

FREEREG

FreeReg at <freereg.rootsweb.com> is another volunteer project, like FreeBMD and FreeCEN, which aims to put UK genealogy data online 'to provide free internet searches of baptism, marriage, and burial records, which have been transcribed from parish and nonconformist church registers in the UK'. However, the project seems to be dormant – the search page, which announces that the database is still in preparation, has not been updated since 2000, and there have been no new messages in the archives of the FREEREG mailing list at <**archiver.rootsweb.com/th/index/ FREEREG/**> since July 2003.

▌MARRIAGE WITNESS INDEX

Ted Wildy's UK Marriage Witness Index is a well-known pre-web index, started in 1988. Originally, online access to the index was only via email to the maintainer, Faye Guthrie, but early in 2003 it was put on the web as one of RootsWeb's user-submitted databases at <**userdb.rootsweb.com/ uki/**>. It has around 80,000 entries, which include the names of witnesses, groom and bride, together with the date and place of the marriage, and the name and address of the genealogist who submitted the information.

Unfortunately, you cannot search RootsWeb specifically for this database, but data from it will be included in any search for UK marriage records. There is, however, still an advantage in emailing the maintainer – the RootsWeb version of the material does not include the contact details of the original submitter, who may well be someone researching the family involved. Further information about the MWI will be found at <**members. optushome.com.au/guthrigg/mwi.htm**>.

▌SCOTLAND

Unlike England and Wales, Scotland has collected most of its parish registers in one place, the GROS, and the births/baptisms and banns/marriages dating from 1553 to 1854 (the start of general registration) are all available online at ScotlandsPeople <**www.scotlandspeople.gov.uk**>, described above (p. 41). Currently all events have been indexed, and images of the original pages will start being added to the site during 2005. No completion date is given.

The GROS website has information on Scottish parish registers at <**www.gro-scotland.gov.uk/famrec/hlpsrch/opr.html**> and provides a 'List of the Old Parochial Registers' at <**www.gro-scotland.gov.uk/famrec/ hlpsrch/opr-cov.html**> with links to a number of files in PDF format covering individual counties or groups of counties.

There are no deaths or burials from the OPRs at ScotlandsPeople and the site gives no indication whether or when they might be included. A Scottish National Death and Burial Index, aiming to index all recorded pre-1855 deaths and burials in Scotland, is being created by the Scottish Association of Family History Societies in conjunction with its member societies and the GROS. It will be available on CD-ROM, but it is not clear whether it will ever be made available online. Some very basic information on the project is available at <**www.gwsfhs.org.uk/projects. html**>.

The Anglo-Scottish Family History Society has compiled a Scottish Strays Marriage Index, i.e. an index of marriages that took place outside Scotland, where at least one of the partners was born in Scotland. The index, which has around 6,000 entries, is available free of charge as a series of PDF files at <**www.mlfhs.org.uk/AngloScots/**>.

▌IRELAND

There is almost no Irish parish register material online apart from a small amount at FamilySearch. However, there are a number of places to look for the little other material that is available:

- RootsWeb has a small number of user-submitted databases with Irish parish register material listed at <**userdb.rootsweb.com/regional.html**> – note there are *two* sections for Ireland, one of which is under 'United Kingdom'
- The Irish Ancestors site has links to online resources for individual counties at <**scripts.ireland.com/ancestor/browse/links/counties/**>, which includes some parish register material
- The Genuki county pages for Ireland, linked from <**www.genuki. org.uk/big/irl/**> have sections devoted to Church Records.

There is, however, useful information online about the location of church records. IrelandGenWeb at <**www.irelandgenweb.com**> and NorthernIrelandGenWeb at <**www.rootsweb.com/~nirwgw/**> have county pages which often include details of the parishes whose registers have been filmed by the LDS. Fianna has a convenient list of LDS microfilm numbers for Irish parishes at <**www.rootsweb.com/~fianna/county/ldspars.html**>, though of course this information can also be gleaned from the Family History Library catalogue (see p. 126).

PRONI has details of its microfilm holdings of Church of Ireland and Presbyterian records at <**www.proni.gov.uk/records/private/cofiindx.htm**> and <**www.proni.gov.uk/records/private/presindx.htm**> respectively.

▌OTHER INDEXES

Two important and rare paper collections from the SoG are available on the British Origins site at <**www.britishorigins.com**>:

- Boyd's Marriage Index: 1538–1837 (over seven million names)
- Boyd's London Burials (300,000 names).

Origins is described in detail on p. 35.

Ancestry at <www.ancestry.co.uk> has Pallot's baptism and marriage indexes for England, covering the period 1780–1837, the originals of which are held by the Institute of Heraldic and Genealogical Studies. This has 200,000 baptisms and 1.5 million marriages, mainly from Middlesex and the City of London, but with some material from other counties. Ancestry is described on p. 43.

Many individual genealogists also have computerized indexes, particularly for marriages. Little of this material has made its way online as yet, and most is accessible only for postal searches. However, it is likely that this material will start to appear on pay-per-view sites in the longer term.

Genuki has many links to online indexes and transcriptions for individual counties and places.

CHAPTER 8

OTHER RECORDS ONLINE

There are, of course, many types of record of interest to the family historian other than those discussed in the foregoing chapters. This chapter looks at some of the most important, but there is much more than can be covered here. Where these are official records, the websites of the national archives will give details of any large-scale plans for digitization (see p. 117ff.). But even where there are no such plans, many individuals and groups are publishing small collections of data from other records online. These tend to be piecemeal indexes and transcriptions, rather than the publication of complete national datasets, and some are discussed under the relevant topic in Chapter 11 or under 'Local and social history' in Chapter 13.

This chapter can only cover the main types of other record. A number of the commercial data services have significant collections of material from sources other than civil registration, census and parish registers:

- Ancestry at <**www.ancestry.co.uk**>
- FamilyHistoryOnline at <**www.familyhistoryonline.net**>
- National Archivist at <**www.nationalarchivist.com**>
- Origins at <**www.origins.net**>.

All of these are discussed in Chapter 4. RootsWeb has a facility for users to upload data into its user-submitted data area. There are about three dozen small datasets for the British Isles, details of which are at <**userdb. rootsweb.com/contributors.html**>.

In addition, the archives and libraries discussed in Chapter 9 have details of other records which may or may not have been digitized.

WILLS

Wills are an important source for family historians and there has been a considerable increase in the number of wills available online in the last few years. Wills have been proved in many different places, and locating the right source for the potential will of a particular ancestor can sometimes be difficult, so it is important to look at the general information about probate records before looking for a specific will.

ENGLAND AND WALES

Very basic information about wills in England and Wales can be found on the FamilyRecords gateway at <www.familyrecords.gov.uk/topics/wills.htm>. But for more detail, consult the National Archives' three Research Guides relating to wills:

- Wills, Probate Records <www.catalogue.nationalarchives.gov.uk/Leaflets/ri2241.htm>
- Wills before 1858: where to start <www.catalogue.nationalarchives.gov.uk/Leaflets/ri2302.htm>
- Wills and Death Duty Records after 1858 <www.catalogue.nationalarchives.gov.uk/Leaflets/ri2301.htm>.

Probate records since 1858 are under the jurisdiction of the Probate Service, which has pages on the Court Service website at <www.hmcourts-service.gov.uk>. There is a 'Guide to obtaining probate records' at <www.hmcourts-service.gov.uk/cms/1176.htm> and a page on 'Probate Records and Family History' at <www.hmcourts-service.gov.uk/cms/1183.htm>. A recent review of probate business by the Court Service (<www.hmcourts-service.gov.uk/cms/files/rop-final-report.pdf>) concluded that the full Probate Calendar from 1858 should be online by April 2006.

For pre-1858 wills, the most important site is DocumentsOnline at <www.nationalarchives.gov.uk/documentsonline>. This offers images of over one million wills from the Prerogative Court of Canterbury, the largest probate court for England and Wales, for the period 1384–1858. Detailed information on coverage is given at <www.nationalarchives.gov.uk/documentsonline/wills.asp>. Each will costs £3.50 to download, regardless of length.

Another source of wills for England and Wales is British Origins at <www.britishorigins.com> (see p. 35) which has the following currently available:

- Bank of England Will Extracts Index 1717–1845 (61,000 names)
- Archdeaconry Court of London Wills Index 1750–1800 (5,000 names)
- Prerogative Court of Canterbury Wills 1750–1800 (208,000 records)
- York Medieval Probate Index 1267–1500 (over 10,000 wills)
- York Peculiars Probate Index 1383–1883 (over 25,000 wills).

There is a page with information on each of these collections, which should enable you see whether they will be worth checking in a particular instance.

Most pre-1858 wills were proved in local diocesan courts, whose records are now in County Record Offices. It is, therefore, a good idea to check the website of a likely CRO for information on the relevant court or courts for parishes in the county. Among CRO-based projects to digitize wills are:

- Cheshire's Wills Database Online at <**www.cheshire.gov.uk/Recordoffice/ Wills/Home.htm**>
- The Wiltshire Wills project at <**www.wiltshire.gov.uk/mainindex/ heritage/wsro/wiltshirewills.htm**>.

FamilyHistoryOnline at <**www.familyhistoryonline.net**> (see p. 39) has indexes to several thousand wills for Wiltshire, Shropshire, Montgomery- shire and Stoke-on-Trent.

There are online indexes to two related resources: the Death Duty Reg- isters available on the National Archivist site at <**www.nationalarchivist. com**>, covering the years 1796 to 1903; an Inheritance Disputes Index 1574–1714 with over 26,000 lawsuits on British Origins.

SCOTLAND

The official source for Scottish wills is ScotlandsPeople at <**www. scotlandspeople.gov.uk**> (see p. 41). The site offers an index of over half a million entries to the testaments (wills) of Scots recorded in the Registers of Testaments from 1500 to 1901. Unlike the other material on ScotlandsPeople the wills are not part of the pay-per-view system, but scans can be purchased at £5 each via an online shop (all wills cost the same, regardless of length). Searching the indexes is free and the index entries themselves give quite detailed information about testators.

The site also has some examples of wills from each 50-year period covered by the index – click on 'What's in the Database', then 'Record Types & Examples'. A selection of wills of famous Scots can be viewed free of charge in the Features section of the site (Figure 8-1 shows the will of Robert Burns). For those unfamiliar with Scottish probate records and terminology, the FAQ pages at <**www.scotlandspeople.gov.uk/content/ faqs/**> provide a comprehensive introduction to all aspects of the records. Further help is available in the 'Research Tools' area (under 'Help & Other Resources'), which includes material on handwriting, abbreviations found in wills and occupations.

IRELAND

General information about wills and probate in Ireland will be found on the Irish Ancestors site at <**scripts.ireland.com/ancestor/browse/records/ wills/**>. Ancestry.com has two articles on Irish wills by Sherry Irvine at <**www.ancestry.com/learn/library/article.aspx?article=2515**> and PRONI has basic information about wills for Northern Ireland at <**www.proni. gov.uk/records/wills.htm**>.

Irish Origins at <**www.irishorigins.com**> has an index to pre-1858 wills held at the National Archives of Ireland, and Ancestry has indexes to Irish

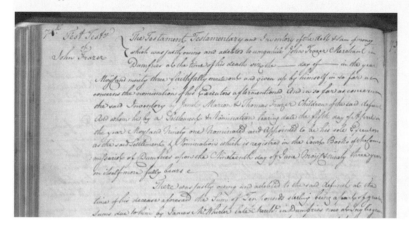

Figure 8-1 Will of Robert Burns at ScotlandsPeople

Wills taken from published indexes – details at <**www.ancestry.co.uk/ search/db.aspx?dbid=7287**>.

You can also expect to find local transcriptions done by volunteers. For example, there is an index to wills for the Diocese of Raphoe, Donegal at <**freepages.genealogy.rootsweb.com/~donegal/wills.htm**>, while Ginni Swanton has scanned images of the published index to Irish Wills for the Dioceses of Cork and Ross at <**www.ginnisw.com/Indexes%20to%20Irish %20Wills/Thumb/Thumbs1.htm**>. Other sites with Irish wills can be found from the 'Locality Specific' section on the 'Wills and Probate' page of Cyndi's List at <**www.cyndislist.com/wills.htm**> or by using a search engine.

CEMETERIES AND MONUMENTAL INSCRIPTIONS

While monumental inscriptions (MIs) are not official records, their close connection with the deceased means that they can provide family information not given by a death certificate, and can make up for a missing entry in a burial register. Similar information can come from obituaries, which are covered on p. 110, below.

The best starting point for cemeteries and MIs is Guy Etchells's Tombstones & Monumental Inscriptions site at <**www.framland.pwp. blueyonder.co.uk**>. This aims to 'provide a photographic record of the various churches, churchyards and cemeteries for the benefit of those genealogists who live some distance away', but it also has a comprehensive collection of links to related sites for the UK and other English-speaking countries, as well as links for war memorials. Cyndi's List has a 'Cemeteries & Funeral Homes' page at <www.cyndislist.com/cemetery.htm> with a number of links for UK sites and many general resources for cemeteries.

Quite a few family history societies have projects to transcribe monumental inscriptions, and this material is starting to find its way online via the FamilyHistoryOnline site (see p. 39) at <www.familyhistoryonline.net>, which already has MI material for Cornwall, Glamorgan, Norfolk and Wiltshire.

Examples of other county-based projects are:

- Dyfed FHS's list of Burial Grounds in Cardiganshire, Carmarthenshire and Pembrokeshire, with links to a number of MI transcriptions, at <www.dyfedfhs.org.uk/register/burials.htm>
- Cornish Cemeteries at <freepages.genealogy.rootsweb.com/~chrisu/cemeteries.htm> with material for around a dozen cemeteries and churchyards in Cornwall.

There is quite a lot of material for London. GenDocs has a list of Victorian London Cemeteries at <www.gendocs.demon.co.uk/cem.html>, with addresses and dates, while London Cemeteries is a project to provide a photographic record of all the capital's cemeteries at <www.londoncemeteries.co.uk>. It has a useful page of links to the cemetery web pages of the London Boroughs at <www.londoncemeteries.co.uk/?page=links>. The London Burial Grounds site at <www.londonburials.co.uk> has details of many London burial grounds.

There are also countless small volunteer transcriptions. For example, the England Tombstone Project at <www.rootsweb.com/~engcemet/> has transcriptions for a number of cemeteries including four from London. Interment.net at <www.interment.net> has collections of MI transcriptions for some UK cemeteries. These are individual user-submitted records, and only some of the materials represent complete transcriptions for a cemetery or churchyard.

Apart from the general resources mentioned above, good ways to see if there is anything for a particular place or church is to look at the relevant Genuki parish page if there is one, or simply use a search engine to find pages with the place name and the phrase 'monumental inscriptions'.

British-Genealogy has pages on recording and publishing memorial inscriptions at <www.british-genealogy.com/resources/graves/>. The Welsh Family History Archive has a useful page on Welsh Words and Phrases on Gravestones at <home.clara.net/wfha/wales/welsh-phrases.htm>. For help with Latin inscriptions, see p. 212.

Roll of Honour at <www.roll-of-honour.com> is a site dedicated to listing those commemorated on war memorials. Currently the site has details of over 600 memorials in around half the counties of England. For each memorial the site gives not only the names of the individuals but also, where available, personal details drawn from the Debt of Honour Register (see below) or other publications. There are photographs for many of the memorials.

Wall to Wall at <www.walltowall.co.uk>, the television production company responsible for *Who Do You Think You Are?*, have announced a TV series on the First World War, in connection with which they are 'looking to create an online directory of war memorials and those commemorated on them, consolidating and complementing existing information'.

There are many mailing lists relating to cemeteries and monumental inscriptions. Those most relevant to the British Isles are:

- UK-CEMETERIES, subscription details at <lists.rootsweb.com/index/intl/UK/UK-CEMETERIES.html>
- MI-ENGLAND at <lists.rootsweb.com/index/intl/ENG/MI-ENGLAND.html>
- SCOTLAND CEMETERIES at <lists.rootsweb.com/index/intl/SCT/SCOTLAND-CEMETERIES.html>
- SCT-TOMBSTONE-INSCRIPTIONS at <lists.rootsweb.com/index/intl/SCT/SCT-TOMBSTONE-INSCRIPTIONS.html>
- IRELAND-CEMETERIES at <lists.rootsweb.com/index/intl/IRL/IRELAND-CEMETERIES.html>
- IRL-TOMBSTONE-INSCRIPTIONS at <lists.rootsweb.com/index/intl/IRL/IRL-TOMBSTONE-INSCRIPTIONS.html>.

DEBT OF HONOUR REGISTER

One of the first important collections of genealogical data for the UK to go online was the Debt of Honour Register on the website of the Commonwealth War Graves Commission at <www.cwgc.org>, launched in 1998. This is a database of the names of 1.7 million members of the Commonwealth forces who died in the First and Second World Wars.

For all those listed there is name, rank, regiment and date of death, with details either of place of burial or, for those with no known grave, of commemoration. The burial information gives not only the name of the cemetery but also the grave reference and instructions on how to get to the cemetery. Some records have additional personal information, usually including the names of parents and the home address. With many cemeteries holding the dead from particular battles and campaigns, there is often historical information which puts the death in its military context. The database also includes information on 60,000 civilian casualties of the Second World War, though without details of burial location.

Figure 8-2
Debt of Honour Register
search form

CWGC
COMMONWEALTH
WAR GRAVES
COMMISSION

		Home

Casualty Search Results

Here are the results of your enquiry. There are **148** records which match your search criteria.

Select a name to see more details

No	Surname	Rank	Service	Date Of Death	Age	Regiment	Nationality	Grave/Memorial Ref.	Cemetery/Memorial Name
61	OWEN, WILFRED EDWARD SALTER	Lieutenant		04/11/1918	25	Manchester Regiment	United Kingdom	A. 3.	ORS COMMUNAL CEMETERY
62	OWEN, WILLIAM FOSTER	Private	20814	07/06/1917	0	Royal Fusiliers	United Kingdom	Panel 6 and 8.	YPRES (MENIN GATE) MEMORIAL
63	OWEN, WILLIAM GLYNN	Private	202670	25/11/1917	21	Welsh Regiment	United Kingdom	Panel 7.	CAMBRAI MEMORIAL, LOUVERVAL
64	OWEN, WILLIAM GEORGE	Private	1226	10/08/1915	25	Cheshire Regiment	United Kingdom	Panel 75 to 77.	HELLES MEMORIAL
65	OWEN, WILLIAM GEORGE	Private	39318	18/07/1916	0	Welsh Regiment	United Kingdom	Pier and Face 7 A and 10 A.	THIEPVAL MEMORIAL
66	OWEN, WALTER GLYN	Private	42308	31/10/1918	21	Labour Corps	United Kingdom	III. O. 4.	ARRAS ROAD CEMETERY, ROCLINCOURT
67	OWEN, W G	Private	156427	03/10/1918	0	Machine Gun Corps (Infantry)	United Kingdom	XVI. E. 3.	GREVILLERS BRITISH CEMETERY
68	OWEN, WILLIAM	Private	45003	26/10/1917	0	Northumberland Fusiliers	United Kingdom	XIII. E. 24.	CEMENT HOUSE CEMETERY
69	OWEN, WILLIAM GEORGE	Serjeant	4870	22/04/1918	40	Gloucestershire Regiment	United Kingdom	I. D. 11.	PERNES BRITISH CEMETERY
70	OWEN, W G	Lance Corporal	18831	19/03/1916	0	11th (Prince Albert's Own) Hussars	United Kingdom	Screen Wall. 89. 32276.	NUNHEAD (ALL SAINTS) CEMETERY
71	OWEN, W H	Sapper	360920	10/12/1918	39	Royal Engineers	United Kingdom	XLVII. C. 16.	ETAPLES MILITARY CEMETERY
72	OWEN, WILLIAM HENRY	Lance Corporal	36838	26/08/1917	23	Machine Gun Corps	United Kingdom	XXII. Q. 2A.	ETAPLES MILITARY CEMETERY
73	OWEN, WILLIAM HERBERT	Private	G/67396	06/11/1918	19	The Queen's (Royal West Surrey Regiment)	United Kingdom	I. A. 22.	AULNOYE COMMUNAL CEMETERY

Figure 8-3 Debt of Honour Register search results

The initial search form on the home page allows you to specify surname, initials, war or year of death, force (i.e. army, navy, etc.) and nationality. Unless you are looking for an unusual name, it is best to enter as much detail as possible. Figure 8-2 shows a search for the record of the war poet Wilfred Owen. From the details given, the database reports there are 148 records, which can be viewed 25 to a page (Figure 8-3). If you know the

CWGC COMMONWEALTH WAR GRAVES COMMISSION	
Home	Casualty Details
Latest News	
About the CWGC	**Name:** OWEN, WILFRED EDWARD SALTER
Architecture	**Initials:** W E S
Horticulture	**Nationality:** United Kingdom
Organisational Structure	**Rank:** Lieutenant
	Regiment: Manchester Regiment
	Unit Text: 5th Bn.
Education	**Age:** 25
Publications	**Date of Death:** 04/11/1918
Community Involvement Initiative	**Awards:** MC
	Additional information: Son of Mr. and Mrs. Tom Owen, of "Mahim", Monkmoor Rd., Shrewsbury. Native of Oswestry. Enlisted in The Artists' Rifles in October 1915. Commissioned into the Manchester Regiment in June 1916. Was a poet of repute, although during his lifetime, only a few of his poems appeared in print. The 'Atheneum' of December 1919, nominated Owen's work "Strange Meeting" as the finest of the war.
Finance	
Careers	**Casualty Type:** Commonwealth War Dead
Useful Information	**Grave/Memorial Reference:** A. 3.
Links	**Cemetery:** ORS COMMUNAL CEMETERY [View Details]

Figure 8-4 Debt of Honour Register individual record

regiment and approximate rank of the person you're looking for, it should not take too long to identify the relevant record. Knowing that Wilfred Owen was an officer, and that he was killed near the end of the war, it is relatively easy to identify him as the lieutenant in the Manchester Regiment who died on 4 November 1918.

The list of search results links to a page giving the details for each soldier listed. In the case of Wilfred Owen (see Figure 8-4), in addition to the basic details of rank, regiment and date of death, the record shows the names of his parents and their address, along with some further biographical information. The bottom part of the screen gives details of the cemetery and grave, as well as information about the campaigns from which the cemetery holds the dead.

Because the search results give only the initials of the individuals, it can be quite time-consuming to search for someone whose regiment is unknown, though in some cases an age is given. Unfortunately, next of kin are not always named, so for common names you may need to look at army records to confirm the identity of a particular entry.

You can also search for individual cemeteries and access a list of graves. For many cemeteries there are plans and photographs.

PROPERTY RECORDS

Property records are important in showing a place of residence before the start of the census or where, as in Ireland, census records are missing. Even those too poor to own property may be recorded as occupiers, though of course only a head of household will be given.

Many of the records are held at local level, so it is worth checking the relevant county record office website for information. There are few national projects in this area, but many small transcriptions for individual parishes.

TITHES

Tithe records and in particular the nineteenth-century tithe maps are important for both owners and occupiers of land. A very thorough discussion of tithe records will be found in the National Archives' Research Guide 'Tithe Records: A Detailed Examination' at <**www.catalogue. nationalarchives.gov.uk/Leaflets/ri2148.htm**>. The National Library of Wales also has comprehensive pages on this topic at <**www.llgc.org.uk/dm/ dm0030.htm**>. County Record Office websites often give information about tithe maps and schedules in their collections, and these are obvious candidates for digitization. Devon and Worcester have projects to index their tithe maps – these both have mammoth URLs of over 100 characters, so follow the links on the site for this book or search from the county council home pages at <**www.devon.gov.uk**> and <**www.worcestershire. gov.uk**> respectively.

A major tithe records project is the University of Portsmouth's Tithe Survey of England and Wales at <**tiger.iso.port.ac.uk:7778/pls/www/web. html?p=tithe_intro**>, which also offers data for seven parishes. Digital Handsworth at <**www.digitalhandsworth.org.uk**> (see p. 201) includes images of tithe maps, and indexes to the schedules.

There are many individual transcriptions of tithe schedules. The best way to find them is probably to search on the word 'tithes' or the phrase 'tithe map' and the relevant place name.

GRIFFITH'S VALUATION

For Ireland, the nineteenth century property records are all the more important because of the destruction of census records. The sites referred to for Irish census material in Chapter 6 have information on these records, usually under the heading 'Census substitutes'. Among the most important is Griffith's Valuation, and there is a range of material from this source online.

The Irish Origins site at <**www.irishorigins.com**> has an index to Griffith's Valuation and images of the original documents, in a joint venture with the National Library of Ireland and Irish CD-ROM publisher Eneclann. Another subscription site for Irish genealogy, Otherdays, has the Valuation online at <**www.otherdays.com**>, and offers correlation of entries with the Ordnance Survey maps.

There are also many local transcriptions, for example:

- The LEITRIM-ROSCOMMON Griffith's database at <www. leitrim-roscommon.com/GRIFFITH/> has a selection of material for parishes in Galway, Leitrim, Limerick, Mayo and Roscommon
- <freepages.genealogy.rootsweb.com/~tyronc/parishes/griffiths/> has some material for Co. Tyrone
- <www.rootsweb.com/~irlker/griffith.html> has some material for Co. Kerry
- From-Ireland has material for Carlow, Laois and Leitrim at <www. from-ireland.net/gene/griffithsval.htm>, which also has links to other sites with Griffith's data.

Links to such material will be found on the Genuki pages for Ireland at <www.genuki.org.uk/big/irl/>, and on the Ireland pages of Census Finder at <www.censusfinder.com/ireland.htm>.

The PRONI has a guide to using Griffith's Valuation at <www.proni.gov. uk/research/family/griffith.htm>.

INSURANCE RECORDS

Useful sources of information on property in London are the surviving fire insurance policies. The Guildhall Library holds records for many insurance companies, and over 50,000 policies from the Sun Fire Office for 1816–1831 have been indexed. The index can be found on the Access to Archives website at <www.a2a.org.uk>, and detailed instructions on using it are available at <www.history.ac.uk/gh/sun.htm>. The index comprises the name and address of the policyholder, his occupation or status, and the location of property insured. There is general information on the Guildhall Library's Fire Insurance records at <www.history.ac.uk/gh/ fire.htm>.

NEWSPAPERS

The most important site for British newspapers is that of the British Library Newspaper Library at <www.bl.uk/collections/newspapers.html>. Under the heading 'Newspaper, Journalism, and Media Internet Resources', this page has links for present-day newspapers online including: London National Newspapers, Scottish Newspapers, Irish Newspapers, English and Welsh Newspapers, Channel Islands and Isle of Man Newspapers, Newspapers Around the World, and Other Newspaper Libraries and Collections.

The BL Newspapers Catalogue at <www.bl.uk/catalogues/newspapers/> includes over 52,000 newspaper and periodical titles from all over the world, dating from the seventeenth to the twenty-first century. Each entry

NEWSPAPERS CATALOGUE

About | Search tips | Date search | Main

Search results

print   Search for: **liverpool** with sort by date

home

site search   Date ranges show the earliest and latest copies held, but this does not necessarily mean
that we hold all intervening copies. Click on the title for its full details.

back   Go to Page: 1 ▾ 60
Results 1 - 50 of 439   next 50

search tips   **1756-1759**
new search   Williamson's Liverpool Advertiser and Mercantile Register
modify search   Liverpool; Merseyside; England
              1759-1793
                  Williamson's Liverpool Advertiser and Mercantile Chronicle
                  Liverpool; Merseyside; England
              1766-1766
                  Williamson's Liverpool Advertiser and Mercantile Chronicle
                  Liverpool; Merseyside; England
              1767-1768
                  Liverpool Chronicle (The)
                  Liverpool; Merseyside; England
              1794-1795
                  Liverpool Phoenix or, Ferguson's Weekly Gazette
                  Liverpool; Merseyside; England
              1794-1828
                  Billinge's Liverpool Advertiser and Marine Intelligencer
                  Liverpool; Merseyside; England
              1795-1795
                  Gore's Liverpool General Advertiser

Figure 8-5 Search results for "Liverpool" in the Newspaper Library catalogue, sorted
by date

in the web catalogue contains full details of the title (including any title
changes), the place of publication (the town or city and the country) and
the dates which are held. The results can be sorted by any of these fields,
which means you can get a historical list of newspapers for a particular
town (see Figure 8-5). Further information about the BL's newspaper
collection will be found on p. 105.

The websites for other major libraries and archives discussed in Chapter
9 will have sections on their newspaper holdings. Unfortunately Familia
(see p. 124) does not include newspaper holdings for pubic libraries.

A particularly useful site is Newsplan, which gives details of newspapers
and information on libraries and record offices where they can be
consulted. At present Newsplan has websites for two regions:

- London and the South East at <laser.newsplan.co.uk> – 2,500 titles
- West Midlands at <wm.newsplan.co.uk> – 1,100 titles.

Figure 8-6 shows a sample record in Newsplan. Newsplan is a long-
established programme for cataloguing and preserving local newspapers,
so there is a reasonable chance that additional regions will be covered in
due course.

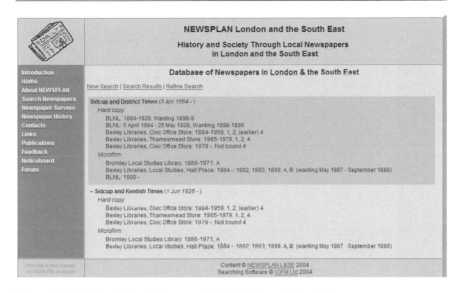

Figure 8-6 Details of the *Sidcup and District Times* in Newsplan

While historical editions of most newspapers must be read in the libraries, there is some material online. The Genuki county pages are a good way of finding links to local newspapers on the web, and Cyndi's List has a 'Newspapers' page at <www.cyndislist.com/newspapr.htm>. There are, of course, many sites relating to present-day newspapers, including Kidon Media-link, which has links to the websites of UK newspapers at <www.kidon.com/media-link/unitedkingdom.shtml>, and All the World's Newspapers, which has comprehensive listings for all countries at <www.onlinenewspapers.com>.

The British Library Online Newspaper Archive is a pilot project at <www.uk.olivesoftware.com> which has digitized copies of a number of editions of:

- *Daily News*
- *News of the World*
- *Penny Illustrated*
- *Manchester Guardian*
- *Weekly Despatch*.

There are a number of short runs of each paper for individual years. Each newspaper page comes up as a separate image in the browser window (Figure 8-7). In this view, only the headlines are easily legible but clicking on an article brings up an enlarged version so you can read the body text. There is also a text search facility, which brings up only the individual articles. You may need to use Internet Explorer to view this site.

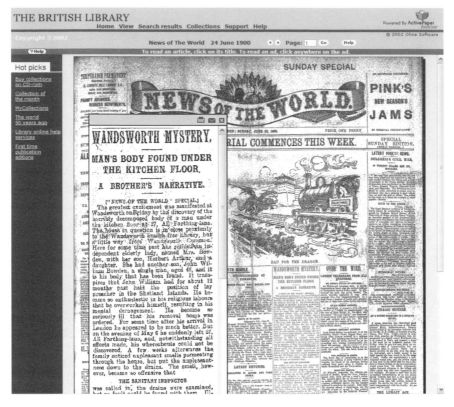

Figure 8-7 British Library Online Newspaper Archive

British Newspapers 1800–1900 is a much more comprehensive digitiz-ation project announced by the British Library in June 2004. The titles to be digitized will include two national papers, *The Morning Chronicle* and *The Morning Post*, as well as a range of regional and local papers from all parts of the UK. The completed project is intended to go online at the end of 2006, though it is possible that some material may be made available earlier. Details are at **<www.bl.uk/collections/britishnewspapers1800to1900. html>**, and a list of potential local papers for inclusion is at **<www.jisc.ac.uk/ index.cfm?name=form&formid=449045718>**.

The Scotsman has an online archive of its entire collection of printed issues from the first edition of 25 January 1817 at **<archive.scotsman.com>**. At the time of writing, the archive only goes up to 1950, but this will be extended to the present day in due course. Initial searches are free, but access to articles requires a subscription, and various subscription periods are available, costing from £7.95 for 24 hours to £159.95 for a full year. Access to the entire contents of the very first edition of the paper, however, is free.

Another important site for historical newspapers is Gazettes Online at <www.gazettes-online.co.uk>. This is a major project to make the entire archive of the London, Edinburgh, and Belfast Gazettes available on the web – these are the UK's official newspapers of record, stretching back to 1665. So far, the period 1900–1979 is covered, but the ultimate aim is to have all 56,000 editions online. Among the material of interest to family historians are awards of civilian and military medals, military promotions, and insolvency notices.

To access the archive go to the home page for the edition you want to search and select 'Archive' on the navigation bar. Each page of each edition comes as a separate PDF file. The site seems to be designed to work only in Internet Explorer on the PC – some Mac users have reported the site to be unusable, and it does not display properly in some other PC browsers.

Another online collection of historical newspaper material is the Internet Library of Early Journals at <www.bodley.ox.ac.uk/ilej/>, a joint project by the universities of Birmingham, Leeds, Manchester and Oxford to place online digitized copies of eighteenth- and nineteenth-century journals, in runs of at least 20 years. The project comprises:

- *Gentleman's Magazine*
- *The Annual Register*
- *Philosophical Transactions of the Royal Society*
- *Notes and Queries*
- *The Builder*
- *Blackwood's Edinburgh Magazine.*

Alongside these projects there are some online indexes to individual editions of newspapers. These are generally the work of individuals and therefore inevitably limited in scope:

- *The Belfast Newsletter* is served by an index for the period 1737–1800 at <www.ucs.louisiana.edu/bnl/> and a number of digitized copies for 1796–1803 on the Act of Union site at <www.actofunion.ac.uk/news. php>
- There is a surname index for *The Surrey Advertiser* for 1864–7 at <www.newspaperdetectives.co.uk>
- Indexes for 12 West Country newspapers, covering several years each, are at <freespace.virgin.net/paul.mansfield1/paul001.html>.

The most important British newspaper index online is for *The Times*, covering the whole period since its first edition in 1784. The online version of this is available only on a corporate subscription – see <www.galegroup.com> – so you would need to find a public library which subscribes. During the (US) National Library Week 2005 there was a week-long free trial period, which will perhaps be repeated.

OBITUARIES

There are a number of sites with information about newspaper obituary notices. Cyndi's List has a page devoted to obituaries at <**www.cyndislist. com/obits.htm**>, though almost all the sites listed relate only to the USA.

Free Obituaries On-Line at <**www3.sympatico.ca/bkinnon/obit_links6. htm**> has links to sites providing obituaries – many are newspaper sites – for Australia, Canada, England, Ireland, Jamaica, New Zealand, Scotland, and the USA.

The Obituary Daily Times is a daily index of published obituaries at <**www.rootsweb.com/~obituary/**>, which has over 10 million entries, mainly from US newspapers. The site is an index only – you need to refer to the original newspaper to see the text. A database of the Irish extracts (over 50,000) from this service is provided by the Irish Ancestral Research Association (TIARA) at <**tiara.ie/obframe.htm**>.

Obituary Lookup Volunteers at <**freepages.genealogy.rootsweb.com/ ~obitl/**> holds lists of those prepared to look up obituaries in particular newspapers or libraries. There are separate pages listing volunteers for England, Wales, Scotland and Ireland, as well as a number of other countries.

▌DIRECTORIES

Alongside newspapers the other major printed source, particularly for ancestors who were in trade, are nineteenth-century directories. Many of these have been digitized and published on CD-ROM, but an increasing number are available either complete or in part on the web.

Rod Neep's British-Genealogy site has some general information about trade directories and how they can help with your research at <**www. british-genealogy.com/resources/books/directories/**>. There are individual pages listing the published directories for the following counties: Bedfordshire, Berkshire, Buckinghamshire, Cornwall, Cumberland, Derbyshire, Gloucestershire, Nottinghamshire, Oxfordshire, and Staffordshire. An article by David Tippey, 'Using Trade Directories in your Research' is available at <**www.genealogyreviews.co.uk/tippey_directories.htm**>.

The major site for directories is the Digital Library of Historical Directories' site at <**www.historicaldirectories.org**>. This is the fruit of a Heritage Lottery Fund project based at the University of Leicester. The aim of the project is to place online digitized trade directories from England and Wales from 1750 to 1919. It is intended to be representative rather than comprehensive, with one directory for each county and each major town for the 1850s, 1890s and 1910s, with additional decades to follow.

You can browse by county or decade, or you can select the keyword option to do a more advanced search. This allows you to specify, if you

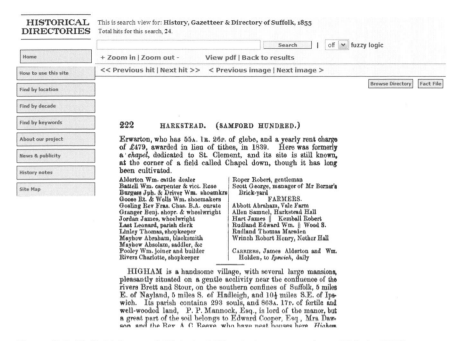

Figure 8-8 Digital Library of Historical Directories: a page from White's 1855 *History, Gazetteer & Directory of Suffolk*

wish, a county, a decade, a publisher, and any names or other terms (a particular occupation, perhaps). The search results list all matching directories, but do not list the pages with individual hits – you need to select the directory you want to examine. This will bring up the title page of the directory and tell you how many occurrences of your keywords there are. To examine the relevant pages, you need to click on the 'Next hit' button. You can also simply browse the directory, page by page. The display shows a page at a time, and pages can be printed or saved (see Figure 8-8).

Although this is by far the largest collection of directories, there are many other sites which have material from directories. In some cases, there is simply a name index to the printed volume, such as that for Pigot's *Commercial Directory for Surrey* (1839), which is on the Genuki Surrey site at <homepages.gold.ac.uk/genuki/SRY/>. This provides text files with page references for names and places. While not a substitute for online versions of the directories, these listings at least indicate whether it is worth locating a copy of the directory in question. Another approach is to place scanned images on the web, along with a name index, as on Nicholas Adams's site, which provides Pigot's 1830 and 1840 directories for Herefordshire at <freepages.genealogy.rootsweb.com/~nmfa/genealogy.html>. Finally, some sites offer a full transcription, with or without a name index, such as Rosemary Lockie's pages devoted to the 1835 Pigot's *Commercial Directory for Derbyshire* at **<www.genuki.org.uk/big/eng/DBY/Pigot1835/about.html>**.

There are also some partial transcriptions, usually for individual towns or cities, such as Brian Randell's material for Exeter at **<genuki.cs.ncl.ac.uk/DEV/Exeter/White1850.html>** taken from White's *Devonshire* directory of 1850, or Ann Andrews's extracts for a group of Derbyshire parishes from Kelly's 1891 directory at **<ds.dial.pipex.com/town/terrace/pd65/dby/kelly/>**. David Foster's Direct Resources site at **<www.direct-resources.uk.com>** has brief extracts from a large number of directories online, with the full transcriptions available on CD-ROM.

Since directories were compiled on a county basis, the easiest way to find them online is to look at the relevant county page on Genuki. Alternatively, you could use a search engine to search for, say, [Directory AND Kelly AND Norfolk] or [Directory AND Pigot AND Lancashire] to locate the publications of the two main nineteenth-century directory publishers. (See Chapter 16 for information on search engines and formulating searches.) You may also find information about county directories on county record office websites, while Familia lists the directory holdings for many public libraries (see Figure 9-7).

Directories relating to the military and the professions are discussed in Chapter 11.

CHAPTER 9

ARCHIVES AND LIBRARIES

Archives and libraries are often seen as the antithesis of the internet, but this is largely illusory, certainly from the genealogical point of view. Only a limited range of British genealogical resources are reproduced as images on the web, and most types of material are available, if at all, in the form of online indexes. This means that you will need to go to the relevant record office or a suitable library to check the information you have derived from online sources against original documents (or microfilms of them). It will be years before all the core sources are completely available online. Technologically, it is in fact a trivial matter to take records which have already been microfilmed and put images of them online. But to be usable, such online images need to be supported by indexes, and the preparation of these requires substantial labour and investment. As mentioned in Chapter 4, delivering images via the web has implications for running costs, even where production costs are minimal.

If you are going to look at paper records, then catalogues and other finding aids are essential. Traditionally, these have been available only in the reading rooms of record offices themselves, so a significant part of any visit has to be spent checking the catalogues and finding aids for whatever you have come in search of. But the web has allowed repositories to make it much easier to access information about their collections and facilities. At the very least, the website for a record office will give a current phone number and opening times. Larger sites will provide descriptions of the holdings, often with advice on how to make the most of them. Increasingly, you can expect to find catalogues online and, in some cases, even place orders for documents so that they are ready for you when you visit the repository.

All this means you can get more out of a visit to a record office, because you're able to go better prepared. You can spend more time looking at documents and less trying to locate them. And if you can't get to a record office, you will be able to give much more precise information than previously to someone visiting it on your behalf.

This chapter looks at what the major national repositories and the various local bodies provide in the way of online information.

▍GATEWAYS TO ARCHIVES

There are a number of sources of information about repositories and the archival collections they hold.

The ARCHON Directory at <**www.archon.nationalarchives.gov.uk/ archon/**> acts as a gateway for all British archives. The site is hosted by the National Archives (see p. 117) and its intention is to provide 'information on all repositories in the United Kingdom and all those repositories throughout the world which have collections of manuscripts which are noted in the indexes to the UK National Register of Archives'. There is a page devoted to each archival repository in the British Isles, including the Republic of Ireland. In addition to basic details such as contact information, opening times, and a link to any website, it also provides links to catalogue entries in the National Register of Archives (see p. 117).

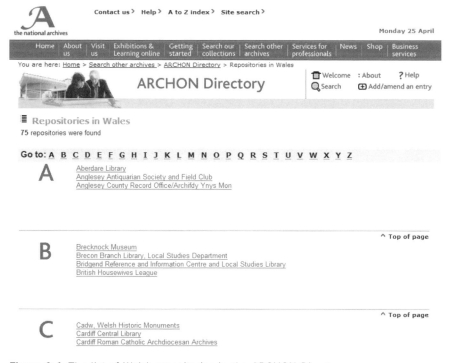

Figure 9-1 The list of Welsh repositories in the ARCHON Directory

There are also search facilities which make it possible to search across the directory, so, for example, you could search for all archives in a given town or county. Although it is probably easier to use the Genuki county pages to find County Record Offices (see p. 123), the ARCHON Directory is better for locating other repositories and archives with relevant material.

Access to Archives (A2A) is a national project, funded by government and the Heritage Lottery Fund, to 'create a virtual national archives catalogue, bringing together a critical mass of information about the rich national archival heritage and making that information available globally from one source via the World Wide Web'. The website at <www.a2a.org. uk> offers search facilities across almost 400 catalogues with 7.5 million items. This includes material from many county record offices. The search allows you to look for a word or phrase (which includes names) in a specific repository, over a whole region, or indeed over all regions. You can also restrict the search to material you have not previously seen by searching only for items added since a particular date. The site is due to move to <www.nationalarchives.gov.uk/a2a/> but no date has yet been announced for this move.

North of the border, the Scottish Archive Network (SCAN) at <www. scan.org.uk> has a similar remit – among its aims are 'the linking of archives large and small, public and private, throughout Scotland, and the creation of a unique knowledge base on Scottish history and culture'. It has a directory with contact details for all Scottish repositories at <www. scan.org.uk/directory/contactdetails.htm>. There is an online catalogue at <www.dswebhosting.info/SCAN/> (though this URL has the appearance of a temporary location) which provides consolidated access to the catalogues of over 50 repositories in Scotland, with over 20,000 archives. The Research Tools pages at <www.scan.org.uk/researchrtools/> include examples of documents, a glossary of Scottish terms, and material on handwriting. There is also a Knowledge Base with answers to questions frequently asked in Scottish archives. Oddly, this does not have its own page but is available as a pop-up link from other pages, such as the Research Tools page.

The ScottishDocuments site at <www.scottishdocuments.com> was originally launched by SCAN as a home for digitized Scottish wills. In June 2005, these were moved to ScotlandsPeople (see p. 98) and future plans for ScottishDocuments are unclear as this book goes to press, though it seems likely that it will house further collections of digitized documents.

Archives Network Wales at <www.archivesnetworkwales.info> is a similar site for Wales, with descriptions of archival collections in Welsh record offices, universities, and other bodies.

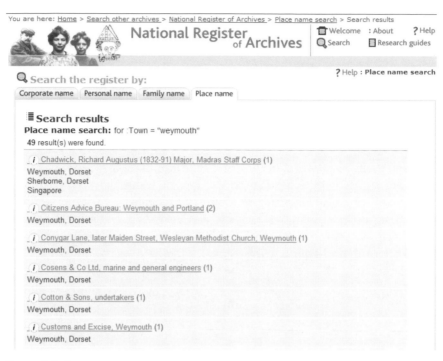

Figure 9-2 Place name search for "Weymouth" in the National Register of Archives

Figure 9-3 Full entry for a record in the NRA

THE NATIONAL REGISTER OF ARCHIVES

The National Register of Archives (NRA) has an online index at <www. nra.nationalarchives.gov.uk/nra/>. This contains reference details for around 150,000 people, families and corporate bodies relating to British history, with a further 100,000 related records. The materials themselves are held in record offices, university libraries and specialist repositories. The search engine allows you to search by:

* Corporate Name – combined search of the Business Index and the Organizations Index
* Personal Name – combined search of the Personal Index and the Diaries and Papers Index
* Family Name
* Place Name – lists businesses, organizations and other corporate bodies by place.

Figure 9-2 shows the results of a place name search in the NRA, while Figure 9-3 shows the full details for one of the search results. Note that it not only gives the repository but also the reference number used by the record office in question. An obvious use of the NRA is to locate the parish registers for a particular place. It is important to note that unlike A2A, the NRA catalogue cannot be used to search for the contents of archives, only the description and location, so a search on family name will only find archives deposited by or relating to the family, not individual documents which mention someone with that surname.

NATIONAL ARCHIVES

THE NATIONAL ARCHIVES

The National Archives is the main national repository for the UK, and its website at <www.nationalarchives.gov.uk> has a number of sections relevant to genealogists. There is a main 'Family History' page at <www. nationalarchives.gov.uk/familyhistory/>. For detailed information on the National Archives' records for individual areas of interest, there are over 300 Research Guides, all of which are online, all linked from an alphabetical index at <www.catalogue.nationalarchives.gov.uk/ researchguidesindex.asp>. For a more informal introduction to family history research at the National Archives, see the 'Family History' pages at <www.nationalarchives.gov.uk/pathways/familyhistory/>, under 'Learning guides'. A list of the topics in this area is given on p. 9. The 'Visit Us' menu links to pages with all you need to know when visiting the National Archives, including details of opening hours. Probably the most important if you have never previously visited TNA is the advice on planning your visit at <www.nationalarchives.gov.uk/visit/plan.htm>.

There is much on the site that is relevant to genealogists and these resources are not described here but in the relevant chapters. There are links to the online data collections (the 1901 census and DocumentsOnline) from the 'Search our collections' menu and the 'Family History' page.

The Catalogue

One of the most important facilities on the National Archives website is PROCAT, the online catalogue at <**www.catalogue.nationalarchives.gov. uk**>, with almost 10 million entries. There are two ways to use the catalogue: you can browse or you can search.

In browsing, you start from the list of all the department codes denoting the various government departments which created the records in question, and you will then get a list of all the individual document series from that department. Figure 9-4 shows the start of the list of all the document series for Home Office Records (Department code HO), which would be of interest if you had an ancestor who was a criminal or was naturalized. The titles of the series are sometimes rather terse, but clicking on the title will bring up a detailed description of the series. Clicking on the series number itself opens up a menu listing of all the individual pieces within that series. Figure 9-5 shows the start of the list for HO8, records for the prison hulks.

Reference	Hierarchy			
		Title/Scope and content	Covering dates	Last Piece Ref.
📂 HO		ⓘ Records created or inherited by the Home Office, Ministry of Home Security, and related bodies	1700-1996	
				Next ⊙ ⊗
+☐ Division within HO		ⓘ Aliens and Immigration, Denization and Naturalisation, Community Relations, Community Programmes and ...	1789-1999	
+☐ HO 1		ⓘ Home Office: Denization and Naturalisation Papers and Correspondence	1789-1871	176
+☐ HO 2		ⓘ Home Office: Aliens Act 1836: Certificates of Arrival of Aliens	1836-1852	236
+☐ HO 3		ⓘ Home Office: Aliens Act 1836: Returns and Papers	1836-1869	102
+☐ HO 4		ⓘ Aliens Office and Home Office: Original Patents of Denization	1804-1843	51
+☐ HO 5		ⓘ Aliens Office and Home Office: Aliens' Entry Books	1794-1921	142
+☐ Division within HO		ⓘ Criminal Department	1782-1980	
+☐ HO 6		ⓘ Home Office: Judges' and Recorders' Returns	1816-1840	25
+☐ HO 7		ⓘ Home Office: Convicts, Miscellanea	1785-1835	3
+☐ Division within HO		ⓘ Prison Department and Inspectorate	1802-1981	
+☐ HO 8		ⓘ Home Office: Convict Prisons: Quarterly Returns of Prisoners	1824-1876	207
+☐ HO 9		ⓘ Home Office: Convict Prison Hulks: Registers and Letter Books	1802-1849	16
+☐ Division within HO		ⓘ Criminal Department	1782-1980	
+☐ HO 10		ⓘ Home Office: Settlers and Convicts, New South Wales and Tasmania: Records	1787-1859	64
+☐ HO 11		ⓘ Home Office: Convict Transportation Registers	1787-1870	21

Figure 9-4 Series list for Home Office records (HO)

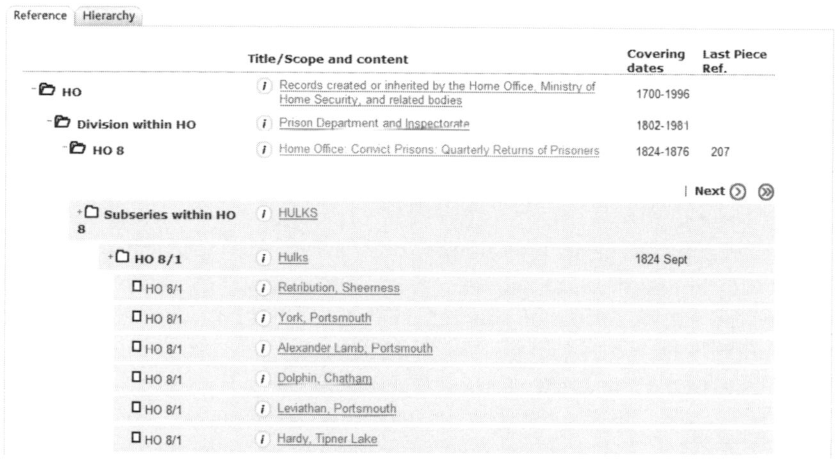

Figure 9-5 List of piece numbers for the class HO8

Figure 9-6 Search results in series WO 97 (Royal Hospital Chelsea: Soldiers Service Documents)

Of course, this is all very well if you are familiar with the records in question, or are working with a reference book. If not, it is probably easier to enter the catalogue via the Search option. You can search on up to three keywords, and the results will list every relevant document together with its full catalogue reference for all the series whose titles or descriptions contain the relevant words. If there are a lot of matches in different series, the results page will list the series and the number of results in each; clicking on that number will bring up a list of the individual documents. You can also specify a series to narrow down the search. Where a document relates to a specific individual, it is indexed under that person's name, so you can, rather surprisingly, search the catalogue for an individual ancestor. Figure 9-6 shows an entry for my great-great-great-grandfather Christopher Christian in series WO 97 (Royal Hospital Chelsea: Soldiers Service Documents). Note that to search on two keywords, you need to link them with AND; if you just type in two words, they are treated as a phrase.

In itself, the online catalogue is very straightforward to use, but it cannot simplify the organization of the actual records, which have been created independently by individual government departments over 900 or so years. In order to make the most of the catalogue, you will need to be familiar with the way in which the records you are looking for are organized. Research Guides, linked from <www.catalogue.nationalarchives.gov.uk/researchguidesindex.asp>, cover all the major series of records of interest to genealogists. *Tracing Your Ancestors in the Public Record Office* and specialist books on individual series of record are recommended reading. A useful feature of the online catalogue search is that the search results pages start with a drop-down list of relevant Research Guides.

Other catalogues

In addition to PROCAT, there are a number of specialist catalogues on the site. Those of most interest to genealogists are:

- The E179 database at <www.nationalarchives.gov.uk/e179/> – this catalogues tax records relating to lay people and clergy in England, c.1200–1688, with over 25,000 documents.
- The Equity Pleadings database at <www.nationalarchives.gov.uk/equity/> – this currently contains details of around 30,000 Chancery Pleadings.
- The Hospital Database at <www.nationalarchives.gov.uk/hospitalrecords/> – this includes the location and covering dates of administrative and clinical records.
- The Manorial Documents Register (MDR) at <www.mdr.nationalarchives.gov.uk/mdr/> – this shows the whereabouts of manorial documents in England and Wales. The following county sections are so far included: Hampshire, Isle of Wight, Norfolk, Surrey, Middlesex, the three Ridings of Yorkshire, and all of Wales.

NATIONAL ARCHIVES OF SCOTLAND

The National Archives of Scotland has a website at <www.nas.gov.uk>, with a Family History section at <www.nas.gov.uk/family_history.htm>. The material in the NAS is indexed in the SCAN online catalogue (see p. 115).

The site offers a comprehensive collection of fact sheets in Adobe Acrobat (PDF) format, covering: adoption, buildings, crafts and trades, crime and criminals, customs and excise, deeds, divorce, education, emigration, estate records, inheriting lands and buildings, lighthouses, military records, the poor, sasines, taxation records, valuation rolls, and wills and testaments. There is also a Family History FAQ page covering the National Archives' holdings and services relevant to family historians.

A redesigned NAS site is due to be launched in autumn 2005, so expect to see an expansion of this material.

THE PUBLIC RECORD OFFICE OF NORTHERN IRELAND

The Public Record Office of Northern Ireland (PRONI) has a website at <www.proni.gov.uk>. The site offers extensive information for genealogists, including descriptions of the major categories of record and about two dozen leaflets on various aspects of Irish genealogical research. Links to all these aids are provided on the 'Records Held' page at <www.proni. gov.uk/records/records.htm>. The 'Introductions to the Major Collections' page at <www.proni.gov.uk/records/listing.htm> links to descriptions of the main collections of private papers held by PRONI. There is also an FAQ page at <www.proni.gov.uk/question/question.htm>.

The site does not offer a full online catalogue, but has four online indexes of use to genealogists:

- The Geographical Index (for locating any administrative geographical name, with Ordnance Survey Map reference number)
- The Prominent Person Index
- The Presbyterian Church Index
- The Church of Ireland Index.

The last two cover only those records which have been microfilmed by PRONI. There are plans to add other church records, school records and pre-1858 wills. All are linked from <www.proni.gov.uk/records/USING/using.htm>.

PRONI has two important online databases of primary records:

- A database of half a million men and women who signed the Ulster Covenant and Declaration in 1912 at <www.proni.gov.uk/ulstercovenant/> with scanned images of the signatures
- Freeholders' Records at <www.proni.gov.uk/freeholders/>, which indexes pre-1840 voter registration records.

NATIONAL ARCHIVES OF IRELAND

The National Archives of Ireland has a website at <www.nationalarchives. ie>. Among other things, this has help for beginners, information on the main types of Irish genealogical record, and a good list of links to websites for Irish genealogy. The NAI has no online catalogue, but there are two online databases of interest to genealogists:

- Ordnance Survey Parishes Index
- Ireland-Australia Transportation.

These can be accessed from <**www.nationalarchives.ie/research/databases. htm**>. There is a collection of guides to various aspects of Irish genealogy at <**www.nationalarchives.ie/genealogy/begin.htm**>.

The site was redesigned in 2004. Unfortunately the new navigation doesn't work on all browsers, so you may need to use Internet Explorer or switch to the text-only version at <**www.nationalarchives.ie/text/**> to access the Genealogy area of the site.

▌ NATIONAL LIBRARIES

The British Library has a number of collections of interest to genealogists. The home page of the BL website is at <**www.bl.uk**>, while the Integrated Catalogue is at <**catalogue.bl.uk**>. The catalogue is also included in COPAC, discussed on p. 125. A number of catalogues to specific collections are linked from <**www.bl.uk/catalogues/listings.html**>.

The British Library Newspaper Library at Colindale has a website at <**www.bl.uk/collections/newspapers.html**> and its online catalogue at <**www.bl.uk/catalogues/newspapers**> includes over 52,000 newspaper and periodical titles from all over the world. The Newspaper Library is discussed in more detail on p. 105.

The India Office Records held by the British Library do not have their own online catalogue, but a description of holdings will be found at <**www. bl.uk/collections/orientaloffice.html**>, and some of the material can be found on Access to Archives <**www.a2a.org.uk**> – on the Search page select 'British Library, Oriental & India Office' from the 'Location of Archives' field. The NRA at <**www.nra.nationalarchives.gov.uk/nra/**> also contains entries for material in the India Office Records.

The National Library of Scotland has a website at <**www.nls.uk**> and its main catalogue is linked from <**main-cat.nls.uk**>. Among the other catalogues, Scots Abroad at <**www.nls.uk/catalogues/online/scotsabroad/**> will be of interest to those descended from Scottish emigrants.

The National Library of Wales website at <**www.llgc.org.uk**> provides links to a number of online catalogues from <**www.llgc.org.uk/cronfa/ index_s.htm**>. The most useful of these for genealogists are:

- ISYS and CAIRS – catalogues of archives catalogued before and after 1999. ISYS includes an index of applicants for marriage licences from 1616 to 1837.

- Crime and Punishment – information about crimes, criminals and punishments included in the gaol files of the Court of Great Sessions in Wales.
- Welsh Biography Online.

Another useful though not genealogical database is Wales on the Web, which is a gateway of web resources relating to all aspects of Wales.

The National Library of Ireland has a website at <www.nli.ie>, with a family history section at <www.nli.ie/fr_servfamily.htm>. This covers all the main sources in the library which are of use to family historians, and has lists of parish registers. There are several online catalogues, searchable separately or combined, all linked from <hip.nli.ie>. There is also a newspaper catalogue at <www.nli.ie/newsplan/>. There are catalogues of the photographic collections, linked from the family history page. The site also hosts the web pages of the Office of Chief Herald at <www.nli.ie/fr_offi2.htm>.

For access to online catalogues of the UK national libraries, see the information on COPAC, p. 125, below.

COUNTY RECORD OFFICES

There are several ways to locate a county record office (CRO) website. Each Genuki county page provides a link to relevant CROs, and may itself give contact details and opening times. Mark Howells has links to record office websites for:

- England <www.oz.net/~markhow/englishros.htm>
- Wales at <www.oz.net/~markhow/welshros.htm>
- Scotland at <www.oz.net/~markhow/scotsros.htm>.

The ARCHON Directory (see p. 114) allows you to locate a record office by county or region. Finally, CROs can be found via the website of the relevant county council (you may even be able to make a guess at its URL, as it will often be something like <www.essexcc.gov.uk>) or via the UK government portal at <www.direct.gov.uk> (see p. 17), which links to the websites of all arms of national and local government.

There is a wide variation in what CROs provide on their websites. At the very least, though, you can expect to find details of location, contacts, and opening times, along with some basic help on using their material. However, increasingly they offer background material on the area and specific collections, and even online catalogues. Even better, a number of CROs are engaged on major digitization projects, some of which are mentioned elsewhere in this book. Much of the manuscript material held by CROs is catalogued on ARCHON (see p. 114).

The FFHS has a leaflet 'You And Your Record Office: A Code Of Practice For Family Historians Using County Record Offices' at <www.

ffhs.org.uk/General/Help/Record.htm>, which offers advice on preparing for a visit and what to expect.

PUBLIC LIBRARIES

Public libraries, although they have little in the way of manuscript collections, have considerable holdings in the basic sources for genealogical research. For example, many central libraries have microfiche of the GRO indexes and microfilm of local census returns, as well as local printed material.

The UK Public Libraries page at <**dspace.dial.pipex.com/town/square/ac940/ukpublib.html**> is a general site devoted to public libraries. At <**dspace.dial.pipex.com/town/square/ac940/weblibs.html**> it provides links to library websites, and to their OPACs (Online Public Access Catalogues) where these are available over the internet.

For public libraries in the Irish Republic, Ireland's public library portal has links to the websites and online catalogues at <**www.library.ie/public/**>.

However, for genealogists, a more useful starting point is the Familia website at <**www.familia.org.uk**>. This is designed to be a comprehensive guide to genealogical holdings in public libraries, with a page for every local authority in the UK and the Republic of Ireland, listing the principal public libraries within the authority which have family history resources, along with contact details, opening times, etc. It then outlines the genealogical holdings under the following main headings:

- Births, deaths and marriages
- Census records
- Directories
- Electoral registers
- Poll books
- International Genealogical Index
- Unpublished indexes
- Parish registers
- Periodicals
- Published transcripts
- Other materials.

There are also details of any research services offered. While not all local authorities have provided detailed information on their family history material via Familia, around 85% of them have. Figure 9-7 shows part of the entry for Bath Central Library, with details of its directory and electoral register holdings.

6. Directories

6(a) County and Regional Directories

Somerset, 1805 to 1969/70 (incomplete), some on microfiche
Gloucester, 1822 to 1969/70 (incomplete), some on microfiche
Wiltshire, 1805 to 1969/70 (incomplete), some on microfiche

6(b) City and Town Directories

Bath: 1783 to 1973/4: Post Office directory, 1858 to 1940: Kelly's directory, 1929 to 1973/4 (incomplete)
Bristol: Morris directory, 1872: Wright's, 1912; 1915 to 1917: Kelly's, 1923 to 1973: Town and Country, 1935/6 to 1969/70

6(c) Telephone Directories

7. Electoral registers and polls books

7(a) Electoral Registers

Register of electors, Bath, 1908 to 1915; 1918 to 1939
Civilian residence electors list, 1945
Bath register of electors, 1948 to 1954; 1956 to date
Bathavon, 1960 to 1989; 1991/2 to 1995/6
Bath & North East Somerset, 1996/7-

7(b) Poll Books

Bath: 1832; 1835; 1837; 1840; 1841; 1847; 1851; 1851/2; 1855; 1857; 1859; 1868

Figure 9-7 Part of the Familia page for Bath & North East Somerset

▌UNIVERSITY LIBRARIES

While university libraries are not of major importance for genealogical research, all have special collections which may include personal papers of notable individuals. They are also likely to have collections of local material which, while probably not of use in constructing a pedigree, may be of interest to the family historian looking for local topographical and historical information.

There is no single central index to university library holdings but COPAC is a major consortium of 24 university libraries, including three of the four copyright libraries (Cambridge University Library, the Bodleian in Oxford, and Trinity College, Dublin), as well as the British Library, and the National Libraries of Scotland and Wales (see p. 122). The COPAC website at <www.copac.ac.uk> provides access to a consolidated catalogue for all member institutions.

All university libraries are included on the ARCHON site at <www.archon.nationalarchives.gov.uk/archon/>, which provides contact details and has catalogue entries for archival material (i.e. not books or periodicals) relating to individuals, families and organizations. The Archives Hub at <www.archiveshub.ac.uk> is a site which offers descriptions of archival collections in around 100 academic libraries.

Bear in mind that university libraries are not open to the general public and that you will normally need to make a written application in advance in order to have access, particularly in the case of manuscript material.

FAMILY HISTORY CENTRES

The LDS Church's Family History Centres (FHCs) are valuable not just because they hold copies of the IGI on CD-ROM, microfiche copies of the GRO indexes, and other materials, but because any UK genealogical material which has been microfilmed by the Church can be ordered for viewing in an FHC, and this includes many parish registers.

Contact details for FHCs are available at the FamilySearch site at <www.familysearch.org> – clicking on the 'Library' tab (at the top of most main screens) and then selecting 'Family History Centers' will lead to a search page. Genuki provides a quick way to get listings from this search facility: the page at <www.genuki.org.uk/big/LDS/> has links which will search automatically for all FHCs in England, Scotland, Ireland and Wales on the FamilySearch site. The site of the LDS Church in the UK at <www. lds.org.uk> has a database of FHCs, reached by following the 'Chapel Location' link in the menu, which will give the FHCs in a particular city or region, or search for those nearest to a particular postcode.

The key to exploiting this immense wealth of material is the Family History Library (FHL) catalogue, which can be consulted online at the FamilySearch site. The search page at <www.familysearch.org/Eng/Library/ FHLC/frameset_fhlc.asp> offers searches by place, surname, or, for published works, author. If you search by place, you will get a list of the various types of records available for it. Figure 9-8 shows the initial results of a place search for Lenham in Kent, while Figure 9-9 shows the expanded entry for Church Records, with descriptions of the various items available.

Place Details	FAMILY HISTORY LIBRARY CATALOG	THE CHURCH OF JESUS CHRIST OF LATTER-DAY SAINTS

View Related Places

Place:	England, Kent, Lenham
Topics:	England, Kent, Lenham - Census England, Kent, Lenham - Church records England, Kent, Lenham - Church records - Indexes England, Kent, Lenham - Land and property England, Kent, Lenham - Manors England, Kent, Lenham - Manors - Court records England, Kent, Lenham - Occupations England, Kent, Lenham - Poorhouses, poor law, etc. England, Kent, Lenham - Taxation

Figure 9-8 Search results for Lenham, Kent in the FHL catalogue

Topic Details	FAMILY HISTORY LIBRARY CATALOG	THE CHURCH OF JESUS CHRIST OF LATTER-DAY SAINTS
Topic:	England, Kent, Lenham - Church records	
Titles:	Archdeacon's transcripts, 1564-1813; Bishop's transcripts, 1611-1905 Church of England. Parish Church of Lenham (Kent)	
	Births and baptisms, 1779-1837 Independent Church (Lenham)	
	Bishop's transcripts, 1874-1908 Church of England. Chapelry of Charing Heath (Kent)	
	Churchwarden accounts and vestry minutes, 1681-1918 Church of England. Parish Church of Lenham (Kent)	
	Parish register extracts, 1559-1905 Church of England. Parish Church of Lenham (Kent)	
	Record of members, 1849-1860 Church of Jesus Christ of Latter-day Saints. Lenham Hill Branch (Kent)	
	Record of members, ca. 1795-1877 Church of Jesus Christ of Latter-day Saints. Bromley Branch (Kent)	

Figure 9-9 Search results for Lenham, Kent in the FHL catalogue – Church records

Title Details	FAMILY HISTORY LIBRARY CATALOG	THE CHURCH OF JESUS CHRIST OF LATTER-DAY SAINTS
		View Film Notes
Title:	Archdeacon's transcripts, 1564-1813; Bishop's transcripts, 1611-1905	
Authors:	Church of England. Parish Church of Lenham (Kent) (Main Author)	
Notes:	Microreproduction of original records housed at the Canterbury Cathedral Archives, Canterbury, Kent.	
	Some early pages damaged	
	The church was named for St. Mary.	
	Canterbury Cathedral Archives no.: DCa/BT/112; DCb/BT1/141; DCb/BT2/174	
Subjects:	England, Kent, Lenham - Church records	
Format:	Manuscript (On Film)	
Language:	English	
Publication:	Salt Lake City : Filmed by the Genealogical Society of Utah, 1991-1992	
Physical:	on 4 microfilm reels ; 35 mm.	

Figure 9-10 FHL catalogue search – Title Details

In order to find the microfilm reference for one of the entries, you need to click on it to bring up the 'Title Details' screen (Figure 9-10). This tells you the repository where the material is held (or was at the time of filming), together with the repository's reference for the material. This means you could even use the FHL catalogue as a partial catalogue to county record offices.

Film Notes	FAMILY HISTORY LIBRARY CATALOG	THE CHURCH OF JESUS CHRIST OF LATTER-DAY SAINTS

View Title Details

Title:	Archdeacon's transcripts, 1564-1813; Bishop's transcripts, 1611-1905
Authors:	Church of England. Parish Church of Lenham (Kent) (Main Author)

Note	Location Film
Archdeacon's transcripts: Baptisms, marriages and burials 1564-1813 (missing: 1565/6, 1570/1, 1573/4, 1578/9, 1594/5, 1629/30, 1633/4, 1640/1-1660/1, 1664/5, 1665/6, 1670/1, 1774/5, 1775/6)	FHL BRITISH Film 1751918 Item 3
Bishop's transcripts: Baptisms, marriages and burials 1611-1813 (missing: 1613/4, 1621/2, 1627/8, 1631/2, 1640/1, 1642/3-1662/3, 1716/7, 1795/6)	FHL BRITISH Film 1736839 Item 3
Bishop's transcripts contd.: Baptisms,marriages and burials 1813-1824	FHL BRITISH Film 1786623 Item 6
Bishop's transcripts contd.: Baptisms and burials 1824-1873, 1876-1882, 1897-1898, 1904-1905 Marriages 1824-1837	FHL BRITISH Film 1786624 Item 1

Numbers 1-4 of 4 film notes

Figure 9-11 FHL catalogue – Film Notes

Finally, clicking on the 'View Film Notes' button at the top left brings up detailed information on the microfilms relating to this item (Figure 9-11) with an exact description of what is on each film, together with the film reference which you can now use to order the film at an FHC.

THE SOCIETY OF GENEALOGISTS

The Society of Genealogists is home to the premier genealogical library in the country. Its library catalogue has been converted to an OPAC system with the aid of a Heritage Lottery Fund grant and has recently been made available online at <**www.sog.org.uk/sogcat/**>.

There are two types of search: the default browse search takes you to the first item in the catalogue which matches your search criteria, or the "Power Search" allows you to select items based on up to three fields. The online catalogue is still quite new and a number of features, such as the ability to save searches, had not yet been implemented at the time of writing.

In order to use the Library, you need to be a member of the Society or pay a search fee, see <**www.sog.org.uk/visit.html**>. But even if you are not in a position to use the library itself, the comprehensive nature of the Society's collections makes the catalogue a valuable guide to which parish registers, for example, have been transcribed, or what has been published on a particular surname.

If you are not already familiar with the Library and its catalogue, it will be worth looking at the tutorial, particularly if you want to search for place names or surnames.

The site also has extensive information about the library at <**www. sog.org.uk/library/**> which includes the quarterly lists of library accessions printed in the *Genealogists' Magazine* at <**www.sog.org.uk/library/ accessions.html**>.

BEYOND THE BRITISH ISLES

If you need to consult archives outside the UK and Ireland the best general starting points will be the pages for individual countries on Cyndi's List – each of these has a section headed 'Libraries, Archives & Museums'. This will have links to not only the national archives, but also major provincial archives. Of course, if the country is not English-speaking you may not be able to make full use of the site, but you will often find at least some basic information in English and an email address for enquiries.

The UNESCO Archives Portal, which has the unwieldy URL <**portal. unesco.org/ci/en/ev.php-URL_ID=5761&URL_DO=DO_TOPIC&URL_ SECTION=201.html**>, provides links to national and other archives around the world.

The Family History Centres have microfilmed records from many countries, and searching on a country in the Family History Library Catalog will list the various types of record and what has been filmed (see p. 126).

FUTURE DEVELOPMENTS

The Archives Portal on the National Archives site at <**www.portal. nationalarchives.gov.uk/portal/**> has a database of current archival projects, searchable by name, region or keyword. Many of these projects are not of direct relevance to genealogists, but selecting the keywords 'Family History' or 'Genealogy' will bring up a list of those that are.

In 2004, the Museums, Libraries and Archives Council published a report titled *A Digital Future for Archives*, which envisages the internet as an essential component in the future of archives and repositories. A summary and the full report are available in PDF format at <**www. mla.gov.uk/action/archives/atf.asp**>. (One interesting aspect of the report is the visitor numbers cited for some of the major archive-related websites.) The report's primary recommendation is the creation of 'a digital Gateway to UK Archives that will give everyone the opportunity to participate in the archival heritage'. How and when this will be achieved remains to be seen, but while it may be a very long time before all genealogical records are online, it looks as if there will be within the foreseeable future a comprehensive network of catalogues and finding aids for archives and the repositories that hold them.

CHAPTER 10

SURNAME INTERESTS AND PEDIGREES

The resources discussed in Chapters 4–8 contain direct transcriptions of, or indexes to, primary genealogical sources. But alongside these are 'compiled' sources, the material put together by individual genealogists. Many people are now putting their pedigrees on the internet on a personal website – Chapter 17 explains how to do this yourself, and Chapter 16 looks at how to locate such material. But there are a number of sites to which people can submit details of the surnames they are interested in, or even entire pedigrees, so that others can contact them. Sites devoted to surname origins and distribution are discussed in Chapter 13.

SURNAME INTERESTS

One of the best ways to make progress with your family tree is to make contact with others who are interested in the same surnames. In some cases you will end up encountering cousins who may have considerable material relating to a branch of your family, but at the very least it is useful to discover what resources others have looked at. If you find someone who is doing a one-name study, they may even have extracts from primary sources which they might be prepared to share with you.

Before the advent of the internet, making such contacts was quite difficult. It involved checking a range of published and unpublished sources, looking through the surname interests in family history magazines, and consulting all the volumes of directories such as the annual *Genealogical Research Directory*. You will still need to do all this, of course, not least because quite a few genealogists are still not online and this is the only way to find out about *their* researches. The SoG's leaflet 'Has it been done before?' at <www.sog.org.uk/leaflets/done.html> provides a comprehensive overview of the various offline resources to check. But the internet now offers a much easier way both of locating and inviting such contacts.

COUNTY SURNAME LISTS

If you have already made some progress with your family history and have got back far enough to know where your ancestors were living 100 or so years before your birth, then you should check the relevant county surname list – a directory of genealogical research interests for a particular county.

Surname lists do not provide genealogical information as such: they are just registers of interests, like a printed research directory, and give for each surname the email address of the researcher who submitted it, and usually a date range for the period of interest (see Figure 10-1). Some lists also have links to the websites of submitters.

There is at least one surname list for almost every county in the UK and Ireland, and Genuki keeps a central list of these at <**www.genuki.org. uk/indexes/SurnamesLists.html**>. Many counties are included in Graham Jaunay's national Online Names Directories for England, Wales, Ireland and Scotland at <**www.list.jaunay.com**>, which are run in connection with Genuki. These cover around 70% of the British Isles – all Welsh counties, most Scottish and Irish counties, and half the English counties. Within each national directory, you can search on an individual county or do a general search. Figure 10-1 shows the results of a search for any name in Huntingdonshire in the Online English Names Directory. Clicking on the name in the 'Subscriber' column will bring up a mail window in your

Online English Names Directory

Search in the County of '**HUN**' for the keyword ''.

Names 1-102 of 102

County	Family name	Place	Date range	Subscriber	Submitted
HUN	**ABBESS**	Fenstanton	1700-1900	Heather Thomas	12 Jun 2004
HUN	**ABBOTT**	Ramsey	1775-1850	Ray Lines	5 Sep 2004
HUN	**ALLIN**	All County	1750-now	Sophia Antoniazzi	23 Apr 2005
HUN	**ARCHER**	Leighton Bromswold	1775-1825	B Horne	26 Feb 2005
HUN	**BACON**	Location: ?	1825-1850	Maureen Thomas	19 Mar 2005
HUN	**BANNISTER**	Sawtry	1875-onwards	Kym Bannister	30 Oct 2004
HUN	**BARKER**	St Neots	1800-1925	Ian Barker	9 Apr 2005
HUN	**BASS**	All County	1800- 1900	Suzie Switzer	9 Oct 2004
HUN	**BEETHAM**	Hartford	1900-1925	Diana Sweeney	12 Mar 2005
HUN	**BELLAMY**	Sawtry	1775-1975	M.mclaughlin	4 Sep 2004
HUN	**BERRIDGE**	Great Catworth; Little Catworth	1800-onwards	Peter Sharp	4 Dec 2004

Figure 10-1 Huntingdonshire entries from the Online English Names Directory

browser with the email address of the person to contact, or you can read the email address from the status bar at the bottom of the browser when you move your mouse over the link. Surname lists for Australia and New Zealand are also available on this site.

Alongside Graham Jaunay's lists, there are around 40 other county-based surname lists, with a few for smaller areas. Although these lists are not formally connected with Genuki, many of them have long-standing links with the relevant Genuki county page. Links to any lists relevant to a county will be found on the Genuki county page as well as on the central surname list page.

For other countries, Cyndi's List has links to further surname lists at <www.cyndislist.com/database.htm#Locality>, but do not expect to find the same level of coverage as there is for the UK.

In addition to the county surname lists, there are a number of surname lists relevant to UK emigration and immigration. These are discussed in Chapter 11 (see p. 166 ff).

You should consider submitting your surname interests to the relevant national or county lists so that other people can contact you. The exact method of doing this varies from list to list: on some there is a web page with a submission form; on others you will need to email the list maintainer. Be sure to follow the instructions, as many list maintainers expect you to submit your interests in a particular format (to make processing of submissions easier to automate) and may ignore something sent in the wrong format.

One problem with surname lists is that someone who has made a submission may forget to update their entries if they subsequently change their email address, so you will occasionally find contact details that are no longer valid. Unfortunately there is nothing you can do about this – it is a fact of life on the internet – and there is no point in asking the surname list manager where a particular submitter can be contacted if their stated email address is no longer valid. Obviously if you change your own email address, you'll need to contact the owner of any surname list you have submitted to. For Graham Jaunay's lists, there are online forms for changing an email address, and you will need to 'refresh' your entries annually to keep them listed.

THE GUILD OF ONE-NAME STUDIES

The Guild of One-Name Studies at <www.one-name.org> is an organization for those who are researching all people with a particular surname, rather than just their own personal pedigree. It has a searchable Register of One-Name Studies online at <www.one-name.org/register.shtml>, which gives a contact address (not necessarily electronic) for each of the 7,000 or so surnames registered with the Guild.

Unlike the county lists, the surname interests registered with the Guild cover the whole world – this is, in fact, a requirement for membership. So, even though the person who has registered a particular one-name interest may not have ancestors in common with you, there is still a good chance that they have collected material of interest relating to your surname. In particular, a Guild member is likely to have a good overview of the variants of their registered surname. This makes the Guild's list of surnames worth checking even, or especially, if you are only just starting your researches, whereas the county surname lists are probably not very useful until you have got back at least three generations.

ROOTSWEB

One of the most useful sites for surname interests is RootsWeb at <**www.rootsweb.com**> which has a wide range of surname-related resources, all linked from <**resources.rootsweb.com/~clusters/surnames/**>. There is a separate page for each listed surname with:

- Links to personal websites at RootsWeb which include the name
- Search forms for a number of databases hosted by RootsWeb
- Links to any mailing lists for the surname (see below).

The most general surname resource at RootsWeb is the Roots Surname List (RSL) at <**rsl.rootsweb.com**>. This is a surname list attached to the ROOTS-L mailing list, the oldest genealogy mailing list on the internet, and contains over a million entries submitted by around 200,000 individual genealogists. You can enter a geographical location to narrow your

Surname	From	To	Migration	Submitter	Comment
Jeffery	1600	1650	Southease,SSX,ENG	hstvns	
Jeffery	1600	now	Hartland>Northam>DEV,ENG	ldeleuw	
Jeffery	1650	1750	Frant,SSX>Goudhurst,KEN,ENG	bjashton	Robert 1664-1715
Jeffery	1650	1860	"Medstead,HAM,ENG"	Mswitzer	
Jeffery	1680	1796	CAM,ENG	ruddles1	
Jeffery	1682	1820	Folkestone,KEN,ENG	alkira	
Jeffery	1700	1850	SSX,ENG	mavlodge	
JEFFERY	1710		Camborne, Cornwall, ENG	brendan1	
Jeffery	1724	1816	Kenwyn/Wendron,CON,ENG	lsaleeba	
Jeffery	1745	now	ENG	deannz	Anne JEFFERY m. Thomas RICHARDS
Jeffery	1750	1790	StBotolph,Aldgate,LND,ENG	rijames	
Jeffery	1750	1900	OXF, ENG	rhoare	Oxford city, and Cowley.
Jeffery	1770	1800	Coaton,NTH,ENG	digbyw	
Jeffery	1780	1840	CON,ENG	awegner	
Jeffery	1791	1805	CON,ENG	dralphne	John m.Sarah

Figure 10-2 Search results in the Roots Surname List

search, using Chapman county codes and/or three-letter country codes – there is a list of standard codes at <helpdesk.rootsweb.com/codes/>. However, you may need to do a couple of searches to make sure you find all relevant entries as some people spell out English counties in full or use the two-letter country code UK instead of ENG. If you check the list regularly, a useful feature is that you can restrict your results to those added or updated recently. Submitter details are not given on the search results page, but there is a link to them from the user ID of the submitter.

DISCUSSION FORUMS

Mailing lists, newsgroups and other types of discussion forum are described in detail in Chapter 15, but it is worth noting here that there are many groups devoted to individual surnames. Even if you do not participate in any of them, it will still be well worth your while to look through the archives of past messages to see if anyone else is working on the same family or on the same geographical area.

John Fuller's list of mailing lists has information on those dedicated to individual surnames at <www.rootsweb.com/~jfuller/gen_mail. html#SURNAMES>. Many of these surname lists are hosted by RootsWeb and can also be found from the general list of mailing lists at <lists. rootsweb.com> or via the individual surname pages at <resources. rootsweb.com/~clusters/surnames/>.

Alongside the surname mailing lists, there are web-based message boards or discussion forums for individual surnames. One of the largest sites hosting such discussion lists is GenForum at <genforum.genealogy.com>, which must have message boards for at least 10,000 surnames. Ancestry. com and RootsWeb also have a common set of surname message boards at <boards.ancestry.com> or <boards.rootsweb.com> – follow the link to 'United Kingdom and Ireland', and then the link to the relevant part of the UK.

In many cases, these boards relate to a surname mailing list hosted by RootsWeb. This means that you can contribute your own query, via the web, without having to subscribe to a mailing list. A particularly useful feature is that the individual boards can be searched, which makes it possible to find messages relating to particular places, something which is essential for common and widespread surnames.

On the other hand, newsgroups, discussed in Chapter 15, are of little use for finding surname interests. Although there are newsgroups devoted specifically to the posting of surname interests – the group for British surnames is soc.genealogy.surnames.britain – these have been defunct since June 2000. There are nearly 150 groups in the hierarchy alt.family-names (e.g. alt.family-names.johnson), but these have few messages in them, most of which are spam in any case, so they are very unlikely to be useful to you.

FAMILY HISTORY SOCIETIES

Every family history society has a register of members' interests, and it will be worthwhile checking the societies which cover the areas where your ancestors lived. If you're lucky, the list will be available online. For example, the Shropshire FHS offers a database of 20,000 members' interests at <www.sfhs.org.uk/memberinterests.asp>, which can be browsed, or searched for a specific surname. The Sussex Family History Group at <www.sfhg.org.uk> has both a public members' interests area and a more extensive one for members only. Bear in mind that not all these members will be contactable by email and societies generally do not publish members' postal addresses online, so you may need to consult the society's journal for contact details. For a list of FHS websites consult the 'Family History and Genealogy Societies' page on Genuki at <www.genuki.org.uk/Societies/>.

PERSONAL WEBSITES

Many genealogists have a personal website (see Chapter 17), and locating such sites can be a useful step in making contact with someone who shares your genealogical interests or even some of your ancestors. Cyndi's List has pages listing sites for Surnames, Family Associations and Family Newsletters, all linked from <www.cyndislist.com/surnames.htm>. The Online Genealogical Database Index at <www.gentree.com/gentree.html> specifically links to personal sites with databases.

Both of these sites link to only a fraction of the personal genealogical websites, and really you need to use a search engine to get more inclusive coverage. Unfortunately just typing a surname in a search engine will not be very helpful. You need to search for a surname and the word genealogy and/or the phrase 'surname list' (see Chapter 16).

PEDIGREE DATABASES

The surname interest resources do not provide genealogical information, they simply offer contact details for other genealogists who may share your interests. But there are several sites which allow genealogists to make their pedigrees available on the web. You can, of course, do this by creating your own website, as discussed in Chapter 17, particularly if you want to publish more comprehensive information. But if you just want to make your pedigree available online, these sites provide an easy way to do it. Even if you do not make your own pedigree available, many others have, and it is worth checking these sites for overlap with your own family tree.

There are two ways of getting your own pedigree into one of these databases. Some of them have facilities for you to create your pedigree entirely online, while the commoner method is to upload a GEDCOM file containing your pedigree. Information about GEDCOM files and how to create them will be found on p. 279, Chapter 17.

There is not space here to give more than a brief account of some of the most important sites, but for a comprehensive list of pedigree databases consult the 'Databases – Lineage-Linked' page on Cyndi's List at <**www.cyndislist.com/lin-linked.htm**>.

FREE DATABASES

FamilySearch at <**www.familysearch.org**> has been discussed as a source of record transcriptions in Chapter 7 (p. 89), but the site also includes two data collections with user-submitted information. Ancestral File goes back to 1978, starting life as a CD-ROM collection, initially as a way for members of the LDS Church to deposit the fruits of their researches but in fact open to submission from anyone with genealogical information. The Pedigree Resource File is a more recent database compiled from submissions to the FamilySearch website and also published on CD-ROM.

In Ancestral File a successful search on an individual name brings up an individual record with links, on the left, to a full pedigree, a family group record and submitter details (see Figure 10-3). Unfortunately, there is only a postal address for the submitter, no email address, and it may well be out of date, considering the age of some of the data.

In the Pedigree Resource File a search produces a similar individual record with details of the submitter, but no link to a pedigree. A useful feature is that it gives you the submission number – clicking on this will

Figure 10-3 An individual record in Ancestral File

do a search for all individuals in the same submission. The submitter details will include a postal address, and may also have a link to the submitter's website. As discussed in Chapter 7, you can search all four FamilySearch databases at once by selecting All Resources from any of the search pages (see Figure 7-1), and the results are then listed separately for each database.

Probably the largest collection of pedigrees is on RootsWeb, whose WorldConnect data has a home page at <worldconnect.genealogy.rootsweb. com>. It currently contains over 360 million names, submitted by about a quarter of a million users. Ancestry's World Tree provides access to the same database at <www.ancestry.myfamily.com/trees/awt/> (this is freely accessible and does not require a subscription to Ancestry).

The initial search page form provided on RootsWeb allows you to search on surname and given name, and the search results pages then list each matching entry with further details and offer a link to the home page for the database in which the entry is found or to the specific person. If you get too many results to cope with, a more detailed search form provides options to narrow down your search with dates, places, names of parents, etc.

Figure 10-4 shows a page of search results on WorldConnect. Clicking on the name of the individual takes you to their data, while the link on the right takes you to details of the submitted database in which this individual is found, including the email address of the submitter. On the Ancestry site you need to register with your name and email address, free

Results 1-20 of 50

Name	Birth/Christening Date	Place	Death/Burial Date	Place	Database
Ede, Amy	1886	Bognor, Sussex, England			3065435
🔍 🖼	Father: Charles Ede Mother: Sarah Ide				
Ede, Ann	29 Jun 1791	Horsham, Sussex Co., England	Bef. 1822		1794533
🔍 📖 👤	Spouse: Henry Constable				
Ede, Ann	29 JUN 1791	Horsham, Sussex Co., England	BEF. 1822		steele_blue1947
🔍 🖼 📖 👤	Father: ? Ede Mother: Sarah ? Spouse: Henry Constable				
EDE, Ann	ABT 1676	<Cuckfield, Sussex, England>			bevangenealogy25
🔍 👤	Spouse: James SAYERS				
Ede, Caroline Eliza	13 APR 1878	Hyde St., Southsea, Sussex, England	12 MAR 1958	White Rock, Hastings, Sussex, England	raviac
🔍 🖼 📖 👤	Father: Edward Ede Mother: Caroline Raven Spouse: Willie Herbert Raven				
Ede, Catherine	1876	Cuckfield, Sussex			dawnscotting
🔍 🖼	Father: Thomas Ede Mother: Mary Ann Unknown				
Ede, Catherine	1876	Cuckfield, Sussex, England			parks
🔍 🖼	Father: Thomas Ede Mother: Mary Ann Unknown				
Ede, Catherine	25 Feb 1810	Cuckfield, Sussex, England			jesm87
🔍 🖼	Father: John Ede Mother: Mary Harvey Spouse: William Parsons				

Figure 10-4 Search results on WorldConnect

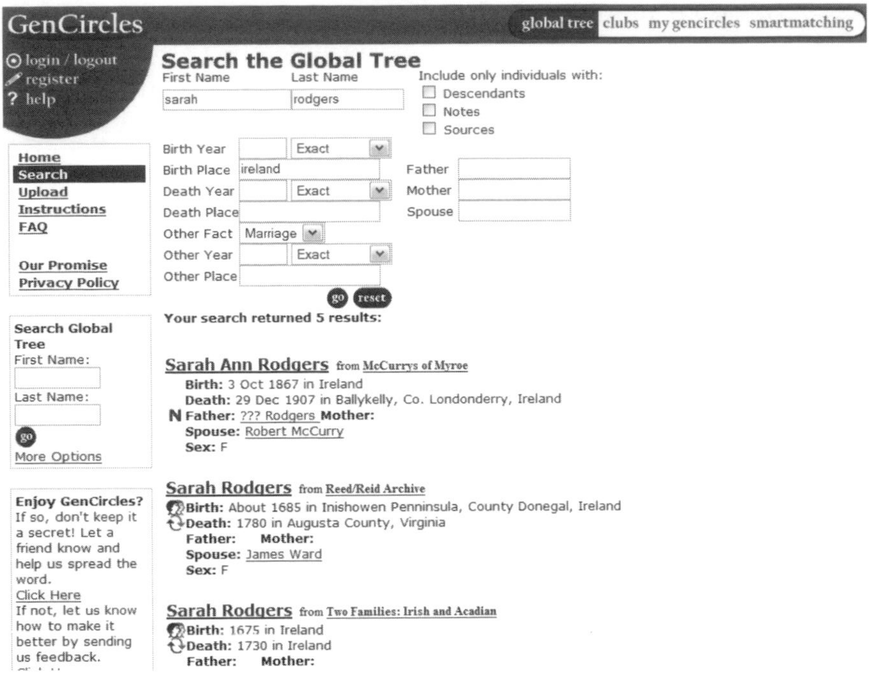

Figure 10-5 Search results in GenCircles

of charge, before you can search. However, the initial search form is more comprehensive. Data from World Tree are also included in general searches carried out on the Ancestry site at **<www.ancestry.myfamily.com/search/main.htm>**.

GenCircles at **<www.gencircles.com>**, started by Cliff Shaw in 2001, is a free service that currently has over 90 million individuals (see Figure 10-5). You need to register before using, but there's no subscription. GenCircles offers a facility called SmartMatching, which compares the individuals in your file against all other individuals submitted to detect any matches.

Another free service is GeneaNet, a French-run site at **<www.geneanet.org>** which started in 1996. This allows you to upload a GEDCOM file, but it also has its own free software, GeneWeb, which you can either use on the site or download. It has entries for more than 350 million individuals. Additional facilities are available as part of 'privileged membership' for €40 per year.

A potentially interesting development is WikiTree at **<wikitree.org>**, a collaborative project launched in April 2005 to develop an online pedigree database.

SUBSCRIPTION DATABASES

Alongside the free pedigree databases, there are a number of commercial services, all of which require a subscription. I should perhaps point out that I have not subscribed to any of these services and the material in this section is based on the publicly available information the sites provide.

GenServ at <www.genserv.com>, started by Cliff Manis in 1991 as an email only service – this was before the invention of the web – is among the oldest pedigree databases on the internet, with over 25 million individuals in around 17,000 GEDCOM files. It is a slightly unusual service in that you *must* submit some of your own material in order to subscribe. Once you have done this you can have a free 60-day trial subscription, while a regular subscription is $12/£8 per year, which allows you to do unlimited searches (though only so many per day). Details of how to subscribe are given at <www.genserv.com/gs/gsh2sub.htm>. A more limited trial (one surname search for any one email address) is available under the 'Sample Search' option at <www.genserv.com/gs3/samplesearch.html>.

World Family Tree is a subscription database (also available on CD-ROM) at <familytreemaker.genealogy.com/wfttop.html> with about 180 million individuals in around 270,000 pedigrees. There is a free search facility (which requires registration, but not subscription), but in order to view any matching pedigrees found by your search you will need to sign up. The site has been criticized for charging for access to freely submitted pedigrees, and the charges ($9.99 per month, $49.99 per year) are quite high if you are only going to use the site occasionally, though they have been reduced since the last edition of this book. However, the free search can also be treated as an index to the CD-ROMs – you can buy, or look for in a library, any which hold material of interest to you.

OneGreatFamily at <www.onegreatfamily.com> was launched in the summer of 2000 and now claims over 150,000 users sharing over 42 million ancestors. It represents a more sophisticated approach to online pedigrees. Rather than just seeing itself as a repository for a copy of your data, it acts as a substitute for a traditional genealogy program. Like GenCircles, it has facilities for matching your own data with other trees on the site. Subscriptions are $14.95, $29.95 and $74.95 for one, three and twelve months respectively. There is also a seven-day free trial, though you have to give credit card information in order to sign up for this, and it automatically turns into a subscription if you do not cancel. To view pedigrees on the site you need to download the Genealogy Browser, which is a plug-in for your web browser. To find out more, it is worth reading Dick Eastman's very positive account of using the site at <**www.onegreatfamily. com/static-tpls/pr-eastman06-21-00.htm**>.

GENESREUNITED

Halfway between the free and the subscription services is GenesReunited at <**www.genesreunited.co.uk**>. The site, launched in November 2002, is an offshoot from the very successful FriendsReunited. (In fact it was launched as GenesConnected but the name was changed in 2004 to make the link more obvious.) I have termed it 'semi-free' because it is a mix of a free and a subscription service. You do not have to subscribe in order to enter or upload your pedigree, nor to carry out searches on the database. But you need to be a subscriber in order to make contact with the person who submitted an individual you find a possible match with. GenesReunited does not give you the email address of a submitter; instead you type in a message on the site and GenesReunited actually sends it. This offers some measure of privacy protection, since subscriber email addresses are not visible on the site and are never given out. The subscription is £10 per year.

The site provides several message boards and there are brief articles for the novice genealogist. It *appears* to offer census and civil registration records but all that happens is that you are taken to the site of Ancestry at <**www.ancestry.co.uk**> (see p. 43).

One irritating problem is that individuals are listed only with a birth year. Christening dates are not used, even in the absence of a birth date, so there will be no date given for that individual if there is only a christening date in the GEDCOM file.[8]

Currently GenesReunited claims to have over 30 million names. Although this is a smaller figure than World Family Tree or OneGreat Family, the UK focus of GenesReunited means you are much more likely to find matches with your own British or Irish ancestors here.[9] Another consideration is the connection with FriendsReunited (with around 11 million registrations). This suggests GenesReunited probably contains many submissions from people who do not regard themselves as serious family historians and who are unlikely to use any of the other resources discussed in this chapter. It may, therefore, be better for contacting reasonably close cousins, particularly if there are recent branches of your family you have lost touch with, than for finding people who have a shared ancestor 300 years ago. On the other hand, there may also be entries from people who will not bother to respond to a contact.

---

8 A fudge to get round this, more or less, is to do a search and replace in your GEDCOM file before uploading it, substituting 1 BIRT for every occurrence of 1 CHR. This is preferable to entering a guessed at birth year for everyone in your database, which is both bad practice *and* hard work.

9 A survey in April 2005 found that GenesReunited was visited by 60% of those in the UK using the web for genealogy – see <**www.netratings.com/pr/pr_050524_uk.pdf**>.

Figure 10-6 Search results in GenesReunited.

RECORD MATCHING

A new approach to matching individuals is taken by LostCousins at <www.lostcousins.com> launched in September 2004. In this service, you don't submit general details of ancestors for matching, but the full reference to the record of an ancestor in the 1881 census index (see p. 85). This means that matching will be very accurate and unambiguous. In the future, the scope will be expanded to include other censuses. Unfortunately, the site gives no indication of how many individuals have been submitted, so it's not possible to assess the likelihood of a match – a May 2005 press release suggests 1 in 10 new submitters find an immediate match. Since matches can only be made on ancestors alive in 1881, you will not get any contacts with anyone more remotely related to you than about fourth cousins.

To use the site requires registration and login. Once you have entered details of an ancestor you will automatically receive an email when a match is found. Registration is free, though it seems there are plans to introduce a small annual subscription. This, however, will not relate to registration and submission of ancestors, both of which will remain free.

LIMITATIONS

One point to bear in mind is that the majority of the individuals in these databases were born in the US, so in spite of the amount of material you should not be surprised if you do not find matches for your UK ancestors in them. However, as many American pedigrees have some roots in the British Isles, it is still well worth checking them. Also, as more British genealogists submit their family trees to such sites, they become more useful for British genealogy.

The material on these sites consists entirely of submissions from individual genealogists. The completeness and accuracy of information is therefore highly variable, though some sites do basic checks in order to detect obvious errors, such as a death date earlier than a birth date. It is therefore best to regard these databases as a way of contacting people with similar interests, rather than as direct resources of data (which is in fact how GenesReunited presents itself). It would be very unwise to incorporate such material directly into your own genealogy database without thorough checking. The obvious exception here is LostCousins, where matching is tied to a specific index of a particular census record, and you in fact don't have access to a pedigree as such.

In some cases checking will be simple – the example in Figure 10-3 gives a christening date and parish, which should be easy to check; in others the information may be of little value, perhaps just a year and a country. There is no way to tell for certain in any of these databases what sources the submitter has drawn their information from. But that does not lessen the advantage of these databases over the surname resources discussed earlier in this chapter, namely that they provide information about individuals and families, not just about surnames. This should make it fairly easy to establish whether the submitter is interested in the same family as you, something that may be particularly important for a common surname.

The problem with all compiled sources is that there is no guarantee of reliability, and indications of the original source for an event may be missing or simply wrong. The errors in indexes to primary sources will normally be restricted to misreadings of original documents or mistyping of the entries, but in the individual submissions information is often fragmentary – years rather than full dates, for example – and errors can be more serious. Some of the submissions are obviously nothing more than guesswork.

To get an idea of how badly wrong some of the information is, it is instructive to look for someone whose details are well known. Charles Darwin was born near Shrewsbury on 12 February 1809 and baptized at St Chad's, Shrewsbury. He married Emma Wedgwood on 29 January 1839, and died at Downe, Kent on 16 April 1882. A search for Charles Darwin in the IGI produces a whole host of results. Among them is the baptism entry from the registers of St Chad's, but the remainder are all from individual submissions, and some are bizarre indeed. One is for a 'Carlos Roberto Darwin', with the correct birth and death years, but the place given simply as England; another has him born in 'Shrewsbury, Northampton, England'; and one has Charles Darwin, born 1809, Downe, Kent, died 16 April 1682, and married to Julia Wedgwood.

Within limits, even inaccurate data can be useful if it's backed up by an accurate source citation – at least you get a pointer to a document that might be worth consulting. But in most cases the only source information in these collections is the name and address of the submitter. If you're lucky, you may also get a current email address, or even a link to a personal genealogy website (particularly with the Pedigree Resources File, which has the most recent submissions). But often the contact details are merely postal addresses which, if they come from the IGI, could be as much as 20 years old. If you're very unlucky, you may even find *no* useful submitter details: some IGI entries simply say something like, 'Record submitted after 1991 by a member of the LDS Church. No additional information is available. Ancestral File may list the same family and the submitter. No source information is available.'

RIGHTS

If you are intending to submit your own pedigree to one of these databases, there is one important issue you need to be aware of. On some sites, when you upload material to a database you grant the site ownership of your pedigree or unlimited rights to use the material as they see fit. This is not necessarily as unreasonable as it might sound. With FamilySearch your data file will be permanently archived in the LDS Church's Granite Mountain Records Vault, ensuring preservation, and it is unrealistic to expect an archive to keep track of the legal ownership of thousands if not millions of files over many decades. Also, FamilySearch makes the data freely accessible online and its CD-ROMs are sold more or less at cost. On the other hand, it is perhaps understandable that some people baulk at allowing the fully commercial exploitation of their data without royalty by some sites, when they are already paying a subscription.

It is therefore important to check the terms and conditions of any pedigree database before you submit your own material. Of the sites mentioned here, RootsWeb, GenCircles, GenesReunited and GenServ make no claim on material submitted, and you retain complete rights over your GEDCOM, including editorial control.

PRIVACY

Another issue in placing your pedigree online is the privacy of living individuals. This is nothing to do with data protection, as is often thought –

much of your information comes from public sources and there can be no legal bar in the UK to publishing it online, or indeed in any other medium, as long as it is accurate. The real issue is that many people can be distressed, understandably, if they find their personal details published online by someone else. Because of this all the online pedigree databases have a policy on publishing information about living individuals. Here are some typical policies:

- RootsWeb has facilities which make it possible for you to remove living people entirely, or clean their entries of specific pieces of information, but it does not check your efforts
- GenesReunited and OneGreatFamily have conditions that you do not include living individuals without their permission, but they do not check or modify the submitted data
- World Family Tree removes all details of living people apart from name, gender and family links
- GenCircles uses a number of techniques for identifying individuals and then ensures that they are not displayed, though the submitter can still see the information.

If you're going to submit to a site that doesn't have its own privacy protection mechanism, you will need to remove living individuals or at least their details. Most genealogy software programs have facilities for doing this: it may be an explicit option in the Export to GEDCOM process, or you may have to select those people who are to be included. If in doubt, excluding everyone born less than 100 years ago is a sensible policy. Figure 10-7 shows how this is done in Personal Ancestral File, using the **Advanced Focus/Filter** option on the **Search** menu.

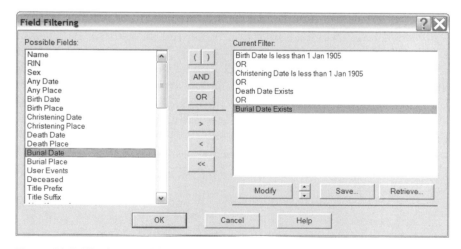

Figure 10-7 Filtering out living persons in Personal Ancestral File

There are a number of standalone tools for purging GEDCOM files of sensitive information – see the 'Software & Computers' page on Cyndi's List at <**www.cyndislist.com/software.htm#Privacy**>. Note that this is something that will also be necessary if you put a pedigree on a personal website (see Chapter 17).

DNA TESTING

The ease and affordability of DNA testing has improved rapidly in recent years, giving rise to all sorts of expectations about what this can do for the genealogist. This is not the place to debate the merits and limitations of DNA testing in validating pedigrees, never mind the technicalities, but it clearly provides a method of confirming or establishing links between individuals.

There is plenty of online information about DNA testing aimed at a genealogical audience. For example:

- Genuki has a concise page on 'DNA testing for Genealogy' at <**www. genuki.org.uk/big/bigmisc/DNA.html**>
- Chris Pomery, author of *DNA and Family History*, has a DNA Portal at <**freepages.genealogy.rootsweb.com/~allpoms/genetics.html**>, which, although not updated for some time, has a lot of useful information
- Historical Genetics at <**www.historicalgenetics.com**>
- The World Families Network has useful FAQs at <**www.worldfamilies. net/faqs.htm**>.

The first three of these provide links to the websites of testing companies.

There are hundreds of DNA testing projects based on individuals with a shared surname, and many have a website and/or mailing list, which should give you the possibility of discussing whether there might be a connection, even if you're not involved in the project.

The majority of these projects concentrate on Y-DNA, so are only relevant to the paternal line and only to male descendants. This does mean, however, that it is closely related to surname inheritance. MtDNA testing, which relates to the maternal line and is applicable to descendants of both sexes, is also available, though of course it cannot relate to a particular surname.

In a search engine, entering the phrase "surname DNA project" along with the surname of interest should be adequate to locate most of these. If you get no initial results, repeat the search but without the quote marks. There is a substantial list of projects at <**worldfamilies.net**>, though all of them seem to be done via a single testing company, so it is not comprehensive. This site also provides free web pages for DNA projects.

If you have had a DNA test carried out, there are also sites where you can post the details of your own genetic markers in the hope of a match, or search for matches from the existing submissions, for example:

- Ybase at <ybase.org>
- Mitosearch at <www.mitosearch.org>.

This means that you do not need to be part of a surname project in order to make use of DNA testing.

There is a general mailing list devoted to this topic, GENEALOGY-DNA, details of which will be found at <lists.rootsweb.com/index/other/DNA/GENEALOGY-DNA.html>. RootsWeb also hosts mailing lists for a number of individual DNA projects, listed at <lists.rootsweb.com/index/other/DNA/>.

LOCATING LIVING PEOPLE

The surname lists and databases already discussed will put you in touch with other genealogists who have made their researches – or at least their research interests – public, but you can also use the internet to locate long-lost relatives or their descendants, or simply people with a particular surname.

PHONE NUMBERS AND ADDRESSES

BT provides an online directory enquiry service at <www2.bt.com/edq_resnamesearch>, and this will give you an address, postcode and phone number. 192.com at <www.192.com> provides more extensive searching, including electoral rolls. This is a commercial service, though the initial free registration allows you to conduct 10 searches per day. A list of UK dialling codes can be found at <www.brainstorm.co.uk/uk_std_code_search.htm>.

The internet is particularly useful for foreign phone numbers, since only a small number of major reference libraries in the UK have a full set of international directories. Infospace has worldwide telephone listings available from <www.infospace.com/home/white-pages/world>. Infobel's 'Telephone Directories' pages at <www.infobel.com/teldir/> has links to Yellow Pages, White Pages, business directories, email addresses and fax listings from 184 countries. International dialling codes are at <kropla.com/dialcode.htm>.

EMAIL ADDRESSES

Finding email addresses is not straightforward. For a start, there is no single authoritative directory of email addresses in the way that the phone book is for phone numbers. There are simply too many email addresses and they are changing all the time. Also, there is no single place to register them. However, there are a number of directories of email addresses on the web.

The Yahoo directory has links to many sites providing general or specific email address searches at <**uk.dir.yahoo.com/Reference/Phone_Numbers_ and_Addresses/Email_Addresses/**>. Cyndi's List has a 'Finding People' page at <**www.cyndislist.com/finding.htm**>.

One point to bear in mind is that it is easy for these databases to add an email address by extracting it from a message sent to a mailing list or newsgroup, or if it is provided on a web page. However, it is quite impossible for a database to know when the address ceases to be valid (perhaps because the person concerned has changed their internet provider), so the databases are full of old, no longer valid email addresses as well as current ones. Except for fairly unusual names, you will find multiple entries, and since email addresses often give no clue to the geographical location of the person it may be hard to identify the one you are looking for. Also, people posting messages to newsgroups often give fake email addresses to prevent spam (i.e. unsolicited bulk mail), though these should be easy to spot if you are familiar with the way email addresses are constructed. All in all, these sites are much less useful than they might seem at first sight.

Another way to find an email address is simply to use a standard search engine to look for the relevant name, but success will depend on the person concerned having a web page and having sent messages to a publicly archived mailing list or newsgroup, or contact details on someone else's, and the search could be time-consuming.

ADOPTION AND CHILD MIGRATION

While the resources discussed so far can be useful for tracing people when you know their names they may be of little use in the case of adoption or child migration, and you may need to go to sites specifically devoted to these issues.

The FamilyRecords portal has brief information on UK adoption records at <**www.familyrecords.gov.uk/topics/adoption.htm**> and more information, including details of the Adoption Contact Register, is available on the GRO site at <**www.gro.gov.uk/gro/content/adoptions/**>. The FFHS has a leaflet 'Tracing The Birth Parents Of Adopted Persons In England And Wales' (relevant to the period since 1927) at <**www.ffhs.org.uk/General/ Help/Adopted.htm**>. GROS has a page on 'Adoption in Scotland' at <**www.gro-scotland.gov.uk/regscot/adoption.html**>.

For Ireland, a National Adoption Contact Preference Register was launched early in 2005 – details at <**www.adoptionboard.ie/preferenceRegister/ index.php**>. Searching in Ireland has a page for Irish-born adoptees at

<www.netreach.net/~steed/search.html>. The newsgroup alt.adoption is for all issues relating to adoption.

The Salvation Army offers a Family Tracing Service. Unfortunately, this is another site with montrous nonsense URLs, so you'll need to go to the home page at <www.salvationarmy.org.uk> and select Family Tracing from the Quick Links. Alternatively, there is a direct link from the website for this book.

The UK Birth Adoption Register at <www.ukbirth-adoptionregister. com> is a site for adoptees and birth parents to register their interest in making contact. A one-off registration fee of £10 is required to place your details in the database. LookUpUK at <www.lookupuk.com> is a general site for tracing missing persons and those separated by adoption, with a number of message boards and other resources. Cyndi's List has a page devoted to Adoption resources at <www.cyndislist.com/adoption.htm>, and John Fuller has an extensive list of mailing lists relating to adoption at <www.rootsweb.com/~jfuller/gen_mail_adoption.html>.

For child migration, the Department of Health's very comprehensive leaflet 'Former British child migrants' at <www.dh.gov.uk/assetRoot/04/ 09/00/30/04090030.pdf> is the essential starting point. This provides information on the various agencies involved in child migration from the UK (and the relevant dates), with contact details and links to websites. Government sites in the receiving countries are also likely to have information relating to local records. For example, the National Archives of Australia has a fact sheet on 'Child migration to Australia' at <www. naa.gov.au/Publications/fact_sheets/FS124.html>. Library and Archives Canada has an online database of Home Children (1869–1930) at <www. collectionscanada.ca/02/020110_e.html>.

Child Migrants at <www.childmigrants.com> provides a history of child migration, a message board, and links to websites of many organizations for former child migrants. BRITISHHOMECHILDREN is a mailing list for 'anyone who has a genealogical interest in the 100,000 British Home Children who were emigrated to Canada by 50 child care organizations 1870–1948' – details at <lists.rootsweb.com/index/intl/can/ BRITISHHOMECHILDREN.html>.

A more general resource which may be of use is Look4them at <www. look4them.org.uk>, an umbrella site run by nine organizations involved with tracing missing people.

CHAPTER 11

SOCIAL GROUPS

Earlier chapters have covered the major sources of primary genealogical data online which, because they are common to all our forebears, are of use to every family historian. However, our ancestors did much more than be born and buried, or be discovered living in a certain place by the census enumerator, and when it comes to questions of occupation, religious persuasion and geographical mobility, there is great variety. The aim of this chapter is to cover some of the more important of these social groupings. Unlike the sites mentioned in the earlier chapters, the material discussed here is mostly general historical information, but there are still a number of sites which include data extracts for particular groups of people. Each of these topics is a large subject in itself, so this chapter can only hint at the range of online resources available.

CHURCHES AND CLERGY

Records relating to parish registers are covered in Chapter 7. However, most of the available material relates to the Anglican Church, though FamilySearch does include some Catholic and nonconformist registers. Beyond the major sources mentioned in Chapter 7 you should not expect to find much parish register material online. Nonetheless, there is some useful information on the web about churches, religious denominations and clergy.

John Fuller has a page for mailing lists relating to individual churches and denominations at <www.rootsweb.com/~jfuller/gen_mail_religions.html>.

ANGLICAN CHURCHES

The official websites for the Anglican churches of the UK are:

- Church of England <www.cofe.anglican.org>
- Church in Wales <www.churchinwales.org.uk>
- Church of Ireland <www.ireland.anglican.org>

- Church of Scotland <www.churchofscotland.org.uk>
- Scottish Episcopal Church <www.scotland.anglican.org>.

You can expect these to provide information about individual parishes, usually organized by diocese or accessible via a search facility such as the CofE's Church-Search site at <www.church-search.com>.

A useful web directory of Christian sites is Praize.com at <www.praize. com>. This offers a directory page for each Christian denomination at <www.praize.com/engine/Denominations/>. Church Net at <www. churchnet.org.uk> offers similar links, just for the UK, though they are mostly to the websites of individual congregations at <www.churchnet. org.uk/cgi-bin/directory.cgi?sectionid=354>.

Many individuals have placed pictures of local churches online, and these are discussed in Chapter 14, 'Photographs', p. 222.

ROMAN CATHOLIC CHURCH

The official websites for the Roman Catholic Church in the British Isles are:

- England and Wales <www.catholic-ew.org.uk>
- Scotland <www.scmo.org/_titles/bishops_conference.htm>
- Ireland <www.catholicireland.net>.

The National Archives has a Research Guide on 'Catholic Recusants' at <www.catalogue.nationalarchives.gov.uk/Leaflets/ri2173.htm>, which gives a guide to the relevant official records. The Catholic Record Society at <www.catholic-history.org.uk/crs/> is the main publishing body for Catholic records, while the Catholic Central Library has a guide to its collections at <www.catholic-library.org.uk>. The Catholic Archives Society has a website at <www.catholic-history.org.uk/catharch/>.

Information about the Catholic Family History Society will be found at <www.catholic-history.org.uk/cfhs/>, and the Catholic History site at <www.catholic-history.org.uk> also hosts three regional Catholic FHS websites.

The Local Catholic Church History and Genealogy Research Guide and Worldwide Directory at <home.att.net/~Local_Catholic/> is a comprehensive research guide to Catholic records. It has details of individual churches and links to online information, with very thorough pages for the UK and Ireland. The Fianna website has a guide to Roman Catholic records in Ireland at <www.rootsweb.com/~fianna/county/parishes.html> taken from Brian Mitchell's *A Guide to Irish Parish Registers*.

Useful links for the British Isles will be found on the Catholic Genealogy site at <www.catholic-genealogy.com>, which also offers discussion groups for (paid) subscribers. Cyndi's List has over 200 links to Catholic resources at <www.cyndislist.com/catholic.htm>.

NONCONFORMIST CHURCHES

The Spartacus Internet Encyclopaedia has a brief history of the most important religious groups at <www.spartacus.schoolnet.co.uk/religion. htm>, with links to details of individual reformers and reform movements. Cyndi's List has individual pages devoted to Baptist, Huguenot, Methodist, Presbyterian and Quaker materials, and links to many other relevant resources on the 'Religion and Churches' page at <www.cyndislist.com/ religion.htm>. Many of the denominational mailing lists at <www. rootsweb.com/~jfuller/gen_mail_religions.html> are for dissenting groups. (Huguenot immigration is covered on p. 176.)

For details of the records, consult the FamilyRecords portal's fact sheet on 'Nonconformist Registers' at <www.familyrecords.gov.uk/frc/pdfs/ nonconformist_registers.pdf>. For Scotland and Ireland, look at Sherry Irvine's article 'Protestant Nonconformity in Scotland' at <www.genuki. org.uk/big/sct/noncon1.html>, and Fianna's guide to 'Baptist, Methodist, Presbyterian and Quaker Records in Ireland' at <www.rootsweb.com/ ~fianna/county/churches.html>.

GenDocs has lists of London churches for a number of nonconformist denominations on its 'Victorian London Churches' page at <www.gendocs. demon.co.uk/churches.html>.

Societies which are relevant for those with nonconformist ancestors are:

- The Quaker Family History Society <www.rootsweb.com/~engqfhs/> which has details of Quaker records and their location, with a page for each county
- The Baptist Historical Society at <www.baptisthistory.org.uk>, which has no general genealogical material but docs have information on Baptist ministers.

There are a number of libraries which specialize in nonconformist material. The John Rylands University Library in Manchester has a strong nonconformist collection, particularly for the Methodist Church. A description of the main resources will be found at <rylibweb.man.ac.uk/ data2/spcoll/intchris.html> and the home page of the Methodist Archives and Research Centre is at <rylibweb.man.ac.uk/data1/dg/text/method. html>.

Dr Williams's Library is an essential repository for those researching English nonconformist ancestors. Its website at <www.dwlib.co.uk> has information about the library and its holdings, as well as a family history area with a brief introduction to nonconformist records and an explanation of which denominations are and are not covered by the library. The ARCHON Directory at <www.archon.nationalarchives.gov.uk/archon/> (see p. 114) has an entry for the Library with links to the materials catalogued in the National Register of Archives, including papers relating to around 200 clergymen.

The official Quaker website has information about the collections in the library at Friends House at <www.quaker.org.uk/library/>, with details of genealogical sources at <www.quaker.org.uk/library/guides/libgenea.html>.

CLERGY

Lambeth Palace Library has a very comprehensive leaflet, 'Biographical sources for Anglican clergy' at <www.lambethpalacelibrary.org/holdings/Guides/clergyman.html>. The definitive resource for England is the Clergy of the Church of England Database. This project, based at King's College, London, aims to construct and publish online a database of all the Church's clergy from 1540 to 1835. The database was launched in Spring 2005 at <www.theclergydatabase.org.uk>, with material for six of the CofE dioceses. Figure 11-1 shows an entry for an individual clergyman. The Institute of Historical Research already has an online version of the *Fasti Ecclesiae Anglicanae*, which gives basic biographical information on the 'higher clergy' up to 1837 at <www.history.ac.uk/fasti/>. The first two volumes of the Scottish equivalent, *Fasti Ecclesiae Scoticanae*, have been transcribed and indexed at <www.dwalker.pwp.blueyonder.co.uk/Ministers%20Index.htm>.

Mundus at <www.mundus.ac.uk> describes itself as a 'gateway to missionary collections in the UK', and will be worth checking if you have

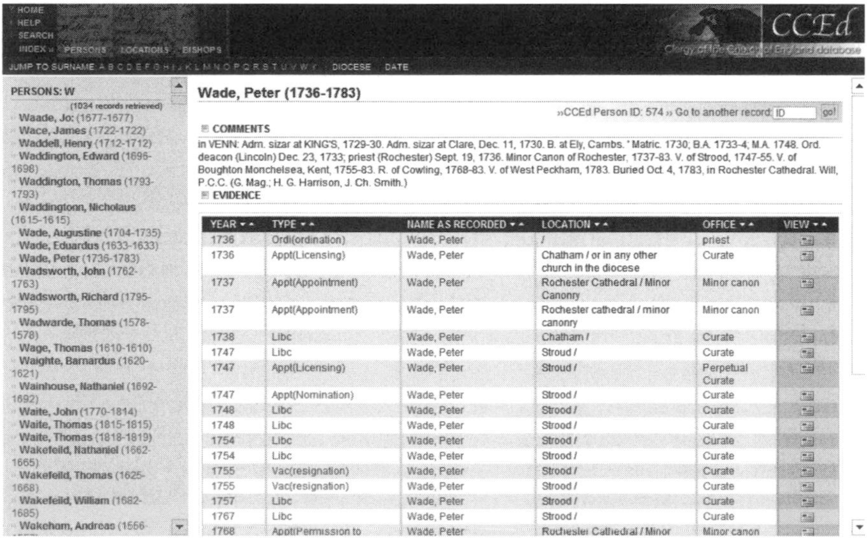

Figure 11-1 An entry from the Clergy of the Church of England Database

missionary ancestors. The site provides information on over 400 collections of overseas missionary materials held in institutions in the United Kingdom, including collections of personal papers.

There are two discussion groups for those with clerical ancestors:

- The CHURCHMEN-UK mailing list, details at <lists.rootsweb.com/index/other/Occupations/CHURCHMEN-UK.html>
- The Clergymen forum at <www.british-genealogy.com/forums/forumdisplay.php?f=39>.

▌OCCUPATIONS

Occupational records have on the whole not formed part of official state records, so they do not feature strongly in the major online data collections. The National Archives' Family History Guide (see p. 7) includes material on occupations, under the title 'People at Work' at <www.nationalarchives.gov.uk/pathways/familyhistory/gallery2/apprentices.htm>, with pages devoted to apprentices, the police, customs and excise officers, coastguards and the legal profession. The National Archives has Research Guides on the following occupations and professions for which there are state records:

- Royal Warrant Holders and Household Servants
- Lawyers
- Tax and Revenue Collectors
- Metropolitan Police
- Royal Irish Constabulary

- Teachers
- Nurses
- Railway Staff
- Civil Servants
- Coastguards

There is also a guide on Apprentices. All are linked from the Research Guides home page at <www.catalogue.nationalarchives.gov.uk/researchguidesindex.asp>.

Genuki has an 'Occupations' page at <www.genuki.org.uk/big/eng/Occupations.html> with a number of links for particular occupations, and links to all the National Archives' Research Guides mentioned. Cyndi's List has a page of resources relating to occupations at <www.cyndislist.com/occupatn.htm> and many other pages which have information on occupations related to particular topics – for example the Prisons page at <www.cyndislist.com/prisons.htm> includes links to Police sites.

The largest set of occupational records online is the apprenticeship material on the British Origins site at <www.britishorigins.com>: the London City Apprenticeship Abstracts 1442–1850 (100,000 records with 300,000 names of apprentices, their parents, and masters) and the Apprentices of Great Britain 1710–74 (350,000 records, about 20% of which relate to Scotland). The site has additional information about apprenticeship records and a list of City Livery Companies at <**www. britishorigins.com/help/popup-aboutbo-lonapps2.htm**>. More information about the Livery Companies will be found on the Corporation of London site at <**www.cityoflondon.gov.uk/Corporation/leisure_heritage/livery/**>.

The Modern Records Centre at the University of Warwick holds records relating to 'labour history, industrial relations and industrial politics'. While it has not put any records online, the main genealogy page at <**www2.warwick.ac.uk/services/library/mrc/holdings/genealogy/**> has links to genealogical guides for the following occupations:

- Bookbinders
- Bricklayers
- Brushmakers
- Bus and Cab Workers
- Carpenters
- Carvers
- Compositors
- Gilders
- House Decorators
- Ironfounders
- Joiners
- Miners
- Painters
- Picture-frame makers
- Plasterers
- Printing workers
- Quarrymen
- Railwaymen
- Seamen
- Steam Engine Makers
- Stonemasons
- Tramway Workers
- Woodworkers

There are many sites devoted to individual occupations, sometimes with just historical information, sometimes with a database of names. Examples of the latter are the Database of Sugar Bakers and Sugar Refiners at <**www. mawer.clara.net/intro.html**> and the Biographical Database of British Chemists at <**www.open.ac.uk/ou5/Arts/chemists/**>.

The Coalmining History Resource Centre at <**www.cmhrc.pwp. blueyonder.co.uk**> has lists of mines at various dates, reports from an 1842 Royal Commission on child labour in the mines, and a database of mining deaths with 90,000 names. The Institute of Historical Research has pages with names of Royal Office Holders in Modern Britain at <**www.history. ac.uk/office/**> ('modern' here meaning 'post-medieval').

The British Book Trade Index, hosted by the University of Birmingham at <**www.bbti.bham.ac.uk**>, is an index of people who worked in the book trade in England and Wales up to 1851 (see Figure 11-2). There is a similar project for Scotland run by the National Library of Scotland at <**www.nls. uk/catalogues/resources/sbti/**>.

The National Archivist (see p. 44) has a small number of professional directories at <**www.nationalarchivist.com**>. Information on 'Tracing your Medical Ancestors' is provided by the Royal College of General Practitioners at <**www.rcgp.org.uk/history/rcgparchives/genealogy.asp**>, and it

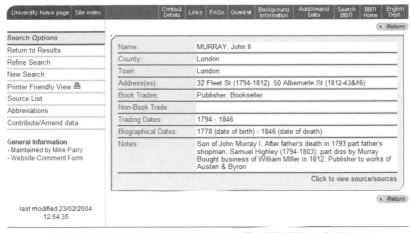

Figure 11-2 John Murray II in the British Book Trade Index

will be worth checking the websites of other professional bodies for historical information about membership. The National Archives have a page on 'Lawyers in the family' at <www.nationalarchives.gov.uk/pathways/familyhistory/gallery2/lawyers.htm>.

There are an increasing number of mailing lists devoted to occupations. These are listed at <www.rootsweb.com/~jfuller/gen mail_occ.html> and those most relevant to UK family historians are:

- BLACKSMITHING
- BRITISH_HATTERS
- CANAL-PEOPLE
- CIRCUS-FOLK
- COALMINERS
- DOCTORS-NURSES-MIDWIVES
- ENG-CANAL-PEOPLE
- ENG-PUBS-INNS
- ENG-THAMESWATERMEN
- Itinerantroots
- LIGHTHOUSE-KEEPERS
- MUSIC-OCCUPATIONS
- ORGAN-BUILDERS

- PAPER-MILLS-MAKERS
- POLICE-UK
- POSTALWORKERS-UK
- RAILWAY-UK
- SCOTLAND-TINKS-HAWKERS
- SCOTTISH-MINING
- THEATRE-UK
- TOWNCRIERS-UK
- UK-COALMINERS
- UK-PHOTOGRAPHERS
- UK-WATCHMAKERS
- VIOLIN-MAKERS
- WOODWORKERS

Many of these are hosted by RootsWeb, where details and archives will be found, linked from <lists.rootsweb.com/index/other/Occupations/>. There is also a general OCCUPATIONS list.

British-genealogy has a general Occupations discussion forum as well as forums for specific occupations:

- Canals and Watermen
- Clergymen
- Coastguards
- Mariners
- Photographers and old photographs
- Railwaymen

All are linked from <**www.british-genealogy.com/forums/forumdisplay. php?f=4**>.

Resources relating to merchant seamen are discussed along with those for the Royal Navy, on p. 160. Trade directories are an important source of occupational information, and these are discussed on p. 110. Photographers are covered on p. 224. A number of resources for clergymen are mentioned earlier in this chapter.

OCCUPATIONAL TERMS

Brief explanations of terms for past occupations are provided in John Hitchcock's 'Ranks, Professions, Occupations and Trades' page at <**www. gendocs.demon.co.uk/trades.html**> and John Lacombe's 'A List of Occupations' at <**cpcug.org/user/jlacombe/terms.html**>. These are quite similar in coverage with around 1,600 occupational terms. The 'Dictionary of Ancient Occupations and Trades, Ranks, Offices, and Titles' at <**freepages. genealogy.rootsweb.com/~dav4is/Sources/Occupations.html**> is a smaller collection of around 750 terms.

For the period before parish registers Olive Tree's list of 'Medieval And Obsolete English Trade And Professional Terms' at <**olivetreegenealogy. com/misc/occupations.shtml#med**> may be useful, especially since it includes medieval Latin terms for many occupations, and some older English spellings.

The most comprehensive listing of occupational terms, with something like 30,000 entries and descriptions, is the Open University's *Dictionary of Occupational Terms*. However, this is available only on CD-ROM and is not online.

CRIME AND PUNISHMENT

The official records of crime are those of the courts and the prison system, and these will be found in the National Archives, which has a number of Research Guides devoted to the subject, including:

- Outlawry in Medieval and Early Modern England
- Criminal Trials, Old Bailey and the Central Criminal Court
- Criminal Trials at the Assizes
- Convicts and Prisoners 1100–1986.

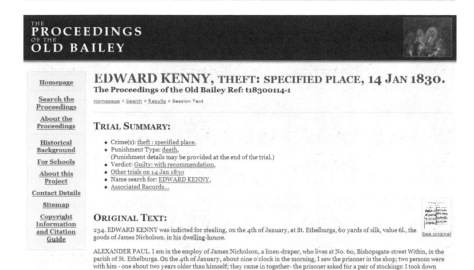

Figure 11-3 Proceedings of the Old Bailey

All of these are online at <www.catalogue.nationalarchives.gov.uk/researchguidesindex.asp>. The National Archives also has material on 'Ancestors and the Law' in its 'Family History' section at <www.nationalarchives.gov.uk/pathways/familyhistory/>.

Cyndi's List has a page devoted to 'Prisons, Prisoners & Outlaws' at <www.cyndislist.com/prisons.htm>. Genuki lists relevant resources under the headings Court Proceedings and Correctional Institutions on national and county pages.

A major online resource is the Proceedings of the Old Bailey site at <www.oldbaileyonline.org>, which contains details of 100,000 trials from 1674 to 1834, with transcriptions and scanned images from the contemporary printed proceedings free of charge. Sophisticated search facilities allow trials to be selected by keyword, name, place, crime, verdict and punishment, or you can browse the trials by date. The text of trials also contains the names of defendants, victims, jurors and judges, which can be found via the name search, so the site is not only of interest to those with criminal ancestors.

In addition to the records themselves, the site has extensive background material about particular communities, which will be of general interest:

- Black Communities of London
- Gypsies and Travellers
- Homosexuality
- Irish in London
- Jewish Communities
- Huguenot London.

Additional background includes material on the various types of verdict and punishment.

Other crime records online include Jeff Alvey's page on 'Newgate Prison' at <**www.fred.net/jefalvey/newgate.html**> which has a list of names taken from an 1896 book on the subject. The same site lists some of the executions in England from 1606 at <**www.fred.net/jefalvey/execute.html**>.

For information on prisons, the Rossbret Prisons website at <**www. institutions.org.uk/prisons/**> is an essential resource. This has a list of prisons organized by county with historical information and details of the relevant records. There is a PRISONS-UK mailing list, details of which will be found at <**lists.rootsweb.com/index/intl/UK/PRISONS-UK.html**>.

Records relating to crime and punishment in Scotland are held by the NAS (see p. 120), which has a fact sheet, 'Crime and Criminals', at <**www.nas.gov.uk/miniframe/fact_sheet/crime.pdf**>.

There are many resources online relating to convict transportation to the colonies, and these are discussed under Colonies and Migration on p. 166 ff.

THE ARMED FORCES

There are two official sites for information on the armed forces and their records: the National Archives and the Ministry of Defence (MoD). The National Archives provides an extensive series of Research Guides to help you understand how the historical records are organized and how to locate and understand them. These can be found at <**www.catalogue. nationalarchives.gov.uk/researchguidesindex.asp**>. The 'Family History' pages have material on the army and navy at <**www.nationalarchives. gov.uk/pathways/familyhistory/gallery3/army.htm**>.

The MoD site at <**www.mod.uk**>, while mainly devoted to the present-day forces, has detailed pages on the location of recent service records, and provides many contact addresses. Each branch of the services has its own website within the MoD's internet domain: <**www.royal-navy.mod. uk**>, <**www.army.mod.uk**> and <**www.raf.mod.uk**>. Beyond these central bodies, there are the individual regiments, ships, squadrons and other units, many of which have their own web pages with historical information. The easiest way to find these is from the site for the relevant arm of the services, which has links to its constituent units. The MoD site does not offer information about individuals.

The most important collection of online data relating to service personnel is the Debt of Honour Register at <**www.cwgc.org**>, discussed in Chapter 8 (p. 101), which lists the Commonwealth war dead from the two world wars. However, there are other small collections of data at some of the sites for individual branches of the services. The National Archives has not yet announced any project to make military records available online, other than the medal records discussed below, but several series of military record are among the materials recommended for potential digitization projects – see the final page of <www.nationalarchives.gov. uk/business/pdf/licensed_associateships.pdf>. The London Gazette (see p. 109) contains details of appointments in the armed forces, and the text search facility on the site at <www.gazettes-online.co.uk> can be used to do a name search.

The Scots at War site at <www.fettes.com/scotsatwar/> concentrates mainly on the twentieth century. It has a Commemorative Roll of Honour with service and biographical information on Scottish servicemen, and detailed genealogical help pages which will be of interest to anyone with Commonwealth military ancestors.

Genuki has pages devoted to Military Records at <www.genuki.org.uk/ big/MilitaryRecords.html> and Military History at <www.genuki. org.uk/big/MilitaryHistory.html>. Cyndi's List has a page devoted to UK Military at <www.cyndislist.com/miluk.htm>, which covers all branches of the services, while her 'Military Resources Worldwide' page at <www. cyndislist.com/milres.htm> has more general material.

If you need to identify medals, a good starting point is MedalNet at <www.medal.net> which is devoted to Commonwealth medals. There are also sites devoted to the holders of gallantry medals, particularly the Victoria Cross, for which lists of recipients can be found at <www. victoriacross.net/> and <www.victoriacross.org.uk/vcross.htm>. Stephen Stratford has information on gallantry medals, with photographs at <www.stephen-stratford.co.uk/gallantry.htm>. The Gazettes Online website, described in more detail on p. 109, has a facility to search the online issues for awards of medals at <www.gazettes-online.co.uk/honours.asp>.

The National Archives has two main Research Guides on military medals and their records:

- Campaign Medals and other Service Medals at <www.catalogue. nationalarchives.gov.uk/Leaflets/ri2296.htm>
- Gallantry Medals <www.catalogue.nationalarchives.gov.uk/Leaflets/ ri2297.htm>.

DocumentsOnline at <www.nationalarchives.gov.uk/documentsonline> includes digital images of over five million First World War medal index cards and medal records of over 100,000 Second World War Merchant Seamen. Images of the index cards can be purchased, though it may be that the online index provides sufficient information.

The Imperial War Museum at <www.iwm.org.uk> has a family history section at <www.iwm.org.uk/server.php?show=nav.00100a>, and links to many military museums, while the MoD has a comprehensive listing of

British military museums at <**www.army.mod.uk/ceremonialandheritage/ museums_main.htm**>. The IWM also has an online database with parts of its collections catalogued at <**www.iwmcollections.org.uk**>. Digitized extracts from some of the materials are available on the site.

In addition to the data in the Debt of Honour Register (see p. 101), the Officers Died site at <**www.redcoat.info/memindex3.htm**> lists officers killed in a whole range of wars from the North American Wars of the eighteenth century to Afghanistan and Iraq in 2004, compiled from various books, casualty lists, medal rolls, newspapers, and memorials. The same site has pages devoted to Soldiers Memorials at <**www.angelfire.com/mp/ memorials/memindz1.htm**>. Roll of Honour at <**www.roll-of-honour. com**> (see p. 101) is a site dedicated to listing those commemorated on war memorials. Britains Small Wars at <**www.britains-smallwars.com**> covers the period from 1945 up to the present and has extensive information about each war, including in many cases lists of casualties.

There are quite a few sites devoted to particular wars or battles, such as the pages on the Battle of Culloden <**www.electricscotland.com/history/ culloden**>. Some are devoted to a war as a whole, such as the Trenches on the web site at <**www.worldwar1.com**>,which is subtitled 'An Internet History of The Great War'. Others are devoted to a particular aspect – for example, The Second Battle of the Marne at <**batmarn2.club.fr/ menuseng.htm**> offers information about all the British divisions involved in this engagement and what they did.

RootsWeb has a number of mailing lists devoted to particular wars, including:

- NAPOLEONIC
- CRIMEAN-WAR
- BOER-WAR
- GREATWAR
- WORLDWAR2
- KOREAN-WAR

WW20-ROOTS-L is devoted to 'genealogy in all 20th century wars'. All these lists are hosted by RootsWeb and details will be found by following the various military links in the Other box on the main Lists page at <**lists. rootsweb.com**>.

British-genealogy has discussion forums devoted to the following conflicts:

- English Civil War
- American War of Independence
- Napoleonic Wars
- American Civil War
- Crimean War
- Boer War
- World War 1
- World War 2

Links to these forums will be found at <**www.british-genealogy.com/**>.

THE ROYAL NAVY AND MERCHANT NAVY

The official Royal Navy site at <**www.royal-navy.mod.uk**> has separate sections for ships, the Fleet Air Arm, submarines, the Royal Marines and naval establishments. Historical information is in a section called 'Navy Life' at <**www.royal-navy.mod.uk/static/pages/211.html**>.

Although the merchant navy is not an arm of the state, it has long been subject to government regulation and many maritime ancestors will have served in both the Royal Navy and the merchant fleet.

The most important gateway to British maritime resources on the web is the National Maritime Museum's Port site at <**www.port.nmm.ac.uk**>. In addition to a search facility, there is an option to browse by subject or historical period. The site offers a detailed description of each resource it links to. The focus of this gateway is not primarily genealogical, but a search for 'genealogy' turns up almost 200 resources. The site includes a range of research leaflets for all aspects of ships and the sea, including a number on tracing people in the Royal Navy and merchant marine. In addition, the research leaflets on uniforms and medals may be useful. The list of leaflets will be found at <**www.port.nmm.ac.uk/research/ research.html**>.

Another site with many links, though again it is not specifically genealogical, is Peter McCracken's Maritime History on the Internet site at <**ils. unc.edu/maritime/mhiweb/webhome.shtml**>. There is a useful collection of links to other official naval sites at <**www.royal-navy.mod.uk/static/pages/ 2090.html**>.

Genuki has a page of merchant marine links at <**www.genuki.org.uk/ big/MerchantMarine.html**>, while the Royal Navy is included in its Military Records and Military History pages mentioned above.

The MARINERS mailing list is for all those whose ancestors pursued maritime occupations. The list has its own website at <**www.mariners-l. co.uk**> with sections devoted to individual countries, as well as more general topics such as wars at sea and shipping companies. The site also has a guide to ranks in both the Royal and merchant navy at <**www. mariners-l.co.uk/GenBosun's Locker.html**>. The MERCHANT-MARINE list covers Merchant Marines of all countries involved in the Second World War, and details will be found at <**lists.rootsweb.com/ index/other/Military/MERCHANT-MARINE.html**>. There is also a BRITISH-MARINERS list – details at <**lists.rootsweb.com/index/other/ Military:_Naval/MERCHANT-MARINE.html**>.

In addition to the NMM's site at <**www.nmm.ac.uk**>, the Royal Navy site has links to this and UK naval museums on its links page at <**www. royal-navy.mod.uk/static/pages/2090.html**>, while almost 300 maritime museums are listed at <**www.cus.cam.ac.uk/~mhe1000/marmus.htm**>.

Records

Since the majority of naval records are held by the National Archives, one of the best places to find out about them is the collection of online Research

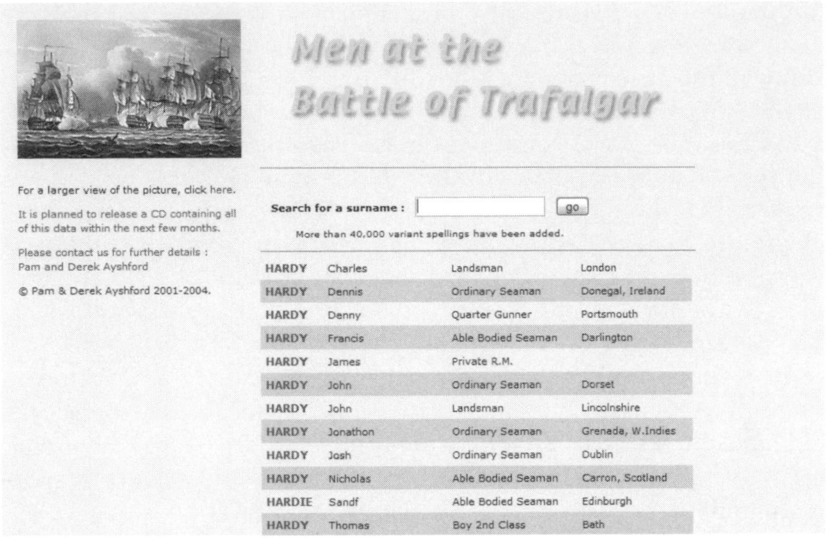

Men at the Battle of Trafalgar

For a larger view of the picture, click here.

It is planned to release a CD containing all of this data within the next few months.

Please contact us for further details : Pam and Derek Ayshford

© Pam & Derek Ayshford 2001-2004.

Search for a surname : go

More than 40,000 variant spellings have been added.

HARDY	Charles	Landsman	London
HARDY	Dennis	Ordinary Seaman	Donegal, Ireland
HARDY	Denny	Quarter Gunner	Portsmouth
HARDY	Francis	Able Bodied Seaman	Darlington
HARDY	James	Private R.M.	
HARDY	John	Ordinary Seaman	Dorset
HARDY	John	Landsman	Lincolnshire
HARDY	Jonathon	Ordinary Seaman	Grenada, W.Indies
HARDY	Josh	Ordinary Seaman	Dublin
HARDY	Nicholas	Able Bodied Seaman	Carron, Scotland
HARDIE	Sandf	Able Bodied Seaman	Edinburgh
HARDY	Thomas	Boy 2nd Class	Bath

Figure 11-4 The Age of Nelson: Database of men at Trafalgar

Guides at <**www.catalogue.nationalarchives.gov.uk/researchguidesindex.asp**>, where the relevant materials are grouped under Royal Navy and Merchant Navy. An introduction to the records of merchant seamen will be found at <**www.nationalarchives.gov.uk/pathways/familyhistory/gallery3/seamen.htm**>.

The Royal Navy site has details on obtaining service records for those who joined the Navy from 1924 onwards at <**www.royal-navy.mod.uk/static/pages/1034.html**> (earlier records are at the National Archives).

For a more discursive guide to naval records, Fawne Stratford-Devai's articles on the Global Gazette site are recommended, 'British Military Records Part 2: THE ROYAL NAVY' at <**globalgenealogy.com/globalgazette/gazfd/gazfd48.htm**> and 'Maritime Records & Resources' in two parts, at <**globalgenealogy.com/globalgazette/gazfd/gazfd50.htm**> and <**globalgenealogy.com/globalgazette/gazfd/gazfd52.htm**>. Among other things, these articles have very useful lists of some of the main groups of records (mainly from the National Archives) which have been microfilmed by the LDS Church and can therefore be consulted at Family History Centres.

Other guides to tracing seafaring ancestors include Bob Sanders's site at <**www.angelfire.com/de/BobSanders/**> which has an extensive collection of material on 'Tracing British Seamen & their ships', including not only naval occupations but also Fishermen, Customs & Excise Officers and Coastguards. Len Barnett has what he calls 'a realistic guide to what is available to those looking into merchant mariners' careers' at <www.barnettresearch.freeserve.co.uk/main.htm>.

Apart from the Commonwealth War Graves Commission's Debt of Honour Register at <www.cwgc.org>, almost all online data transcriptions relating to seamen will be found on the websites of individuals. For example, Bob Sanders has an index to O'Byrne's *Royal Navy Biography* of 1849 with details of Royal Navy officers, linked from <www.angelfire.com/de/BobSanders/Site.html>, as well as many other small data collections. The Naval Biographical Database is an ambitious project at <www.navylist.org> to 'establish accurate biographical information on those individuals who have served, or supported the Royal Navy since 1660'. So far the site has details of around 12,000 people and 5,000 ships.

The National Archives has a Trafalgar Ancestors database, launched on the 200th anniversary of the battle, at <www.nationalarchives.gov.uk/trafalgarancestors/> with over 18,000 names drawn from a wide range of sources. The Age of Nelson at <www.ageofnelson.org> has a complete Navy List for the period of the Napoleonic Wars. It also has a project to trace the descendants of those who fought at Trafalgar, as well as its own Trafalgar Roll. The Trafalgar Roll Call is one of the datasets promised by the National Archivist site at <www.nationalarchivist.com> (see p. 44).

The National Archives are planning to add Seamen's Records 1853–1924 (record series ADM 188) to DocumentsOnline (see p. 97) in Autumn 2005.

Ships

There are a number of sites relating to the ships rather than the seamen who served on them, and these can be useful for background. For example, Gilbert Provost has transcribed details of vessels from the Lloyd's Register of British and Foreign Shipping from 1764 up to 2001 at <www.reach.net/~sc001198/Lloyds.htm>. Michael P. Palmer maintains the Palmer List of Merchant Vessels at <www.geocities.com/mppraetorius/> which has descriptions of hundreds of merchant vessels, compiled from a variety of sources. Both sites provide names of masters and owners as well as information on the ships themselves. Steve Johnson provides a 'photographic A to Z of British Naval warships, submarines, and auxiliaries from 1880 to 1950' at <freepages.misc.rootsweb.com/~cyberheritage/>.

If you suspect that an ancestor was on a naval vessel, either in port or at sea, on census night in 1901, you should find Jeffery Knaggs's index to the location of Royal Navy ships at <homepage.ntlworld.com/jeffery.knaggs/RNShips.html> of interest. Bob Sanders has a similar list of Ships in UK Ports for the 1881 census at <www.angelfire.com/de/BobSanders/81Intro.html>.

THE ARMY

In addition to the detailed information about army records in the National Archives' Research Guides mentioned above, there is basic information about locating records in the National Archives for individual soldiers at <**www.nationalarchives.gov.uk/familyhistory/military/army/**>. Genuki has a page devoted to British Military History at <**www.genuki.org.uk/big/MilitaryHistory.html**>, and an article by Jay Hall on 'British Military Records for the 18th and 19th centuries' at <**www.genuki.org.uk/big/MilitaryRecords.html**>. The FFHS provides some basic information in the online version of its leaflet 'In search of your Soldier Ancestors' at <**www.ffhs.org.uk/General/Help/Soldier.htm**>; and there is a useful article by Fawne Stratford-Devai devoted to 'British Military Records Part 1: The Army' in *The Global Gazette* at <**globalgenealogy.com/globalgazette/gazfd/gazfd44.htm**>.

While the National Archives does not have individual army service records online, the online catalogue (see p. 118) includes the names of individual soldiers from documents in series WO 97, which comprises discharge papers for the period 1760–1854. The National Archivist has a number of Army Lists available at <**www.nationalarchivist.com**>, and more are in the pipeline. The site also has a free searchable database of Officers in the Grenadier Guards for the period 1656 to 1874.

The crucial piece of information about any ancestor in the army is the regiment or unit he served in. A useful area of the army site at the MoD is that devoted to the organizational structure of the army at <**www.army.mod.uk/unitsandorgs/**>, which has links to the web pages for the individual regiments, as well as to the special units and the Territorial Army. On the page for each regiment is a brief history and a list of its main engagements.

However, over the centuries, regiments have not been very stable in either composition or naming and you are likely to need historical information about the particular period when an ancestor was in uniform. Apart from the official material on the MoD site, the essential resource for regimental history is T. F. Mills's Land Forces of Britain, the Empire and Commonwealth site at <**www.regiments.org**>. The site not only provides detailed background information on the regimental system at <**regiments.org/milhist/uk/forces/bargts.htm**>, but also lists the regiments in the army in particular years since the eighteenth century. For an overview of regimental name changes and amalgamations, see Cathy Day's listing of 'Lineages of all British Army Infantry Regiments' at <**members.ozemail.com.au/~clday/regiments.htm**>.

The Scots at War site has a list of Scottish regiments at <**www.fettes.com/scotsatwar/regpages.htm**> with pages devoted to each one.

Many individuals have put up pages on individual regiments, sometimes in relation to a particular war or engagement. There is no single comprehensive listing of these, but you should be able to find them by entering the name of the regiment in a search engine.

There is a britregiments mailing list, details of which will be found at <groups.yahoo.com/group/britregiments/>. Note that this is a military rather than genealogical discussion forum.

If you need to identify a cap badge, you could have a look at <www. egframes.co.uk/indexbadge.htm>, which is a commercial site offering badges for sale but has photographs of current badges and a searchable database of regiments. If you want to know what uniform an ancestor wore, or are trying to identify a photograph, the illustrations from two booklets by Arthur H. Bowling on the uniforms of British Infantry Regiments 1660–1914 and Scottish Regiments 1660–1914 are online at <geocities.com/Pentagon/Barracks/3050/buframe.html>.

Otherwise, you will need to browse through some of the online photographic collections, such as Photographs of Soldiers of the British Army 1840 to 1920 at <www.members.dca.net/fbl/>.

For army museums, the MoD has a comprehensive listing on its web-site at <www.army.mod.uk/ceremonialandheritage/museums_main.htm>, which can be viewed alphabetically or by special interest covered. The National Army Museum in Chelsea has a website at <www.national-army-museum. ac.uk>. A list of Scottish military museums is provided on the Scottish Military Historical Society's website at <www.btinternet.com/~james.mckay/ disp_018.htm>. Regimental museums can be found via the regiment's page on the Army website.

THE ROYAL AIR FORCE

The official RAF site is at <www.raf.mod.uk>, with a list of units and stations at <www.raf.mod.uk/stations/>. The 'Histories' section at <www. raf.mod.uk/history/histories.html> offers historical material on individual squadrons and stations, with images of squadron badges and details of battle honours and aircraft. If you have an ancestor who took part in the Battle of Britain, you will want to look at the operational diaries at <www.raf.mod.uk/bob1940/bobhome.html>. The 'Links' page at <www. raf.mod.uk/links/> has links to the websites of individual squadrons and stations. The MoD site has (non-electronic) contact details for RAF Personnel records at <www.mod.uk/contacts/raf_records.htm>.

The RAF Museum has a website at <www.rafmuseum.org.uk>, and the pages for the museum's Department of Research & Information Services at Hendon has information on archive and library material at <www. rafmuseum.org.uk/london/research/>.

There do not seem to be any genealogical mailing lists specifically for the RAF, though the general lists for twentieth-century wars mentioned on p. 160 above will cover RAF interests.

COLONIES AND MIGRATION

Former British colonies are genealogically important for British and Irish family history for three reasons: they have been the destination of emigrants from the British Isles (both voluntary and otherwise), the source of much immigration, and a place of residence and work for many British soldiers, merchants and others. There have, of course, been other sources of immigration and some of the most significant are discussed towards the end of this section.

There is not space here to deal with internet resources relating to the individual countries, or to overseas records unrelated to immigration or emigration, but good places to start are Cyndi's List at <**www.cyndislist. com**>, which has individual pages for all the countries or regions, and the GenWeb site for the country at <**worldgenweb.org**> (see p. 24).

Genuki has links relating to both emigration and immigration at <**www. genuki.org.uk/big/Emigration.html**>. Resources relating to child migration are covered in 'Adoption and child migration' on p. 147.

For the official British records of emigration, the National Archives' 'Emigration' Research Guide is the definitive online guide at <**www. catalogue.nationalarchives.gov.uk/Leaflets/ri2272.htm**>. For convict transportation, there are Research Guides relating to North America and the West Indies at <**www.catalogue.nationalarchives.gov.uk/Leaflets/ri2234. htm**>, and to Australia at <**www.catalogue.nationalarchives.gov.uk/ Leaflets/ri2235.htm**>.

Key general records for emigration from the British Isles are passenger lists, and there are a number of sites with information about surviving passenger lists, or with data transcribed from them. Cyndi's List has a 'Ships and Passenger Lists' page at <**www.cyndislist.com/ships.htm**>. Among other information, this has links to many passenger lists and lists of ship arrivals.

The Immigrant Ships Transcribers Guild at <**www.immigrantships.net**> has transcribed over 6,500 passenger lists and is adding more all the time. These can be searched by date, by port of departure, port of arrival, passenger name or captain's name. In addition to its own material, the 'Compass' area of the site at <**immigrantships.net/newcompass/pcindex. html**> has an enormous collection of links to other passenger list sites. For Irish emigration, the ScotlandsClans site has many links at <**www. scotlandsclans.com/irshiplists.htm**>. There are a number of mailing lists for immigrant ships, but the most general is TheShipsList, which has its

Figure 11-5 Material on Irish Migration from MovingHere

own website at <www.theshipslist.com>. Details of other lists relating to emigration and immigration will be found at <www.rootsweb.com/~jfuller/gen_mail_emi.html>.

The National Archives has an introduction to naturalization records for family historians at <www.nationalarchives.gov.uk/familyhistory/naturalisation/>, and there are Research Guides for 'Immigration' at <www.catalogue.nationalarchives.gov.uk/Leaflets/ri2156.htm> and 'Naturalisation' at <www.catalogue.nationalarchives.gov.uk/Leaflets/ri2257.htm>.

Probably the most important site for information on immigration to the British Isles is Moving Here at <www.movinghere.org.uk>. This covers Caribbean, Irish, South Asian and Jewish immigration to England over the past two centuries and the subsequent history of the immigrant communities. The site has a catalogue of resources as well as general historical material and individual historical testimony. There is specifically genealogical information in the 'Tracing Your Roots' gallery at <www.movinghere.org.uk/galleries/roots/>.

Another good general site is The Channel 4 Guide to Genealogy, which has material on tracing an ancestor who was an immigrant at <www.channel4.com/history/microsites/U/untold/resources/geno/geno3.html> covering Jewish, African-American, West Indian, African, and Asian immigration.

A useful starting point for all ethnic groups is The Open Directory (see p. 28) at <www.dmoz.org> which has pages for many groups linked from <dmoz.org/Society/Ethnicity/>. The links collected here are primarily to historical and cultural material, however, and you should not expect to find any genealogical resources beyond what is already on Cyndi's List. For more specifically British resources, it is worth going to <dmoz.org/Regional/Europe/United_Kingdom/Society_and_Culture/Ethnicity/> which links to pages for 13 immigrant communities.

There is a Museum of Immigration at Spitalfields in London which has a website at <www.19princeletstreet.org.uk>. The British Empire & Commonwealth Museum in Bristol has a website at <www.empiremuseum.co.uk> with information on the museum and its collections.

There are a number of general mailing lists relating to migration from and within the British Isles, including:

- ENGLISH-EMIGRANTS <lists.rootsweb.com/index/other/Ethnic-English/ENGLISH-EMIGRANTS.html>
- WELSH-EMIGRANTS <lists.rootsweb.com/index/other/Ethnic-Welsh/WELSH-EMIGRANTS.html>
- IRISH-IN-UK <lists.rootsweb.com/index/other/Ethnic-Irish/IRISH-IN-UK.html>, with a website at <www.connorsgenealogy.com/IrishUK/>.
- IRISH-SCOTS <lists.rootsweb.com/index/other/Ethnic/Irish/IRISH-SCOTS.html>
- SHIPS_FROM_ENGLAND <lists.rootsweb.com/index/other/Immigration/SHIPS_FROM_ENGLAND.html>.

NORTH AMERICA

The American colonies were the first dumping ground for convicts, and the National Archives' Research Guide 'Transportation to America and the West Indies, 1615–1776' at <www.catalogue.nationalarchives.gov.uk/Leaflets/ri2234.htm> gives details of the records. More general information about colonies on the other side of the Atlantic will be found in 'The American and West Indian Colonies Before 1782' at <www.catalogue.nationalarchives.gov.uk/Leaflets/ri2105.htm>. For post-colonial emigration to the US, see 'Emigrants to North America After 1776' at <www.catalogue.nationalarchives.gov.uk/Leaflets/ri2107.htm>. The US National Archives and Records Administration has information on immigration records at <www.archives.gov/genealogy/immigration/> and naturalization records at <www.archives.gov/genealogy/naturalization.html>.

For other links relating to emigration to North America, the best starting point is the 'Immigration and Naturalization' page on Cyndi's List at <www.cyndislist.com/immigrat.htm>.

US sites of course have a wealth of data relating to immigrants. Ancestry at <www.ancestry.com>, for example, has databases of Immigrants to

New England 1620–33, Irish Quaker Immigration into Pennsylvania, New England Founders, New England Immigrants, 1700–75, New England Irish Pioneers and Scots-Irish in Virginia. A number of immigration datasets are included in a subscription to Ancestry's UK record collection, but for most a subscription to the US Immigration Collection is required (see p. 43). For the late nineteenth and early twentieth centuries, Ellis Island Passenger Arrivals (the American Family Immigration History Center) at <www.ellisislandrecords.org> has a searchable database of passengers who entered America through Ellis Island between 1892 and 1924.

There are many sites devoted to individual groups of settlers, for example the *Mayflower* Passenger List at <members.aol.com/calebj/passenger. html>. The immigration page on Cyndi's List is the easiest way to find such sites. The 'Immigration And Ships Passenger Lists Research Guide' at <home.att.net/~arnielang/shipgide.html> offers help and guidance on researching ancestors who emigrated to the USA.

There is less material online for Canada. Marjorie Kohli's Immigrants to Canada site at <www.ist.uwaterloo.ca/~marj/genealogy/thevoyage. html> has an extensive collection of material, and links to many related resources. The National Archives of Canada has information on immigration at <www.genealogy.gc.ca/10/1008_e.html>, covering both border entry and passenger lists. There is a pilot online database for the passenger list records for the years 1925–35 at <www.collectionscanada.ca/ archivianet/020118_e.html>. The inGeneas site at <www.inGeneas.com> also has a database of passenger lists and immigration records; the National Archives of Canada Miscellaneous Immigration Index is free; the index to other material can be searched free, but there is a charge for record transcriptions.

AFRICAN AND CARIBBEAN

Good starting points for researching Black British ancestry are the BBC and Channel 4 websites. The Channel 4 Guide to Genealogy has already been mentioned (see p. 8 and p. 167) and includes material on African, West Indian and African-American genealogy. The BBC website offers an introduction to Caribbean family history by Kathy Chater at <www.bbc.co. uk/history/your_history/family/caribb_family_1.shtml>, which gives some historical background and discusses the relevant records.

CaribbeanGenWeb at <www.rootsweb.com/~caribgw/> has areas devoted to all the islands of the Caribbean. Though there are considerable differences in scope, as each island site has its own maintainer, all have message boards to make contact with other researchers, and many have substantial collections of links. You should also find information on civil registration, parish registers and other records. Another useful collection of genealogy links for the Caribbean will be found on the Candoo site at

<www.candoo.com/genresources/>, including lists of relevant microfilms in the LDS Church's Family History Centres.

For anyone with Caribbean ancestry, the Caribbean Surnames Index (CARSURDEX) at <www.candoo.com/surnames/> will be an essential resource. It has over 4,000 surname interests with surname, island and an email contact address, and there is an online form for submitting your own surnames.

There is a newsgroup for discussion of Caribbean ancestry, soc. genealogy.west-indies, which is gatewayed with the CARIBBEAN mailing list (see <lists.rootsweb.com/index/other/Newsgroup_Gateways/ CARIBBEAN.html>). Details of other West Indies mailing lists will be found at <www.rootsweb.com/~jfuller/gen_mail_country-wes.html>. The GEN-AFRICAN-L mailing list, gatewayed with the soc.genealogy. african newsgroup, also covers the genealogy of Africa and the African diaspora. There are also genealogical mailing lists for individual African countries – see <www.rootsweb.com/~jfuller/gen_mail_african.html>. The CARIBBEAN-FREEDMEN and ENGLAND-FREEDMEN mailing lists may be of interest to descendants of freed slaves. Details of both are linked from <lists.rootsweb.com/index/other/Ethnic-African/>.

While there is still relatively little specifically genealogical material online for those with Black British ancestry, the web offers an increasing amount of general historical information relating to black immigration and the history of black communities in Britain.

The Black Presence in Britain at <www.blackpresence.co.uk> is devoted to Black British history and has articles on a number of aspects, including parish and military records. Both the BBC and Channel 4 sites have areas devoted to this topic. Resources relating to the BBC's *Windrush* season, broadcast in 1998, at <www.bbc.co.uk/history/society_culture/ multicultural/windrush_01.shtml> include a factfile and oral testimony from those who came to Britain on the *Windrush*. This is part of the 'Multiculture' area of the BBC's site which has a range of material relating to Black History and the British Empire. Channel 4's Black and Asian History Map at <www.channel4.com/history/microsites/B/ blackhistorymap/> provides a large number of links to sites with biographical and historical information on Black and Asian immigrants to Britain. There is a timeline to provide an overview, a map which allows you to select links for particular parts of the UK, and a search facility.

An important site is the Black and Asian Londoners Project (BAL). This project of the London Metropolitan Archives (LMA) is creating an online database of Black and Asian Londoners between 1536 and 1840, with names and area of residence based on information from church registers, family papers in the LMA and material from the British Library and the India Office. The home page is at <www.corpoflondon.gov.uk/

Corporation/lma_learning/dataonline/lz_baproject.asp> and the database can be searched on name, street, borough, place of origin, or occupation. The results of a search are images of the original records (see Figure 11-6).

The PortCities sites for Bristol and Liverpool, linked from <**www. portcities.org.uk**>, have material on the slave trade centred on these ports, while the London site has pages devoted to the capital's Somali and Swahili-speaking communities.

It's worth using a search engine searching for the phrase 'black history' with the name of a town. This will turn up sites such as Birmingham Black History at <**www.birminghamblackhistory.com**>, or Brighton and Hove Black History at <**www.black-history.org.uk**>.

CASBAH is a project which aims to identify and map national research resources in the UK library and archives sectors that are relevant to Caribbean studies and the history of Black and Asian peoples in Britain. The CASBAH website at <**www.casbah.ac.uk**>, while aimed primarily

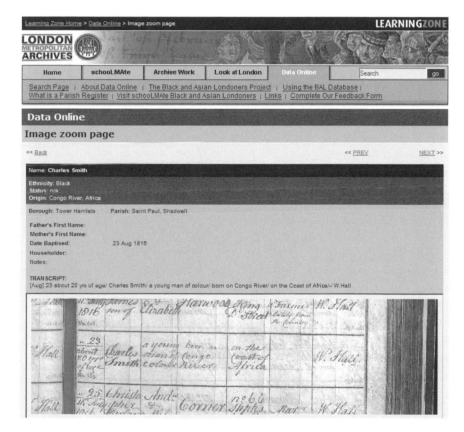

Figure 11-6 An entry from the BAL database: the baptism of Chas. Henry Smith, 'a young man of colour', at St Paul, Shadwell

at academic researchers, is useful to anyone researching Black History in Britain because it provides links to around 120 other relevant websites, particularly libraries with relevant collections.

A number of relevant organizations have useful websites, for example the Archives & Museum of Black Heritage at <**www.aambh.org.uk**> (this requires Macromedia Flash) and the Black and Asian Studies Association <**www.blackandasianstudies.org.uk**>.

The Open Directory's African-British page at <**dmoz.org/Society/ Ethnicity/African/African-British/**> is a good starting point for web resources relating to African and Afro-Caribbean immigration into Britain, though the listing does not specialize in genealogical sources.

Black Search at <**www.blacksearch.co.uk**> is a UK-based web directory of Black websites around the world. It has a genealogy page, which can be found by following the 'History and Culture' link from the home page. There are also headings in this section for Africa, African-American, Black British, and Caribbean.

For convict transportation to the West Indies, see the National Archives' Research Guides mentioned under 'North America' above.

INDIA

A number of the resources mentioned in the previous section cover Asian immigration to Britain as well as Black immigration, particularly the Database of London's Black and Asian History. The Channel 4 Guide to Genealogy has material on tracing Indian and other Asian ancestry at <**www.channel4.com/history/microsites/U/untold/resources/geno/geno3e. html**>.

The British Library has a whole set of pages devoted to 'Sources relating to Asians from the Indian Subcontinent' at <**www.bl.uk/collections/ britasian/britasia.html**>, including an outline of Asian immigration and contemporary material from various walks of life.

The BL site is also useful for ancestors from the British Isles who lived or worked in India, as it includes the India Office website. This has pages for family historians at <**www.bl.uk/collections/oiocfamilyhistory/ family.html**>, with information on the various types of genealogical source.

Another good starting point for genealogical research into British India is Cathy Day's Family History In India site at <**members.ozemail.com.au/ ~clday/**>, which provides a comprehensive guide for 'people tracing their British, European and Anglo-Indian family history in India, Burma, Pakistan and Bangladesh'. It has extensive material relating to the British Army in India and many small data extracts.

The Families in British India Society has a website at <**fibis.org**> with a free online database of selected records of the India Office and East India Company held by the British Library and elsewhere. The records include transcriptions of civil, ecclesiastical, maritime and military records covering the period from 1737 to 1947. Amongst over 100,000 records included are details of ships sailing to India, and their occupants, of use to maritime historians plus births, marriages and deaths of persons in British-administrated territories in India which will be used by family and social historians. Many records are of soldiers of the Indian Army and of the British Army regiments which served in India. The database can be searched from <search.fibis.org>.

The National Archivist site (see p. 44) has a number of datasets relating to British India at <**www.nationalarchivist.com**>, including the East India Company's Commercial Marine Service Pensions List 1793 to July 1833, and the Indian Army & Civil Service List July 1873.

There are two genealogical mailing lists relevant to the Indian subcontinent, BANGLADESH and INDIA. Details will be found at <**lists. rootsweb.com/index/intl/BGD/BANGLADESH.html**> and <**lists.rootsweb. com/index/intl/IND/INDIA.html**> respectively. RootsWeb hosts genealogical mailing lists for a number of other Asian countries, listed at <**lists. rootsweb.com/index/**>. There is also an INDIA-BRITISH-RAJ list, though this is devoted to general historical and cultural topics rather than to genealogical issues as such. Subscription details and a link to the archive of messages will be found at <**lists.rootsweb.com/index/intl/IND/ INDIA-BRITISH-RAJ.html**>.

AUSTRALASIA

There are extensive materials online relating both to convict transportation to Australia, and to later free emigration to Australia and New Zealand. Good starting points are the Australia and New Zealand pages on Cyndi's List at <**www.cyndislist.com/austnz.htm**> and <**www.cyndislist. com/newzealand.htm**> respectively. Another worthwhile site is the Australian Family History Compendium, which has a list of online sources at <**www.cohsoft.com.au/afhc/netrecs.html**>. For information on the official records held by the British state, see the National Archives' Research Guides.

Convict lists for the first, second, and third fleets will be found on Patricia Downes's site at <**www.pcug.org.au/~pdownes/**>. The National Archives of Ireland has a database of Transportation Records 1788–1868 at <**www.nationalarchives.ie/search01.html**> (see Figure 11-7). In addition to the passenger list sites mentioned above, links to passenger lists for Australasia will be found at <**www.nationalarchives.ie/genealogy/ transp.htm**>.

Australian government agencies have much information relating to convicts and free settlers online. The National Archives of Australia website at <**www.naa.gov.au**> has a family history section, which includes material

The National Archives of Ireland

Search results

Found 1 record matching **O'Brian**. Printing first 1 of 1 records.

The document reference in each entry below is the National Archives of Ireland reference to the original document in the archive: The microfilm reference number refers to the set of microfilms presented to Australia in 1988.

Record 1 of 1

```
SURNAME: O'BRIAN                      OTHER NAMES: MARGARET
     AGE:  25          SEX: F              ALIAS:

PLACE OF TRIAL: Co. Antrim                  TRIAL DATE: 21/10/1839
PLACE OF IMPRISONMENT:                      DOCUMENT DATE:

     CRIME DESCRIPTION: Larceny
     SENTENCE: Transportation 7 yrs
     SHIP:

PETITIONER:                           RELATIONSHIP:

DOCUMENT REFERENCES:  TR 3, p 193
MICROFILM REFERENCES:
COMMENTS:
```

Figure 11-7 An entry from the National Archives of Ireland's Transportation Records

on immigration at <www.naa.gov.au/The_Collection/Family_History/immigrants.html>. The Victoria Public Record Office has an online database of Immigration to Victoria 1852–89 at <proarchives.imagineering.com.au>. The Archives Office of Tasmania, at <www.archives.tas.gov.au>, has a Colonial Tasmanian Family Link Database with about 500,000 entries and an Index to Naturalisation Applications for 1835–1905. New South Wales has all nineteenth-century civil registration indexes online at <www.bdm.nsw.gov.au/familyHistory/searchHistoricalRecords.htm> and Indexes to Assisted Immigrants 1839–96 at <www.records.nsw.gov.au/indexes/immigration/introduction.htm>, though the full records are not online. Comprehensive links to Australian archives are on the Archives of Australia site at <www.archivenet.gov.au>.

Archives New Zealand has a website at <www.archives.govt.nz> with a 'Migration Reference Guide' at <www.archives.govt.nz/docs/pdfs/Ref_Guide_Migration.pdf>. The Registrar General's site at <www.bdm.govt.nz> has information on births, deaths and marriages but no online data.

The online Encyclopedia of New Zealand at <www.teara.govt.nz> has considerable material relating to settlement, with sections devoted to particular communities. There is extensive coverage of English, Scots, Welsh and Irish settlement.

There are dozens of mailing lists for Australian and New Zealand genealogy, all listed at <www.rootsweb.com/~jfuller/gen_mail_country-aus.html> and <www.rootsweb.com/~jfuller/gen_mail_country-nez.html>. The main general lists are AUSTRALIA and NEW-ZEALAND, while the remainder are devoted to specific topics: AUS-CONVICTS, AUS-IMMIGRATION-SHIPS, AUS-IRISH, AUS-MILITARY, AUS-NSW-COLONIAL-HISTORY, convicts-australia, TRANSCRIPTIONS-AUS and TRANSCRIPTIONS-NZ. There are also lists for individual states, regions, and even towns. The newsgroup soc.genealogy.australia+nz is gatewayed with the GENANZ mailing list.

JEWS

There are many sites devoted to Jewish genealogy, though not many are specifically concerned with British Jewry. A general history of Jews in Britain is provided in Shira Schoenberg's Virtual Jewish History Tour, which has a page devoted to England at <www.jewishvirtuallibrary.org/jsource/vjw/England.html>. The JewishGen site at <www.jewishgen.org> is a very comprehensive site with a number of resources relevant to Jewish ancestry in the British Isles. These include an article on researching Jewish ancestry at <www.jewishgen.org/infofiles/ukgen.txt>, and the London Jews Database <www.jewishgen.org/databases/UK/londweb.htm>, which has over 9,000 names, compiled principally from London trade directories. The Jewish genealogical magazine *Avotaynu* has a 'Five-minute Guide to Jewish Genealogical Research' at <www.avotaynu.com/jewish_genealogy.htm>. The National Archives has a Research Guide 'Anglo-Jewish History, 18th–20th Centuries: Sources in the National Archives', online at <www.catalogue.nationalarchives.gov.uk/Leaflets/ri2183.htm>. As usual, Cyndi's List has a good collection of links at <www.cyndislist.com/jewish.htm>.

The Jewish Genealogical Society of Great Britain's website at <www.jgsgb.org.uk> has a substantial collection of links to Jewish material in Britain and worldwide. It also has a number of data files available for downloading at <www.jgsgb.org.uk/downl2.shtml>. *Avotaynu* has a Consolidated Jewish Surname Index at <www.avotaynu.com/csi/csi-home.html> with over half a million names. There is a varied collection of material relating to London Jews on Jeffrey Maynard's site at <www.jeffreymaynard.com>. The Channel 4 Guide to Genealogy has material on tracing Jewish ancestry at <www.channel4.com/history/microsites/U/untold/resources/geno/geno3a.html>.

The JewishGen Family Finder (JGFF) at <www.jewishgen.org/jgff/> is a 'database of ancestral towns and surnames currently being researched by Jewish genealogists worldwide', with around 80,000 surnames submitted by 60,000 Jewish genealogists.

The Holocaust Martyrs' and Heroes' Remembrance Authority has made its central database of Shoah Victims' Names available online at <www.yadvashem.org>. The database contains some three million names of Holocaust victims. Basic searches can be made on surname, forename and locality, while the advanced search facilities offer more precise matching possibilities using year of birth and death, as well as permitting up to four locations to be specified.

The newsgroup soc.genealogy.jewish is devoted to Jewish genealogy. This group is gatewayed with the JEWISHGEN mailing list and John Fuller lists another three dozen mailing lists for Jewish genealogy at <**www. rootsweb.com/~jfuller/gen_mail_jewish.html**>. Most are specific to particular geographical areas, and JEWISHGEN and JEWISH-ROOTS are the only general interest lists. There are two discussion forums specifically relevant to Jewish communities in the British Isles:

- The BRITISH-JEWRY mailing list, details at <**lists.rootsweb.com/ index/other/Ethnic-Jewish/BRITISH-JEWRY.html**>
- The Jewish-Roots forum on British-Genealogy at <**www.british-genealogy. com/forums/forumdisplay.php?f=187**>.

HUGUENOTS

Cyndi's List has links to Huguenot resources at <**www.cyndislist.com/ huguenot.htm**>, while basic information on the Huguenots will be found on Olive Tree Genealogy at <**olivetreegenealogy.com/hug/overview.shtml**>.

There are two main mailing lists: HUGUENOTS-WALLOONS-EUROPE and a general HUGUENOT mailing list, both hosted at Roots-Web (subscription details at <**lists.rootsweb.com/index/other/Religion/**>). The former has its own website at <**www.island.net/~andreav/**> with a good collection of links and its own surnames list.

The Huguenot Surnames Index at <**www.aftc.com.au/Huguenot/ Huguenot.html**> will enable you to make contact with others researching particular Huguenot families. The Huguenot Society of Great Britain & Ireland has a website at <**www.huguenotsociety.org.uk**>. Information about the Huguenot Library, housed at University College London, will be found at <**www.ucl.ac.uk/Library/huguenot.htm**>, and information on the French Protestant Church of London is on the Institute of Historical Research site at <**www.history.ac.uk/ihr/associnstits/huguenots.mnu.html**>.

GYPSIES

There are two starting points on the web for British gypsy ancestry. The Romany & Traveller Family History Society site at <**www.rtfhs.org.uk**>, apart from society information (including a list of contents for recent issues of its magazine), has a page on 'Was Your Ancestor a Gypsy?'. This lists typical gypsy surnames, forenames and occupations. The site also has a good collection of links to other gypsy material on the web. The Gypsy Collections at the University of Liverpool site at <**sca.lib.liv.ac.uk/**

collections/gypsy/intro.htm> has information about, and photographs of, British gypsy families as well as a collection of links to other gypsy sites.

Directories of gypsy material can be found in the Open Directory at <dmoz.org/Society/Ethnicity/Romani/>, and there is more specifically genealogical material on Cyndi's List at <www.cyndislist.com/peoples. htm#Gypsies> on a page entitled 'Unique Peoples & Cultures'. BBC Kent has a Romany Voices site at <www.bbc.co.uk/kent/voices/>, which has a family history section and useful links to other Gypsy websites.

There is a UK-ROMANI mailing list for British gypsy family history, details of which will be found at <lists.rootsweb.com/index/intl/UK/ UK-ROMANI.html>.

ROYAL AND NOTABLE FAMILIES

The web has a wide range of resources relating to the genealogy of royal houses and the nobility, as well as to famous people and families. For initial orientation, Genuki's page on 'Kings and Queens of England and Scotland (and some of the people around them)' at <www.genuki.org.uk/ big/royalty/> provides a list of Monarchs since the Conquest, Kings of England, Kings of Scotland, Queens and a selection of the most notable Queens, Kings, Archbishops, Bishops, Dukes, Earls, Knights, Lords, Eminent Men, Popes and Princes. There is also a detailed table of the Archbishops of Canterbury and York, and the Bishops of London, Durham, St David's and Armagh, from AD 200 to the present day, at <www.genuki.org.uk/big/eng/History/Archbishops.html>.

Cyndi's List has a page with over 200 links relating to Royalty and Nobility at <www.cyndislist.com/royalty.htm>.

The best place for genealogical information on English royalty is Brian Tompsett's Directory of Royal Genealogical Data at <www3.dcs.hull.ac. uk/public/genealogy/royal/catalog.html>, which contains 'the genealogy of the British Royal family and those linked to it via blood or marriage relationships'. The site provides much information on other royal families, and includes details of all English peerages at <www.dcs.hull.ac.uk/public/ genealogy/royal/peerage.html>. It can be searched by name, by date, or by title. Another massive database devoted to European nobility will be found on the WW-Person site at <www8.informatik.uni-erlangen.de/html/ww-person.html>.

The official website of the royal family is at <www.royal.gov.uk> which, among other things, offers family trees of the royal houses from the ninth-century kingdom of Wessex to the present day in PDF format linked from <www.royal.gov.uk/output/Page10.asp>.

Burke's Peerage & Gentry at <www.burkes-peerage.net> have a series of indented lineages of the rulers of England and subsequently Great Britain among the free resources on its website at <www.burkes-peerage.net/sites/common/sitepages/roking.asp> covering the period from James I to George IV. This area of the site has information on all rulers of England, Scotland and Great Britain. The main material on the site is available via its subscription service, and includes data from the published books, including

- *Burke's Peerage & Baronetage*
- *Burke's Landed Gentry Scotland*
- *Burke's Landed Gentry Ireland*
- *Burke's Landed Gentry England & Wales.*

Genuki has part of *The English Peerage* (1790) online at <www.genuki.org.uk/big/eng/History/Barons/>, with information on a number of barons and viscounts of the period. Leigh Rayment's Peerage Page at <www.angeltowns.com/town/peerage/> has comprehensive information on the peerages, baronetage, House of Commons, the orders of chivalry and the Privy Council.

Royal and noble titles for many languages and countries are explained in the 'Glossary of European Noble, Princely, Royal, and Imperial Titles' at <www.heraldica.org/topics/odegard/titlefaq.htm>.

Alongside royalty and nobility, you can almost certainly find information on the web on any other genealogically notable group of people. Thus there are sites devoted to everyone from the *Mayflower* pilgrims (<www.mayflowerhistory.com/Passengers/passengers.php>) to the *Bounty* mutineers (<www.lareau.org/genweb.html>). There are countless sites devoted to biblical genealogies.

Mark Humphrys has a site devoted to the Royal Descents of Famous People at <www.compapp.dcu.ie/~humphrys/FamTree/Royal/famous.descents.html>, while Ulf Berggren provides genealogical information on many notable people from Winston Churchill to Donald Duck (really!) at <www.stacken.kth.se/~ulfb/genealogy.html>. The ancestry of the US presidents will be found on a number of sites, and <www.dcs.hull.ac.uk/public/genealogy/presidents/presidents.html> provides a tree for each of them.

The Bolles Collection has the index and epitome for the 1903 edition of the *Dictionary of National Biography* online, containing brief biographies of over 30,000 notable individuals – follow the link to the DNB from <www.perseus.tufts.edu/cache/perscoll_Bolles.html>. The easiest way to locate a particular individual is to use the search facility on this main page.

There are number of relevant mailing lists including:

- GEN-ROYAL
  <lists.rootsweb.com/index/other/Royalty_and_Nobility/GEN-ROYAL.html>

- BRITISH-NOBILITY
  <lists.rootsweb.com/index/intl/UK/BRITISH-NOBILITY.html>
- PLANTAGENET
  <lists.rootsweb.com/index/intl/UK/PLANTAGENET.html>
- SCT-ROYAL
  <lists.rootsweb.com/index/intl/SCT/SCT-ROYAL.html>
- GEN-ANCIENT
  <lists.rootsweb.com/index/other/Miscellaneous/GEN-ANCIENT.html>.

Lists for further countries will be found at <www.rootsweb.com/~jfuller/ gen_mail_nobility.html>. Yahoo has almost 100 discussion groups for royal and noble genealogy, listed at <dir.groups.yahoo.com/dir/Family_ Home/Genealogy/Royal_Genealogies>.

CLANS

Information on Scottish clans will be found among the surname resources discussed in Chapter 10, but there are also some general sites devoted to clans. The Scottish Tourist Board offers some general information about clans from its 'History' page at <www.visitscotland.com/aboutscotland/ history/>, while ScotlandsClans at <www.scotlandsclans.com> has links to sites for individual clans, as well as a message board and a mailing list. Another mailing list is CLANS, details of which can be found at <lists. rootsweb.com/index/intl/SCT/CLANS.html>, and RootsWeb has many mailing lists for individual clans, listed at <lists.rootsweb.com/index/intl/ SCT/>. However, none of these seems to be particularly thriving. There is a newsgroup, alt.scottish.clans. The Gathering of the Clans site at <www. tartans.com> has pages devoted to individual clans (with a brief history, badge, motto, tartan, etc.) and a 'Clan Finder' which matches surnames to clans. Clan maps are mentioned in Chapter 12, p. 197.

HERALDRY

Heraldry is intimately connected with royal and noble families, and there is quite a lot of material relating to it on the web. The authoritative source of information about heraldry in England and Wales is the website of the College of Arms at <www.college-of-arms.gov.uk>. Its FAQ page deals with frequently asked questions about coats of arms. The SoG has a leaflet on 'The Right to Arms' at <www.sog.org.uk/leaflets/arms.html>. For Scotland, the Lord Lyon King of Arms is the chief herald, with a website at <www.lyon-court.com>. The National Archives of Scotland is currently digitizing the armorial and genealogical information in the Lord Lyon's Public Register of All Arms and Bearings in Scotland, though no date has been announced for its online availability. Information on heraldry in Ireland will be found on the National Library of Ireland's website at <www.nli.ie/fr_offi2.htm>.

The Heraldry on the Internet site at <www.digiserve.com/heraldry/> is a specialist site with a substantial collection of links to other online heraldry resources, and Cyndi's List has a page of heraldry links at <**www. cyndislist.com/heraldry.htm**>. The British Heraldry site at <**www.heraldica. org/topics/britain/**> has a number of articles on heraldry. The Heraldry Society will be found at <**www.theheraldrysociety.com**>, while the Heraldry Society of Scotland has a site at <**www.heraldry-scotland.co.uk**>.

For the meaning of terms used in heraldry, an online version of Pimbley's 1905 *Dictionary of Heraldry* is at <**www.digiserve.com/heraldry/pimbley. htm**>, while there is an online version of James Parker's *A Glossary of Terms used in Heraldry* (1894) at <**www.heraldsnet.org/saitou/parker/**>. Burke's Peerage has a 'Guide to Heraldic Terms' taken from the 106th edition of *Burke's Peerage & Baronetage* at <**www.burkes-peerage.net/ sites/common/sitepages/heindex.asp**>. Heraldic terms will also be found in the 'Knighthood, Chivalry & Tournament Glossary of Terms' at <**www. chronique.com/Library/Glossaries/glossary-KCT/glssindx.htm**>.

CHAPTER 12

GEOGRAPHY

Maps and gazetteers are essential reference tools for family historians, and while the internet cannot offer the wealth of material available in reference libraries and record offices, let alone the British Library Map Library (website at <www.bl.uk/collections/maps.html>), there are nonetheless many useful resources online. Historical maps are quite rare, and the web has proved an ideal medium for making them much more readily accessible.

Good starting points for online maps and gazetteers are the 'Maps, Gazetteers & Geographical Information' page on Cyndi's List <www.cyndislist.com/maps.htm> and the Genuki county pages.

GAZETTEERS

While your more recent ancestors perhaps all came from places you are familiar with, the more lines you follow the more likely you are to come across somewhere you've never heard of or don't know the location of. Although your local library will have some suitable gazetteers to help you locate them, you will almost certainly find that online sources offer a much wider range of information.

MODERN

As you'd expect, one site that provides a gazetteer is the Ordnance Survey, which has a link to its place name gazetteer on its home page at <www.ordnancesurvey.co.uk>, or you can go direct to <www.ordnancesurvey.co.uk/freefun/didyouknow/>. This claims to have 250,000 place names. The search results will give you the county or unitary authority in which the place is located, a grid reference, latitude and longitude, with a link to the OS Get-a-map facility (see p. 189) showing a 2 km square area around the chosen place from the 1:25,000 OS map, which is approximately 2½ inches to the mile. Although the search does not allow wild cards you can give part of the name – as little as two letters – if you're not sure of the spelling, or you suspect you've got an old spelling. Obviously, the fewer letters you enter, the longer the search will take and the more results you'll need to examine. 'Place' is a very broad concept in this gazetteer – it covers not only towns and villages, but even many individual farms and named geographical features.

Given the comprehensive nature of the OS gazetteer, it might seem there would be little scope for competition. But the Gazetteer of British Place Names at <**www.gazetteer.co.uk**>, although it includes a mere 50,000 names, has more details about the present-day administrative divisions a place belongs in. It also includes 'commonly accepted alternative spellings and Welsh and Gaelic versions'.

Although created for a very different purpose, Archaeology UK's UK Placename Finder at <**www.digital-documents.co.uk/archi/placename. htm**> may be useful. It includes around 160,000 places and provides a sophisticated search facility. Search results show counties and grid references, with a link to two general mapping sites discussed below, Multimap and StreetMap.

HISTORICAL

Of course, a significant problem in using present-day gazetteers for the family historian is that the information they give may not be appropriate for earlier historical periods. In particular, the county name given for a place will be its modern administrative county, and for places now in a unitary authority a modern gazetteer will not even indicate which county a place used to be in. For this reason historical gazetteers are an essential online resource.

The most important historical gazetteer for the UK is A Vision of Britain through Time at <**www.visionofbritain.org.uk**>. This is the public face of the Great Britain Historical GIS ('Geographical Information System'), which is described as 'a unique body of information about the towns and villages of Britain, combining statistical information from the Census of Population between 1801 and 2001 with historical maps and descriptions'.

The site has two facilities to help with places. The Administrative Unit Search provides information on the administrative units. For an individual village, for example, it will tell you not only which county it is (or rather was) in, but the Poor Law or Registration District, any ancient hundred it was part of and the like. While none of this will help you locate a place on the map, it will indicate which records may have information on a place.

Another major part of the site is the Descriptive Gazetteer, which will eventually contain the entire text of three nineteenth-century gazetteers:

- John Goring's *Imperial Gazetteer of England and Wales* (1870–72) (still in progress)

- Frances Groome's *The Ordnance Gazetteer of Scotland* (Edinburgh: Thomas C. Jack, Grange Publishing Works, 1882–5)
- The first edition of *John Bartholomew's Gazetteer of the British Isles* (1887).

The Bartholomew descriptions are fairly concise (particularly for smaller places), while Goring's are more extensive. Note that the Bartholomew gazetteer includes the present-day Republic of Ireland. To access the entries from these, you need to go to the Descriptive gazetteer search at <**www.visionofbritain.org.uk/Search-DG/gazetteersearch.jsp**>.

Genuki has a number of historical gazetteers which are likely to be useful for family history. The main Genuki Gazetteer at <**www.genuki.org.uk/big/Gazetteer/**> (see Figure 12-2) is intended in the first instance to make it easier to locate the appropriate page on Genuki for information about a particular place. It includes the locations of nearly all the civil parishes at the time of the start of civil registration in 1837 (which form the basis of Genuki's town and parish pages), but smaller places are gradually being added and for some counties coverage is *very* comprehensive, e.g. Cornwall with over 13,000 places.

Figure 12-1 A Vision of Britain

The Genuki Church Database at <www.genuki.org.uk/big/churchdb/search.html> (see Figure 12-3) provides the locations of all churches within a given distance of a particular place (the default is three miles). Results link to the Genuki parish page, if there is one.

Genuki also has a searchable database of places in the 1891 census at <www.genuki.org.uk/big/census_place.html> (covering England, Wales and the Isle of Man only). The results give the county, district, sub-district as well as the piece number and the LDS microfilm number. There is a limited wild card facility, in that you can truncate a name to as little as the first four letters. If you type in the name of a district or sub-district, you get a list of all the places it comprises, with their piece numbers.

Darren Wheatley has a Parish Finder at <www.parishfinder.co.uk>. This allows you not only to search for the county and grid reference for any parish, but you can also search for neighbouring parishes and discover the distances between parishes.

GENUKI
Contents

GENUKI Gazetteer

Place name	County	Search type	
kingston	- Any - ⌄	Complete word ⌄	New Search

County	OS Grid ref	Parish or Township	Place
Buckinghamshire	SP900380	Kingston	
Berkshire	SU407984	Kingston Bagpuize	
	SU325870	Sparsholt	Kingston Lisle
Cambridgeshire	TL340550	Kingston	
Cheshire	SJ940950	n/k	Kingston
Cornwall	SX360750	n/k	Kingston
	SX360750	n/k	Kingston Consols Mines
	SX360758	n/k	Kingston Farm
Devon	SX903515	Brixham (St Mary)	Kingston
	SY066877	Colaton Raleigh	Kingston
	SX846540	Dittisham	Kingston
	SX635478	Kingston	
	SX795654	Staverton	Kingston House
Dorset	ST950000	Kingston Lacy	
	SY710910	Kingston Maurward	
	SY570890	Kingston Russell	

Figure 12-2 The Genuki Gazetteer

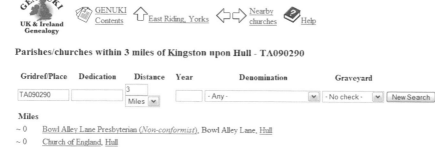

GENUKI
UK & Ireland
Genealogy

GENUKI
Contents   East Riding, Yorks   Nearby
churches   Help

Parishes/churches within 3 miles of Kingston upon Hull - TA090290

Gridref/Place	Dedication	Distance	Year	Denomination	Graveyard
TA090290		3 Miles ⌄		- Any - ⌄	- No check - ⌄ New Search

Miles

~ 0   Bowl Alley Lane Presbyterian (*Non-conformist*), Bowl Alley Lane, Hull

~ 0   Church of England, Hull

~ 0   Holy Trinity (*Church of England*), Hull

~ 0   Providence Independent (*Non-conformist*), Hull

~ 0   Sculcoates,All Saints (*Church of England*), Hull

~ 0   Sculcoates,Christchurch (*Church of England*), Hull

~ 0   St James (*Church of England*), Hull

~ 0   St Mary (*Church of England*), Hull

~ 1 N   Hull Chapel Catholic (*Roman Catholic*), Sculcoates

~ 2 E   Church of England, Drypool

~ 3 NE   Church of England, Sutton on Hull

Figure 12-3 The Genuki Church Database

SCOTLAND & IRELAND

While Scotland is included in many of the gazetteers already mentioned, there is also a major project for a specifically Scottish gazetteer based at the University of Edinburgh and accessible at <**www.geo.ed.ac.uk/ scotgaz/**>, the Gazetteer for Scotland, which is described as 'a vast database of information on places, people and families in Scotland'. Although there is a 'place search', this cannot actually be used to find towns and villages. Instead you need to use the 'any words' search at <**www.geo.cd.ac. uk/scotgaz/Anyword.html**>, and select parishes and settlements – or you could even try Attractions, Council Areas, Families, Famous People, Geographical Features or Historical Counties. This takes you to a descriptive entry for the place with details of location, and a link to a very schematic county map, though no grid reference is given. The site includes many entries from Groome's *Ordnance Gazetteer for Scotland* (1882–85) – a 'quill and parchment' icon on a place entry indicates a link to an extract from Groome.

For Ireland, there are a number of online sources to help you locate historical places. The National Archives of Ireland has an OS Parish List Index at <**www.nationalarchives.ie/cgi-bin/naigenform02?index=OS+ Parish+List**> (or go to the Finding Aids page at <**www.nationalarchives. ie/research/databases.htm**> and follow the Ordnance Survey link). The Irish Times' Irish Ancestors site has a place name search at <**scripts.ireland. com/ancestor/placenames/**>. The IreAtlas at <**www.seanruad.com**> is a database of all Irish townlands, with details of the county and civil parish. It does not give map references.

The Public Record Office of Northern Ireland has a 'Geographical Index of Northern Ireland', at <**www.proni.gov.uk/geogindx/geogindx.htm**>, which lists counties, baronies, poor law unions, dioceses, parishes, and townlands. The index is only browsable, not searchable, but there are several different routes through the material to help you find a specific place. However, I couldn't find any way of getting a single listing of all the places with a particular name.

COUNTIES AND TOWNS

As well as these national gazetteers, there are many resources for counties and larger towns. It is not possible here to give a comprehensive listing – the easiest way to find them is to go to the Genuki page for the relevant county at <**www.genuki.org.uk/big/**>. A number of local government sites provide gazetteers of their area, for example:

- Gazetteer of Greater Manchester at <**www.manchester2002-uk.com/towns/gazetteer1.html**>
- Devon Library Services have a Historic Devon Gazetteer at <**www.devon.gov.uk/library/locstudy/gazet.html**>
- The North West Kent Family History Society provides a West Kent Parish Gazetteer at <**www.nwkfhs.org.uk/PARINDEX.HTM**>
- Clare County Library has a transcription of the entries for Clare places in the *Parliamentary Gazetteer of Ireland, 1845* at <**www.clarelibrary.ie/eolas/coclare/history/parliamentary_gazeteer_1845.htm**>.

There are also many small-scale scans and transcriptions for individual places of material from historical gazetteers. If there is a Genuki page for a particular town or village, it will normally start with a brief description taken from a nineteenth-century source. Trade directories, discussed on p. 110, will also give the location of a place and other information.

For London, see p. 195.

ADMINISTRATIVE GEOGRAPHY

All towns and villages in the British Isles have a place in the administrative geography of the constituent counties, and this has not necessarily remained constant over the last few hundred years. A number of the gazetteers already mentioned include information on the administrative units to which towns and villages belong, but there are also some resources specifically devoted to this issue, which is important because it has a bearing on where records are likely to be found.

Genuki provides a general overview of Administrative Regions and, as well as pages for the individual counties, has material on 'Local Government Changes in the United Kingdom' at <**www.genuki.org.uk/big/**

Regions/UKchanges.html> with detailed tables for England, Wales, Scotland and Northern Ireland. The situation in the Republic of Ireland is more straightforward as the pre-independence counties remain. The Association of British Counties has maps of the old counties as well as the new counties and unitary authorities at <www.abcounties.co.uk/newgaz/>. It is also well worth looking at their 'Additional notes for historians and genealogists' at <www.abcounties.co.uk/newgaz/cen.htm>, which explains the difference between the historic counties, the 'registration counties' used by the GRO, and the nineteenth- and twentieth-century administrative counties and county boroughs.

Genuki has maps of the counties of England, Wales and Scotland at <www.genuki.org.uk/big/Britain.html> and of Ireland at <www.genuki.org.uk/big/Ireland.html>. Each Genuki county page also has a description of the county, usually drawn from a nineteenth-century directory or similar source.

If you are from outside the UK and are not familiar with the counties and other administrative divisions you will find Jim Fisher's page 'British Counties, Parishes, etc. for Genealogists' at <homepages.nildram.co.uk/~jimella/counties.htm> useful.

Where counties have changed their boundaries over the years, the individual Genuki county pages will provide relevant details. The complex set of changes which, in less than a hundred years, saw parts of the home counties, and indeed the whole of Middlesex, incorporated into the capital are dealt with on the Genuki London site at <homepages.gold.ac.uk/genuki/LND/parishes.html>. The major local government reorganization of 1974 saw the creation of new counties and boroughs. The former Department of the Environment, Transport and the Regions had a useful page on the current structure of local government. It is no longer officially available but cached versions are still available at Google and Yahoo Search – links are available on the website for this book.

Genealogists almost always refer to pre-1974 counties, and any genealogical material on the internet is likely to reflect that. This is why there are no pages on Genuki for Tyne and Wear or the present-day Welsh counties. But non-genealogical sites will tend to locate places in their current counties, even if the material is from the nineteenth century – a number of the sites with photographs discussed in Chapter 14 do this, for example.

Counties are often referred to by three-letter abbreviations, the Chapman County Codes, e.g. SFK for Suffolk. A list of these can be found on Genuki at <www.genuki.org.uk/big/Regions/Codes.html>.

OVERSEAS

Gazetteers may be even more important if you have ancestors who migrated. It is not possible here to cover individual countries outside the

British Isles, but there are a number of places to look. As you would expect, Cyndi's List has links to many online gazetteers. They are included in the 'Maps, Gazetteers & Geographical Information' page at <www.cyndislist.com/maps.htm> under two distinct headings: 'Historical Maps, Atlases & Gazetteers' and 'National Gazetteers & Geographic Information', of which the latter has the most useful entries.

The National Library of Australia has a useful page devoted to Gazetteers of the World and Beyond at <www.nla.gov.au/map/worldgazetteers. html> (the 'Beyond' indicates the inclusion of a planetary gazetteer). This includes not only links to online sources, but to some gazetteers available in print and on CD-ROM.

The most comprehensive world gazetteer is the Getty Thesaurus of Geographic Names Online at <www.getty.edu/research/conducting_ research/vocabularies/tgn/>. Even for the UK this is useful, since it includes geographical, and some historical information (see Figure 12-4). However, it is not intended to be comprehensive and concentrates on larger places. For example, it gives only one place in Ireland called Inch, while the Irish Ancestors site lists a dozen.

If these resources fail to find your place, then see if there is a mailing list devoted to the country you are interested in – listed by John Fuller at

Figure 12-4 The Getty Thesaurus of Geographic Names

<www.rootsweb.com/~jfuller/gen_mail.html> – and post a query. There will almost certainly be people on the list with suitable reference works to hand or even local knowledge.

MODERN MAPS

As with gazetteers, the OS website at <www.ordnancesurvey.co.uk> is the obvious starting point for any information about present-day mapping of the British Isles. This provides a facility called Get-a-map at <www.getamap.co.uk>, which allows you to call up a map centred on a particular place. You can search by place name, postcode, or OS grid reference. Alternatively, you can just click on the map of the UK and gradually zoom in to your chosen area. The maps are free for personal use (including limited use on personal websites). There is also an option to go to the nineteenth-century OS maps discussed in 'Historical maps', below.

A relatively unknown source of OS maps for England is the MAGIC (Multi-Agency Geographic Information for the Countryside) site at <www.magic.gov.uk>. The site is designed to provide information for countryside management, shown in a number of layers, over a base map, which is a monochrome modern OS map. MAGIC has a number of advantages over the Get-a-map service. The first is that you can get a much higher level of detail – the Get-a-map site at a scale of 1:25,000 while MAGIC

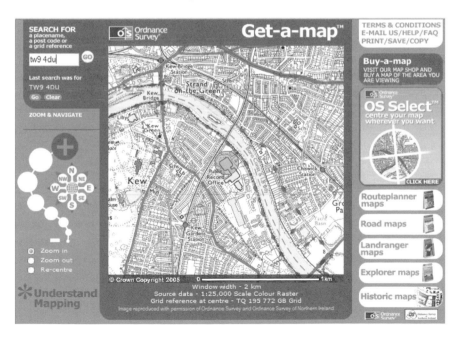

Figure 12-5 The National Archives in Get-a-map

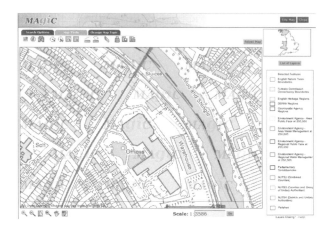

Figure 12-6
The National Archives
in MAGIC

allows you to go up to 1:101.[10] Also, it shows a much larger area: a rectangle 6×4 km, compared with a 2 km square in Get-a-map.

Another useful feature of MAGIC is that it shows modern civil parish boundaries. While it is true that in urban areas these won't match historical ecclesiastical boundaries, for rural areas the site provides the closest thing we have to an online parish map. Because this site is designed for specialist use, it is more complex to use than those designed for the general public. To access the maps, from the home page you need to choose Interactive Map, then choose Administrative Areas from the top field, and enter a place, postcode or grid reference in the lower. There are many options once you are viewing a map. A Map Tools tab gives access to a a range of tools, including the ability to identify an area, and to save a map as a GIF file. You can also bookmark the current view.

There are three main sites that provide free UK streetmaps. Streetmap at <**www.streetmap.co.uk**> allows searches by street, postcode, place name, OS grid, Landranger grid, latitude/longitude, or telephone code. Multimap at <**uk.multimap.com**> offers similar facilities: the initial search option offers place or postcode, while the advanced search includes building and street. Google Maps launched a UK map site in spring 2005 at <**maps.google.co.uk**>. So far this only shows streets, and doesn't indicate even quite major landmarks (e.g. Canterbury Cathedral, Stonehenge).

Genuki has instructions on 'How to find a present day house, street or place in the U.K. (or to find only the Post Code)' by using the Royal Mail site or the Multimap site at <**www.genuki.org.uk/big/ModernLocations.html**>.

Both Streetmap and Multimap provide aerial photographs, often at quite a high level of detail, for cities and some other parts of the country. On

---

10 The British Library has a useful page showing different map scales at <**www.bl.uk/collections/map_scale.html**>.

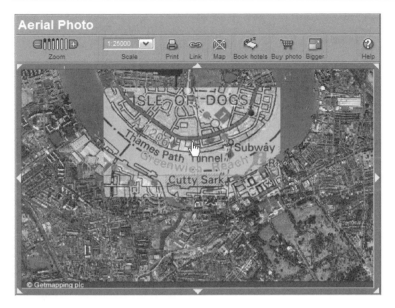

Figure 12-7 Multimap: an aerial photograph of Greenwich, with OS map overlay

the Multimap photographs, the cursor allows you to move a transparent overlay of the OS map, which is useful for identifying places and streets (see Figure 12-7). Google Maps has a satellite mapping option covering the whole country (and indeed the whole world), though resolution varies from area to area. There are various levels of zoom, options to rotate and tilt the images, and very quick panning. The same images can be viewed in Google Earth, a free downloadable viewer for satellite maps at <earth.google.com>. This has the advantage of an overlay showing roads and streetnames. It also offers a 'placemark' facility. Because of the amount of data transferred, Google Earth requires a broadband connection and a fairly recent Windows PC. With an older machine you will need to check whether your graphics card is supported before downloading.

HISTORICAL MAPS

The best-known site for historical maps is Old-maps at <www.old-maps. co.uk>. This is a free site, run by a commercial mapping company, which has scans of the First Series of 6-inch Ordnance Survey maps of England, Wales and Scotland. These maps date from the latter half of the nineteenth century.

You can either do a place name search to locate the map for the area you are interested in, or use the county gazetteer to select from a list. The initial map image that comes up when you select a place is too small to see any but the most obvious geographical detail, but once you zoom in,

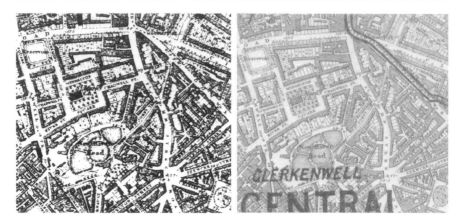

Figure 12-8 Old-maps and the Boundary Commission maps compared

the resolution is sufficient to read the smallest text. In all but the most heavily built-up areas, individual buildings and plots of land can be made out clearly. However, while the resolution is good, the scans are black and white rather than greyscale, which tends to give poor results where the original has shading or where text is overlaid on map detail.

There are also options to see a modern map of the same area – the OS 1-inch map – or a modern aerial photograph (though this option is not available for Scotland). Your browser will allow you to save the map to a file for subsequent cropping or editing.

Another site with nineteenth-century Ordnance Survey maps is the London Ancestor's collection of maps from the report of the 1885 Boundary Commission, which includes Ireland as Old-maps does not. All are linked from the 'Genealogy Documents' page at <**www.londonancestor. com/misc/misc.htm**>. For Wales and Scotland, only a selection of counties and towns are included. Because these maps have been scanned as greyscale images, they are generally preferable to the scans on Old-maps when looking at urban areas. However, since the aim of these maps was to show the names and boundaries of electoral divisions, detail is sometimes obscured by overwritten text or hand-drawn lines. Figure 12-8 offers a comparison using the area south of the Angel Islington: on the left is the black and white scan at Old-maps, while on the right is the same area in greyscale on the London Ancestors site.

The Boundary Commission county maps are at a larger scale and therefore less detailed than the 6-inch maps on Old-Maps, which means they are less good for rural areas, though they do have the advantage of showing parish boundaries very clearly.

There are two particularly useful volunteer-run sites that offer a wide selection of historical maps of the British Isles. Genmaps at <**freepages.**

genealogy.rootsweb.com/~genmaps/> covers England, Wales and Scotland and has an enormous collection of maps for the counties, as well as many for individual towns and cities. The site doesn't give a figure for the total number of maps available, but it must be well over 1,000 – there are 100 just for Yorkshire, and even Rutland is represented by 40 maps. Genmaps also has an extensive collection of links to other historical map sites, including those of several dozen commercial map-dealers, many of whom have low resolution scans on their sites.

A smaller but nonetheless very worthwhile collection is that of Your Maps Online at <www.yourmapsonline.org.uk>. This site invites users to submit scans of out-of-copyright maps in their possession, and currently boasts around 250 maps. There is an index page for each county with thumbnails of the images available, which link to the full-size images. There is also an alphabetical index to the whole collection. Many of the maps have been scanned at very high resolution, so you need to be prepared for some long downloads if you have a dialup connection. This site also has its own user forums.

Apart from these two major sites, many other individuals have scanned classic historical maps and map editions. For example, Tom Arnold has put on his personal website scans of all Samuel Lewis's county maps of Wales and Ireland dating from around 1840. These are linked from <homepage.ntlworld.com/tomals/index2.htm>. John Speed's early seventeenth-century maps of around 30 English towns and cities (plus Edinburgh) have been digitized by Professor Maryanne Horowitz of Occidental College, Los Angeles and are available at <faculty.oxy.edu/horowitz/home/johnspeed/>. Maproom.org has maps from Cary's Traveller's Companion of 1790, showing main roads and distances, at very high resolution at <www.maproom.org/maps/britain/cary/turnpikes/>.

There are also maps from some more modern printed works which are likely to be of interest. For example, Alan Gresley has scanned the town plans from the 1910 edition of Baedeker's *Great Britain Handbook for Travelers* at <contueor.com/baedeker/great_britain/>.

There is no online map collection from the British Library, though the BL's Images Online website at <www.imagesonline.bl.uk> includes some digitized maps. These can be found by selecting the 'Maps and Views' link from the Subject Index.

Another source for historical maps online may be the sites of commercial map-dealers, many of whose websites have scans of the maps they have for sale. For example, Heritage Publishing at <www.heritagepublishing.com> has scans of some of John Speed's 1610 maps of the British counties. It is well worth using a search engine to locate sites which have the phrase 'antique maps' and the town or county of your choice.

LOCAL PROJECTS

In addition to the sections for individual counties on Genmaps and Your Maps Online, there are many sites with map collections for individual counties and towns.

The University of Portsmouth's Geography department hosts two county collections each with a very comprehensive range of historical county maps going back to the sixteenth century:

- Old Hampshire Mapped at <www.geog.port.ac.uk/webmap/hantsmap/hantsmap/hantsmap.htm>
- Old Sussex Mapped at <www.envf.port.ac.uk/geo/research/historical/webmap/sussexmap/sussex.html>.

For County Durham, Pictures in Print at <www.dur.ac.uk/picturesinprint/> is a collaborative project between the British Library and the various holders of map archives in Durham to produce an online catalogue for the maps of the county along with digital images (see Figure 12-9). To view the images, you will need to download a plug-in.[11]

Tomorrow's History at <www.tomorrows-history.com> is a local history site for the North East of England, with a map viewing system which allows you to compare maps from any two periods since the mid-nineteenth century.

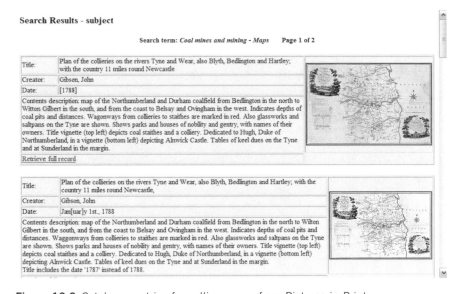

Figure 12-9 Catalogue entries for colliery maps from Pictures in Print

---

11 The plug-in downloads automatically for Internet Explorer, but may need to be manually installed for other browsers.

Here's History Kent at <www.hereshistorykent.org.uk> has maps of historic towns with historical areas and buildings marked on an overlay over the OS map or an aerial view – search for a town then select 'GIS Mapping' from the sidebar.

Since Tithe Maps are primary sources for genealogists they are discussed in Chapter 8 on p. 104.

PARISH MAPS

Maps of the ancient ecclesiastical parishes are among the most useful for the family historian. Of the national collections, the London Ancestor's Boundary Commission maps and MAGIC show more recent parish boundaries, but there is no guarantee that these match the older boundaries.

The definitive parish maps for an older period are those published in *Historic Parishes of England & Wales*, available on CD (details at <www.ex.ac.uk/geography/research/boundaries.html>). The reason for mentioning them here is that the authors, Roger Kain and Richard Oliver, allow the maps to be published online, and you will find a number of them available on Genuki parish pages, such as Brian Randell's pages for Devon parishes at <www.genuki.cs.ncl.ac.uk/DEV/indexpars.html> and my own for Sussex at <homepages.gold.ac.uk/genuki/SSX/parishes.html>.

Many other Genuki county pages have a map showing the parishes within the county, and each family history society has a map showing the location of the parishes for their area, which many of them make available on their website. Look at Genuki's list of FHSs at <www.genuki.org.uk/Societies/>.

LONDON

There is an enormous wealth of online maps for London, many of which show individual streets. Genmaps has scans of around 70 historical maps, plans and panoramas of London at <freepages.genealogy.rootsweb.com/~genmaps/genfiles/COU_Pages/ENG_pages/lon.htm> from the 1560s to 1920, including John Roque's detailed 24-sheet map of 1746, and many plans of City wards. The site also has many county maps for Middlesex, though these are mostly not at the same level of detail.

The Collage server at <collage.cityoflondon.gov.uk> includes many maps and plans among its 20,000 or so images, mainly drawn from the Guildhall Library's Print Room. Particularly useful is the place search, which links to plans of individual City wards and parishes. There are also many views of individual streets, as well as insurance plans showing the locations of individual buildings. High resolution digital files of the images can be purchased online.

If you are trying to find a London street mentioned in a census but which no longer appears on the A–Z, then the Lost London Streets site

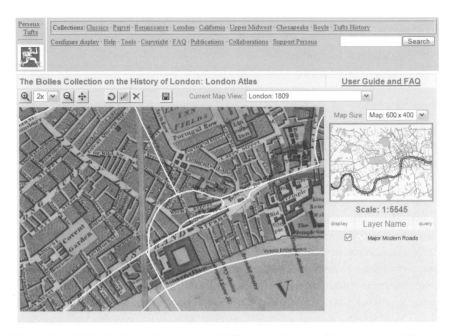

Figure 12-10 The Bolles collection: An 1809 map of London (Drury Lane and the Strand) with an overlay of the modern street plan (showing the later position of Kingsway and the Aldwych).

at <members.aol.com/WHall95037/london.html> will be worth visiting. This gives an A–Z reference with details of what happened to the street. It covers over 3,500 streets that have undergone a name change or have disappeared altogether over the last 200 years. GenDocs' Victorian London Street index will be found at <www.gendocs.demon.co.uk/lon-str.html>. For over 61,000 streets this gives a postal district or locality and metropolitan borough, but no more precise location. For an earlier period, The London Ancestor has a street index to W. Stow's 1722 *Remarks on London: Being an Exact Survey of the Cities of London and Westminster, Borough of Southwark, and the Suburbs and Liberties contigious to them, shewing every Street, Lane, Court, Alley, Green, Yard, Close, Square, or any other Place, by what Name soever called, is situated in the most Famous Metropolis* at <www.londonancestor.com/stow/stow-strx-all. htm>.

The Bolles Collection London Map Browser at <www.perseus.tufts.edu/ cgi-bin/city-view.pl> has digitized copies of two dozen maps of London from the seventeenth to the nineteenth century. There is an optional overlay of the modern street pattern and the ability to identify streets and major buildings by location or name (see Figure 12-10). Once you have chosen a particular grid square to view, you can then select different maps to see how the area looked at different periods. There is also a London Atlas.

MOTCO has historical maps and panoramas of London from 1705 onwards at <www.motco.com/map/>. Some maps have place indexes – for example Stanford's 1862 Library Map of London and its Suburbs has an index to around 5,000 streets with a link to the relevant portion of the map.

One of the most famous London maps, Charles Booth's 1889 Map of London Poverty is available on the LSE's Charles Booth site at <**booth.lse. ac.uk**>, which shows Booth's original map against a modern one.

SCOTLAND

Scotland is particularly well served by historical map digitization projects, and there are two outstanding sites for maps of Scotland.

Charting the Nation at <**www.chartingthenation.lib.ed.ac.uk**> is run by the University of Edinburgh Library and has maps for the period 1550–1740. (In fact, there are some later maps, as the site includes The Board of Ordnance collection of military maps and architectural plans dating from around 1690 to about 1820.) While some of the maps are at too small a scale to be of any genealogical utility, there are others, such as the 1792 map of Glasgow (Figure 12-11) which are detailed enough to show individual streets and street names.

The other major site for Scottish maps is that of the National Library of Scotland which has four map collections in its Digital Library at <**www.nls.uk/digitallibrary/map/**>

• Maps of Scotland 1560–1928 (around 1,300 maps)
• Pont's Maps of Scotland c.1583–c.1596
• Military Maps of Scotland (eighteenth century)
• Ordnance Survey town plans 1847–1895.

To view many of the maps requires a plug-in (called ExpressView) which you will need to download.

The Maps of Scotland area of the site includes many county maps and town plans. The OS town plans are probably the most useful to the family historians, covering 62 towns in over 1,900 sheets at an extraordinary level of detail. The quality of the scans is excellent.

Other notable items include Bartholomew's 1912 *Survey Atlas of Scotland*. Of specifically genealogical interest is Lizars' 1822 'Map of the Highlands of Scotland denoting the districts or counties inhabited by the Highland Clans'. Each can be found by going to Maps of Scotland and choosing the publisher from the 'Surveyor/Mapmaker/Engraver' dropdown list.

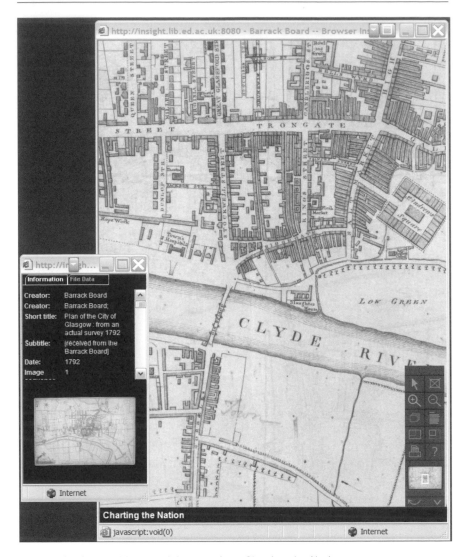

Figure 12-11 A 1792 plan of Glasgow from Charting the Nation

Another map of the clans is provided by Scot Roots at <**www.scotroots. com/clan-map.htm**>.

IRELAND

Probably the most useful set of maps of Ireland for the genealogist are the Boundary Commission county maps on the London Ancestor site at <**www. londonancestor.com/maps/maps-ireland.htm**>. For Counties Roscommon and Leitrim, there is a very comprehensive set of maps showing Roman

Catholic and civil parishes, as well as poor law unions at <www. leitrim-roscommon.com/LR_maps.html>.

The University of Wisconsin-Madison has some maps of Ireland, including a Poor Law map, at <history.wisc.edu/archdeacon/famine/ map.html>. The Perry-Castañeda Library has a 1610 town plan of Dublin at <www.lib.utexas.edu/maps/historical/dublin_1610_1896.jpg>.

MAP COLLECTIONS

For guides to archival map collections, the British Cartographic Society's 'A Directory of UK Map Collections' at <www.cartography.org.uk/Pages/ Publicat/Ukdir/UKDirect.html> is a very comprehensive starting point.

The catalogues of the archives and libraries mentioned in Chapter 9 include map holdings. The National Archives has a Research Guide 'Maps in the Public Record Office' at <www.catalogue.nationalarchives.gov.uk/ Leaflets/ri2179.htm>, while PRONI's map holdings are described at <www.proni.gov.uk/records/maps.htm>.

The national libraries all have significant map collections which are described on their websites:

- The British Library <www.bl.uk/collections/maps.html>
- The National Library of Scotland <www.nls.uk/collections/maps/>
- The National Library of Wales <www.llgc.org.uk/dm/dm0067.htm>
- The National Library of Ireland <www.nli.ie/co_maps.htm>.

FINDING MAPS

Of course, there are many more maps online than it has been possible to mention here, particularly for local areas. Some of the larger sites mentioned have good collections of links, but there are two other obvious places to look for links to other online maps. First, the Genuki page for a county or parish (start from <www.genuki.org.uk/big/>) should have a range of links to relevant maps and some of the parish pages have a map of the parish.

For older maps on a worldwide basis, probably the best starting point is the Map History gateway at <www.maphistory.info/webimages.html>, maintained by Tony Campbell, former Map Librarian of the British Library. The Europe page at <www.maphistory.info/imageeur.html> has links to over 60 sites with individual maps or map collections for the British Isles.

For map collections of local coverage it will always be worth checking the websites of the relevant record offices, whose online catalogues are also good places to start looking for details of the maps which aren't online.

CHAPTER 13

HISTORY

While family history is concerned mainly with individual ancestors, both their lives and the documents that record them cannot be understood without a broader historical appreciation of the times in which they lived. The same can be said of the historical documents essential to genealogical research. The aim of this chapter is to look at some of the general historical material on the internet that is likely to be of use to family historians.

LOCAL AND SOCIAL HISTORY

LOCAL HISTORY

For introductory material on local history the Local History page on the BBC History site at <**www.bbc.co.uk/history/lj/locallj/index.shtml**> is a good starting point. As well as describing what is involved in local history, it looks at how to approach the history of a factory, a landscape and a village, by way of example. The National Archives site has a local history section at <**www.nationalarchives.gov.uk/localhistory/**> with introductory material and a guide to the relevant national records.

If you want guidance on where to find information and sources, then the 'Getting Started' page on the *Local History Magazine* website at <**www.local-history.co.uk/gettingstarted.html**> will prove useful. Sites with information on repositories which hold sources for local history are covered in Chapter 9.

It would be unrealistic to expect much of the printed material on local history to be available online, but the *Victoria County History* at <**www. englandpast.net**> has a lottery-funded project to create an online edition. This project is still in the early stages – there are 14 county websites with varying amounts of material, all linked from <**www.englandpast.net/ vch_counties.html**>.

The British History Online site, run by the University of London's Institute for Historical Research, has an increasing number of volumes from the VCH online at <www.british-history.ac.uk> as well as a number of other local history sources.

Chris Phillips, who runs the very useful Medieval English Genealogy site at <www.medievalgenealogy.org.uk>, has compiled an index to place names mentioned in the titles of topographical articles in the published volumes of the VCH. This can be found at <www.medievalgenealogy. org.uk/vch/>.

For Scotland, the *Statistical Accounts of Scotland* at <edina.ac.uk/ statacc/> are a major source. These accounts, dating from the 1790s and 1830s, are descriptive rather than financial, and offer 'a rich record of a wide variety of topics: wealth, class and poverty; climate, agriculture, fishing and wildlife; population, schools, and the moral health of the people'. The site has images of every page of the original printed volumes, and there is an index by county and parish to take you straight to the place of interest.

There is an increasing amount of material online for individual cities, towns and villages. County record offices are among those exploiting the web to publish online resources for local history, and there are a number of lottery-funded projects to put local history material online. Some of the more notable sites are:

- Knowsley (Lancs) Local History <history.knowsley.gov.uk>
- Digital Handsworth <www.digitalhandsworth.org.uk> (see Figure 13-1)
- Wiltshire Community History <www.wiltshire.gov.uk/community/>
- The Kingston Local History project at <localhistory.kingston.ac.uk/ contributePages/klhp.html> (Kingston-on-Thames)
- Tomorrow's History <www.tomorrows-history.com> (North East of England)
- PortCities <www.portcities.org.uk> (ports of Bristol, Hartlepool, Liverpool, London, Southampton)
- Powys Heritage Online <history.powys.org.uk>
- Swansea History Web at <www.swanseahistoryweb.org.uk>
- The Gaelic Village <www.ambaile.org.uk/en/> (Scottish Highlands and Islands).

Some of these have online data as well as general historical material. See also the local photographic collections mentioned on pp. 220.

The easiest way to see if there are any lottery-funded local history projects in progress for a place you are interested in is to go to the EnrichUK website at <www.enrichuk.org.uk>. Selecting the 'Browse' option, then 'Geographic', then the region and sub-region of your choice, will bring up a list of all projects for the locality.

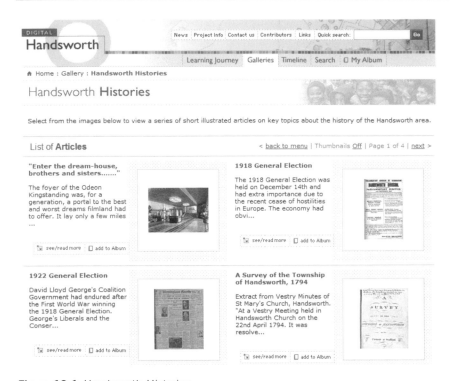

Figure 13-1 Handsworth Histories

There are many examples of small data extracts for local areas. They include:

- Tithe Titles for Kelsall, Cheshire <www.the-dicksons.org/Kelsall/kelsall/tithespg.htm>
- Tithe Book of Bolton with Goldthorpe, 1839 <www.genuki.org.uk/big/eng/YKS/WRY/Boltonupondearne/TitheBook/>
- The English Surnames Survey has a number of local datasets at <www.le.ac.uk/elh/pot/intro/intro3a.html>, including Lay Subsidy transcriptions for Lincolnshire (1332) and Rutland (1296/7), and some Poll Tax databases.

A more comprehensive approach is represented by the Online Parish Clerk (OPC) schemes. Each county scheme has volunteers transcribing historical records for individual parishes. So far, there are schemes for Cornwall, Cumberland & Westmorland, Devon, Dorset, Kent, Lancashire, Sussex and Wiltshire. Links to the websites of these projects, which will link in turn to the pages for individual parishes, will be found on Genuki's OPC page at <www.genuki.org.uk/indexes/OPC.html>. The Genuki county and parish pages themselves include descriptive extracts from historical directories and have links to other local transcriptions.

David Hawgood's book *One-Place Genealogy* is designed to help genealogists find studies about the places their ancestors lived. The entire text of the book is online at <www.hawgood.co.uk/opg/>, with a list of studies by county at <www.hawgood.co.uk/opg/counties.htm> which is kept up to date. There is a ONE-PLACE-STUDY mailing list for those involved in studying a single parish or group of parishes, details of which can be found at <lists.rootsweb.com/index/other/Miscellaneous/ONE-PLACE-STUDY. html>. British-Genealogy hosts a number of discussion forums for one-place studies, listed under the individual counties at <www.british-genealogy. com/forums/forumdisplay.php?f=2>.

An interesting resource is the English Accents and Dialects collection at <www.collectbritain.co.uk/collections/dialects/>, which includes sound recordings of speakers from the northern counties of England talking about their lives. Quite apart from their linguistic interest – local vocabulary is listed – the interviews are a source of oral history for local historians, with each speaker's name, age and locality given.

Curious Fox at <www.curiousfox.com> is a site which provides message boards for local history and genealogy. While most mailing lists are county-based, this is different in that it is based on a gazetteer of over 50,000 town and villages in the British Isles (including 3,000 in Ireland), each with its own page. You can search for the settlement name, generate lists of nearby villages and hamlets, and link to the exact location on Multimap and Old-maps. You can also search by family name. The site calls itself 'semi commercial': you can join and use the site free of charge, but a subscription of £5 provides additional facilities, including an automatic email when someone adds a message relating to a town or village you have stored as a place of interest. Without a subscription you can only contact subscribers.

SOCIAL HISTORY

Although the web provides material on any aspect of social history you care to name, from slavery to education, it is difficult to know what you can expect to find on a given topic in terms of quality and coverage. In view of the large number of possible subjects which come under 'social history', and the very general application of these headings (education, poverty, etc.), using a search engine to locate them can be quite time-consuming. However, if you know any terms that refer only to historical material (1840 Education Act, Poor Law, etc.) this may make searching easier. Also, local history sites such as those discussed above are likely to include some material on social history and local museums, and may provide useful links to non-local material.

For more recent local and social history, local newspapers are an important source, and these are discussed on p. 105.

Where aspects of social history are bound up with the state, you can expect to find some guidance on official sites. The National Archives, for example, has Research Guides on Education, Enclosures, Lunacy and Lunatic Asylums, Outlawry, and the Poor Law, among other subjects – see <www.catalogue.nationalarchives.gov.uk/researchguidesindex.asp>. Records relating to crime and punishment are discussed on pp. 156f.

A comprehensive guide to social history sites is beyond the scope of this book, but the following examples may give a taste of some of the resources on the internet.

Professor George P. Landow's Victorian Web includes an overview of Victorian Social History at <www.scholars.nus.edu.sg/landow/victorian/> with a considerable amount of contemporary documentation. This site, incidentally, was one of the first to use the web to make linked historical materials available.

The Workhouses site at <www.workhouses.org.uk> provides a comprehensive introduction to the workhouse and the laws relating to it, along with lists of workhouses in England, Wales and Scotland, and a guide to workhouse records (see Figure 13-2). The Rossbret Institutions site at <www.institutions.org.uk> has information not only on workhouses but on a wide range of institutions, including Asylums, Almshouses, Prisons, Dispensaries, Hospitals, Reformatories, and Orphanages.

GenDocs has a list of 'Workhouses, Hospitals, Lunatic Asylums, Prisons, Barracks, Orphan Asylums, Convents, and other Principal Charitable Institutions' in London in 1861 at <www.gendocs.demon.co.uk/institute.html>.

Hidden Lives at <www.hiddenlives.org.uk> is a site devoted to children in care between 1881 and 1918. It has details of around 170 care homes and many histories of individual children (not named). There are useful links to other online sources relating to children and poverty.

The Powys Heritage Online project mentioned above has sections devoted to crime and punishment, education and schools, religion in Wales, and care of the poor, at <history.powys.org.uk/history/intro/themes.html>, which make use of original documents and photographs.

Scots Origins has a number of articles on aspects of Scottish social history at <www.scotsorigins.com/help/popup-resarticles-so.htm>.

Electric Scotland has a substantial account of the 'Social History of the Highlands' at <www.electricscotland.com/history/social/> taken from a nineteenth-century work. The site has much other material on Scottish history.

Finally, the Spartacus Educational site at <www.spartacus.schoolnet. co.uk> is a model of what can be done with historical material on the

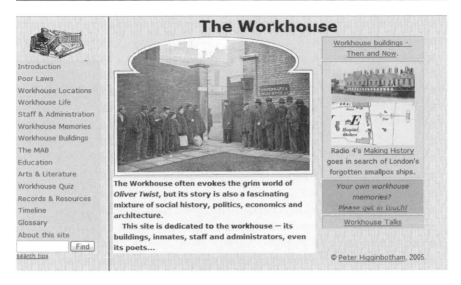

Figure 13-2 The Workhouse site at <**www.workhouses.org.uk**>

web. It has information on many topics in social history since the mid-eighteenth century, such as child labour, the railways, the textile industry and female emancipation. The site contains both general information and historical documents. The pages devoted to the textile industry, for example, at <**www.spartacus.schoolnet.co.uk/Textiles.htm**>, contain general information on the machinery, the various occupations within the industry and the nature of daily life in the textile factory, but also include biographical material on individual inventors, entrepreneurs and factory workers, the latter taken from interviews before a House of Commons Committee in 1832.

SOCIETIES

There are at least as many groups devoted to local history as there are family history societies, though of course not all of them have websites. A comprehensive listing for all parts of the UK and Ireland is provided by *Local History* magazine in the Local History Directory at <**www. local-history.co.uk/Groups/**>. This gives contact details including email addresses and websites where available. But you should note that many of the entries in this listing have not been updated for some time, so quite a few links no longer work and it is probably not a reliable guide to which societies have *no* web presence. Knowing the name of a society, however, it is a simple matter to use a search engine to see if it has its own site. The British Association for Local History has a select list of links to local history society websites at <**www.balh.co.uk/links.htm**>.

MAILING LISTS

Most of the genealogical mailing lists for counties, areas, and individual places are useful for local history queries, and there are some lists which specifically include local history in their remit. For example, the sussex-past group on Yahoo Groups at **<groups.yahoo.com/group/sussexpast/>** describes its interests as 'Discussions and questions/answers on archaeology, local history, museums and architecture in Sussex.' HAMPSHIRE-LIFE, which has its own website at **<freepages.genealogy.rootsweb.com/ ~villages/>**, is for discussion not only of genealogy but also the 'history of towns and villages; folklore; songs, poetry and sonnets; and nostalgic pictures'.

LOCAL-HISTORY is a general mailing list for the British Isles, which is hosted by JISCmail, the national academic mailing list service. You can see the archive of past messages for the list at **<www.jiscmail.ac.uk/lists/ local-history.html>** and there are also instructions on how to subscribe. RootsWeb is host to a list for Wales – details at **<lists.rootsweb.com/index/ intl/WLS/WALES-LOCAL-HISTORY.html>**.

▌ N A M E S

ORIGINS

A regular topic on mailing lists and newsgroups is the origin of surnames. When talking about surnames, though, the term 'origin' has two distinct meanings: how the name came about linguistically (its etymology); and where it originated geographically (its home). Unfortunately there is little reliable information on the web relating to the first of these. The definitive sources for British surname etymologies are the modern printed surname dictionaries, which are not available online. If you are lucky you may find a surname site that quotes and gives references for the relevant dictionary entries for your particular surname, but in the absence of source references you should treat etymological information given on genealogy websites as unreliable. Even where sources are given, you should be cautious – some of the older surname dictionaries cited are the work of amateurs rather than scholars.

An Ancestry subscription will give you access to Bardsley's 1901 *Dictionary of English and Welsh Surnames* (see **<www.ancestry.co.uk/ search/db.aspx?dbid=7300>**). William Arthur's 1857 *An Etymological Dictionary of Family and Christian Names With an Essay on their Derivation and Import* is used as the source for surname dictionaries at Ancestor Search at **<www.searchforancestors.com/surnames/origin>** and, without acknowledgement, Last Name Meanings at **<www.last-names.net>**. Neither of these is a substitute for a modern surname dictionary, though

William Arthur's 'Essay On The Origin And Import Of Family Names' at <www.searchforancestors.com/surnames/origin/essay.html> is still a useful brief introduction to the general sources of surnames.

There are two mailing lists devoted to discussion of surname etymology. SURNAME-ORIGINS-L is a US-based list devoted to the etymology and distribution of surnames, and details can be found at <members.tripod. com/~Genealogy_Infocenter/surname-origins.html>. The English Surname List (ESL) is a forum for discussion of the etymology, history and significance of surnames in England. It has a website at <www.jiscmail.ac.uk/ lists/esl.html> with an archive of past messages and a web form for joining the list.

Cyndi's List has a page devoted to surnames in general at <www. cyndislist.com/surn-gen.htm>.

VARIANTS

There is no definitive online source to help you to decide whether surname X is in fact a variant of surname Y, or what variant spellings you can expect for a surname. However, if a name has been registered with the Guild of One-Name Studies the Guild's online register at <www.one-name. org/register.shtml> may give some indication of major variants, and it will be worth contacting the person who has registered it. Posting a query about variants on one of the many surname mailing lists and query boards (see Chapter 15) would also be a sensible step.

The Thesaurus of British Surnames is a project to develop an online thesaurus of British surname variants. The ToBS website at <www.tobs. org.uk> does not have details of individual variants as yet but has a number of resources relating to the issues of surname matching, including papers on the problems of identifying surname variants, and a comprehensive bibliography on the subject.

There are a number of computerized surname-matching schemes. The most widely used, though it has severe shortcomings, is Soundex, which is described at <www.archives.gov/genealogy/census/soundex.html>. A more recent development is the proprietary NameX, which is used by Origins and 1837online, which is briefly described at <www.imagepart- ners.co.uk/Thesaurus/AboutNameX.htm>. The ToBS web-site has links to online versions of some of these at <www.tobs.org.uk/links/online. html>.

DISTRIBUTION

Looking at the geographical distribution in a major database such as FamilySearch at <www.familysearch.org> can sometimes be helpful, though you should be cautious about drawing etymological inferences from distributional information in this sort of database.

Harry Wykes has a site devoted to Surname Distribution Analysis at <**www.wykes.org/dist/**>, which produces distribution maps for individual surnames. To use the site, you need to have the 1881 census on CD-ROM, and you can then extract and upload the data for a surname, from which the site will create a distribution map, which you can then download (Figure 13-3). There are also distribution maps for around 300 surnames in the 1881 census at <**members.lycos.co.uk/ancestors/surnamedistribution.html**>.

Barry Griffin has surname distribution maps for Cornwall, the Isle of Man, Ireland and Scotland at <**baz.perlmonk.org**> (though you'll have to scroll past some political material).

GRO(S) has an Occasional Paper on 'Surnames in Scotland over the last 140 years' linked from <**www.gro-scotland.gov.uk/statistics/library/geninfo/**>. There are lists of the ten most common surnames in each county, according to the 1901 census, at <**www.gro-scotland.gov.uk/files/01surnames_tablea7.pdf**>

Philip Dance's Modern British Surnames site at <**homepages.newnet.co.uk/dance/webpjd/**> is designed as a guide to the resources for the study of surname frequency and distribution. The site also includes discussion of the various approaches to surname origins, and has interesting statistical material. A site covering local names is Graham Thomas's Gloucestershire Names and their Occurrence at <**www.grahamthomas.com/glocnames.html**>.

FORENAMES

Behind the Name at <**www.behindthename.com**> is a very comprehensive site devoted to the etymology and history of first names. In addition to English and Irish names it has details for a number of other countries and regions, as well as a listing of Biblical names.

About.com has a page of links for 'Naming Patterns for Countries & Cultures' at <**genealogy.about.com/od/naming_patterns/**>, which includes links for British and Irish names, as well as many others. A search for ["naming patterns"] in a search engine will reveal many other sites devoted to this topic. Anne Johnston has a useful list of diminutives for common Christian names at <**www.nireland.com/anne.johnston/Diminutives.htm**>. The website for the OLD-ENGLISH mailing list (see pp. 211 and 213) has a listing of Latin equivalents of common forenames at <**homepages.rootsweb.com/~oel/latingivennames.html**>.

For present-day forename frequencies, the authoritative sources are government sites. The National Statistics site at <**www.statistics.gov.uk**> has a number of reports on the current and historical frequency of first names. If you enter *name* in the search box on the home page, you will

get a list of relevant documents. GRO(S) has a paper on 'Popular Forenames in Scotland, 1900–2000' at <www.gro-scotland.gov.uk/statistics/
library/occpapers/popular-forenames-in-scotland-1900-2000.html>.

Image Partners has a forename thesaurus which attempts to match variant forename spellings at <www.imagepartners.co.uk/Thesaurus/Forenames.
aspx>.

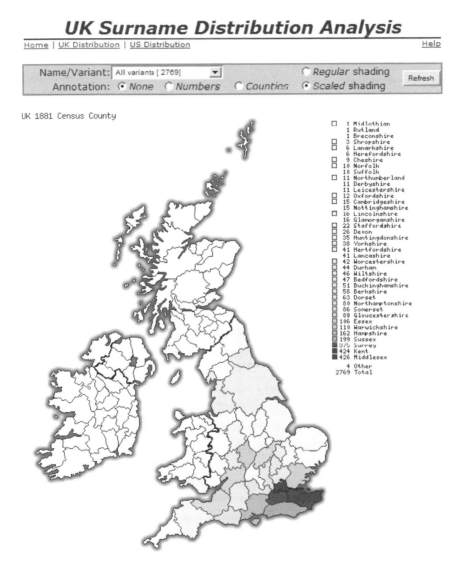

Figure 13-3 Distribution of the surname Woodham(s) as displayed by UK Surname
Distribution Analysis

UNDERSTANDING OLD DOCUMENTS

If the queries on genealogy mailing lists are anything to go by, one of the main things genealogists need help with is making sense of old documents, whether it is a census entry or a sixteenth-century will. In some cases it's just a matter of deciphering the handwriting, in others it is understanding the meaning of obsolete words, and in older documents the two problems often occur together. While the internet hardly provides a substitute for the specialist books on these subjects, there are quite a few resources online to help with these problems.

HANDWRITING

As the mistakes in census transcriptions show, even fairly modern handwriting can often be problematic to read, and once you get back beyond the nineteenth century the difficulties become ever greater. Few genealogists bother to go on palaeography courses, but there are some outstanding online resources to help you.

The English Faculty at Cambridge University has an online course on English Handwriting 1500–1700 at **<www.english.cam.ac.uk/ceres/ehoc/>** with high quality scans of original documents. There are extensive examples of every individual letter in a variety of hands as well as examples of the many abbreviations found in documents of this period. A series of graded exercises gives you an opportunity to try your own skills at transcribing original manuscripts.

The National Archives also has an online palaeography tutorial at **<www.nationalarchives.gov.uk/palaeography/>**. The interactive part of the site offers ten graded documents to try your hand at transcribing, with a popup alphabet for the hand, and there are another 30 example documents on the site. The 'Where to start' page offers tips for transcribing and covers some common abbreviations.

The Scottish Archive Network site has a dedicated palaeography website, Scottish Handwriting at **<www.scottishhandwriting.com>**, concentrating on the period 1500–1750 (see Figure 13-4). This includes a '1 Hour Basic Tutorial' and has detailed pages devoted to the forms of some of the more challenging individual letters. A problem solver suggests techniques for making sense of problem words and letters.

Dave Postles of the University of Leicester has materials relating to an MA in Palaeography online at **<paleo.anglo-norman.org>**. The site has two areas, one devoted to medieval and the other to early modern palaeography.

Dianne Tillotson has a site devoted to all aspects of Medieval Writing at **<medievalwriting.50megs.com/writing.htm>** and the material on

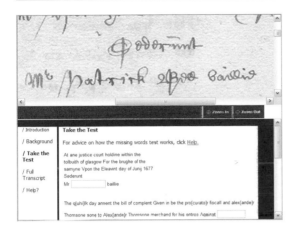

Figure 13-4
ScottishHandwriting.com

abbreviations at <medievalwriting.50megs.com/scripts/abbreviation/abbreviation1.htm> looks as if it will be useful when complete.

The OLD-ENGLISH mailing list website at <homepages.rootsweb.com/~oel/> includes pages on Old Law hands and Court hand, with scans of plates from Andrew Wright's 1776 *Court Hand Restored* showing examples of all the common letter shapes of the period. Both are linked from <homepages.rootsweb.com/~oel/contents.html>.

While most palaeography sites deal with the early modern and medieval periods, there is also help for those struggling with Victorian hands. For example, The FreeBMD page on 'Reading the Writing' at <www.freebmd.org.uk/handwriting.html> shows how the shape of nineteenth-century pen nibs affects the thickness of the stroke, and also looks at how to deal with difficult scans. The website of the 1901 Census of Ottawa and Carleton Project has a page devoted to reading handwriting in the census at <www.ogsottawa.on.ca/1901census/ReadingHandwriting.htm> and shows how to create a table of upper case letters as a basis for accurate transcription.

DATES AND CALENDARS

There are a number of useful resources on the web to help you make sense of the dates and calendars used in older genealogical sources.

There are two particular types of dating which are generally unfamiliar to modern readers. The first is the dating of documents, particularly legal ones, by regnal years, i.e. the number of years since the accession of the reigning monarch (so 1 January 2005 is 1 January 52 Eliz. II). The Regnal Year Calculator at <www.albion.edu/english/calendar/regnal.htm> will convert regnal years for the period from the Norman Conquest to George I. There is a useful table of regnal years up to Queen Victoria at <www.amostcuriousmurder.com/kingdateFS.htm>.

Saints' days are also frequently encountered in early documents, and the On-line Calendar of Saints' Days at <members.tripod.com/~gunhouse/calendar/home.htm> should enable you to decode these. The Catholic Encyclopedia's Dates And Dating page at <www.newadvent.org/cathen/04636c.htm> is also useful.

In September 1752 Britain switched from the old Julian calendar to the Gregorian. For information on this change see Mike Spathaky's article 'Old Style And New Style Dates And The Change To The Gregorian Calendar' at <www.genfair.com/dates.htm>. Calendars through the Ages has the text of the Calendar Act of 1751, which instituted this change, at <webexhibits.org/calendars/year-text-British.html>. Steven Gibbs has a conversion routine for the Julian and Gregorian calendars at <www.guernsey.net/~sgibbs/roman.html>, which may be useful if you are consulting records from countries which switched either earlier (most of Europe) or later (Russia) than the UK. Calendopaedia, the Encyclopaedia of Calendars, at <www.geocities.com/calendopaedia/> has extensive information on calendars, including information on the dates lost in the switch from the Julian to the Gregorian calendar for all the individual countries in Europe at <www.geocities.com/calendopaedia/gregory.htm>.

To find out what day a particular date fell on, consult Genuki's Perpetual Calendar at <www.genuki.org.uk/big/easter/>, which also gives the dates of Easter. The years 1550 to 2049 are covered.

Chris Phillips provides a comprehensive guide to chronology and dating at <www.medievalgenealogy.org.uk/guide/chron.shtml>, as part of a site devoted to medieval genealogy, while the Ultimate Calendar web page at <www.ecben.net/calendar.shtml> has over 250 links to online resources for all contemporary and historical calendars.

LATIN

For medieval genealogy and for legal records up to the 1730s, you will often encounter texts written in Latin. Even in English texts Latin phrases or, worse, abbreviations for them are not uncommon. Latin has also, of course, been much used for inscriptions.

General help in reading Latin documents will be found at <italiangenealogy.tardio.com> – follow the relevant link on the home page – while there are Latin dictionaries at <kuhttp.cc.ku.edu/ftp/pub/history/latwords.html> and <www.nd.edu/~archives/latgramm.htm>. The latter also provides a grammar and links to other useful resources. Be warned, however, that these cover classical Latin and not the Latin of medieval and early modern Britain. Lynn H. Nelson's 'Latin Word List' at <www.ku.edu/ftp/pub/history/latwords.aid> seems to be based on the Vulgate and will therefore be of use for Christian Latin terms. There is a Java applet based on this dictionary at <www.sunsite.ubc.ca/LatinDictionary/> which gives Latin→English and English→Latin for a word entered.

There is a list of 'Hard Little Words: Prepositions, Adverbs, Conjunctions (With Some Definitions of Medieval Usage)' at <www.georgetown.edu/faculty/irvinem/classics203/resources/latin.lex>. The Latin Primer at <www.xmission.com/~nelsonb/latin.htm> has a concise list of essential vocabulary for genealogists. Ancestry solutions has a list of 'Latin terms found in genealogical and historical records' at <www.ancestrysolutions.com/Defslatin.html> with a link to a brief guide to reading Latin. Eva Holmes has three articles on translating Latin at <www.suite101.com/welcome.cfm/italian_genealogy>.

These sites do not include feudal land-tenure terms, and will not be sufficient to enable you to translate a medieval charter, but they can certainly help with Latin words and phrases embedded in English prose.

Latin abbreviations are often used, particularly in set phrases, and the FAQ for the soc.genealogy.medieval newsgroup has a list of some of those commonly found in genealogical documents at <users.erols.com/wrei/faqs/medieval.html#GN13>.

There is a LATIN-WORDS mailing list which is for 'anyone with a genealogical or historical interest in deciphering and interpreting written documents in Latin from earliest to most recent twentieth century times, and discussing old Latin words, phrases, names, abbreviations and antique jargon'. Subscription details will be found at <www.rootsweb.com/~jfuller/gen_mail_trans.html> and the list archive is at <archiver.rootsweb.com/th/index/LATIN-WORDS>.

TECHNICAL TERMS

Genealogists encounter technical terms from many specialist areas, and have the additional difficulty that it may not be apparent whether a term is just specialized or in fact obsolete. The definitive resource for such questions remains the *Oxford English Dictionary*, but this is available online at <www.oed.com> only via a very hefty subscription (£230 as of summer 2005).

Other places to turn when you encounter this sort of problem include the rather inappropriately named OLD-ENGLISH mailing list, which is for 'anyone who is deciphering old English documents to discuss interpretations of handwriting and word meanings', or the OLD-WORDS mailing list, 'for the discussion of old words, phrases, names, abbreviations, and antique jargon useful to genealogy'. Details of how to subscribe to these lists are at <www.rootsweb.com/~jfuller/gen_mail_trans.html>. You can also browse or search the archives for them at <archiver.rootsweb.com/th/index/OLD-ENGLISH> and <archiver.rootsweb.com/th/index/OLD-WORDS> respectively. Bear in mind that the contributors to the lists have widely varying expertise, and you will need to evaluate carefully any advice you receive. However, the companion website for the OLD-ENGLISH list at <homepages.rootsweb.com/~oel/> has an excellent collection of material, as well as some useful links at <homepages.rootsweb.com/~oel/links.html>.

The Dictionary of the Scots Language site at <www.dsl.ac.uk/dsl/> provides electronic editions of two key works of Scottish lexicography, the *Dictionary of the Older Scottish Tongue* (DOST) and the *Scottish National Dictionary* (SND). Between them, these two dictionaries cover the use of Scots words from the twelfth century to the present day. A search can be conducted in either or both works. Quite apart from their general interest, an obvious use for genealogists is to help with understanding Scottish wills and other legal documents. A wide-ranging glossary of Scottish terms will be found on The Wedderburn Pages at <pro.wanadoo.fr/euroleader/wedderburn/glossary.htm>, including both archaic and modern terms.

Guy Etchells has a list of 'Leicestershire Agricultural Terms' taken from a work of 1809 at <freepages.genealogy.rootsweb.com/~framland/framland/agterm.htm>. Old terms for occupations are discussed on p. 156.

Legal

Even where they are not written in Latin many early modern texts, particularly those relating to property, contain technical legal terms that are likely to mean little to the non-specialist, but which may be crucial to the understanding of an ancestor's property holdings or transactions. A useful list of 'Legal Terms in Land Records' will be found at <users.rcn.com/deeds/legal.htm>, while the equivalent but distinct terminology for Scotland is explained in the Customs & Excise notice 'Scottish Land Law Terms' (the URL is 159 characters long, so follow the link from the website for this book). These are both guides to present-day usage, but in view of the archaic nature of landholding records this should not be a hindrance. A more specifically historical glossary is provided on the Scottish Archive Network site at <www.scan.org.uk/researchrtools/glossary.htm> and legal terms are included in The Wedderburn Pages mentioned above. The Manorial Society of Great Britain has a glossary of manorial terms at <www.msgb.co.uk/glossary.html>.

Medical

Death certificates of the last century, and earlier references to cause of death, often include terms that are unfamiliar. Some can be found in one of the online dictionaries of contemporary medicine, such as MedTerms at <www.medterms.com> or the University of Newcastle's On-line Medical Dictionary at <cancerweb.ncl.ac.uk/omd/>. But for comprehensive coverage of archaic medical terms, Paul Smith's Archaic Medical Terms site at <www.paul_smith.doctors.org.uk/ArchaicMedicalTerms.htm> is a more suitable place to go. In addition to the terminology, it has a list of recorded epidemics for the UK and USA. Another useful site is Antiquus Morbus at <www.antiquusmorbus.com>, which has old medical terms in English, Latin, German, French, and many other European languages. Each entry comes with a bibliographical reference, and there are links to around twenty further online sources for the medical terms. Within the English section, there are individual lists for occupational diseases, poisons, and alcoholism; there is also a separate list of Scots terms. Cyndi's List has a 'Medical & Medicine' page at <www.cyndislist.com/medical.htm>.

Measurements

Leicester University's palaeography course materials, mentioned on p. 210, include a number of useful lists covering terms likely to be found in old legal documents: land measurement terms, the Latin equivalents of English coinage, and Roman numerals. See the medieval palaeography pages at <paleo.anglo-norman.org/medfram.html>.

Steven Gibbs's site, mentioned on p. 212, has facilities for converting to and from Roman numerals at <www.guernsey.net/~sgibbs/roman. html>.

Details of old units of measurement (though not aerial measurements) can be found at <www.fergusoncreations.co.uk/home/shaun/metrology/english.html>, while both linear and aerial measures are covered by <www.johnowensmith.co.uk/histdate/measures.htm>. There is a comprehensive Dictionary of Measures at <www.unc.edu/~rowlett/units/> which includes a useful article on 'English Customary Measures' at <www.unc.edu/~rowlett/units/custom.html>. Cyndi's List has a page devoted to 'Weights and Measures' at <www.cyndislist.com/weights.htm>.

Medieval

There are a number of general guides to medieval terms, including NetSERF's Hypertext Medieval Glossary at <netserf.cua.edu/glossary/home.htm>, and The Glossary Of Medieval Terms at <cal.bemidji.msus.edu/History/mcmanus/ma_gloss.html>. Resources for the terminology of heraldry are discussed on p. 179.

VALUE OF MONEY

A very frequent question on genealogy mailing lists is the present-day equivalent of sums of money in wills, tax rolls and the like. While there can be no definitive answer – goods are now cheaper than ever, while labour much more expensive – there is plenty of material online to give you an idea of what things were worth.

There is a very detailed analysis of the historical value of sterling in a House of Commons Research Paper 'Inflation: the Value of the Pound 1750–1998', which is available online in PDF format at **<www.parliament. uk/commons/lib/research/rp99/rp99-020.pdf>**. For a longer time span, there are two tables covering the period from the thirteenth century to the present day at **<www.johnowensmith.co.uk/histdate/moneyval.htm>**.

Alan Stanier's 'Relative Value of Sums of Money' page at **<privatewww. essex.ac.uk/~alan/family/N-Money.html>** has statistics for the wages of various types of worker, mainly craftsmen and labourers, but also domestic servants and professionals.

The Economic History Services' site has a page at **<eh.net/hmit/ ppowerbp/>**, which enables you to find the modern equivalent of an amount in pounds, shillings and pence in a particular year. This is part of a 'How much is that?' section at **<eh.net/hmit/>** which also has information on UK and US inflation rates since the 1660s and the pound–dollar conversion rate for the last 200 years. If you are too young to remember the pre-decimal system of pounds, shillings and pence, then 'What's A Guinea?' at **<www.wilkiecollins.demon.co.uk/coinage/coins.htm>** will enlighten you.

1710 - 1911

Nominal Annual Earnings for various Occupations in England and Wales

Source: _Williamson, 1982_

The figures given are in current pounds sterling, and relate to adult males.

Occupation	1710	1737	1755	1781	1797	1805	1810	1815	1819
Agricultural Labourers	17.78	17.18	17.18	21.09	30.03	40.40	42.04	40.04	39.05
General Labourers	19.22	20.15	20.75	23.13	25.09	36.87	43.94	43.94	41.74
Messengers and Porters (exc. govt.)	31.15	34.75	33.99	33.54	57.66	69.43	76.01	80.69	81.35
Government low-wage	21.58	28.79	28.62	46.02	46.77	52.48	57.17	60.22	60.60
Police, Guards, Watchmen	13.28	26.05	25.76	48.08	47.04	51.26	67.89	69.34	69.18
Miners	22.46	27.72	22.94	24.37	47.79	64.99	63.22	57.82	53.37
Government high-wage	62.88	84.04	78.91	104.55	133.73	151.09	176.86	195.16	219.25
Skilled in Shipbuilding	36.26	37.00	38.82	45.26	51.71	51.32	55.25	59.20	57.23
Skilled in Engineering	40.73	41.56	43.60	50.83	58.08	75.88	88.23	94.91	92.71
Skilled in Building Trades	28.50	29.08	30.51	35.57	40.64	55.30	66.35	66.35	63.02
Skilled in Textiles	33.59	34.28	35.96	41.93	47.90	65.18	78.21	67.60	67.60
Skilled in Printing Trades	43.29	44.17	46.34	54.03	66.61	71.11	79.22	79.22	71.14
Clergymen	99.66	96.84	91.90	182.65	238.50	266.42	283.89	272.53	266.55
Solicitors and Barristers	113.16	178.18	231.00	242.67	165.00	340.00	447.50	447.50	447.50
Clerks (exc. govt.)	43.64	68.29	63.62	101.57	135.26	150.44	178.11	200.79	229.64
Surgeons, Medical Officers	51.72	56.85	62.02	88.35	174.95	217.60	217.60	217.60	217.60

Figure 13-5 Nominal Annual Earnings for various Occupations **<privatewww.essex. ac.uk/~alan/family/N-Money.html>**

The Scottish Archive Network (see p. 115) provides a Scots Currency Converter at <**www.scan.org.uk/researchrtools/scots_currency.htm**> (though this requires Internet Explorer).

For the most recent period, the Retail Price Index is the official source, and its home is the Office for National Statistics, which has a home page for the RPI at <**www.statistics.gov.uk/cci/nugget.asp?id=21**>, and an Adobe Acrobat file with data going back to the birth of the RPI in June 1947 at <**www.statistics.gov.uk/downloads/theme_economy/Rp02.pdf**>.

An excellent collection of links to sites with information on the historical value of the pound and other currencies is Roy Davies's 'Current value of Old Money' page at <**www.ex.ac.uk/~RDavies/arian/current/howmuch. html**>, which includes an extensive list of printed sources.

There is an Excel spreadsheet with data on the 'Wages and the cost of living in Southern England 1450–1700' linked from <**www.iisg.nl/hpw/ dover.html**>, with individual figures for Oxford, Cambridge, Dover, Canterbury and London.

CHAPTER 14

PHOTOGRAPHS

Among the many reasons for the success of the web is the ease with which it can be used to make images available to a wide audience. The questions of cost and commercial viability that face the printed photograph do not really apply on the web – apart from the labour involved, it costs effectively nothing to publish a photograph online. The widespread availability of inexpensive scanners and the popularity of the digital camera mean that more and more people have the equipment to create digital images. While no archive is in position to publish a significant fraction of its photographic holdings in print, online image archives are mushrooming.

Photographs are, of course, primary historical sources. But you are not particularly likely to come across a picture of your great-great-grandmother on the web (unless she was, say, Queen Victoria), so for the genealogist online photographs mainly provide historical and geographical background to a family history, rather than primary source material.

The web is also a good source of information for dealing with your own family photographs, and there are sites devoted to dating, preservation, restoration, and scanning.

Cyndi's List has a page with links for 'Photographs and Memories' at <**www.cyndislist.com/photos.htm**>, covering all aspects of photography and family history. Information on using search engines to locate images online is covered in Chapter 16 on p. 265. Present-day aerial photographs tend to be provided by mapping sites and are covered in Chapter 12, p. 190.

NATIONAL COLLECTIONS

For photographs of historic buildings, there are two national sites. The National Monuments Register's (NMR) Images of England site at <**www. imagesofengland.org.uk**> is intended to be 'an internet home for England's listed buildings' with good-quality photographs and descriptions of every listed building in the country. So far around half the 370,000 listed properties are included on the site.

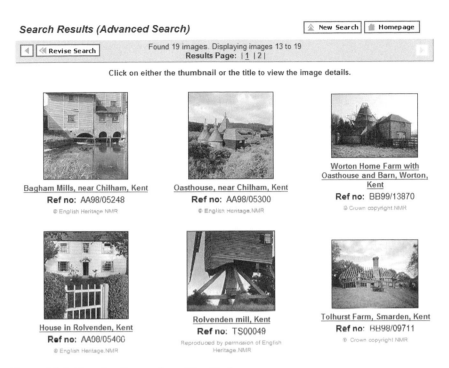

Figure 14-1 Thumbnail page from ViewFinder

You can do a quick search without further ado (retrieving a maximum of 50 images), while the free registration gives you access to more sophisticated standard and advanced searches. Search facilities include search by county or town, building type, period, or person (an architect or other individual associated with a building). Thumbnail images link to full size images with a description.

ViewFinder is run by English Heritage at <viewfinder.english-heritage. org.uk>. This aims to make part of the NMR's image archive available online. Whereas Images of England contains contemporary photographs, the ViewFinder images are older. The site has around 25,000 images in a number of collections drawn from individual photographers. The largest collection, with over 13,000 photographs, represents the work of Henry W. Taunt, an important Oxford photographer of the late nineteenth and early twentieth century. London is well served by these collections, with many street views and material relating to the Port of London. There is also a project relating to 'England at Work', with 5,000 images illustrating England's industrial heritage. The photographs come in three sizes: a small thumbnail, a basic view of about 450×300 pixels, which you can save, and an enlarged view of around 700×480 pixels which your browser won't let you save. Even though the images are historical, the search is based on present-day counties, not the pre-1974 counties.

A new and very different type of collection is the National Photo Album at <**www.nationalphotoalbum.co.uk**>, launched by computer manufacturer HP at the start of 2005. This is designed as a photo archive for public submissions. Users are invited to submit photos of 'individuals, families, workplaces, events, outings, cities, towns and villages; anything which reveals something of the way we have lived over the past hundred years or so'. There is a mixture of contemporary and historical photos. You can browse the album by category (the most interesting for family historians will be 'Workers and the workplace', 'Family history and friends', and 'Buildings, places and landmarks') or search on a particular word or name. Some of the photos can be downloaded, others not. Even though the site is still quite new, there are already some interesting photographs of old occupations and workplaces. An online form makes it easy to upload photographs for the curators to consider for adding to the album. The site also offers tips on archiving photos and editing digital photos.

An interesting approach, though only for contemporary photographs, is taken by Geograph at <**www.geograph.co.uk**>, which invites people to submit photographs of the main geographical features for every 1 km grid square of the British Isles.

LOCAL COLLECTIONS

Record offices and libraries have substantial collections of photographic material, and this is increasingly being made available online, in many cases with lottery funding. Some of these collections are purely photographic, while others include scanned prints, drawings and even paintings. The following will give you some idea of the sort of material available.

For London, there is PhotoLondon at <**www.photolondon.org.uk**>, designed to highlight and promote historic photographs of London in the capital's libraries, museums and archives. The core of the material is from the collections of the Guildhall Library, the London Metropolitan Archives, Westminster City Archives, the Museum of London and the National Monuments Record, but there are also smaller selections from individual boroughs with descriptions of the holdings from which they are taken.

Collage (see Figure 14-2) is the Guildhall Library's contribution to PhotoLondon at <**collage.cityoflondon.gov.uk**>, and has around 20,000 images of the capital. As well as maps, plans and photographs of places, there is a large collection relating to trades and industries, including the City livery companies.

For suburban London, the Ideal Homes site at <**www.ideal-homes. org.uk**> includes historical photographs for the six South-East London Boroughs. Thumbnails link to larger images with a description.

Figure 14-2 Photograph of Fleet Street from Collage

Glasgow's Mitchell Library, which houses the City Archives, offers the 'Virtual Mitchell Collection' at <www.mitchelllibrary.org/vm/> – note the three l's in the URL – which is a selection from the images in the collection covering 'street scenes and buildings, but also scenes of past working lives and of social life in the city'. Searches can be made by street name or subject.

West Sussex Record Office has an online database at <www2.westsussex. gov.uk/RO/DB/pick.asp> with details of 31,000 photographs held in the record office, of which around 2,000 are available online. The online database provides record office references so that scans of photographs can be requested if the image is not already online. According to the home page, 'as resources permit, more images will be added to the database and eventually there will be 150,000 entries consisting of photographs, prints and drawings'.

Picturesheffield.com at <www.picturesheffield.com> is an online version of Sheffield Local Studies Library's computerized image system. Funded from the Heritage Lottery Fund, the site currently contains around 8,500 photographs, but will hold around 10,000 when complete. Low resolution images (typically around 350×200 pixels at 72 dots per inch) can be downloaded from the site free of charge, and high resolution photographic prints can be purchased.

Picture The Past at <www.picturethepast.org.uk> is the website for the North East Midlands Photographic Record, a project run by the local

Figure 14-3 A Nottingham entry from Picture The Past

authorities of Derby, Derbyshire, Nottingham and Nottinghamshire, and intended to 'conserve and make publicly accessible the photographic heritage of the North East Midlands'. The site currently holds around 20,000 images. There is a comprehensive search facility – you can specify a county or a place, and enter individual keywords (though the site does not indicate what keywords are used in the database). Individual images are presented on-screen at around 250×190 pixels, and you can order high quality prints online. A useful feature of the database is that each image has a link to a present-day map showing the approximate location. Many pictures are accompanied by quite detailed historical notes (see Figure 14-3). There is also a facility for those with local historical knowledge to contribute additional information.

It is always worth checking a relevant record office website for photographic collections. Even if there is little or no material on the web, you can expect to find information about their holdings – for example, Greater Manchester CRO has details of its Documentary Photography Archive at **<www.gmcro.co.uk/Photography/DPA/dpa.htm>**, which is an important collection for family historians because it includes many family photographs up to the 1950s. Photographs are usually an important part of official local history sites for specific places (see p. 200).

▋PERSONAL SITES

Alongside these efforts by public bodies, there are many images published on the web by individuals. In particular, there are many present-day photographs of parish churches, for example:

• Richard's Church Album at **<www.thirdman.ukhq.co.uk>** has photographs of over 2,000 churches in all parts of England

- The Old Scottish Borders Photo Archive at <www.ettrickgraphics.com/bordersindex.htm> has views of border towns
- Kevin Quick has photographs of Bedfordshire and Buckinghamshire churches, as well as general views of Bucks towns and villages at <www.countyviews.com>.

The best way to find such sites is to go to the relevant Genuki county page.

COMMERCIAL PHOTOGRAPHS

The commercial picture libraries have not been slow to exploit the web as a means of providing a catalogue for prospective purchasers of their material or services. The reason that these resources are useful to non-professional users is that access to the online catalogues and databases is usually free, though the image size and quality is likely to be reduced, and the scans may have some overprinting to prevent them being used commercially.

For example, PastPix <www.pastpix.com> is a subscription service with over 20,000 historical photographs, mainly from the UK, but the collection can be searched free of charge. There is a whole range of photographs of places and occupations, though the picture size for casual visitors is quite small (registered users have access to larger images).

Perhaps the most important commercial site with old photographs for the UK is the Francis Frith Collection at <www.francisfrith.com>. Frith was a Victorian photographer whose company photographed over 7,000 towns and villages in all parts of the British Isles, from 1860 until the company closed in 1969. The entire stock was bought by a new company, which now sells prints. While the aim of the website is to act as a sales medium, it has reasonable size thumbnails (under 400×274 pixels) of all 100,000 odd pictures in the collection, which can be located by search or via a listing for each (present-day) county without the need to make a purchase. There are also some historic aerial photographs. The site allows you set up an 'album' to store the pictures you want to view again. If you're using a browser other than Internet Explorer, you may find the text display problematic on some pages.

Frith's photographs and many other commercial photographs of towns and villages were issued as postcards, which means that postcard sites may have material of interest. For example, Data Wales has a number of early twentieth-century postcards of various parts of Wales at <www.data-wales.co.uk/postcard.htm>; there is a collection of Isle of Wight postcards at <members.lycos.co.uk/bartie/>; Eddie Prowse has an online collection of postcards of Weymouth and Portland at <www.eprowse.fsnet.co.uk>; Photo-Ark at <www.photo-ark.co.uk> has postcards (as well as other

Figure 14-4 An 1886 photograph of Manchester from the Francis Frith Collection

photographs) for Derbyshire, Lancashire, Lincolnshire, Nottinghamshire and Yorkshire. Postcardworld at <www.postcardworld.co.uk> is a commercial site with postcards of all parts of the UK, with good quality scans on the site.

PROFESSIONAL PHOTOGRAPHERS

In one sense, professional photographers are just another occupational group. But their role in creating a unique part of the recent historical record makes them of interest not just to their descendants. Information about their working lives can be important in dating and locating family photographs.

A useful site for information on UK photographers is the New Index of Victorian, Edwardian & Early 20th Century UK Photographers at <www.users.waitrose.com/~rodliffe/>. This has a database of photographers (which, however, can only be searched by county) and links to many other sites. Roger Vaughan has a list of several hundred Victorian photographers at <www.cartes.fsnet.co.uk/cartefs.htm>, while PhotoLondon (see p. 220) has a Directory of London Photographers 1841–1908 at <www.photolondon.org.uk/directory.htm>. Another site with lists of photographers, with towns and dates, is Victorian Photographers of Britain 1855–1901 at <mywebpage.netscape.com/hibchris/instant/aboutme.html>.

The 'Photographs and Memories' page on Cyndi's List at <www.cyndislist.com/photos.htm> lists a number of other sites with dates and places for British professional photographers, including some for specific towns or counties (including Ayrshire, Liverpool and Sussex).

UK-PHOTOGRAPHERS is a mailing list for the discussion and sharing of information regarding the dating of photographs produced by professional photographers in England and Wales between 1850 and 1950. Information on subscribing will be found at <lists.rootsweb.com/index/ other/Occupations/UK-PHOTOGRAPHERS.html>, which has a link to the archive of past messages.

PORTRAITS

While most of the online historic photographs are of places, there are some photographs of individuals. The military is particularly well represented. For example, Fred Larimore's site devoted to Nineteenth Century British And Indian Armies And Their Soldiers at <www.members.dca.net/fbl/> has a collection of photographs for the period 1840–1920, in some cases with information about the individual shown and commentary on uniform details. Other sites with military photographs are mentioned on p. 165.

The website of the Roger Vaughan Picture Library at <www.rogerco. freeserve.co.uk> has around 3,000 Victorian and Edwardian studio photographs, with links to other sites with many more. Most of the subjects aren't named, so this is more useful for help with dating and information on professional photographers.

Many school photographs will be found online. For a simple example, see Kennethmont School's page at <www.kinnethmont.co.uk/k-school. htm>, which offers a selection of group photos from 1912 onwards with many pupils identified by name (yes, the site and the school differ in spelling!). Jeff Maynard has a more extensive collection for Harrow County School with form and sports team photos going back to the 1920s at <www.jeffreymaynard.com/Harrow_County/photographs.htm>.

A good way to find photographs for particular schools is to check the website of the school itself (most have the format <www.*name-of-school. name-of-localauthority*.sch.uk> or do a general search on the school name. A local history site may include school photographs, too. (Incidentally, if you come across a site called World School Photographs, ignore it – it seems to be solely designed to collect personal information, and has *no* school photographs.)

As well as these individual efforts, there are online photo archives to which you can contribute scans of your own material. Perhaps the best known is DeadFred at <www.deadfred.com>, which has almost 50,000 records for around 12,000 surnames, but the 'Photographs and Memories' page on Cyndi's List at <www.cyndislist.com/photos.htm> has many more, under the heading 'Lost & Found'.

▌DATING, PRESERVATION, RESTORATION

The web can be useful in connection with your own photographs, if you need to date them or if you need advice on preservation or restoration.

For help with the dating of old photographs, look at the BBC's History website, which has articles on Victorian Studio Photographs at <www.bbc.co.uk/history/your_history/family/victorian_photo1.shtml>. Andrew J. Morris's site 19th Century Photography at <ajmorris.com/roots/photo/> is a more detailed account of the various types of photographic process and technique. The Roger Vaughan Picture Library has a section devoted to dating portraits at <www.cartes.freeuk.com/time/date.htm> with examples of (approximately) dated photographs for years between 1860 and 1952.

If you are interested in preserving and restoring old photographs, Colin Robinson has information about their care and conservation at <www.colinrobinson.com>, while David L. Mishkin's article on 'Restoring Damaged Photographs' at <www.genealogy.com/10_restr.html> covers the various approaches to restoration. If you want to scan photographs and restore them digitally, it is worth looking at Scantips <www.scantips.com>, which not only has extensive advice about scanning in general but also includes a page on 'Restoration of genealogical photos' at <www.scantips.com/restore.html>. About.com has a series of articles by Kimberley Powell on 'creating and editing digital photos' at <genealogy.about.com/cs/digitalphoto/a/digital_photos.htm>.

These sites offer advice not just on the obvious topic of repairing the signs of physical damage but also on correcting tonal problems with faded originals. Sites devoted to digital restoration generally assume you are using Adobe Photoshop, but the principles transfer to other graphics editing packages, though there may be some differences in terminology.

A general source of help with old photographs is the RootsWeb mailing list VINTAGE-PHOTOS, which is devoted to 'the discussion and sharing of information regarding vintage photos including, but not restricted to, proper storage, preservation, restoration, ageing and dating, restoration software, photo types and materials used, restoration assistance, and scanning options'. Information on how to join the list will be found at <lists.rootsweb.com/index/other/Miscellaneous/VINTAGE-PHOTOS.html>, which also provides links to the list's archives. The GenPhoto list at Yahoo Groups is a photographic mailing list specifically for family historians. Its coverage includes identifying old photographs, and using digital photography and scanning to share and preserve family photos. You can read archived messages and join the group at <groups.yahoo.com/group/genphoto/>. The Photo Identification Discussion Group is also on Yahoo Groups, at <groups.yahoo.com/group/photoid>, and is devoted to 'techniques for identifying the date and subjects of old photographs'. Archived messages can be read only once you have joined the group.

There are a number of newsgroups devoted to photography (rec.photo and others in the same hierarchy), but none specifically relating to old photographs.

DIGITAL PRESERVATION

While modern digital photographs don't need 'preservation' as such, appropriate archiving is essential if future generations are to see them. Digital photographs may not get torn or faded, but image files can easily become corrupted or destroyed. Also, it's a lot easier to write a name and a date on the back of a print than to attach the same information securely to a file. A good starting point for all matters to do with this issue is the Archiving Digital site at <www.archivingdigital.com>, maintained by Christopher Auman, author of a book on the subject. The site is still quite new and the main content at present is the author's blog, which includes a series of articles covering the basics.

If you're serious about digital preservation, then an important consideration is the long-term stability of the storage media. Authoritative guidance is available in a report from the US National Institute of Standards and Technology at <www.itl.nist.gov/div895/gipwog/StabilityStudy.pdf> – the conclusions are probably all you need.

CHAPTER 15

DISCUSSION FORUMS

One of the most useful aspects of the internet for anyone researching their family history is that it is very easy to 'meet' other genealogists online to discuss matters of common interest, to exchange information and to find help and advice. The specific issues of locating other people with interests in the same surnames and families are dealt with in Chapter 10. This chapter looks at the three main types of online discussion forum: mailing lists, newsgroups and web-based forums.

MAILING LISTS

Electronic mailing lists provide a way for groups of people to conduct online discussions via email. They are simply a logical extension of your electronic address book – instead of each member of a group having to keep track of the email addresses of everyone else, this list of email addresses is managed by a computer called a 'list server'. This arrangement allows people to add themselves to the list, or remove themselves from it, without having to contact all the other members.

You join a list by sending an email message to a list server. Thereafter you receive a copy of every message sent to the list by other list members; likewise, any message you send to the list gets circulated to all the other subscribers.

FINDING LISTS

The first genealogical mailing list, ROOTS-L, goes back to a period long before the internet was available to the general public – its first message was posted in December 1987. There must be well over 50,000 English-language mailing lists devoted to genealogy.

Every mailing list is hosted on a specific server, and a large proportion of the genealogy lists are hosted by RootsWeb (over 28,000), whose main mailing lists page will be found at <**lists.rootsweb.com**>. General, not geographically specific, lists for the UK (which includes those for occupations, for example) are linked from <**lists.rootsweb.com/index/intl/ UK/**> while there are individual pages for England, Ireland, Scotland and Wales, with links to lists for local interests. There is no master listing of all RootsWeb lists, so it can be hard to find those which do not fall into obvious categories, even if you know the name of the list.

A general mailing list site that hosts many genealogy lists is Yahoo Groups at <**groups.yahoo.com**>. Most of the groups hosted here are listed under the **Family & Home | Genealogy** category, though there are many others for particular countries and areas, which can be found by using the search facility.

In spite of the large number of lists, it is a simple matter to find those which might be of interest to you, as there are two sites which compile this information. The more definitive is John Fuller and Chris Gaunt's Genealogy Resources on the Internet site which has a comprehensive listing of genealogy mailing lists at <**www.rootsweb.com/~jfuller/gen_mail.html**>, subdivided into the following categories:

- Countries Other Than USA
- USA
- Surnames
- Adoption
- African-Ancestored
- Cemeteries/Monuments/ Obituaries
- Computing/Internet Resources
- Emigration/Migration Ships and Trails
- Family History, Folklore, and Artifacts
- Genealogical Material/Services
- General Information/Discussion
- Jewish

- LDS
- Native American
- Newspapers
- Nobility/Heads of State/Heraldry
- Occupations
- Religions/Churches (other than Jewish/LDS)
- Societies
- Software
- Translations and Word Origins
- Vital Records (census, BDM)
- Wars/Military
- Uncategorized

The 'uncategorized' lists include a number devoted to topics of general interest, such as the GEN-MEDIEVAL and SHIPWRECK lists.

However, more useful for those with UK interests is Genuki's Mailing Lists page at <**www.genuki.org.uk/indexes/MailingLists.html**>. This has the advantage of listing only those relevant to British and Irish genealogy, and includes lists which, although of interest to UK genealogists, are not categorized under the UK by John Fuller or RootsWeb – notably war-related lists such as AMERICAN-REVOLUTION, BOER-WAR or WAR-BRIDES. The organization of the Genuki listing makes it easier to find lists of interest: at the top of the page are those devoted to general topics, but the main body of the page gives all the lists for each county in the British

Isles. Another advantage over John Fuller's pages, which give only subscription information, is that the Genuki listing has links to the web page for each list, so you can easily find further information or access the list archives, if they are publicly accessible.

WHAT LISTS ARE THERE?

The most generally useful mailing lists are those for individual counties. RootsWeb has lists for every county in the British Isles and these are the best places to find discussion of or ask questions about the areas where your ancestors lived and about local records.

As well as lists for each county as a whole, there are many devoted to areas in a county, and to particular towns and villages. Staffordshire, for example, is covered not only by a general list, STAFFORDSHIRE, but also by lists for local areas such as the Black Country, as well as a number of individual towns such as Walsall and Sedgley. Staffordshire interests are also covered by the broader MIDMARCH and SHROPSHIRE-PLUS lists.

Alongside such geographically based lists, there are general lists covering particular topics in relation either to the entirety of the British Isles, or to some constituent of it. Examples of these are lists like AUS-CONVICTS, BRITREGIMENTS, RAILWAY-UK and UK-1901-CENSUS. Other lists are mentioned in Chapters 11, 12 and 13.

Of course Genuki and John Fuller only have details of lists relating to genealogy. If you want to find mailing lists on other topics, there is unfortunately no definitive catalogue – in fact such a thing would be impossible to compile and maintain. However, the International Federation of Library Associations and Institutions provides some useful links on its 'Internet Mailing Lists Guides and Resources' page at <**www.ifla.org/I/training/listserv/lists.htm**>. Also, since many mailing lists have either a website of their own or at least a listing somewhere on the web, a search engine can be used to locate them.

There are also many mailing lists for individual surnames. These are discussed in detail on p. 134.

John Fuller has a regular electronic newsletter called NEW-GENLIST which carries announcements of new lists added to his sites. Subscription details will be found at <**lists.rootsweb.com/index/other/Miscellaneous/NEW-GENLIST.html**> which also has a link to the archive of past announcements.

LIST ARCHIVES

Many genealogy mailing lists, including almost all the lists hosted by RootsWeb, have an archive of past messages. The RootsWeb list archives can be found at <**archiver.rootsweb.com**>. Not all list archives are open to non-members of the relevant list, but where a list has open membership it is not very common to find that the archive is closed.

The archives have several uses. First, they allow you to get an idea of the discussion topics that come up on the list and judge whether it would be worth your while joining. In particular, an archive will give you some idea of the level of traffic on the list, i.e. how many messages a day are posted. Also, they provide a basis for searching, whether by the list server's own search facility, or by a general search engine such as those discussed in Chapter 16. This means that you can take advantage of information posted to a mailing list without even joining it, though of course you will need to join to post your own messages.

JOINING A LIST

In order to join a list you need to send an email message to the list server, the computer that manages the list, instructing it to add you to the list of subscribers. The text of the email message must contain nothing but the correct command.

Although the basic principles for joining a list are more or less universal, there are a small number of different list systems and each has its own particular features

Many lists are run on 'listserv' systems (listserv is the name of the software that manages the lists). To join one of these you need to send a message to listserv@*the-name-of-the-list-server*, and the text of the email message should start with the word SUB (short for 'subscribe'), followed by the name of the list and then your first and last names. So to join WW20-ROOTS-L, a list for the discussion of genealogy in all twentieth-century wars, you would send the following message (supposing your name was John Smith):

```
To: listserv@listserv.indiana.edu

SUB WW20-ROOTS-L John Smith
```

You need to specify the list name because this particular list server could be managing many different lists.

On systems such as RootsWeb, however, there may be a separate subscription email address for each list. This is typically formed by adding the word *request* to the list name. So to join the GENBRIT-L list, for example, you send your joining command to GENBRIT-L-request@roots web.com and the text of the message itself only needs to say *subscribe*:

```
To: GENBRIT-L-request@rootsweb.com

subscribe
```

Yahoo Groups uses a similar system – to join the yorkshiregentopics group, you would need to send the following message:

```
To: yorkshiregentopics-subscribe@yahoogroups.com
```

You should not need to worry about which subscription format to use: any site with details of mailing lists, such as Genealogy Resources on the Internet, should give explicit instructions on how to join the lists mentioned. As you can see from Figure 15-1, on Yahoo Groups the home page for each group gives subscription instructions.

Because these messages are processed by a computer, you should send *only* the commands – there is no point in sending a message to an automatic system saying, 'Hello, my name is . . . and I would like to join the list, please.' Also, it is a good idea to remove any signature at the end of your email message, so that the list server does not attempt to treat it as a set of commands.

Incidentally, do not be worried by the word 'subscription'. It does not mean you are committing yourself to paying for anything, it just means that your name is being added to the list of members.

If you have more than one email address you need to make sure that you send your joining message from the one you want messages sent to. Most mailing lists will reject an email message from an address it does not have in its subscriber list. If you want to be able to use more than one email address to post messages to a list, you will need to ask the list administrator to add additional addresses for you.

Some lists have web pages with an online form for joining. In this case you simply type your email address in the box. There is a similar system for the mailing lists at Yahoo Groups, though here you have to register (free) before you can join any of its lists. Once you have signed in, you can click on the subscribe button for any list and it will bring up a page where you can select your subscription options and join the list.

When you join a list you will normally get a welcome message. You should make sure you keep this, as it will give you important information about the list and the email addresses to use. There are few things more embarrassing online than having to send a message to everyone on a mailing list asking how to unsubscribe because you have lost the welcome message which contains the instructions.

There are some circumstances in which you will not be able to join a list by one of the methods discussed here: some lists are 'closed', which means that they are not open to all comers. This is typically the case for mailing lists run by societies for their own members. In this case, instead of sending an email to the list server you will probably need to contact the person who manages the list, providing your society membership number, so that he or she can check that you are entitled to join the list and then add you.

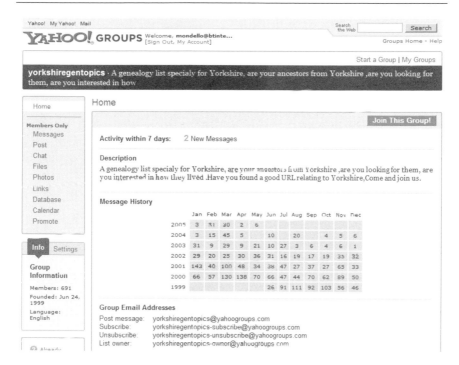

Figure 15-1 Home page for the yorkshiregentopics group on Yahoo

Closed mailing lists are also often used for the management of genealogical projects. In such cases those involved in the project are usually added to a list as soon as they join the project and no outsiders are admitted. Closed lists can also allow geographically remote committee members of a society to keep in touch, as with the trustees of Genuki, who conduct all affairs via a closed mailing list.

SUBSCRIPTION OPTIONS

Many mailing lists have two ways in which you can receive messages. The standard way is what is called 'mail mode', where every individual message to the list is forwarded to you as soon as it is received. However, some older email systems were not able to cope with the potentially very large number of incoming messages, so lists also offered a 'digest mode'. In this a bunch of messages to the list are combined into a single larger message, thus reducing the number of messages arriving in the subscriber's mailbox. Even though few of us nowadays are likely to be affected by this sort of technical limitation, some people do not like to receive the dozens of mail messages per day that can come from a busy list, and prefer to receive the messages as a digest.

However, there are also disadvantages to this. For a start, you need to look through each digest to see the subjects of the messages it contains, whereas individual messages with subject lines of no interest to you can quickly be deleted unread. Also, if you want to reply to a message contained within a digest your email software will automatically include the subject line of the *digest*, not just the subject of the individual message within the digest you are replying to. The result is that other list members will not be able to tell from this subject line which earlier message you are responding to. If your email software automatically quotes the original message in reply, then you will need to delete almost all of the quoted digest if you are not to irritate other list members with an unnecessarily long message, most of which will be irrelevant (see Netiquette, p. 248).

There are a number of different ways of arranging to receive a list in digest form. With the lists on RootsWeb there is a different subscription address, containing -D- instead of -L-, so subscription messages for the digest form of GENBRIT list go to GENBRIT-D-request@rootsweb.com. On listserv systems, once you have joined a list you should send a message with the text set LISTNAME digest to change to digest mode, and set LISTNAME nodigest to switch back to mail mode. On lists with a web subscription form, you may be able to choose between mail and digest on the form.

TEXT FORMATTING

Email software generally allows you to send messages in a number of different formats, and normally you do not need to worry about exactly

Table 15-1 Mailing List Addresses

Address	What it's for
The list server	Automatic control of your subscription to the lists. Messages sent to this address are not read by a human, and can only consist of specific commands.
The list itself	This is the address to be used for contributions to the discussion. Anything sent to this address is copied to all the list members.
	A common beginner's mistake is to send a message meant for the list server to the list address, and hundreds or even thousands of people receive your 'unsubscribe' message.
The list owner/ administrator	This is for contacting the person in charge of the list. For most lists, it should only be needed if there is some problem with the list server (e.g. it won't respond to your messages) or something the automated server can't deal with that requires human intervention (e.g. abusive messages).
	For closed lists, you will probably need to use this address rather than the list server address in order to subscribe.

how your mail software is formatting them. When you start sending messages to mailing lists, however, you may find that this is an issue you need to consider. The reason for this is that some mailing lists will not accept certain types of formatting, and even if they do, some recipients of your formatted messages may have difficulties.

The standard format for an email message is plain text. This can be handled by any list server and any email software. However, most modern email software will let you send formatted text with particular fonts and font sizes, colour, italics and so on, i.e. something much more like what you produce with your word processor, and some software even uses this as the default. The way it does this is to include an email attachment containing the message in RTF format (created and used by word processors) or HTML format (used for web pages).

You may feel that this is exactly how you want your email messages to look. But if someone is using email software that can't make sense of this format they may have trouble with your message. They may even receive what looks like a blank message with an attachment, and many people are, rightly, wary of opening an attachment which could contain a virus, particularly if it's attached to a suspicious-looking blank message. The only way they will be able to read your message is by saving the attachment as a file and then opening it with the relevant piece of software, and no one will thank you for sending a message requiring all that extra work. Indeed, people using text-based email on some systems, such as UNIX, may not even have access to software for reading such files.

Also, messages with formatting are inevitably larger than plain text messages, so people have to spend more time online to download them, which, while trivial for an individual message, could be significant for someone who is a member of a few busy lists. All things considered, there is really no good reason for using formatted text in mailing-list messages.

Different lists and list systems deal with this problem in a variety of ways. Yahoo Groups allows you to choose whether you receive messages from the list as HMTL or as plain text. RootsWeb does not permit the use of HTML or RTF formatting at all, and will not allow messages with formatted text to get through.

If you need to find out how to turn off the formatting features of your email software, RootsWeb has a useful page on 'Sending Messages in Plain Text' at <**helpdesk.rootsweb.com/listadmins/plaintext.html**>. The page shows you how to do this for over 20 of the widely used email packages, but even if it does not include the software you use, it should give you an idea of what to look for in your own email software.

The only formatting feature that can be really useful in an email message is the ability to highlight words to be stressed, and the traditional way of doing this in a plain text message is to put *asterisks* round the relevant word. One thing *not* to do, in genealogy mailing lists anyway, is put words in upper case – this is traditionally reserved for indicating surnames.

FILTERING

If you do not want to subscribe to mailing lists in digest mode, you can still avoid cluttering up your inbox with incoming messages from mailing lists. Most modern email software has a facility for *filtering* messages, i.e. for moving them automatically from your incoming mailbox to another mailbox when it spots certain pieces of text in the header of the message. You will need to consult the online help for your email software in order to see exactly how to do it, but Figure 15-2 shows a filter in Eudora which will move all mail received from the GENBRIT mailing list into a dedicated mailbox called genbrit (in Eudora, filters are created via the **Tools | Filters** menu). This does not reduce the number of messages you receive, but it keeps your list mail separate from your personal mail and you can look at it when it suits you. Since GENBRIT can give rise to as many as 100 messages a day, this is the only practicable way to deal with the volume.

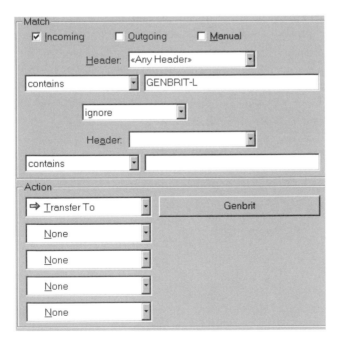

Figure 15-2 This Eudora filter will transfer any incoming mail with a header including the text 'GENBRIT-L' to a dedicated mailbox

Although, in general, mailing lists allow all members to send messages, and messages are forwarded to all members, there are two types of list that work differently.

Some lists are not used for discussion at all, but only for announcements. Typically, this sort of list is used by an organization to publish an email newsletter. It differs from a normal list in that you will not be able to send messages, only receive the announcements. The electronic newsletters mentioned in Chapter 18 (p. 309) are in fact mailing lists of this type.

Normally, mailing lists allow only members of the list to send messages to it, and messages from non-members are rejected. But there are a few lists that accept messages from non-members, for example to allow people to submit information to a project. In a case like this you will not be able to join the list yourself but will be able to send messages to it. Genuki uses a system like this for users to report errors or submit additional information, which is automatically circulated via a mailing list to all Genuki county maintainers. In fact, from the non-members' point of view this is just a special email address, and the fact that it is actually a list is not even apparent.

NEWSGROUPS

While mailing lists are very useful, they do have some disadvantages. Join a big mailing list or a few smaller ones and the number of emails you get in a day will rise drastically. Particularly if you have a slow internet connection, you may feel you do not want to spend ages downloading messages when a good proportion of them may not be relevant to your interests. Even if you have broadband or faster internet connection, you may not want to be swamped.

An alternative type of forum for discussion and questions is the newsgroup. Newsgroups work in a completely different way from mailing lists, and have the great advantage that you do not have to join anything and you do not end up receiving messages which do not relate to your interests.

Whereas a mailing list is like an online club – you really need to be a member to get the best from it – newsgroups are more like electronic notice-boards, where anyone can post a message and everyone can read it. What is good about newsgroups is that you can dip in and out of them as you like. However, there is also the disadvantage that you may miss something useful, since it is up to you to remember to check for new messages – they do not automatically come to you.

NEWS SERVERS

Unlike mailing lists, which are simply a particular way of using email, news is actually a quite separate internet facility which requires special software and which depends on a network of computers around the world called 'news servers'. The way it works is that when you post a message to a newsgroup, the message is uploaded to your local news server, which passes your message on to all the neighbouring news servers. These in turn pass it on to all *their* neighbours until your message has reached every news server on the internet. Within a day, anyone with access to a news server will be able to read your message. One of the advantages of this way of doing things is that the news service as a whole never breaks down, though it might be locally unavailable. This is quite different from a mailing list, whose operation is completely suspended if the particular server that hosts it is out of action, as happens, for example, when RootsWeb from time to time closes down its servers for maintenance over a weekend.

Most subscription ISPs provide a news server for their subscribers, though a free provider may not. If your ISP does not provide a news server, you will need to use one of the web-based news archives discussed below.

NEWSREADING SOFTWARE

In order to look at newsgroups you need a piece of software called a newsreader, or you need to use a web browser or email package that has newsreading facilities. There are several shareware newsreaders and a number of freeware ones available. Forté's Free Agent is a popular freeware newsreader for Windows, while Newswatcher is a freeware Macintosh newsreader. These can be downloaded from <easynet.tucows.com/news95.html> and <easynet.mac.tucows.com/email_news_default.html> respectively. (These pages also list a variety of other shareware and freeware packages.)

Some web browsers and email software includes news reading facilities – check the online help for a mention of newsgroups.

NEWSGROUP HIERARCHIES

Newsgroups are organized in a particular way, which you need to understand in order to use them. With mailing lists, each one is guaranteed to have a unique name because each is hosted on a particular list server, and the people managing the list server make sure that names are distinct (as well as giving some indication of the topic the list is devoted to). Newsgroups are a single global system and they are named in such a way that you can easily see what topic a newsgroup covers; groups devoted to related topics have similar names. Newsgroup names are built up of two or more parts, separated by a dot. The first part of the name indicates the general subject area and each additional part indicates a narrower subject area. Each subject area, or subdivision of one, is called a 'hierarchy'.

Most of the genealogy newsgroups are in the *soc.* hierarchy, which is for social and cultural topics. Their names start soc.genealogy (as opposed to soc.history, soc.culture, etc.), followed by a specific genealogical subject area, for example soc.genealogy.computing or soc.genealogy.ireland. There are many other hierarchies, but the oldest and most important are *alt*, *comp*, *news*, *misc*, *rec*, and *sci*.

GENEALOGY NEWSGROUPS

There are a number of groups dedicated to the genealogy of particular countries, regions or ethnic groups:

- soc.genealogy.african
- soc.genealogy.australia+nz
- soc.genealogy.benelux
- soc.genealogy.britain
- soc.genealogy.french
- soc.genealogy.german
- soc.genealogy.hispanic
- soc.genealogy.ireland
- soc.genealogy.italian
- soc.genealogy.jewish
- soc.genealogy.nordic
- soc.genealogy.slavic
- soc.genealogy.west-indies
- alt.scottish.clans
- wales.genealogy
- wales.genealogy.general

These are the best groups for discussion (in English) of genealogical sources and issues relating to the individual countries, etc.

There are a few non-geographical groups devoted to general genealogical topics:

- alt.genealogy
- soc.genealogy.computing (for anything relating to genealogy software and electronic data)
- soc.genealogy.marketplace (for announcements of commercial services or anything for sale – commercial activity is generally frowned upon in the other genealogy newsgroups)
- soc.genealogy.medieval
- soc.genealogy.methods (for discussion of the techniques and methods of genealogy)
- soc.genealogy.misc

There are a number of groups specifically intended not for general discussion but for the posting of surname interests:

- soc.genealogy.surnames
- soc.genealogy.surnames.britain
- soc.genealogy.surnames.canada
- soc.genealogy.surnames.german
- soc.genealogy.surnames.global
- soc.genealogy.surnames.ireland
- soc.genealogy.surnames.misc
- soc.genealogy.surnames.usa

However, most of these have not been functioning correctly since June 2000 and their only real value is that the archives of past messages may provide contacts for those researching particular surnames, though of course these are increasingly out of date.

There is another range of newsgroups devoted to individual surnames. These are in the alt.family-name and alt.family-names hierarchies, for example alt.family-names.anderson, alt.family-names.lloyd. There are about 150 of these, but they are in practice of doubtful value – they are very little used and have few messages of interest to genealogists. In addition, not all news servers carry them, so their distribution is more restricted than that of other newsgroups. Only the main group alt.family-names seems to be of any use. For specific surnames, a mailing list is much more likely to be useful.

All the groups listed so far are English-language groups, but there are also non-English groups which may be of interest if you have ancestors from another European country. Obviously, the discussion is mostly in the local language, but if you post in English you may well get a response.

- de.sci.genealogie (German)
- dk.historie.genealogi (Danish, little used)
- dk.videnskab.historie.genealogi (Danish)
- fr.rec.genealogie (French)
- fr.comp.applications.genealogie (French, for genealogy software)
- no.fritid.slektsforsking.diverse (Norwegian, general genealogy)
- no.fritid.slektsforsking.etterlysing (Norwegian, searching for relatives/ ancestors)
- no.fritid.slektsforsking.it (Norwegian, software)
- pl.soc.genealogia (Polish)
- se.hobby.genealogi (Swedish)
- sfnet.harrastus.sukututkimus (Finnish).

If you have ancestors from other non-English-speaking countries, you may be able to get some help by posting in an appropriate group in the soc.culture hierarchy – these groups, such as soc.culture.brazil and soc.culture.netherlands, have discussion in English on the country concerned. They may be useful for getting general information about a country from people who are familiar with it, but you should not expect to find specifically genealogical expertise.

Finally, there are two groups for heraldry, alt.heraldry.sca and rec.heraldry, and a group for adoption, alt.adoption, which may be of use in genealogical research.

NEWSGROUP CHARTERS

Every newsgroup has a charter which explains what topics it is intended to cover and what needs it is meant to meet. Charters for all the main genealogy newsgroups can be found at <homepages.rootsweb.com/ ~socgen/>, and this page has other useful information about these newsgroups. The charter for soc.genealogy.ireland is given below as an a example – note the prohibition on things like posting photographs and political discussion.

READING NEWS

Once you have set up your newsreading software there are several different stages in reading news. The very first thing you need to do is get your newsreader to download the list of all the newsgroups that are available on your news server. This can take a good few minutes as there are over 50,000 groups, but it only needs to be done once. Thereafter your software will only need to download the names of any new groups each time it connects to the server. Note that at this stage no messages have been downloaded, just the names of the groups.

CHARTER: soc.genealogy.ireland

Soc.genealogy.ireland is an unmoderated group for genealogy and family history discussion among people researching ancestors, family members, or others who have a genealogical connection to any people in any part of Northern Ireland and The Republic of Ireland.

The group is open to anyone with an interest in genealogy in any of the populations in or from this area, including, but not limited to: people who live, lived, or may have lived there; emigrants; immigrants; and their descendants.

The scope of the group reflects the language, history, migrations, and the realities of researching public records and genealogical data archives, and includes questions of local customs and history, or of regional or national history which affected the lives of these people and which are difficult to research in the present. Posts may be in any language but those seeking replies from a wide spectrum of readers (or at all) would be well advised to post in English.

The focus of the group is on the genealogy of individuals, as members of ethnic groups, and as part of migration patterns. Postings on topics unrelated to genealogy, especially relating to current political or religious topics are not acceptable.

Postings concerning general surnames searches are not welcome and should be directed to the soc.genealogy.surnames.ireland newsgroup. Postings containing MIME attachments, graphics, binary or GEDCOM files, and program listings are also not acceptable.

With a list of groups in your newsreader, you need to decide which ones to read. Newsreaders generally allow you two ways of selecting a newsgroup to read: you can either 'subscribe' to it, or you can just select it. 'Subscribing' simply means that your newsreader keeps a permanent note that you want to look at the group – it does not mean you are 'joining' the group, as you are when you subscribe to a mailing list. The advantage of subscribing is that you don't need to select the group again each time you use your newsreader.

Once you have selected or subscribed to a group, the next stage is to download the message headers – this is not the contents of the messages themselves but simply the details of the messages: who they're from, their subject lines, their date of posting, their size. You have still not downloaded any actual messages, and the idea of this is that you can see which messages are likely to be of interest and look at only those. This is the advantage of a newsgroup over a mailing list: you don't get a copy of every message, just the ones you decide you want to read. The first time you look at a group, or if there are a particularly large number of new messages, you will probably be offered an option to download just some of the headers rather than all of them.

Exactly how you view messages depends on your software. Netscape's built-in newsreader will automatically download and display any message

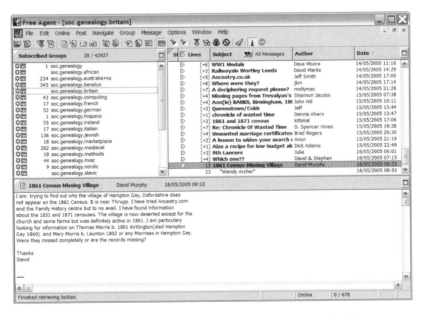

Figure 15-3 A newsreader in action. The top left pane shows the list of newsgroups, the top right pane the message headers. The highlighted message has been downloaded into the bottom pane

your cursor rests on, while in Free Agent you have to double click on a message to display it. Another possibility is to mark all the messages you want to read and then download them in one go. If you do this, you can then disconnect from the internet and read the messages offline, keeping down your connection time and costs. If you regularly want to download all the messages from selected newsgroups you can use your newsreading software in offline mode, or get a dedicated 'offline reader'. However, almost all genealogy groups are also available in mailing list format (see 'Mailing list gateways', below), and this is probably a more convenient way to ensure you get all the messages.

POSTING MESSAGES

One advantage of newsgroups over mailing lists is that you don't need email facilities to read the messages, nor a permanent email address. Your newsreader will post your message straight to the news server and, although it may ask you to configure the software with an email address, you do not need to enter an authentic working email address at all. This means newsgroups are ideal for the occasional internet user and anyone who has not got their own computer and internet connection.

It also means that it is possible to send messages to newsgroups anonymously (which is not to say the computer you are using could not be traced if it were worth someone's time and trouble).

MAILING LIST GATEWAYS

There is a way to read many of the genealogy newsgroups without access to a news server: RootsWeb acts as a gateway that makes the genealogy groups available in mailing list format. This is much more convenient if you want to make sure you don't miss any of the messages in a group. Also, because the mailing lists are available in digest form, this can be a good way of reducing the number of individual messages. Table 15-2 shows each newsgroup and its equivalent mailing list. Full details of the individual lists and how to join them can be found on RootsWeb at <**www. rootsweb.com**>. There is also, of course, an archive of the mailing list messages at <**archiver.rootsweb.com**>.

NEWSGROUP ARCHIVES

While the RootsWeb gateway is useful only for a small number of groups, you can read all newsgroups and post messages to them by using one of the websites devoted to newsgroups. The definitive newsgroup archive is provided by Google at <**groups.google.com**>.

You might think that this sort of service makes dedicated newsreading software and news servers redundant, but in fact there is a big disadvantage to web-based news services: they are very much slower to access.

Table 15-2 Genealogy newsgroups and their equivalent mailing lists

Newsgroup	Gatewayed Mailing List
alt.genealogy	ALT-GENEALOGY
fr.comp.applications.genealogie	GEN-FF-LOG
fr.rec.genealogie	GEN-FF
soc.genealogy.african	GEN-AFRICAN
soc.genealogy.australia+nz	GENANZ
soc.genealogy.benelux	GEN-BENELUX & GENBNL-L
soc.genealogy.britain	GENBRIT
soc.genealogy.computing	GENCMP
soc.genealogy.french	GEN-FR
soc.genealogy.german	GEN-DE
soc.genealogy.hispanic	GEN-HISPANIC
soc.genealogy.ireland	GENIRE
soc.genealogy.italian	GEN-ITALIAN
soc.genealogy.jewish	JEWISHGEN
soc.genealogy.marketplace	GEN-MARKET
soc.genealogy.medieval	GEN-MEDIEVAL
soc.genealogy.methods	GENMTD
soc.genealogy.misc	GENMSC
soc.genealogy.nordic	GEN-NORDIC
soc.genealogy.slavic	GEN-SLAVIC
soc.genealogy.surnames.britain	SURNAMES-BRITAIN
soc.genealogy.surnames.canada	SURNAMES-CANADA
soc.genealogy.surnames.german	SURNAMES-GERMAN
soc.genealogy.surnames.global	SURNAMES
soc.genealogy.surnames.ireland	SURNAMES-IRELAND
soc.genealogy.surnames.misc	SURNAMES-MISC
soc.genealogy.surnames.usa	SURNAMES-USA
soc.genealogy.west-indies	CARIBBEAN

Because the connection between your computer and your ISP's news server is a very short one, a newsreader will respond very quickly to your commands, whereas it will take Google, based in the US, much longer to respond to a keypress from the UK, and the entire screen will have to be redrawn every time, which slows things down even further. Unless you are only an occasional user of news, or do not have access to a news server, using a newsreader will generally be better for normal newsreading.

However, even if you use a newsreader, there are still circumstances when a news archive will be useful. The most important factor is that news servers do not keep messages for ever. Because they have limited disk space, the only way they can make room for gigabytes of new messages every day is to delete older messages, which then become unavailable on the server. Exactly how quickly messages 'scroll off' a news server varies, and partly depends on how busy a particular newsgroup is, but on the whole you should not expect to find messages more than a month old on a server. For older messages, you will need to look at a newsgroup archive. For the genealogy newsgroups the archive of the equivalent mailing list at RootsWeb can be used.

If you want to search for a particular topic across all the newsgroups, this can only be done in a news archive. Your newsreader may have facilities for searching, but these will be restricted to headers and messages you have already downloaded, and there is no way to use a newsreader to search all the messages on the server in the way that an archive's search facility can.

Finally, you may find that your local news server does not carry all the genealogy groups, in which case you will need to go to an archive.

WEB FORUMS

A third type of discussion group is the web-based forum. There is no single term for these but they are often called 'message boards' or 'bulletin boards'. These work in very much the same way as Google's web-based news service: a website acts as a place where people can post messages for others to read. As with newsgroups, this does not clutter up your mailbox and does not require any long-term commitment. And, of course, it does not require you to install or configure software. However, as with Google's news service, these forums can be very slow to use, in comparison with using a newsreader to access a local news server. Also, as there is no way to select a whole group of messages for reading, you have to look separately at every single message of interest, each of which is delivered to you as a separate web page. If you want to read every message, this will be *very* tedious.

Unfortunately, there is no comprehensive list of such discussion forums, as a number of ISPs have a system for their subscribers to set up web-based discussion groups, and there are sites like Yahoo Groups (see p. 229) or Smartgroups at <www.smartgroups.com>, who provide such facilities for all comers. (In fact the distinction between mailing lists and web-based discussion is not absolutely clear-cut. Yahoo Groups, for example, allows you to read messages on the web rather than receiving them as email.)

The main UK site for genealogy discussion forums is British-Genealogy at <www.british-genealogy.com/forums>. This has forums devoted to every

Figure 15-4 Genforum's Isle of Man Genealogy Forum at <genforum.genealogy.com/isleofman/>

county and many individual places, as well as to specific genealogical topics such as occupations and the various types of genealogical record. There are also a few more general forums such as that for genealogy beginners. There is a convenient overview of the available forums at **<www. british-genealogy.com/forums/archive/>**.

One of the major sites providing discussion forum facilities for genealogy is GenForum at **<genforum.genealogy.com>**. There are forums for over 100 countries, including all parts of the British Isles. On the page for each country there is also a link to 'Regions for this Country' which leads to forums for individual counties or major towns, though not every county has its own forum. (Figure 15-4 shows some of the messages on the Isle of Man forum.) There is a forum for each US state, and around 80 devoted to general topics (e.g. emigration, Jewish genealogy, marriage records), including 20 or so devoted to computers and genealogy software. There are thousands of forums relating to individual surnames.

Another site that provides a large number of genealogy forums is Ancestry, which offers over 120,000 genealogy 'message boards' at **<www.ancestry.com/share/>**. There are boards for all parts of the UK and Ireland. There is at least one message board for each county, as well as boards for: most other countries; many of the individual counties in each US state; and thousands of individual surnames. A wide range of general topics have a dedicated message board:

- Adoptions
- Ancestry Daily News
- Ancestry.com
- Cemeteries & Tombstones
- Census
- Crime
- Disasters
- Ethnic/Race
- Folklore, Legends & Family Stories
- Genealogy Software
- Government
- Immigration and Emigration
- Major Events
- Medical
- Medieval History
- Methods
- Migration
- Military
- Newspaper Research
- Occupations
- Organizations and Societies
- Orphans and orphanages
- Pioneer Programs
- Projects
- Religions and Religious
- Research Groups
- Research Resources
- Reunion Announcements
- RootsWeb
- Royalty and Nobility

To assist in finding messages on particular topics and relevant message boards, there is a global search facility.

A site specifically for UK and Irish interests is RootsChat at <www.rootschat.com>. This has discussion forums for England, Wales, Scotland Ireland, and every individual county in the British Isles. TalkingScot provides forums for those with Scottish ancestry at <www.talkingscot.com>. It has separate discussion groups for the various types of genealogical record as well as individual groups for Scottish emigration to particular countries or regions.

Forums on other providers can be found by using a search engine, and a link to any forum relating specifically to UK genealogy should be found on the relevant county page on Genuki.

∎ FREQUENTLY ASKED QUESTIONS (FAQ)

Once you have been on a mailing list or looking at a newsgroup for some time, you will realize that certain questions come up again and again. Needless to say, regular members of a list don't relish the thought of repeatedly taking the time to answer these basic questions, so most newsgroups and general-interest mailing lists (i.e. those not dedicated to particular surnames) have what is called an FAQ, a file of frequently asked questions. The FAQ for a newsgroup is normally posted to the group once a month, but practice varies in mailing lists.

If you are thinking of asking a question in a particular newsgroup for the first time, and especially if you are just starting to research your family tree, it's a good idea to consult the FAQ for the group. This will give you a guide as to what are considered appropriate or inappropriate issues to discuss and above all provide answers to some of the most obvious questions asked by beginners.

The easiest way to find the FAQ for a mailing list or newsgroup is to search the newsgroup archives at Google Groups, or for genealogy groups, the archive of the gatewayed mailing list at RootsWeb.

▌NETIQUETTE

Mailing lists and newsgroups are essentially social institutions and, like face-to-face social institutions, they have a set of largely unwritten rules about what counts as acceptable or unacceptable behaviour. While individual newsgroups and mailing lists may spell some of these out in an FAQ or charter, most of these rules are common to all online discussion groups and are often referred to collectively as 'netiquette'.

Of course, no one can stop you making inappropriate postings to a newsgroup, but breaking the rules will not make you popular: those who repeatedly breach them are likely to be on the receiving end of rebukes, and some people may configure their newsreading software to ignore messages from such miscreants. A mailing list is very likely to make some of these rules explicit conditions for its use, and list owners usually exclude those who persistently ignore them. Even though people are pretty tolerant of mistakes from beginners, it is worth reading the FAQ for a newsgroup or mailing list, and the welcome message from a mailing list.

The culture of newsgroups is rather different from that of mailing lists. The main reason for this is that whereas every mailing list has an owner, no one is in charge of a newsgroup. In fact, newsgroups are one of the few social institutions that are genuinely anarchic. (The only control is that the operator of each news server decides which groups to take and which to ignore.) This means that if people 'misbehave' in a newsgroup, there is no one to appeal to.

Some mailing lists and a very small number of newsgroups are 'moderated'. This can either mean that the messages pass through some sort of editorial control before being posted publicly; or it can mean that those who post inappropriate messages will be reprimanded and possibly, in the case of a list, forcibly unsubscribed.

The complete text of Virginia Shea's book *Netiquette* is online at <**www. albion.com/netiquette/book/**>. Malcolm Austen has some useful 'Notes on List Etiquette' at <**www.mno.org.uk/listiquette**>.

GOOD MANNERS

Manners can be a problem in online discussion forums. The absence of the normal cues we expect in face-to-face interaction seems to make people less restrained (i.e. less polite), and such groups can contain a very diverse mix of individuals, both socially and geographically. This means you cannot rely on instincts developed in the offline world to guide your behaviour. The following are generally accepted rules for electronic discussion forums:

- Make sure that any messages you send are relevant to the topic of the list or group. Some will tolerate the occasional 'off-topic' message, some will not. If the list owner or others in a newsgroup ask you to discontinue a topic, you should do so.
- Be very wary of using humour and irony, particularly if you are new to a group or list. Even those who share your language may not share your cultural norms. You can use a smiley ;-) to signal a joke.
- Don't be rude to others, no matter how ignorant or rude they may seem (an abusive message is called a 'flame'). An apparently stupid question about, say, English counties may be perfectly reasonable if it comes from someone who has limited familiarity with the history and geography of the British Isles.
- Never send an angry message as an immediate response to another message. Allow yourself time to cool down, because once you have sent the message you cannot cancel it when you have second thoughts.
- Avoid politics and religion, except where strictly relevant to a genealogical issue.
- Messages which are all in upper case are very difficult to read. If you post a message all in upper case, people will tell you 'DON'T SHOUT!'. Reserve upper case for highlighting surnames.
- If you are going to criticize, try and be positive and constructive. Much of what is on the internet for genealogists is the result of volunteer projects and individuals giving up their free time. While it is, of course, legitimate to subject any genealogical material or project to criticism, criticizing individuals in the public forum of a newsgroup because they have not done something the way you would have done it is not going to improve the genealogical world. Criticizing commercial services is another matter but, even so, there is no need to be rude. In any case, a defamatory message in an online discussion group could lay you open to a libel prosecution.
- Messages which advertise goods or services are out of place in most mailing lists and all genealogy newsgroups except soc.genealogy. marketplace. They can actually be counter-productive, as people tend to take a dim view of self-promoting commercial postings. However, it is perfectly legitimate to make recommendations about books or software, as long as you are not the author or retailer. Advertising a personal, non-commercial website or any sort of free service is OK as long as it is not done too frequently.

- If you are using one of the twinned newsgroup/mailing lists described above, bear in mind that mailing list messages will reach all members very shortly after the original mailing, but news messages may take some time to make their way around the world. This means that newsgroup users sometimes appear slightly out of touch with the discussion, but that is an artefact of the technology, not a personal failing.
- Don't pass on a virus warning to a list, as almost all virus warnings are hoaxes. If you think it is not a hoax (check at sites like Vmyths <www.Vmyths.com>), mail it to the list owner, and he or she can then post it to the list if it seems to be genuine, i.e. it comes from an authoritative computer security source.
- Don't post messages containing other people's data or data from CD-ROMs. This is more than bad manners, it's copyright infringment.
- Don't forward to a list a message sent to you personally unless you have the original sender's permission or it is obvious from the content that it is meant for wider dissemination.

These last two points are discussed in more detail in Chapter 19 under 'Copyright and privacy' (p. 323f.).

APPROPRIATE REPLIES

One of the basic rules of online discussion is that any reply to a previous message should be 'appropriate'. What this means in practice is:

- Don't post a reply to the list or group if your answer is going to be of interest only to the sender of the original message – email that person directly. So if someone asks how to locate particular records, any reply is likely to be of interest to all; an offer to lend a microfiche reader is only of interest to the person who posted a message asking for one.
- Don't quote the entirety of a previous message in a reply, particularly if your reply comes right at the bottom – just quote the relevant part.[12]
- As mentioned above, if you receive a mailing list as a digest, not only are you going to need to edit out most of the original text in your reply, you will also need to change the subject to something more appropriate. If you don't, people will not know what your message relates to and most will not even look at it.

▌ASKING QUESTIONS

While discussion groups contain much discussion, they also provide places for people to post queries and receive help and advice. One of the reasons

---

12 One of the great religious schisms on the internet is between the 'top-posters' and the 'bottom-posters', who have different views on where in the message one should add one's own remarks when replying.

that the internet is so useful for family historians is that it provides a huge pool of experience and expertise. In fact much of the discussion in genealogy groups arises out of particular queries. If you are asking a mailing list or newsgroup for help or advice, there are a number of things to bear in mind to ensure you get the help you want.

1. Post your query in the right place

There is little point in posting a Scottish query to a Channel Islands mailing list, or asking about a surname in soc.genealogy.computing. For very general queries, newsgroups and their equivalent mailing lists are probably the best places to ask: *any* question relating to British genealogy is within the scope of soc.genealogy.britain, for example. To be sure, check the group's charter (see p. 240). Do not post the same query to a lot of groups or mailing lists – this is called 'cross-posting' and is generally frowned upon. It asks several groups of people to help you and the duplication of effort in replying wastes everyone's time and trouble. (However, cross-posting of announcements is acceptable, as long the message is relevant to each discussion group.)

2. Give an explicit subject line

One of the most important things in any message asking for assistance is making sure people who could assist you notice the message. This applies particularly in a newsgroup or a busy mailing list with many messages a day.

- Make sure your subject line is explicit and helpful. If you use subject lines like 'genealogy' or 'problem' in a genealogy newsgroup or mailing list, few people will even bother to look at your message.
- Put any surnames you are enquiring about in upper case in your subject line. This makes it easy for people who are scanning a list of message headers to notice the surname. Ideally, do this in the body of your message, too.

3. Don't have unreasonable expectations

Some of the more experienced and active members of discussion groups devote considerable time to answering queries from relative beginners, but it is important not to abuse this willingness by having unreasonable expectations of what people will do for you.

- Don't ask a question that is covered in the FAQ if there is one.
- Don't expect people to give you factual information that you can easily look up in a standard reference book or find online for yourself. If you ask, 'Is the Family Records Centre open on Saturdays?' it means you cannot be bothered to use a search engine to find its website (and were not paying attention in Chapter 3!), and are expecting other people to take the time to provide you with the information. If you are

a genealogist living in Britain, you really ought to have a good atlas of the country, so questions like 'Where is Newport Pagnell?' should only come from non-UK residents. On the other hand, questions requiring detailed local knowledge ('Is such and such a building still there?') are entirely reasonable on the county mailing lists.

• Don't expect other list members to teach you the basics of genealogical research. You really need to have a good book on the subject, and should look at the tutorial material discussed in the Introduction (p. 7).

• If you are looking for help with computer software problems (whether specifically genealogical or not), consider looking at the website or discussion forum of the software supplier before asking on a non-technical mailing list or newsgroup.

On the other hand, any request for recommendations and advice is fair enough – the pooling of expertise in a discussion group makes it one of the most sensible places to raise such questions.

❚ STARTING YOUR OWN DISCUSSION GROUP

There are many websites that allow you to start your own discussion group. As mentioned above, you may find that your own ISP provides facilities to set one up on their website. Alternatively, you could look at using Yahoo Groups at <**groups.yahoo.com**> or Smartgroups at <**www.smartgroups. com**>. The advantage of using well-known services like these is that people will be much more likely to come across your group.

RootsWeb hosts an enormous number of genealogical mailing lists and is a good place to create a new one. Details of how to request a new mailing list will be found at <**resources.rootsweb.com/adopt/**>. There is detailed coverage of mailing list administration at <**helpdesk.rootsweb. com/listadmins/**>.

Bear in mind that maintaining a mailing list or discussion group could end up requiring a significant amount of your time if it becomes popular. Unless a list is small, it is certainly much better for it to be maintained by more than one person so that responsibilities can be shared. On the other hand, a mailing list for a particular surname is not likely to generate nearly as much mail as one on a general topic. RootsWeb provides detailed information about the responsibilities of list owners on their system, and other sites that provide discussion forums will do the same.

Starting a new newsgroup is another matter entirely. Generally, a newsgroup can only be set up after the publication of a Request For Discussion (RFD) which outlines the group's proposed purpose (and why existing groups do not meet the same needs), which is then followed by a discussion period. Ultimately a Call For Votes (CFV) is published and all interested can vote for or against the creation of the new group. Clearly, this is not something you could do, as an individual, on the spur of the moment. However, you can set up a newsgroup under the alt. hierarchy without the formal procedure for other groups, though this is not something for the technologically faint-hearted. Given the ease of setting up a mailing list or a web-based discussion forum, it is difficult to see a good reason for setting up a new genealogy newsgroup except by the accepted consensual method.

WHICH DISCUSSION GROUP?

Which mailing lists or newsgroups you read will, of course, depend on your genealogical interests. The main general group for British genealogy is soc.genealogy.britain and its associated mailing list, GENBRIT. If you are not already familiar with mailing lists, you may not want it to be the first one you join – you could be a bit overwhelmed with the 50-plus messages per day arriving in your mailbox, and may prefer to look at the newsgroup rather than the mailing list. Also, it can be a rather boisterous group.

If you know where your ancestors came from, it may be more useful to join the appropriate county mailing lists (see <**www.genuki.org.uk/indexes/MailingLists.html**>). There are fewer messages, and more of the postings are likely to be relevant. You will certainly have a better chance of encountering people with whom you share surname interests, not to mention common ancestors. Other useful lists are those for special interests, such as coalminers or the Boer War.

You might think that the best thing to do is join the lists for your surnames of interest, and there are thousands of lists and web-based forums devoted to individual surnames. However, they differ widely in their level of usefulness. Some have very few subscribers and very few messages, while, particularly in the case of reasonably common English surnames, you may well find lists dominated by US subscribers with mainly post-colonial interests. But with a reasonably rare surname in your family tree, particularly if it is also geographically limited, it is very likely that some other subscribers on a surname list will share your interests. Whereas the relevant county mailing list is certain to be useful, with surname lists it's more a matter of luck.

The simplest way to see whether any discussion forum is going to be worth joining is to look at the archives for the list to see the kind of topics that are discussed. This also has the advantage that you can get a rough idea of how many messages a month you would be letting yourself in for. You could also simply join a group and 'lurk', i.e. receive and read the messages without contributing yourself.

CHAPTER 16

SEARCH ENGINES

One of the most obvious features of the internet that makes it good for genealogical, or indeed any, research is that it is very large, and the amount of material available is rapidly increasing. It is impossible to get an accurate idea of the size of the web, but it would be reasonable to assume at the very least 16,000 million pages, and that does not include any data held in online databases.[13] But the usefulness, or at least accessibility, of this material is mitigated by the difficulty of locating specific pages. Of course, it is not difficult to find the websites of major institutions, but much of the genealogical material on the web is published by individuals or small groups and organizations, which can be much harder to find. Also, since there is no foolproof way to locate material, a failed search does not even imply material is not online.

The standard tool for locating information on the web is a search engine. This is a website that combines an index to the web and a facility to search the index. Although many people do not recognize any difference between directories, gateways and portals on the one hand, and search engines on the other, they are in fact very different beasts (which is why they are treated separately in this book) and have quite different strengths and weaknesses, summarized in Table 16-1.

These differences mean that directories, and particularly gateways and portals, are likely to be good for finding the sites of organizations, but much less well suited to discovering sub-pages with information on individual topics. Even genealogy directories with substantial links to personal

---

13 This is a highly conservative estimate, based on (a) the fact that in summer 2005, Google, the most comprehensive search engine, claimed to cover just over 8,000 million web pages, and (b) the assumption that no search engine indexes more than half the web. A study conducted by Steve Lawrence and C. Lee Giles, 'Accessibility of information on the web' in *Nature*, 8 July 1999, pp. 107–109 (online at <**www.ist.psu.edu/faculty_pages/giles/publications/ Nature-99.pdf**>) found that no search engine covered more than 16% of the web. Although this study is several years old, there has not been any major breakthrough in search engine technology which suggests these results are not still broadly valid.

Table 16-1 Comparison of directories, etc., with search engines

Directories, Gateways and Portals	Search Engines
Directories and gateways list web*sites* according to general subject matter.	Search engines list individual web *pages* according to the words on the page.
Directories are constructed and maintained by intelligent humans. In the case of genealogy gateways you can assume they actually have some expertise in genealogy.	Search engines rely on indexes created automatically by 'robots', software programs which roam the internet looking for new or changed web pages.
Directories and particularly specialist gateways for genealogy categorize genealogy websites intelligently.	While some search engines know about related terms, they work at the level of individual words.
Directories are selective (even a comprehensive gateway like Genuki only links to sites it regards as useful).	Search engines index everything they come across.
Directories, offering a ready-made selection, require no skill on the part of the user.	The number of results returned by a search engine can easily run into six or seven figures, and success is highly dependent on the searcher's ability to formulate the search in appropriate terms.
Gateways often annotate links to give some idea of the scope or importance of a site.	A search engine may be able to rank search results in order of relevance to the search terms, but will generally attach no more importance to the website of an individual genealogist than to that of a major national institution.

websites and surname resources probably don't include more than a fraction of those discoverable via a search engine.

Sometimes it is essential to search for words contained in a page; sometimes it is actually unhelpful. If you were trying to find the opening times of the Family Records Centre, it would be very irritating to retrieve thousands of web pages which mention the Family Records Centre, let alone all those that include the words *family* or *records* or *centre* – for finding a site like this a gateway is ideal. But if you are looking for pages which mention the name of one of your ancestors, there is little point in using a directory or gateway. You have to use a search engine.

There are many different search engines. The main ones (i.e. the largest and most popular) are:

AlltheWeb   <www.alltheweb.com>
AltaVista   <www.altavista.com>
Ask Jeeves   <www.ask.com>
Google   <www.google.com>
Hotbot   <www.hotbot.com>
Lycos   <www.lycos.com>

MSN Search   <search.msn.com>
Teoma   <www.teoma.com>
Yahoo Search   <search.yahoo.com>

There are UK versions of Google at **<www.google.co.uk>**, AltaVista at **<uk.altavista.com>**, Hotbot at **<www.hotbot.lycos.co.uk>**, and Lycos at **<www.lycos.co.uk>**. For a comprehensive set of links to search engines, see Yahoo's listing for Search Engines & Directories at **<dir.yahoo.com/ Computers_and_internet/internet/World_Wide_Web/Searching_the_Web/ Search_Engines_and_Directories/>**.

The nine search engines listed do not in fact represent nine distinct tools. AltaVista and Alltheweb were taken over by Yahoo in spring 2004 and these now use the same index as Yahoo, which leaves them with no independent value. This is a regrettable development for genealogists, because it means that none of the major search engines now offer case sensitive searching or allow 'wild cards', which make it possible to search simultaneously for spelling variations, both of which were useful for surname searches. Ask Jeeves and Teoma use the same index. Hotbot uses the same index as Lycos, though it also offers Google and Ask Jeeves as alternatives, and has more flexible advanced search options (called 'filters').

▌USING A SEARCH ENGINE

In spite of the more or less subtle differences between them, all search engines work in basically the same way. They offer you a box to type in the 'search terms' or 'keywords' you want to search for, and a button to click on to start the search. The example from Yahoo Search shown in Figure 16-1 is typical. Once you've clicked on the 'Search the Web' button, the search engine will come back with a page containing a list of matching web pages (see Figure 16-2), each with a brief description culled from the page itself, and you can click on any of the items listed to go to the relevant web page. Search engines differ in exactly how they expect you

Figure 16-1 The Yahoo Search home page at <search.yahoo.com>

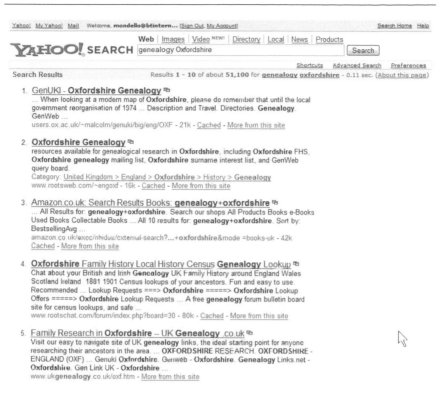

Figure 16-2 Results of a search on Yahoo Search

to formulate your search, how they rank the results, how much you can customize display of the results, and so on, but these basics are common to all.

Most search engines will report the total number of matching web pages found, called 'hits', and if there is more than a pageful (typically 10 or 20), it will provide links to subsequent pages of hits. (In Figure 16-2, you can see this information just above the first search result.) Usually the words you have searched on will be highlighted in some way.

FORMULATING YOUR SEARCH

Your success in searching depends in part on your choice of search engine, which is discussed on p. 269, but is also greatly dependent on your skill in choosing appropriate search terms and formulating your search.

In this chapter I have put search terms between square brackets. To run the search in a search engine type in the text between the brackets *exactly*, but don't include the square brackets themselves. Note that the figures given for the number of hits have indicative status only – they were correct when I tried out these searches, but the indexes used by search engines grow daily, so you will not get identical results. Also, there is no way to verify the accuracy of the figures except where they are very low. But the differences between the various *types* of search and formulation should be of the same order.

BASIC SEARCHING

There are actually several different types of search offered by search engines. In the basic search – the one you get if you don't select any options and just type in words to be searched for – the results will include all web pages found that contain *all* the words you have typed in the search field. This means that the more words you type in, the fewer results you will get. If you type in any surname or place name on its own, unless it's a fairly unusual one you will get thousands of hits. So it's always better to narrow down your search by entering more words if possible. This type of search is called an AND search.

AND and OR are just the most commonly used parts of a general technique for formulating searches called Boolean logic.[14]

LOOKING FOR ALTERNATIVES

One thing to avoid in a basic search is entering a set of alternatives, because then you will miss some, perhaps many relevant pages. Supposing you have ancestors who were Grimsby trawlermen, it might seem a good idea to enter both [trawlerman] and [trawlermen], possibly adding [trawler] for good measure. But each extra word reduces the number of matching pages found. On Google, a search for [Grimsby trawlerman] produces 185 hits, [Grimsby trawlermen] 337 hits, while the combination [Grimsby trawlerman trawlermen] gives only 33. The same will happen if you give alternative surname spellings: for example Google gives around 33,000 hits for [Waymark] and 28,000 for [Wymark], but [Waymark Wymark] produces less than 30, a tiny number of pages which have both variants.

The AND search is not suitable for looking for alternatives, unless you really do require pages that have both on them. What you need instead is an OR search, which will retrieve all pages containing at least one of the search words.

All the main search engines offer the option of doing an OR search. There are normally two ways to do this. First, all search engines have an Advanced Search page (there will be a link to this located near the search

---

14 This topic can be handled only briefly here. For more information on using Boolean expressions for searching, look at the help pages of the search engines or the BrightPlanet tutorial at <**www.brightplanet.com/deepcontent/tutorials/search/part4.asp**>.

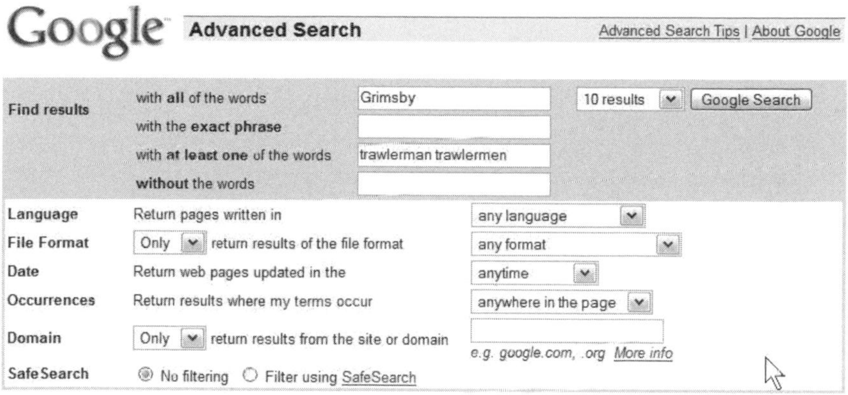

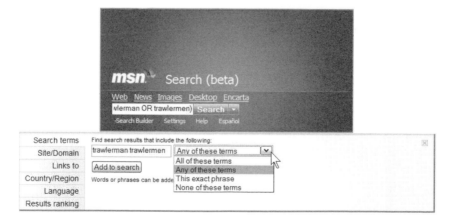

Figure 16-3 An OR search on Google's Advanced Search page

box on the main page, often to the right, as in Yahoo Search, Figure 16-2). This will offer you a wide variety of things to specify about what you are looking for but near the top should be options to 'look for all of the words' and 'look for any of the words'. The first of these is for words which *must* be included, the latter where any *one* of the alternatives you give will do. Figure 16-3 shows how to find your trawlerman ancestors on Google's Advanced Search page at **<www.google.com/advanced_search>**. You'll find very similar options in other search engines. As you'd expect, this gives you more results than any of the individual AND searches.

MSN search has no separate page for an advanced search but has a drop-down panel, activated by clicking on **+Search Builder**, with six tabs which contain all the options normally found on an advanced search page. Figure 16-4 shows how to enter the terms for an OR search. When you

Figure 16-4 Creating an OR search with MSN's Search Builder

click on the 'Add to search' button this is translated into the correct syntax in the search field.

The other way to create an OR search is simply by typing in the correct formulation directly in the search field. Strictly, the correct way to do this is shown in the following example:

[Grimsby AND (trawlerman OR trawlermen)]

But given that the default search is an AND search, this is equivalent to

[Grimsby (trawlerman OR trawlermen)]

which is what the MSN search requires.

However, many search engines are more relaxed. For example, Yahoo, Google and Teoma only require the OR, not the AND or the parentheses:

[Grimsby trawlerman OR trawlermen]

Lycos automatically treats terms in parenthesis as part of an OR expression:

[Grimsby (trawlerman trawlermen)]

All of them also seem to accept the 'correct' syntax, so that will be the best approach if you can't find specific information about this topic on the help pages.

You can use the same principles to construct more complex searches:

[Robinson AND (genealogy OR "family history") AND (Nottingham OR Notts) AND (cobbler OR cordwainer)]

which Google would allow you to enter as

[Robinson genealogy OR "family history" Nottingham OR Notts cobbler OR cordwainer].

EXCLUSION

Often you will find yourself searching on a word that has several meanings or distinct uses, in which case it can be useful to find a way of excluding some pages. The way to do this is to choose a word which occurs only on pages you don't want, and mark it for exclusion, which most search engines do by prefixing with a hyphen. For example [Bath -wash] would be a way to ensure that your enquiry about a town in Somerset was not diluted by material on cleanliness.[15]

---

15 This hyphen is to be regarded as a substitute for the typographically correct minus sign, which your browser would almost certainly ignore and therefore not submit as part of your search.

There is one very common problem when searching for geographical information which this technique can help to alleviate: names of cities and counties are used as names for ships, regiments, families and the like; also, when British emigrants settled in the colonies they frequently reused British place names. This means that many searches which include place names will retrieve a good number of irrelevant pages.

If you do a search on [Gloucester], for example, you will soon discover that there is a Gloucester County in Virginia and in New Brunswick, a town of Gloucester in New South Wales and Massachusetts (not far from the town of Essex), and you probably do not want all of these included in your results if you are looking for ancestors who lived along the Severn. Then there is HMS *Gloucester*, the Duke of Gloucester, pubs called the Gloucester Arms and so on. Likewise, if you're searching on [York], you do not really want to retrieve all the pages that mention New York.

Obviously it would be rather tedious to do this for every possibility, but you could easily exclude those which an initial search shows are the most common, e.g. [Gloucester -Virginia] or [York -"New York"].

Another case where this technique would be useful is if you are searching for a surname which also happens to be that of a well-known person: [Gallagher -Oasis] or [Blair -Tony -Orwell] will reduce the number of unwanted results you will get if you are searching for the surnames Gallagher or Blair, and do not want to be overwhelmed with hundreds if not thousands of hits relating to one or two high-profile bearers of the name. In the first example, [Gallagher] gives over four million hits on Google, while [Gallagher -Oasis] cuts this down to about half as many.

Unfortunately, if you are searching for a surname which is also a place name, e.g. Kent or York, there is no simple way to exclude web pages with the place name, though on p. 270 I suggest a technique for restricting your hits to personal genealogy websites.

STOP WORDS

The reason for putting the Boolean operators AND/OR in upper case, incidentally, is that these are small words which search engines normally ignore, so-called 'stop words': [Waymark OR Wymark] finds 61,000 hits on Google, [Waymark or Wymark] finds only 28 – the 'or' has been ignored and the alternative spellings treated as an AND search.

The counterpart of the - sign for exclusion, is the + sign, indicating that the term *must* be in the pages retrieved. Given that all the main search engines do this by default for all terms you type in, the only real use is to include stop words. For searching on names, places and occupations, this is not likely to be very useful, unless you have ancestors from Oregon (abbreviation 'OR').

In Boolean terms, - is the equivalent of AND NOT, and + the equivalent of AND.

PHRASES AND NAMES

Another important issue when using a search engine is how to group words together into a phrase. If you just type in a forename and surname, or a two-part place name, search engines will treat this as an AND search on the two components.

This *may* not matter, especially if you are looking for something very specific, as search engines tend to put near the top of their listings those hits which include all search terms in the page title. For example, a Google search on [Manorial Documents Register] produces over 14,000 hits, but the MDR area on the National Archives' site, the official home of the MDR, is at the top of the list (see Figure 16-5).

But if you try the same search with the not very dissimilar [National Register of Archives] the results are less satisfactory. For a start Google will tell you that '*of* is a very common word and was not included in your search', and although the official NRA site comes second, it is obviously mixed up with other sites which have the 'National Archives' and the word 'Register' on the same page but not necessarily together. This is just about bearable when you are looking for a particular site or if you are looking for some very specific historical information (try [1834 Poor Law]). But if you are looking for names, it will be hopeless.

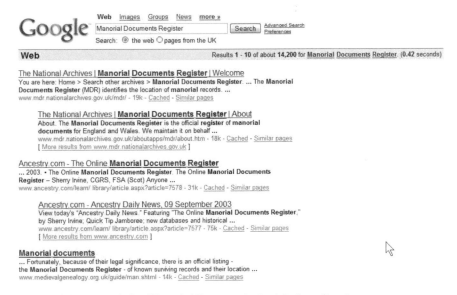

Figure 16-5 A search for [Manorial Documents Register] on Google

The standard way of indicating that your words form a phrase is to surround them with inverted commas, e.g. ["North Shields"] or ["Thomas Walker"] or ["National Register of Archives"]. (Incidentally, stop words are *not* ignored inside inverted commas.) And the difference it can make is enormous: Google gives 1.5 million hits for ["John Smith"] against 23 million for [John Smith].

However, there is a downside: although you are getting more manageable and correct results, the phrase search will miss pages with "Smith, John", "John Richard Smith", so it is not an unmixed blessing. It will also inevitably miss "John, son of Richard and Mary Smith", but with present technology this is simply beyond the capabilities of search engines. Even so, with a reasonably unusual name, the phrase search can produce a list of hits short enough for each one to be checked – for example, a search for ["Cornelius McBride"] on Google produces only 46 hits – which will more than make up for missing a few.

Of course, if your phrase is even slightly wrong, you may get no useful results at all – ["National Archives Register"] won't get you anywhere near the official page of the National Register of Archives, unless you're lucky and find other pages that also don't know its correct title, but do have a link to the official page.

Full Boolean algebra has a NEAR operator which largely solves these problems, but unfortunately it is not supported by any of the major search engines.

NATURAL LANGUAGE SEARCHING

Some search engines claim to offer natural language searching, i.e. you type in your query not as a terse series of keywords, but as a question formulated in a full sentence. This might make you feel marginally less intimidated by the technology, but in fact it will do nothing to improve your search results. All the search engine does is strip out the small, common words and search on the remainder. On Ask Jeeves, for example, at <www.ask.com> the query [where can I find wills for London?] appears to produce exactly the same list of results as [wills London].

REFINING YOUR SEARCH

If you're looking for something very specific, you may find it immediately, as with the search in Figure 16-5. Otherwise, however, you shouldn't assume that your initial search will find what you want and produce a manageable list of results. If, for example, you are looking for individuals or families, or trying to find information on a particular genealogical topic, it is likely that you will have to look at quite a lot of the hits a search engine retrieves before finding what you are looking for. This makes it important to refine your search as much as possible.

The previous pages offer some advice on formulating your search, but however well you formulate it for the first run, you will often be able to refine it once you have looked at the initial results. Search engines provide a search box with your search terms at the top of each page of hits, so it is very straightforward to edit this and re-run the search.

Some search engines offer facilities to refine your search within the results you have already retrieved. In Google, clicking on the 'Search within results' link at the bottom of a results page takes you to another search page where you can specify a narrower search with additional words. Yahoo offers a similar facility, listing alternatives before the first search result. Teoma offers a panel at the side of the page with suggestions for additional phrases to improve your search. However, neither of these actually do anything clever – they just add the new terms and re-run your original search. If you know how to formulate searches, these facilities don't offer anything extra.

▌ SEARCH TIPS

Apart from taking care to formulate your query, there are a number of other things to bear in mind if your searching is going to be successful and not too time-consuming.

First, the better you know the particular search engine you are using, the better the results you will get. Look at the options it offers, and look at the Help or Tips pages. Although I have highlighted the main features of search engines, each has its idiosyncrasies. And while it is quite easy to find what a search engine will do, sometimes the only way to find out what it *will not* do is to see what is missing from the Help pages. It is also worth trying out some different types of query, just so you get a feel for how many results to expect and how they are sorted.

If you carry out searches on your particular surnames on a regular basis, it can be worth adding the URL of the results pages to your bookmarks (Netscape) or favorites (Internet Explorer), making it easy to run the same query repeatedly.

This works because in most search engines the browser submits the search terms as an appendage to the URL, so, for example, when you search Google for [Grimsby AND trawlerman], the browser sends the URL <www.google.com/search?q=Grimsby+trawlerman&btnG=Google+Search>, which is then shown as the address of the first page of results. Bookmarking this page will allow you to retrieve the entire URL and then re-run the search.

There is one simple browser technique which will save you time when searching. Once you have got a list of search results that you want to look at, open each link you follow in a new window or tab so that the original list of search results remains open. (On Windows browsers a right mouse click over the link will bring up a menu with this option; on the Macintosh shift+click). Otherwise, each time you want to go back to your results the search engine will run the search all over again. Another useful trick for a long page of results is to save it to your hard disk so that you can explore the hits at your leisure later.

SEARCHING FOR FILES

Increasingly, search engines can be used for finding other types of material online in addition to web pages. This material falls into two broad categories, which are generally dealt with in distinct ways.

First, there are files with textual material but which are in a proprietary document format rather than the HTML format used for web pages. All the main search engines index such material for a number of file formats, notably Adobe Acrobat (PDF) files, described in more detail on page 293, and Microsoft Word files. This is important because many bodies put longer-term official information online in PDF format.

The content of such files is usually included automatically in the search engine's index, so you do not need to specify a particular file type when searching. However you will be able to choose 'file type' on the advanced search page of most search engines.

Multimedia files are generally handled differently, and the tendency is to have a separate search facility for each format. As you can see in Figure 16-1, Yahoo Search has separate tabs for images, directory, maps (this is actually customizable via the Preferences link), while Google offers the images, groups (i.e. newsgroups) and new tabs above the search box on the home page.

SEARCHING FOR PHOTOGRAPHS

Of the various multimedia file types, those of most interest to genealogists will be the graphics files of scanned or digital photographs. An overview of the sorts of photographs you can expect to find online is given in Chapter 14.

When searching for images, you can't simply use the standard facilities of the search engines, since these look for text. Although any search results *will* include pages with images on them, particularly where there are relevant captions, this will probably not be obvious from the list of search engine results. This might be a way to find sites or pages that are devoted to photographs or postcards, but it will be a time-consuming way to find individual photographs.

Google has an excellent image search facility at <images.google.com>, which claims to have over 880 million images indexed (see <images.

Figure 16-6 Search results in Google Images

google.com/help/faq_images.html>. The search results pages show thumb-nail versions of the images which match your search criteria – clicking on an image takes you to a two-panel page with the image at the top and the page it comes from below. See Figure 16-6, the results of a search for [Chatham dockyard].

Mostly you will just get a normal search box, but if there is an advanced image search this should allow you to be more precise about the sorts of image you want, such as that from Google shown in Figure 16-7.

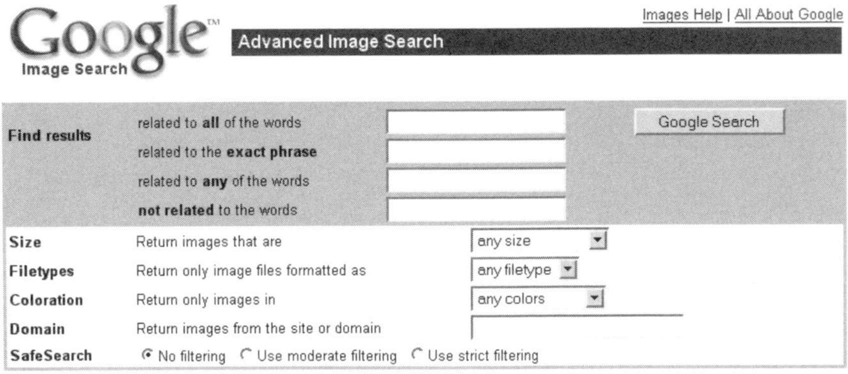

Figure 16-7 Google's Advanced Image Search

For a list of other image search engines, look at the BIG Search Engine Index, which has a list of about 20 image search engines and databases at <www.search-engine-index.co.uk/Images_Search/> with brief descriptions.

The Boston Universities Library site has a brief guide to finding images on the web at <www.bu.edu/library/instruction/findimages/>, which includes information on using standard search engines to find images.

▍SITES AND DOMAINS

Although search engines are mainly used for searching the whole web, they can also be used to search individual websites. Since most major sites have their own search engine, the value of this may not be immediately obvious. But there are two advantages: you don't have to get to grips with a new search engine every time you visit a new site; and the big search engines often have much more sophisticated search facilities than individual sites. For example, the search facility on the National Archives' site has no phrase search, and the results are rather terse. Using a general search engine, you can use the advanced search options to do more complex searches, specify a date range for pages retrieved, look for particular file types, etc. However, the external search results may not be as complete or as up to date as those from an internal search engine.

Most search engines allow you to specify a site as one of the advanced search options – look for the heading 'Domain' on the advanced search page. If you try a search with this you will see that you can in fact specify this in the basic search field by putting a special keyword and a colon before the site's address. The keyword varies from one search engine to another: in most it's 'site', e.g.

["tithe maps" site:www.nationalarchives.gov.uk]

In fact, you do not need to specify a complete site, but can restrict your search to a 'domain'. For example, a search with [site:nationalarchives. gov.uk] will include all National Archives sites, not just the main one. You can specify even less: [site:gov.uk] will conduct a search on pages from *any* UK government website.

▍LIMITATIONS

It is important to bear in mind some of the limitations of search engines. The most important is that no search engine indexes the whole of the web. The study by Lawrence and Giles mentioned at the start of this chapter (p. 254, footnote 13) found that even the best search engines did not index more than 25% of the estimated totality of the web, and not even their combined coverage captured half the web. A secondary point is that many search engines do not index the whole of long pages. In particular, Google does not look beyond the first 100,000 characters. Of course, most pages of interest to the family historian are much shorter, but there are some long surname listings which will be truncated. For these reasons, when you cannot find something with a search engine, it does not mean it is not there – a search engine is not a library catalogue.

Also, do not expect all results to be relevant. Even a fairly precisely formulated query may get some irrelevant results. A particular problem will be pages with long lists of names and places – these will inevitably produce some unwanted matches. For example, a surname interest list which contains an Atkinson from Lancashire and a Chapman from Devon would be listed among the results for a search on [Atkinson Devon]. Particularly if you do not include terms like [genealogy] or ["family history"], or something that occurs more frequently on genealogy sites than elsewhere – ["monumental inscriptions"] or ["parish register"], for example – you will get many irrelevant results. And, of course, searching for a fairly common surname may retrieve numerous genealogical pages that are nothing to do with your own line.

There are ways to cut down on irrelevant results if you are looking for a particular family. The more precise your geographical information the better: if you know your Chapman family came from Exeter, search not for [Chapman Devon] but for [Chapman Exeter Devon]. (Keep Devon in – you do not want Exeter College, HMS *Exeter*, Exeter in New Hampshire, etc.) If you search on both surnames of a married couple, even if they are individually quite common, you are much more likely to get relevant results, for example [Chapman Atkinson Exeter Devon genealogy]. If you use full names, all the better – even ["John Smith" "Ann Williams"] finds fewer than 3,000 pages on Google; if you add [Yorkshire], it comes down to 171! You will still tend to retrieve a few surname listing pages, but there is little that can be done about that.

Another important problem in finding surname material on the internet is that much of it is simply available not in permanent web pages, but in databases. This is part of what is called the 'hidden web'. The only way to find the information is to go to the site with the database and carry out a search. This material *cannot* be retrieved by search engines, and the individual items of data have no place in directories either. This means that the material discussed in Chapters 4–8 will not show up in search engine results. The same is true for much of the material covered in Chapter 10.

Finally, the web is full of spelling errors. For example, Google finds almost 2,000 pages which mention a supposed county of 'Yorskhire', which may elude you in your search for [Yorkshire].

CHOOSING A SEARCH ENGINE

Which is the best search engine depends on a number of factors. The overriding factor is what you are looking for. There are several different aims you might have when using search engines. You might be trying to locate a particular site that you know must exist – you only need one result and you will recognize it when you see it. This is usually a search for a particular organization's website, or some particular resource that you've heard of but can't remember the location of.

Alternatively, you may be trying to find any site which might have information on a particular surname, or even a particular ancestor. The difference between this and the previous search is that there is no way of telling in advance what your search will turn up, and probably the search results will include a certain number, perhaps even a lot, of irrelevant sites. Another difference is that in the first case, you almost certainly have some idea of what the site might be called.

With this in mind, there are three main criteria to consider when deciding which search engine to use:

- the size of the index
- the way in which results are ranked
- the range of search options available.

SIZE

The first of these is the most fundamental. Other things being equal, the search engine with the larger index is more likely to have what you are looking for. However, while this will be very important in looking for pedigree-related information, it will be largely irrelevant if you are looking for something like the Family Records Centre website, which you would expect *all* search engines to have in their indexes.

Since search engines are constantly striving to improve their performance and coverage, there can be no guarantee that what is the most comprehensive search engine at the time of writing will still hold that position when you are reading this. However, Google has consistently had the

Table 16-2 Hits for [genealogy] on a range of search engines (May 2005)

	[genealogy]	[genealogy Oxfordshire]
Google	26.9m	109,000
Teoma	26.3m	59,000
Ask Jeeves	26.3m	58,600
Yahoo	23.2m	82,000
MSN	15.1m	55,000
WiseNut	1.7m	4,800

largest index over the last few years, and is not likely to lose that position overnight.

It's hard to be sure exactly how large search engine indexes are. Some make explicit claims, which are impossible to verify, others don't provide any indication. To give you some idea, Table 16-2 shows the number of hits for searches on [genealogy] and [genealogy Oxfordshire] on some of the larger search engines in May 2005. All the figures should be treated with some caution as there is no way to verify their accuracy, and the disparity between the number of hits for the two searches on Teoma and Ask Jeeves underline this.

RANKING

Unless you get only a handful of hits, one of the issues which will determine the usefulness of search results will be whether the most relevant ones are listed first. In fact poor ranking effectively invalidates the virtues of a large index – a page which is ranked 5,000 out of 700,000 might as well not be included in the results at all because you're never going to look at it.

It's difficult to be specific about how search engines rank their results but they seem to have a measure of relevance based on:

• the frequency of your search terms in the pages retrieved
• the presence of these words in high-profile positions such as the page title, headings, etc.

Google explicitly uses a popularity rating, giving higher priority to pages which many others are linked to, though probably other search engines do this, too. This is good if what you want are recommendations – which is the best site on military genealogy, say. But if you are searching for surnames and pedigrees, which are probably on personal websites, it may be positively unhelpful, as these will automatically rank lower than well-connected commercial sites which happen to have the same surname on them. Almost any surname search will tend to list the major genealogy sites high up, especially those with pages for individual surnames or surname message boards.

It is not straightforward to invert this priority. Of the major search engines, only MSN search has an option to control ranking (shown in Figure 16-8).[16] For personal genealogy pages, the only way I have found of doing this is to include the phrase ["surname list"] in the search terms. The basis for this is that many of the software packages used to create a website from a genealogy database (see Chapter 17) will create a page with

---

16 In June 2005, Yahoo unveiled an experimental search engine at **mindset.research.yahoo. com,** which allows you to vary the relative priority of commercial and non-commercial sites ('shopping' vs 'researching') in the ranking of results.

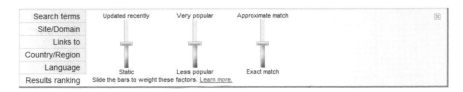

Figure 16-8 MSN Search's ranking controls

this as a title or heading. The results will also include, of course, some non-personal sites such as the county surname lists mentioned on page 131, but the phrase does not seem to be common on non-genealogy sites, and is less likely to be encountered on commercial genealogy sites.

OVERLAP

However, there is an argument that choosing the 'best' search engine is not enough. It's not just that no individual search engine indexes more than half the web. The fact is that each search engine includes in its index some pages which may not be in another search engine's index at all. And there is a very useful tool which illustrates the size of the problem, the Ranking utility at <ranking.thumbshots.com>. This allows you to compare the top 100 hits for a search on any two search engines, and if you try it with something reasonably rare you get a clear indication of the limited coverage.

Figure 16-9 shows the results for the phrase ["bounty migrants"] (i.e. sponsored settlers to Australia) in Google and Teoma. Although the two

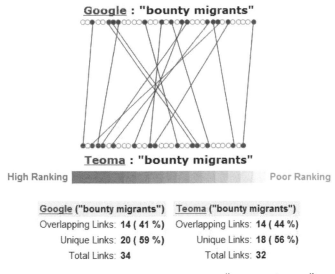

Google ("bounty migrants") Teoma ("bounty migrants")
Overlapping Links: **14 (41 %)**   Overlapping Links: **14 (44 %)**
Unique Links: **20 (59 %)**   Unique Links: **18 (56 %)**
Total Links: **34**   Total Links: **32**

Figure 16-9 Thumbshots: searches for ["bounty migrants"]

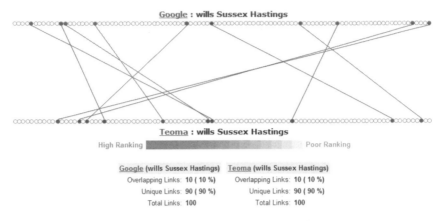

Figure 16-10 Thumbshots: searches for [wills Sussex Hastings]

search engines have similar numbers of results, over half are not found by the other search engine. Of course, there are cases where this won't matter: if you're looking for the site of an organization, for example. But if you're searching, as here, for historical information, or for a particular ancestor by name, you could be missing useful material if you only use one search engine. (If you try this out, you may find this graphic will not display in your browser, unless you are using Internet Explorer.)

What you're missing can be even more startling if you do a more general search. Figure 16-10 compares the results for [wills Sussex Hastings] on Google and Teoma: only 10 of the first 100 results are common to the two search engines, and there's considerable disparity in the ranking of those they do have in common.

The moral is obvious: in a comprehensive web search for individual ancestors and matching surname interests, you cannot afford to use only one search engine, no matter how good.

EVALUATION

There are useful comparative tables of some of the main search engine features on Ian Winship's 'Web search service features' page at <www.unn.ac.uk/central/isd/features.htm> and in Infopeople's 'Search tools Chart' at <www.infopeople.org/search/chart.html>. For evaluation of the different search engines, see the links on the 'Evaluation Of Internet Searching And Search Engines' page at <www.umanitoba.ca/libraries/units/engineering/evaluate.shtml>. Search Engine Watch at <www.searchenginewatch.com> and Search Engine Showdown at <www.searchengineshowdown.com> are good sites devoted entirely to information about search engines and have information on search engine size and ranking.

META-SEARCH ENGINES

One technique for overcoming the fact that no search engine indexes the whole of the web is to carry out the same search on several different search engines. To do this by hand would, of course, be immensely time-consuming, not to mention tedious, but there are two ways of making the task easier.

One is to use an 'all-in-one' search page, which allows you to submit a search to many different search engines. An example of this is Proteus Internet Search at **<www.thrall.org/proteus.html>**, where you type your search terms in the Find box and then select which search engine to submit them to (see Figure 16-11). Proteus keeps a record of your searches in any one session, so you can easily re-run them. You can also choose to have the search results displayed in a new window so that you do not keep having to click on the Back button. Cyndi's List has a small all-in-one search facility on its Search Engines page at **<www.cyndislist.com/search.htm#Forms>**. Here you have to enter your search terms in a different box for each search engine, but you can easily do that by cutting and pasting. Yahoo has a list of All-in-One Search sites. Its URL is 140-odd characters long, so it is best located by going to **<www.yahoo.com>** and running a search for ["All-in-One Search"].

Even more labour-saving are meta-search engines. In these you enter your search only once and it is then automatically submitted to a range of search engines. One of the most popular is DogPile **<www.dogpile.com>**,

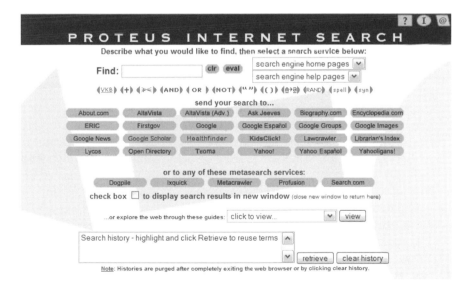

Figure 16-11 Proteus Internet Search, an 'all-in-one' search page

which automatically submits a query to a number of search engines and directories. Another well-known meta-search engine is MetaCrawler at <**www.metacrawler.com**>.

It might seem that these types of search facility make visiting the individual search engines redundant, and they might well do so for certain types of search. But there are important limitations. While you can do an AND search or a phrase search by this method, anything more complex is going to fall down because of the different facilities offered by the different engines. Also, it is important to recognize that, for almost all searches, meta-search engines give *fewer* results than the individual search engines do. This is because meta-search engines select the first few results from each search engine, typically the first ten. In fact, a meta-search engine may retrieve no results at all from a search engine which is slow to respond and is timed out.

For these reasons, meta-search engines are not appropriate for all types of search. They are best when you are looking for a particular site, or want to find the most popular sites devoted to a particular subject. But they are ill-suited to locating pages devoted to particular pedigrees or surnames.

SEARCH SOFTWARE

A similar tool for searching is a 'searchbot', sometimes also called an 'intelligent agent' or a 'desktop search tool'. Rather than a website which you must go to in order to carry out a search, a searchbot is a piece of software that runs on your own computer, allowing you to formulate searches offline and then go online to do the search. Searchbots work like meta-search engines – they submit a query to many different search engines – and have the same strengths and weaknesses. The advantage of a searchbot, though, is that the full results are then stored to your hard disk, and you can examine them at your leisure without re-running the search. It will also store the details of each search, making it easy to repeat.

There are dozens of searchbots, available as shareware or freeware from software archives such as Tucows (see <**tucows.mirrorservice.org/searchbot95.html**> for Windows searchbots). Both Internet Explorer and Mozilla browsers (e.g. Netscape, Firefox) have built-in search facilities. Firefox allows you to choose one of a number of search engines, including Google and Lycos, to submit your searches to. Internet Explorer has a search facility which uses the less comprehensive MSN Search.

GENEALOGY SEARCH TOOLS

The search tools discussed so far have been general-purpose tools, but there are also many special-purpose tools. Some of these are discussed elsewhere in the text: there is a whole range of search engines dedicated to locating living people, by geographical location or email address (see p. 146), and image search tools are discussed earlier in this chapter. Other useful dedicated tools are gazetteers, which allow you to locate places (see p. 181). Chapter 9 covers online catalogues to material which is itself not online. All of these are likely to be better for their particular purpose than the general search engines. However, there are also some search tools devoted solely to genealogy. Two of these are described below, and others will be found on the 'Search Engines' page at <www.cyndislist.com/search.htm# Genealogy>.

GENUKI SEARCH

Probably the most useful search engine devoted to 'official' websites with material on UK genealogy is Genuki Search at <www.genuki.org.uk/ search/>, because it provides an index not only to Genuki itself, but also to the websites of the National Archives, the Society of Genealogists, the Federation of Family History Societies and the Guild of One-Name Studies. Also indexed are the contents of all the family history society websites and county surname interest lists to which Genuki provides links. In addition to the options 'Search for all the words' and 'Search for any of the words', it allows Boolean expressions and phrase searching.

ORIGIN SEARCH

Origins has two dedicated genealogy search engines. Origin Search at <www.originsearch.com> is a free search tool which includes only material identified as relevant to genealogy. However, the search fields are restricted to first and last names. A more sophisticated tool, Origins Search Pro, uses the same index but offers searching across multiple fields and has a facility for saving searches. This is a subscription service (currently £2.50, £6.95 or £12.95 for monthly, quarterly and annual subscriptions respectively).

Origin Search has some sophisticated name-matching techniques which general-purpose search engines don't have. For example, it can recognize a range of variants for both surnames and forenames, and you can specify how exactly names should be matched. The subscription service also allows you to search by category of document, so you can restrict your search to military or immigration pages.

TUTORIALS

Because of the importance of searching to serious use of the internet there are many sites with guides to search techniques and tutorials on searching. In addition to the sites listed under 'Choosing a search engine' on p. 269ff., the University of California at Berkeley has an online tutorial, 'Finding

Information on the Internet', at **<www.lib.berkeley.edu/TeachingLib/ Guides/Internet/FindInfo.html>**, while BrightPlanet has a 'Guide to Effective Searching of the Internet' at **<www.brightplanet.com/deepcontent/ tutorials/Search/index.asp>**. Rice University has a useful and concise guide to 'Internet Searching Strategies' at **<www.rice.edu/fondren/tmp/netguides/ strategies.html>**.

There is a guide to searching specifically for genealogy sites and pages in 'Finding your ancestors on the Internet' at **<genealogy.about.com/ library/weekly/aa041700a.htm>**. You will find the full text of my book *Finding Genealogy on the Internet* online at **<www.spub.co.uk/fgi/>** with links to many relevant sites. The 'Search Engines' page on Cyndi's List at **<www.cyndislist.com/search.htm>** has many links to resources related to search techniques.

CHAPTER 17

PUBLISHING YOUR FAMILY HISTORY ONLINE

So far we have been concentrating on retrieving information and contacting others who share your interests. But you can also take a more active role in publicizing your own interests and publishing the results of your research for others to find.

Some of the ways of doing this have already been touched upon. You can post a message with details of your surname interests to a suitable mailing list or to one of the surnames newsgroups (see Chapter 15). Although your message may be read by only a relatively small number of readers (compared to the total number of people online, that is), it will be archived, providing a permanent record. You can submit your surname interests to the surname lists for the counties your ancestors lived in (see Chapter 10). This will be easier for others to find than material in mailing list archives, since anyone with ancestors from a county is likely to check that archive.

Both of these methods are quick and easy, but they have the limitation that they offer quite basic information, which may not be enough for someone else to spot a link with your family, particularly with more common surnames. The alternative is to publish your family history on the web.

PUBLISHING OPTIONS

There are two ways of putting your family history online: you can submit your family tree to a pedigree database such as those discussed in Chapter 10, or you can create your own website. In fact, these are not mutually exclusive, and there are good reasons for doing both, as each approach has its own merits.

PEDIGREE DATABASES

There are obvious advantages in submitting your family tree to one of the pedigree databases:

- It is a very quick way of getting your tree online.
- The fact that these sites have many visitors and are obvious places to search for contacts means that you are getting your material to a large audience.

But there are some disadvantages to note:

- The material is held in a database, which means it can only be found by going to the site and using the built-in search facilities. It will not be found by anyone using a general web search engine such as those discussed in Chapter 16.
- You can only submit material that is actually held in your genealogy database, and you will not be able to include any other documentary or graphical material relating to your family history.
- Depending on which pedigree database you use, you may be giving up some rights, and your control over the material may be limited (see p. 143).

As long as you check the terms and conditions of any site you use for this purpose, these disadvantages shouldn't discourage you from submitting your pedigree to a database. They simply mean that you might want to consider having your own website as well.

A PERSONAL WEBSITE

Creating your own website may sound like much more work, but there are a number of reasons why it can be better than simply uploading your family tree to a database:

- You can put a family tree on your own site almost as easily as you can submit it to a database.
- You can include any other textual material you have collected which may be of interest: transcriptions of original documents, extracts from parish registers or General Register Office indexes for your chosen names.
- You can include images, whether they are scanned from old photographs in your collection or pictures you have taken of places where your ancestors lived.
- If you submit the address of your site to search engines, all the individuals in your tree and all the other information on your site will be indexed by them, so they can be found by the techniques discussed in Chapter 16. People will not need to be familiar with a particular pedigree database site.

- There will be no issues of rights or the ability to edit or remove material – it will be entirely under your control.

The great thing about a personal website is that it is not like publishing a book: you do not have to do all these things at once. You can start with a small amount of material – a family tree, or even just a list of your surname interests, perhaps – and add to it as and when you like.

But there are a couple of issues to be aware of if you are going to create your own site:

- If you set it up in free web space provided by your ISP you will have to move the whole site if you subsequently switch to another provider. Search engines and everyone who has linked to your site will have to be informed.
- If your site is going to provide more than a basic family tree, you will need to learn how to create web pages.

Both of these issues are tackled later in this chapter.

It is worth pointing out that apart from the major online databases, much of the genealogical material on the web is the result of the efforts of individuals making it available on personal sites. If you have any genealogical information that may be of interest to others, in addition to your personal pedigree, you should consider making it available online.

Whichever of these options you choose, you should avoid publishing information about living people, a topic that is discussed in more detail on p. 143.

FAMILY TREES FOR THE WEB

Probably the most important thing to put on the web is your family tree. This will make it possible for other genealogists to discover shared interests and ancestors, and get in touch with you.

Whether you are going to submit your family tree to a pedigree database or create your own site, you will need to extract the data from your genealogy database software in a format ready for the web. (If you are not yet using a genealogy database to keep a record of your ancestors and what you have discovered about them, look at 'Software' in Chapter 18, p. 312.) The alternative would be to type up the data from scratch, which would be both time-consuming and prone to error.

GEDCOM

GEDCOM, which stands for **GE**nealogical Data **COM**munication, is a standard file format for exchanging family trees between one computer and another, or one computer program and another. It was developed in the 1980s by the LDS Church as a format for users of Personal Ancestral

File (see p. 313) to make submissions to Ancestral File (see p. 136). It has subsequently been adopted and supported by all major genealogy software producers to enable users to transfer data into or out of their programs. It can also be used to download records from the various LDS databases in a format that allows them to be imported into a genealogy program. Although designed by the LDS Church for its own use, it has become the *de facto* standard for exchanging genealogical data electronically.

The reason you need to know about GEDCOM is that all the pedigree databases expect you to submit your family tree in the form of a GEDCOM file. Also, provided your genealogy software can save your pedigree information in GEDCOM format, there are many programs which can automatically create a set of web pages from that file. On the PC, GEDCOM files have the file extension *.ged*.

You do not need to know the technical details of GEDCOM in order to publish your family tree on the web, but Cyndi's List has a page devoted to GEDCOM resources at <www.cyndislist.com/gedcom.htm> with links to explanatory material and technical specifications. Dick Eastman has a straightforward explanation of what GEDCOM is at <**www.eogn.com/ archives/news0219.htm**>, while David Hawgood's *GEDCOM Data Transfer, moving your family tree* is a useful printed guide showing you how to use it to transfer data between genealogy programs (details at <**www.hawgood.co.uk/gedcom.htm**>). For the technically inclined, the GEDCOM specification is at <**homepages.rootsweb.com/~pmcbride/ gedcom/55gctoc.htm**>.

Whatever genealogy software you are using for your family tree, you should be able to find an option to export data to a GEDCOM file. Typically, this option will be found under **Export** on the **File** menu but, if not, the manual or the online help for your program should contain information on GEDCOM export.

GEDCOM CONVERTERS

When you submit your tree to an online pedigree database they will only need the GEDCOM file, and they will have software for indexing it and converting into the right format for the site.

However, if you are using a GEDCOM file because your genealogy software has not got any built-in facilities for creating web pages, you will need to use a special converter program to turn the file into an online pedigree. A large number of such programs are available. All are freeware or shareware and can be downloaded from the web. For those that are shareware, you generally need to pay the registration fee (typically £10 to £20) if you continue to use the program after a trial period of 30 days. There are considerable differences in how these programs create web pages and what the results look like. In addition, there are important differences in the options available. There is not space here to list or discuss all the programs available, but there is a listing on Cyndi's List at <**www. cyndislist.com/construc.htm**>.

At one time, these converters were essential tools for genealogical web publishing. But all the main genealogy database programs now have built-in facilities for creating a web pedigree, and converters are less significant. Indeed, even if you are using an older piece of software without web publishing features there is a very easy way to create a web pedigree without using a converter: just download Personal Ancestral File, Legacy 5.0 or Ancestry Family Tree (all free of charge, see Chapter 18, p. 312). These programs can import a GEDCOM file and turn it into a set of web pages.

Even so, it is well worth having a look at examples of the pages created by the converters, as you may find you prefer their appearance to the output of your genealogy database program. Mark Knight's website at <**help.surnameweb.org/knight/**> shows sample output for most current converters, and the Surname Web has reviews of several GEDCOM converters at <**surnameweb.org/help/conversion.htm**>.

GENEALOGY DATABASES

All recent versions of the main genealogy database programs have facilities to create a set of web pages, including the following:

- Ancestral Quest
- Family Matters
- Family Origins
- Generations
- Kinship Archivist
- Legacy

- The Master Genealogist
- Personal Ancestral File
- Relatively Yours
- Reunion (Macintosh)
- Ultimate Family Tree
- Win-Family

If you have one of these programs, it will be the most straightforward tool to use for turning your pedigree online into a set of web pages.[17]

The programs vary in what they actually produce for a website, but at the very least all will give you:

- a surname index
- an index of individuals
- a series of linked pages with either family groups or details of individuals.

---

17 I have excluded Family Tree Maker from this listing. Although it can create web pages, these can only be uploaded to the manufacturer's website, and in doing so you give them an unlimited right to distribute or sell your data. See <**familytreemaker.genealogy.com/ ftm_uhp_home.html**>.

You should have a choice between an ancestor tree, a descendant tree, or a full pedigree, and there are many options about which individuals, and what information about them, to include.

By way of example, Figure 17-1 shows a page created by Legacy 5.0. This is a web version of a standard descendancy report. Whereas in a printed pedigree you have to turn manually to other pages, here the highlighted names are links which will take you straight to the entries for children. The small superscript numbers link to descriptions of the sources.

FAMILY WEBSITES

Another possibility, half-way between a pedigree database and creating your own website is to use one of the subscription services which act as online genealogy databases. These differ from the pedigree databases in that they provide more sophisticated facilities, such as sharing material with your family while excluding it from general view. They may also have a facility to enter data directly rather than submitting a GEDCOM file, though it's unlikely this would be a useful facility for anyone but the casual family historian. Among the sites which provide this sort of facility are:

- TribalPages at <**www.tribalpages.com**>, which allows you to set up a free website with certain limitations, or you can subscribe $12 or $24 a year for a 'standard' or 'premium' site with greater facilities. The main limitation of the free service is that there are no printable charts. With TribalPages you can choose to have your site password protected, which means you can restrict access to chosen members of your family.

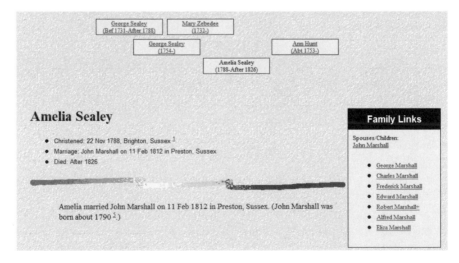

Figure 17-1 Web page created by Legacy

- MyTrees Online at <www.kindredkonnections.com>, a subscription service at $15 for one month and $100 for a year. Details of living people are normally hidden but can be made accessible to family members.

Other services of this type are listed on the 'Genealogy Home Page Construction Kit' on Cyndi's List at <www.cyndislist.com/construc.htm>.

If you just want to share your family tree with your immediate (known) family, these may provide a better solution than trying to password protect an individual website. But they are less well suited to disseminating your pedigree.

█ WEB PUBLISHING BASICS

If you are just going to upload a GEDCOM file to a pedigree database, you do not need to know anything else about web publishing. But if you are going to create your own website you will need to familiarize yourself with what is involved in the process. While it is increasingly possible to create a website without in-depth technical knowledge, it is still essential to have *some* understanding of what is involved. There is not space here to deal with the topic in detail, but this and the following sections cover the basics and there are suggested sources of further information at the end of this chapter.

WHAT IS A WEBSITE?

A website is simply a collection of individual files stored on a web server, which is a computer with (usually) a permanent connection to the web and the capacity to deal with lots of requests for web pages from all over the internet. While larger companies have their own dedicated computers to act as web servers, smaller organizations and home users simply get a portion of the file space on the server belonging to their Internet Service Provider (this is called web hosting).

When you create a website, you first create all the pages on your own computer, then you upload the files to your space on the web server.

Assuming you already have internet access, what you need in order to create a website is:

- web space
- software for creating web pages
- software for uploading the pages to your web space.

If you are going to have photographs or scanned images of documents on your site, you will also need graphics editing software.

One important aspect of web publishing is that it can be done with any computer and a wide range of software. You do not need a specially powerful computer, and you almost certainly have web publishing software on your computer already even if you don't realize it (see p. 288). You will probably be able to use your browser for uploading pages, though there is dedicated freeware and shareware software which will make the process easier.

The other thing you need for a website is time. Even though basic web publishing is not difficult, you will need to learn how it works and you will want to experiment before unleashing your site on the public. You will also need to give some thought to exactly what material you are going to publish, and how best to organize it so that your visitors can find the information they are looking for – just as you would for a book, in fact.

WEB SPACE

In order to have a website you need to have space on a web server for the files which make up your website. If you are paying your Internet Service Provider for your connection to the internet, you will almost certainly find that your subscription includes this facility at no extra cost. It is usual for ISPs to give their customers at least 10Mb of space, and 20Mb or more is not uncommon. Unless you are intending to include many high-quality graphics or a *very* large amount of primary data online this should be more than enough space for a personal genealogy site. It is even quite a respectable amount for a family history society.

While the free ISPs do not always give subscribers free web space, quite a number of them do. If yours does not, there are a number of companies that offer web space entirely free of charge regardless of who your ISP is. FortuneCity <**www.fortunecity.co.uk**>, for example, offers 25Mb with more available on application, while Tripod <**www.tripod.lycos. co.uk**> offers 50Mb. A good place for genealogy sites is RootsWeb <**www. rootsweb.com**> with its 'Freepages', free unlimited web space. Details will be found at <**accounts.rootsweb.com**>. (Other companies can be found by searching Yahoo for the phrase 'free web space', or the Free Webspace directory at <**www.free-webhosts.com**>.) The disadvantage of such services is that they will normally include advertising on your pages, either as a banner ad at the top of a page or as adverts in a separate pop-up window (that's how they can afford to host your site free of charge). There may also be some restrictions on what you can put on your site, though this is unlikely to be of concern to genealogists creating personal sites. The only significant limitation I've encountered is that RootsWeb does not let you upload GEDCOM files – they insist you submit them to WorldConnect instead (see p. 137).

The web address of your site will depend on who is providing your web space and what sort of account you have with them. There are a number of standard formats for URLs of personal websites. The address of my personal genealogy page is <homepages.gold.ac.uk/peter/>, which is the name of the server the site is on, followed by my username on that system. Some providers actually combine the username with the server name directly, which gives you what appears to be your own web server. For example, free web-space provider Tripod gives user sites a name of the format <user-id.tripod.com>.

If you are planning a substantial website with material of general interest rather than simply your own pedigree, or if you are going to set up a site for an organization or genealogy project, it is useful to have a permanent address rather than one that is dependent on your current ISP or web space provider.

- Register your own domain name (see the Nominet site at <www.nic.uk> for information).
- Use a 'redirection service' such as V3 <www.v3.com>. This allocates a permanent free web address of the format <go.to/user-id/>, which redirects people to your actual web space, wherever it currently may be.
- Get another organization to host your material. RootsWeb <www.rootsweb.com>, for example, provides domain names and web space for genealogy projects such as Cemetery Photos at <www.rootsweb.com/~cemphoto/> or the FreeBMD mirror at <freebmd.rootsweb.com>.

Having your own domain name is the ideal solution, but the registration and hosting will require some modest annual expenditure, and you will need to master one or two technical issues. There is a straightforward guide to setting up your own domain in Dick Eastman's newsletters for 25 September and 2 October 2002, archived at <www.eogn.com/archives/news0238.htm> and <www.eogn.com/archives/news0239.htm>.

WHAT IS A WEB PAGE?

When viewed on a web browser, web pages look like a form of desktop publishing and you might think that you need very complex and expensive software to produce a website. In fact the opposite is true. Web pages are in principle very simple – each page is simply a text file with the text that is to appear on the page along with instructions to the browser on how to display the text. The images that appear on a page are not strictly part of it, they are separate files. The page contains instructions telling the browser where to download them from. (This is why you can often see the individual images being downloaded after the text of a page has already appeared in the browser window.) In a similar way, all the links on a web page are created by including instructions to the browser on what page to load when the user clicks on the links. (You can easily get a general idea of how this all works if you load a web page, ideally a fairly simple one, into your browser and use the **View Source** option in Netscape or Internet Explorer, on the **View** menu in both browsers.)

This means that a web page is not a completed and fixed design like the final output of a desktop publishing program on the printed page. It is a set of instructions which the browser carries out. And the reader has a certain amount of control over how the browser does this, telling it not to load images, what font or colour scheme to use, what size the text should be and, most obviously, controlling the size and shape of the browser window it all has to fit into. The reason for this flexibility is that those who view a web page will be using a wide variety of different computer equipment, with a range of screen sizes and resolutions and no guarantee that particular fonts will be available, or even that the reader has a full colour display. Also, readers will be using a range of different web browsers. The web page designer has to create a page that will look good, or at least be readable for all these users.

Figure 17-2 shows the text for a very simple web page. Figure 17-3 shows what this page looks like when displayed in a browser.

```
<HTML>
<HEAD>
<TITLE>This appears at the top of the browser
window</TITLE>
</HEAD>
<BODY>
<H1>Here's the main heading</H1>
<P>Here's a very brief paragraph of text with
<STRONG>bold</STRONG> and <EM>italics</EM>.</P>
<P><IMG SRC="tree.gif">Here's another paragraph with
an image at the start of it.
</P>
<P>Here's a link to the
<A HREF="http://www.nationarchives.gov.uk/">National
Archives</A> Web site.</P>
</BODY>
</HTML>
```

Figure 17-2 The text file for a simple web page

Figure 17-3 The page in Figure 17-2 viewed in a browser

The angled brackets mark the 'tags' which act as instructions to the browser, so the tag <IMG . . .> tells the browser to insert an image at this point. The tags are collectively referred to as 'markup', because they instruct the browser what to do with the text in the same way that an editor marks up a manuscript for typesetting. All the text that is not inside angled brackets appears on the page, but the tags themselves do not. Many of the tags work in pairs, for example the tags <EM> . . . </EM> tell the browser to find a way to emphasize the enclosed text, which is usually done with italics. Links to other websites and other pages on your own site are created by putting the tag <A HREF="site-or-file-name"> . . . </A> round the hotspot, i.e. the text you want the reader to click on, with the web address or file name between the inverted commas ('A' stands for 'Anchor').

You can get a good idea of how this works by saving a copy of the page shown in Figure 17-3 from **<www.spub.co.uk/tgi3/dummypage.html>** and then editing it in Notepad or another text editor to see what happens if you move or delete tags. (Do not try it with a word processor!)

The set of tags that can be used to create web pages is specified in a standard called Hypertext Markup Language (HTML). The standard is controlled by the World Wide Web Consortium (W3C) **<www.w3.org>** on the basis of extensive consultation with those who have an interest in the technology of the web. HTML has been through several versions since its inception in 1991, and the latest is version 4, which came into use at the beginning of 1998.

SOFTWARE

In order to create your website you will need suitable software, and there is quite a range of possibilities. Which is best depends on what software you have already got, what your website is to contain, and how serious you are about your site. One thing to remember is that no matter what software you use, the output is always a plain text file. It is not a file in a proprietary format belonging to a single manufacturer, which is what makes exchanging files between different word processors so problematic. This means you can use a variety of software programs to edit a single page.

Another important point is that you almost certainly do not need to buy additional software – you may well already have some web publishing tools installed on your computer, and if not there are free programs which will provide all the facilities you need.

There are three basic approaches to creating web pages:

- You can create them 'by hand', i.e. by typing in the tags yourself using a text editor.
- You can use a program which works like a word processor but automatically converts the page layout into the appropriate text and tags.
- You can use a program which automatically generates pages from a set of data.

The following sections look at the sorts of software that can be used to create web pages.

EDITORS

In the early days of the web there was no special-purpose software designed for creating sites, and commercial software had no facilities for turning material into web pages. The only way to create a site was with a text editor, typing in both the text of a page and the HTML tags. The surprising thing is that, in spite of the many pieces of software that are now able to create web pages, text editors are still in use among professional web authors. The reason is that these give you complete control and do not make decisions for you. The disadvantage, of course, is that you will need to know what the relevant tags are and how to use them. But even if you mainly use another program to create your web pages, a text editor can still be useful. This is particularly the case where you have been using a program that is not designed specifically for web authoring, but has the facility to save files in HTML format as an add-on. All such programs have *some* failings in their web page output. If you need to correct these, it is easiest to use a text editor.

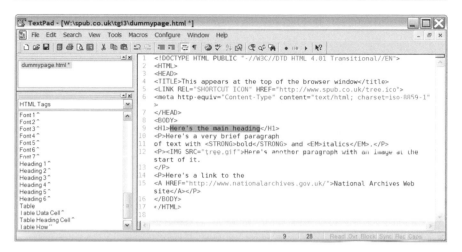

Figure 17-4 Web authoring with an editor: the <H1> tags in the main window were inserted *around* the text simply by selecting the text and then clicking on Heading 1 in the left-hand panel

Although you can use a very basic text editor like the Windows Notepad, you will find it is hard work to create web pages with something so primitive, and it is better to use a more sophisticated editor. Some, like TextPad or NoteTab (downloadable from <**www.textpad.com**> and <**www.notetab. com**> respectively), even though designed as general-purpose text editors, offer a number of features to make web authoring easier. TextPad, for example, allows you to have many documents open at once, and has a comprehensive search and replace function covering all open documents. It has a 'clip library' of the main HTML tags – just clicking on an entry in the library adds the tags to your page (see Figure 17-4).

WORD PROCESSORS

Assuming you have got a reasonably recent version of one of the main word processors, you will be able to use that to create web pages. This way of creating pages is particularly useful if you already have material typed up, because you will be able to turn it into web pages very easily – there should be a **Save as HTML** or **Save as Web Pages** option on the **File** menu. But note that this will not create a web page for each *page* of your word-processed document, it will turn each *document* into a single web page. Once you have saved a page (and thereby given it a file name) you will able to make links to it from other pages.

You might think that with this sort of facility there is no real need for other web authoring software but, unfortunately, word processors are not particularly good at producing web pages that will read well on the wide variety of set-ups internet users have. In particular, they often try to reproduce precisely every nuance of the word-processed document, particularly the page layout, which may have no relevance for a web browser. This can lead to very cumbersome web pages that may download slowly. However, for text-only pages with a straightforward layout, this is a very quick way to get material on to the web.

DESKTOP PUBLISHING

If you have desktop publishing software such as QuarkXPress or Microsoft Publisher, you might think these would be useful for creating websites, since they offer much more sophisticated page layout. Unfortunately, web pages created by such programs are often poor for readers, since they try to reproduce *exactly* what would appear on a printed page. This is quite misguided: on the web, the page designer has no control over the size and shape of the browser window, the absolute sizes of fonts, etc. Pages created by programs like these can be full of problems for readers that a novice web author is unlikely to be able to deal with, even if the hassle were worthwhile.

DEDICATED WEB AUTHORING SOFTWARE

A better all-round option is a piece of dedicated web authoring software. This will provide *only* the layout facilities that are available in HTML. Many such packages offer both a design/layout mode, which looks like a

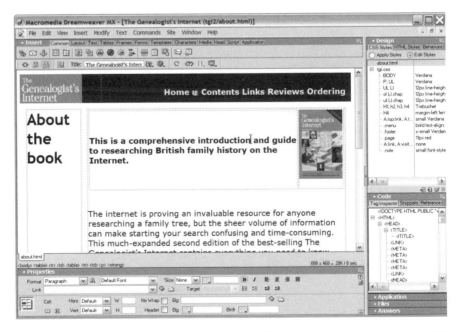

Figure 17-5 Editing the website for the second edition of this book in Dreamweaver MX

word processor, and a text editing mode which allows you to work directly with tags. For the last few years, the most highly regarded commercial program has consistently been Macromedia Dreamweaver (see Figure 17-5). Unfortunately, it is priced for professional users, and it would be difficult to justify the expense for a small personal website. However, a 30-day trial version can be downloaded from the Macromedia website at <www.macromedia.com>, and there are substantial discounts for educational users.

If you are only going to create a fairly simple site, you do not need to pay for a commercial web authoring package, as there are a number of free options.

- *Netscape Composer* is a built-in web editor that comes with Netscape Navigator (to be found on the 'Communicator' menu). This does not have anything like the facilities of Dreamweaver, but it has all you need for doing straightforward pages. It works as a WYSIWYG ('what you see is what you get') editor, with all the main HTML functions available from toolbars and menus. You can view the HTML code but you cannot edit at the text level within Composer, though there is nothing to stop you loading the text into NotePad and viewing both on the screen at once. Netscape can be downloaded free of charge from <www.netscape.com> and is often found on computer magazine CD-ROMs.
- *EvrSoft's FirstPage* can be downloaded free from <www.evrsoft. com>. It is particularly good for those new to web authoring, as long as you don't mind working with tags, as it has Easy, Normal, Expert and Hardcore modes, with more and more complex features available as you progress. Although there is no WYSIWYG editing, there is a preview window which can show you immediately the effect of adding to the page (see Figure 17-6).[18]
- *FrontPage Express* is a cut-down version of Microsoft's web authoring package FrontPage, included with Versions 4 and 5 of Internet Explorer. This was considerably simpler to use than the full commercial version, but rather more flexible than Composer. Unfortunately, since version 5.5 it is no longer included in Explorer or available free from the Microsoft website, but you may still be able to locate a copy online – do a web search for ["FrontPage Express" download]. Some ISPs still have older versions of Internet Explorer in their file download areas, but you should be very wary of installing these on a computer which already has a later version installed.

---

18 Your anti-virus software may object to one of the sample files installed by FirstPage, but the file *does not contain a virus*. You can delete the file to get rid of the warnings without affecting the operation of FirstPage.

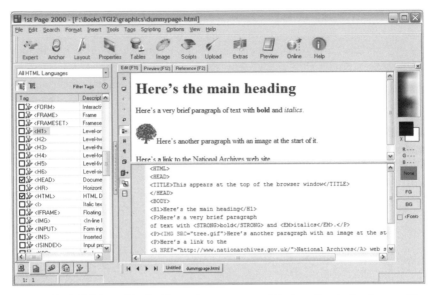

Figure 17-6 Editing with FirstPage. In some ways this is quite similar to an editor like TextPad, but note the preview panel which shows what the page looks like as well as the actual HTML below, and the colour palette at the right

- *OpenOffice.org* is a freeware office suite (with word-processing, spreadsheet, etc.). It includes a good web editor with WYSIWYG and text editing views. Unfortunately, the web editor cannot be downloaded separately, you have to download the whole suite, which is over 60Mb in size. If you have a modem dialup connection this will be impracticable, but you may be able to find a copy on a computer magazine disk.

Trial versions of web authoring packages are frequently to be found on the cover CD-ROMs of computer magazines, and dozens of other shareware packages are available for free downloading. The best place to look is Tucows, which has a wide selection of web authoring software under 'Web Building Tools' at <tucows.mirrorservice.org/internet.html>.

ONLINE SOFTWARE

Some free web space providers have online tools for creating websites directly on the site without having to upload it from your own computer. Obviously, this will not help you convert your family tree for online viewing, but it is a quick way to get a website up and running. Some of the providers offering this facility are:

- Freeservers <www.freeservers.com>
- Tripod <www.tripod.lycos.co.uk>
- Yahoo! GeoCities <geocities.yahoo.com>.

ADOBE ACROBAT

All the software mentioned so far creates pages in HTML. But in fact browsers can cope with files in other formats, either by starting up the relevant application or by using a 'plug-in', an add-on component to display a particular file type.

Adobe Acrobat is a program that can turn any page designed for printing into a document for the web. It does this not by creating a page in HTML, but using a proprietary file format ('PDF', which stands for 'portable document format'). A free reader is available, which can be used as a plug-in by any browser, allowing PDF files to displayed in the browser window when they are encountered. (If you have not already got it installed, the Adobe Acrobat reader can be downloaded free of charge from <**www. adobe.com**>.)

This is not a complete answer to creating a genealogy website – a site consisting solely of PDF files would be very cumbersome, since the files are much larger than plain HTML files and would download slowly. But it is a good way to make existing material that you already have in word-processor files quickly available. It is particularly good for longish documents which people will want to save to disk or print out rather than read on screen. (Web pages do not always print well.) For example, if you want to put online one of the longer reports that your genealogy database can create, turning this into a PDF file would be a good way to do it. Figure 17-7 shows an Ahnentafel report from Personal Ancestral File turned into

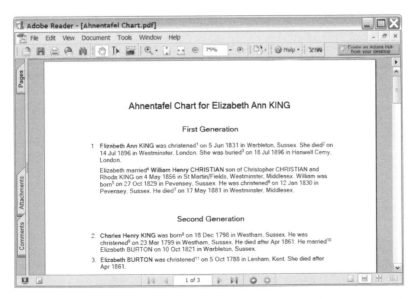

Figure 17-7 An Ahnentafel report from Personal Ancestral File in PDF format

a PDF file – you can view the whole file at <**www.spub.co.uk/tgi3/ eak.pdf**>. This can also be a good solution for putting trees online.

Adobe's own software for creating PDF files is a commercial product costing over £200, an expense it would be hard to justify for a personal website. But there are a number of shareware and freeware programs available which can be used to create PDF files. Though they lack the more sophisticated document management features of Adobe Acrobat itself, they will be perfectly adequate for turning word-processor documents into web pages, or creating PDF files from your genealogy software. You can find a list and downloads at <**tucows.mirrorservice.org/mmedia/pdf95_default. html**>. Dick Eastman's newsletters of 25 February and 7 October 2002 have articles on creating PDF files, which explain the process and look at two of the converters – see <**www.eogn.com/archives/news0208.htm**> and <**www.eogn.com/archives/news0240.htm**>.

DATABASES AND SPREADSHEETS

If you store some of your genealogical information in a spreadsheet or database, there are several ways of putting the data on a website.

First, most recent database and spreadsheet software can create web pages directly (probably via a **File | Export** menu or a **File | Save As** menu option). By way of example, Figure 17-8 shows the first few entries from my database of Sussex parish register entries for the surname Christian as a web page exported from Microsoft Excel.

If this option is not available, there is a reliable fall-back: plain text. Your database or spreadsheet will undoubtedly have a **Save as text** function, and all browsers can display plain text files. This will not look as

Year	Month	Day	Place	Event	Surname	Forenames	Kin
1561	9	28	East Grinstead	C	Christian	William	s. Robert
1577	10	6	East Grinstead	M	Christian	Margaret	widow + Thomas Lullingden
1583	12	28	Lindfield	C	Christian	Jone	d. Rowland
1584	4	26	Lindfield	B	Christian	George	s. Rowland
1586	4	18	Lindfield	C	Christian	Jane	d. Rowland
1589	9	8	East Grinstead	M	Christian	Alice	+ William Goodyer
1595	2	1	East Grinstead	M	Christian	Agnes	+ Charles Adamson
1596	2	26	Pevensey	B	Christian	Joane	wife of Martin
1602	3	6	Waldron	C	Christian	Abraham	s. Martin
1602	6	19	Lindfield	B	Christian		child of Rowland
1606	2	6	Lindfield	M	Christian	Rowland	+ Joan Chantler
1606	12	26	Catsfield	C	Christian	Sara	d. Martin
1611	4	14	Pevensey	C	Christian	Marie	d. of Martine & _
1613	9	10	Lindfield	B	Christian	Rowland	
1613	11	10	Lindfield	B	Christian	Jone	widow
1615	8	10	Pevensey	B	Christian	Martin	
1615	10	19	Hellingly	M	Christian	Elizabeth	+ Steven Bankes
1615	11	13	East Grinstead	M	Christian	Robert	+ Mary Dyvol
1616	8	26	Pevensey	M	Christian	Darothie	+Thomas Harneden
1621	6	11	Pevensey	M	Christian	John	+Jhoane Hencoate

Figure 17-8 A web page exported from Microsoft Excel

good as the example above, but if someone finds an ancestor in your list, that will be the last thing they will be worried about.

You can even take this text file and embed it in a proper web page. There is a special pair of tags, <PRE> . . . </PRE> (for *pre*formatted) which, when put round formatted text like this, will preserve all the line breaks and the multiple spaces, thus maintaining the original format.

DYNAMIC WEBSITES

In an ideal world, all of this would be unnecessary. You would simply upload the database file to your website and people could use their browser to search it, just as you do on your desktop. But the GEDCOM converters and genealogy databases discussed above all produce static web pages. If you make any changes to your family tree, you will need to recreate the web pages from scratch and upload the whole lot to your site again.

A more satisfactory approach is to have a 'dynamic' website. When a visitor clicks on a link within your site, they are not taken to a fixed page, but instead a piece of software looks up the relevant data in a database and extracts the appropriate records to create a web page on the fly. This may be just a plain GEDCOM file or it may be a separate database created from a GEDCOM file, but either way you can easily update the family tree, by uploading a single new file, without having to upload perhaps hundreds of revised pages.

There are two basic ways to access data held in a file:

- When someone visits your site, an applet is downloaded, i.e. a small software application which runs from within your browser. This gets the relevant data from the site and turns it into the page displayed on the screen.
- When someone visits your site, the page is not simply delivered to the user as is but runs a 'script' behind the scenes which incorporates the relevant data from a database or GEDCOM into the page displayed to the reader.

The differences might seem marginal, but are in fact very significant. The disadvantage of the first technique is that it will only work if the user has a recent browser and the Java language installed on their computer, and there may be other compatibility issues in the longer term. It seems that this approach may have a limited future: both the best known Java genealogy programs (JavaGED and WebGED Progenitor) are no longer available, though you will still come across sites that use them.

The disadvantage of the 'scripting' approach is that, while it doesn't make any special demands on the browser, which just gets a perfectly normal web page, special software has to be installed on the web server to make sense of the script. The most likely software requirement is for a scripting language called PHP, often used in combination with MySQL databases. This combination is fairly common in a commercial web hosting environment, but is much less likely to be available in the web facilities provided by consumer ISPs; nor is it something you can simply install in your own web space on your own initiative. However, PHP (and MySQL) facilities are becoming more widespread and the Free Webspace site has a 'power search' at **<www.free-webhosts.com/power-search.php>** which can be used to find hosting services with specific scripting and database facilities.

If PHP is available on the web server hosting your site, there are a number of tools you could look at:

- PhpGedView is an application which can be downloaded free from **<phpgedview.sourceforge.net>**. It has a wide range of charts and the useful ability to create PDF versions of reports. Individual users can be given access to particular areas of a site. A 'portal' page allows visitors to keep track of their own particular ancestors on the site.
- The Next Generation of Genealogy Sitebuilding (TNG), downloadable from **<lythgoes.net/genealogy/software.php>**, requires PHP and access

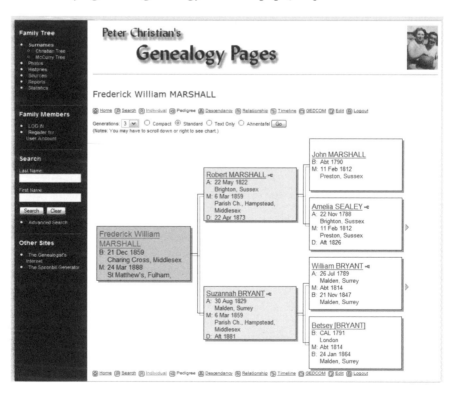

Figure 17-9 A pedigree display from TNG

to a MySQL database. It has a range of reports and the facility to design your own, and can link photos and documents to individuals in your tree. In fact you can have any number of distinct trees, and you can give each registered user access to branches that may not be visible to general visitors. TNG must be purchased – it is not freeware or shareware. Figure 17-9 shows a pedigree display from my own genealogy site, which uses TNG.

- phpmyfamily, which has a home page at <www.phpmyfamily.net>, requires MySQL and is primarily designed to allow family members to collaborate on a family tree. Facilities seem to be more limited than the previous two applications.
- Advanced Genealogy Tool at <netprofx.com/genealogy/> provides a basic tree and individual report.

In such programs, you typically upload all the program files to your website, and then upload the data file for them to work with. You won't need to design any pages as such, though you will be able to customize them in various ways if you wish. While these PHP projects don't require you to be a programmer, you will need to follow instructions about configuring the software for your own site, and will need to have (or develop) some understanding of how files are stored and made accessible on a website. For that reason, these are probably not appropriate tools for the reluctant or timid computer user.

█ WEBSITE DESIGN

Although there is a great deal of material, both in print and online, about website design, for someone publishing family history on the web a few basic principles should suffice. What is important is to work out what the overall structure of your site will be (which other pages is each page going to link to?), and to do so *before* you start creating actual pages. There are also a few technical matters, such as file-naming conventions and file formats for graphics (see below).

There is no single right way to design a website. It depends on what it contains and who it is aimed at. For a personal genealogy site, your main visitors will be other genealogists looking for information on individuals and surnames that might be part of their own ancestry. If you have expertise in a particular area of genealogy, or have collected useful material on a particular topic, people may come looking for general background information. Your main job, then, is to make sure visitors to your site can see whether you have anything useful to them and can access it easily. While it is better, of course, if your site looks good, you should not be worrying about state-of-the-art graphic design, special effects, animation, background music, hit counters, or any of the other things that amateur web authors seem to find irresistible, but which irritate or distract readers and make pages slower to download.

FILENAMES

It is usual to give files for web pages names ending in *.html*. If you call a file *index.html* or *index.htm* it will be loaded by default, i.e. if the URL you have entered in your browser does not specify a particular file. For example, when you go to Genuki's home page at <**www.genuki.org.uk**> you get exactly the same page as when you enter <**www.genuki.org.uk/ index.html**> – in the first instance, the server delivers *index.html* because you have not asked for any specific file. (The filenames *default.html* or *default.htm* are used instead on some servers, such as the National Archives' – try <**www.nationalarchives.gov.uk/default.htm**>). This means your home page should normally be called *index.html* and be placed in the main folder in your web space.

On almost all web servers filenames are case sensitive: *index.html*, *Index.html* and *INDEX.HTML* are different files. To save confusion stick to lower case. If you are using software which automatically generates file-names rather than prompting you for filenames (GEDCOM converters and genealogy databases, for example), look for an option to force filenames to lower case.

GRAPHICS

Web browsers can display graphics in three of the many graphics formats: GIF, JPEG and PNG, of which the last is not widely used. For colour photographs you need to use JPEG as it allows graphics with up to 16.7 million colours and is therefore capable of displaying subtle variations in tone. (JPEG files have the file extension .jpg on the PC). The GIF format, which allows a maximum of 256 colours, is poor for colour photographs but good for black and white photographs, as well as for navigation buttons, logos, maps and the like, which have simple colour schemes. You can compare the strengths and weaknesses of these two formats by looking at the examples at <**www.spub.co.uk/wpg/figures/figure10.html**>.

If you are going to use graphics extensively, you will need a basic graphics editing program such as Photoshop Elements or PaintShop Pro. If you just need to crop images and convert them to GIF or JPEG format, there are freeware or inexpensive shareware tools that will do the job – look under 'Image Tools' at Tucows <**tucows.mirrorservice.org/mmedia. html**> or try the cover CDs of computer magazines.

Each graphic is kept as an individual file on the web server, and any page which uses it has a tag which contains the file name. If you have downloaded *dummypage.html* to your own computer, it will not display the tree unless you also download the file *tree.gif* into the same folder, so that when the browser attempts to interpret the tag <IMG SRC="tree.gif"> it can find the file.

You can use the same graphic on many different pages, so if you have a graphic such as a logo which appears on every page on your site, you only need to put one copy of the file on the server.

ADDING YOUR FAMILY TREE

If you are designing your own site you will need to know how to include the pages showing the family tree you have created from your genealogy database software. Whatever software you use for your genealogy, it will almost certainly create a new folder on your hard disk and put all the created files in it, perhaps in a number of sub-folders.

You need to upload this new folder and all the files it contains on to your website (see 'Uploading your website', below), retaining the filenames and folder structure. If you change filenames or move files you will find that some parts of the tree do not link correctly.

From your home page you will need a link to the index file in the family tree folder. So suppose you have called the folder *johnson* because it contains your Johnson family tree, you would have a link

        <A HREF="johnson">Johnson family tree</A>

on your home page. If you find this does not work, you may need to specify the exact filename of the index file (this should be fairly obvious if you look at the filenames in the family tree folder), for example:

        <A HREF="johnson/default.htm">Johnson family tree</A>

When you are creating a web tree with your genealogy software, it is always worth checking for an option to make filenames lower case. There are other reasons for giving the exact filename, discussed on p. 304.

DESIGN TIPS

The web is a good source of advice about the design of web pages. Here are some of the most important points:

- Have a home page which tells visitors what they will find on the site, and provide links to the main areas of your site.
- Give each page a helpful title and heading, so that if someone book-marks it, or comes to it directly via a link from another site (perhaps a search engine), they can immediately see what the page is about.
- Conversely, make sure that every page has a link back to the home page or some other higher level page, so that if someone comes to your site from a search engine they can get to other pages.

- Don't make your pages too long, and don't include large or unnecessary graphics, as this will only increase the time it takes your pages to download, and potential visitors will be put off.
- Don't use unusual colour schemes. They are unusual for a good reason – they make text unreadable.
- Don't put light text on a dark background on a page with significant information – this can make it impossible to print out from some browsers.
- Put your email address on the site so that people can contact you.

For further advice, look at Webmonkey **<webmonkey.wired.com/webmonkey/ design/>** or the 'Design Tips' area of Usable Web at **<usableweb.com>**.

UPLOADING YOUR WEBSITE

Once you have created a set of pages on your own computer, you need to go online and upload them to your web space. The standard way of doing this is to use a program called an FTP client. FTP stands for File Transfer Protocol, which is a long-established method for transferring files on the internet. There are many free and shareware FTP programs available from software archives like Tucows at **<tucows.mirror.ac.uk>**. CuteFTP and WS-FTP are among the most popular for PC users.

1. Before you connect to the internet to upload, you will want to set up an entry for your website in your FTP client's list of sites. You need to enter:
   - The address of the site. If you are not certain what it is, your ISP/web space provider will be able to tell you, and their help pages will probably provide detailed instructions for uploading files.
   - Your username and password for that site.
2. Next connect to the internet. Once you are logged in, you should see something like Figure 17-10, where I am preparing to upload a family tree to the genealogy folder on my personal website.
3. To upload your files, simply drag the icons for the files to be uploaded across to the right-hand panel. If you drag a folder icon, all the files in that folder will be included in the upload.
4. Finally, start your browser and type in the URL of your site to check it.

Web browsers can also be used to transfer files – see the online help in your browser for details of how to do this.

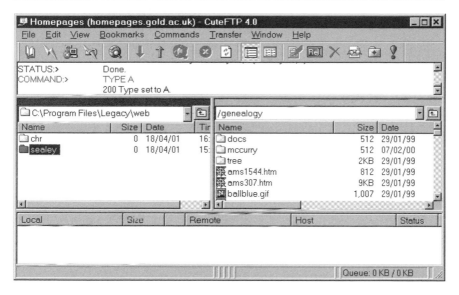

Figure 17-10 Using FTP to upload files to a website (using CuteFTP)

PUBLICITY

Once you have created and uploaded your web pages, you will need to publicize the existence of your site. One simple way to do this is to put its URL in the signature attached to your email messages. Apart from that, there are a number of possible approaches.

SEARCH ENGINES

Making sure your site is known to the main search engines (see Chapter 16) is probably the most effective way to publicize your website. Since search engines index pages automatically, they have no way of knowing what the most important aspects of your site and your individual pages are unless you help them by organizing the material on each page. Among the things search engines look for when estimating the relevance of a page to a search done by a user are:

- Words appearing in the page title and between heading tags
- The initial section of text
- Words which appear frequently on the page.

In addition, there are special tags you can add to a page to provide a brief description of the page and the site. These are <META> tags, which are placed in the <HEAD> section of the page. They will not be visible to someone viewing your page, but they are used by search engines.

```
<META NAME="description" CONTENT="The last will and
testament of Zebediah Poot, died 1687, Wombourn,
Staffordshire, England">
```

When a search engine lists this page in the results of a search, it will normally list its title (i.e. the text between the <TITLE> tags) and your description. If there is no description, it will take the first couple of lines of text from the <BODY> of the page.

You may see reference to a 'keywords' <META> tag, but this is now of limited usefulness as it seems that search engines no longer make use of it in indexing.

Don't expect submission to a search engine to produce a flood of visitors to your site within hours. It can take quite some time for the search engine to visit a new site and index it.

MAILING LISTS AND NEWSGROUPS

A good way to draw immediate attention to a new site is to post a message to appropriate mailing lists and newsgroups. You might think it is a good idea to post to every one you possibly can, to get maximum publicity, but there is little point in posting details of a Yorkshire website to a Cornish list. Choose the county lists relevant to the material you are putting on the web, and any special interest lists. It will be worth notifying the soc.genealogy.britain newsgroup (the GENBRIT mailing list) with an indication of the main surnames and localities covered. There is a special mailing list, NEW-GEN-URL, for publicizing new websites, though it does not now seem to be much used (details at <lists.rootsweb.com/index/other/ Miscellaneous/NEW-GEN-URL.html>).

If there is a mailing list relating to some social group your ancestors belonged to it will be worth notifying that list, so if you have information on coalmining ancestors on your site, for example, it would be worth posting to the COALMINERS list (see Chapter 15).

CYNDI'S LIST

Another useful approach is to submit details of your site to Cyndi's List using the online form at <www.cyndislist.com/newlink.htm>. This may or may not get your site a listing on the relevant category page on Cyndi's List, but it will still have undoubted benefits. First, all submissions to this page are included in the Cyndi's List mailing list (details of which are at <lists.rootsweb.com/index/other/Newsletters/CyndisList.html>), which goes out to a large number of subscribers. This will get a link to your site into the RootsWeb archive at <archiver.rootsweb.com/th/index/ CyndisList/>, and your site will be permanently listed in the 'What's New' pages on Cyndi's List at <www.cyndislist.com/whatsnew.htm>. While it may take some time for your site to be indexed by search engines based on your direct submission, both of these locations are likely to be visited by search engines much more quickly, and the links to your site should be followed automatically.

REQUESTING LINKS

You can request other people to link to your pages, but you need to be realistic about expecting links from other personal sites. People will generally only do this if there is some connection in subject matter between your site and theirs, and if you are prepared to create a link to their site in return. Do not expect major institutions like the National Archives or the SoG to link to a site with purely personal material, just because you have made a link to theirs.

To be honest, if your site contains only personal pedigree information, it is probably not worth bothering to request links from other personal sites, as this will probably not bring any significant number of visitors, certainly compared to the other options discussed so far. However, if your site has material relating to a particular subject, it will be well worth contacting the maintainers of specialist websites relating to that subject, such as those discussed in Chapters 11–13.

If you have transcriptions of original source material of broader interest than extracts for individual surnames you should contact Genuki, who aim to provide links to all UK source material online.

NEWS

Genealogy newsletters will often give a mention to personal websites if you mail the editor (see Chapter 18, p. 306). If you have a website which contains material of sufficiently general interest, i.e. not just your personal pedigree, you may also be able to get a mention in the relevant news section of a family history magazine.

▍PRESERVING YOUR FAMILY HISTORY

While the web is seen as a way of publishing your family history, in one important respect it is not like publishing it in print. A printed family history donated to a genealogy library will be preserved for ever, while your account with your web space provider is doomed to expire when you do, unless you can persuade your heirs otherwise.

But since a website is just a collection of files, there is no reason why all the information cannot be preserved, even if not online. If you copy all the files that constitute your site onto writeable CDs, these can be sent to relatives and deposited in archives just like printed material. The advantage of distributing your material in this way is that people do not need special software – a particular word processor or the same genealogy database as you – in order to view the files, and everyone with a computer has access to a web browser. HTML is a universal, non-proprietary standard which uses plain-text files, and is therefore much more future-proof than the file formats used by most current software.

If you are intending to do this you should make sure that every link gives a specific filename, as mentioned in 'Filenames' on p. 298. A web server knows to deliver a file called *index.html* if a link doesn't specify a filename; a standalone computer doesn't.

Note that you won't be able to do this if your site is dynamic, as you won't be able to run the relevant software from a CD.

❚ HELP AND ADVICE

While you should be able to get help from your ISP or other web host for problems relating to uploading, you are unlikely to be able to get any help from them with the business of creating your website. However, there are countless sources of information online about creating a website online. A good starting point might be Webmonkey's HTML Basics pages at **<webmonkey.wired.com/webmonkey/authoring/html_basics/>**.

An excellent overview of specifically genealogical web publishing with links to relevant software and tutorial materials is Cyndi's 'Genealogy Home Page Construction Kit' at **<www.cyndislist.com/construc.htm>**. The archive of Dick Eastman's newsletter (see p. 310) has a number of articles about creating a website for your genealogy.

The soc.genealogy.computing newsgroup, which is gatewayed with GENCMP-L mailing list, is a good place to look for recommendations and help in putting your pedigree online. British-genealogy has a web pages design discussion forum at **<www.british-genealogy.com/forums/forumdisplay.php?f=226>**.

IN PRINT

If you want a tutorial in print, a search on **<www.amazon.co.uk>** for 'HTML' or 'web publishing' will list the hundreds of general books on the subject, though it's probably best to browse in a physical bookshop to make sure you choose a book at the right technical level. I know of only three books devoted specifically to publishing genealogical information on the web:

- Cyndi Howells, *Planting Your Family Tree Online: How to Create Your Own Family History Website* (Rutledge Hill Press, 2004).

- Peter Christian, *Web Publishing for Genealogy*, 2nd edn (David Hawgood, 1999). There is also a US edition published by the Genealogical Publishing Co. (2000). The website for the book at <**www.spub. co.uk/wpg/**> includes the complete text.
- Richard S. Wilson, *Publishing Your Family History on the Internet* (Writers Digest Books, 1999) <**www.compuology.com/book2.htm**>.

Of these, Cyndi Howells's book is the only one which is reasonably up to date (insofar as such a thing is possible with online material). My own book doesn't cover the most recent developments, but does have the advantage of being available free online, and the general process of creating a website has not changed significantly.

Computers in Genealogy and *Genealogical Computing* are specialist genealogy magazines which regularly carry articles on web publishing. In the case of *CiG* some older articles are available online at <**www.sog.org. uk/cig/**>. The general family history magazines available on the newsstand also have occasional articles on genealogical web publishing.

CHAPTER 18

THE WORLD OF FAMILY HISTORY

Previous chapters have looked at ways of using the internet in direct connection with your own pedigree. This chapter looks at the 'non-virtual' world of family history which exists offline, and how you can use the internet to find out about it.

SOCIETIES AND ORGANIZATIONS

NATIONAL BODIES

There are a number of national genealogical bodies, all of which have websites:

- The Society of Genealogists (SoG) <www.sog.org.uk>
- The Institute of Heraldic and Genealogical Studies (IHGS) <www.ihgs. ac.uk>
- Federation of Family History Societies (FFHS) <www.ffhs.org.uk>
- The Guild of One-Name Studies (GOONS) <www.one-name.org>
- Scottish Genealogy Society <www.scotsgenealogy.com>
- Scottish Association of Family History Societies (SAFHS) <www.safhs. org.uk>
- Association of Family History Societies of Wales <www.fhswales.info>
- Genealogical Society of Ireland <www.familyhistory.ie>.

FAMILY HISTORY SOCIETIES

There are around 200 local family history societies in the UK and Ireland, the overwhelming majority of which have websites. Most of these societies are members of one or more of the three national federations/associations listed above (which are themselves umbrella organizations, not family history societies in their own right). The FFHS includes many member

Society of Genealogists

Family History Library and Education Centre

Click here for
our SHOP !

buy.at/

Search the Society's Website

Latest News	Who, How & Where	Library & Genealogy
• Member's Free Access to the Society's data online - how to access updated 30 March 2005 • Support the Society of Genealogists when you buy on-line. Details	• About the Society of Genealogists • How to join & benefits • e-Publications relating to Governance • Contacting the Society • Visiting the Society • Opening Hours • Links	• Library Info page • Information Leaflets Index • Library Accessions • Library Projects • Internet Access from the Library • Daily search fees

Lectures & Events	Society Online	Society Publications
• Section Index • Calendar of lectures, events etc. • Package deals for	• General Information • *Genealogists' Magazine* • Parish Register Holdings	• Order line Help & Access • Free- Camden and Islington Family

Figure 18-1 The Society of Genealogists

societies from Wales and Ireland, and most English societies are Federation members.

The definitive starting point for finding FHS websites is Genuki's 'Family History and Genealogy Societies' page at <**www.genuki.org.uk/Societies/**>. This lists the national organizations and has links to separate pages for the constituent nations of the British Isles, where details of local societies are to be found.

The individual FHS websites vary greatly in what they offer, but all will have contact details and usually a list of publications. Most do not have their own online shops, but over 60 of them have an online 'stand' at GENfair, the FFHS online shop, at <**www.genfair.com**>.

For genealogical data from family history societies, look at the FamilyHistoryOnline site at <**www.familyhistoryonline.net**> described in detail on p. 39.

▌EVENTS

There is a wide range of genealogical meetings, lectures, conferences and fairs in the UK, from the individual meetings of family history societies to major national events such as the SoG's annual Family History Show. One of the easiest ways to find out about such events is via the web.

The major source for the whole of the UK is the Geneva page (the Genuki calendar of GENealogical EVents and Activities) at <**geneva.weald. org.uk**>, run by Malcolm Austen on behalf of Genuki and the FFHS. This lists events from the SoG's programme, any family history society events submitted, as well as the regional family history fairs regularly held around the country. The National Archives' programme of events, many of which are of interest to genealogists, can be found online at <www.nationalarchives.gov.uk/events/>. The FRC's calendar of events is at <www.familyrecords.gov.uk/frc/news_events/events_calendar.htm>.

Many societies have lectures on internet-related topics, details of which can be found on their websites. The SoG offers a substantial programme of IT-related events, many of which cover the use of the internet for genealogy. Details will be found on the Society's website at <www.sog.org.uk/events/calendar.html>.

▌MAGAZINES AND JOURNALS

Many genealogical publications have a related website, with at least a list of contents for the current issue and in some cases material from back issues.

The website of *Family Tree Magazine* can be found at <www.family-tree.co.uk>, while its sister publication, *Practical Family History*, has a page on the same site at <www.family-tree.co.uk/sister.htm>. Each lists the contents of the current issue. There is an online list of contents for the IHGS's journal, *Family History,* at <www.family-history.org>. *Your Family Tree* has a website at <www.futurenet.com/yourfamilytree/> with contents for the six most recent issues. *Family History Monthly* does not have a website at the time of writing.

The National Archives' *Ancestors* magazine has a website at <www.ancestorsmagazine.co.uk>, which includes extracts from the articles in each issue. There is a regular internet news section and articles about online genealogy. The *Ancestors* website includes a subject index to all issues, and there is a list of the internet topics covered in each issue at <www.spub.co.uk/ancestors.html>.

The SoG's website has a subject and name index to the *Genealogists' Magazine* at <www.sog.org.uk/genmag/>. The Society's computer magazine, *Computers in Genealogy*, has a website at <www.sog.org.uk/cig/> with lists of contents and synopses of articles, though no new material has been added for some years. A number of the articles are available on the site. *Computers in Genealogy* is due to cease publication at the end of 2005.

While *Computers in Genealogy* is the only UK computer genealogy journal, a number of others which cover online genealogy are published in English-speaking countries. Foremost among these is *Genealogical Computing*, a US journal published quarterly by Ancestry.com, which regularly covers the use of the internet for genealogy. Details can be found in the Ancestry.com online bookshop at <shops.ancestry.com>. Copies are available for consultation at the SoG and other major genealogical libraries.

The bimonthly magazine *Local History* has a website at <www.local-history.co.uk> with an index to the contents of past issues back to 1984 at <www.local-history.co.uk/Issues/>, as well as the usual listing for the latest issue. The site also provides links to other local history resources on the web, and a useful listing of local history societies at <www.local-history.co.uk/Groups/>.

The most comprehensive online listing is the 'Magazines, Journals, Columns & Newsletters' page on Cyndi's List at <www.cyndislist.com/magazine.htm>. Subtitled 'Print & Electronic Publications for Genealogy', this page provides links to websites for many print magazines, though many of course will be of interest only to those with North American ancestry.

PERSI, the Periodical Source Index, at <www.ancestry.com/search/rectype/periodicals/persi/main.htm> is a subscription database at Ancestry.com containing 'a comprehensive subject index to genealogy and local history periodicals written in English and French (Canada) since 1800'.

History in Focus is an online history magazine at <www.history.ac.uk/ihr/Focus/> (note the upper-case *F*) published by the Institute of Historical Research in London. It takes a thematic approach to history, with each issue designed to 'provide an introduction to the chosen topic and to help stimulate interest and debate – the series will concentrate on highlighting books, reviews, websites and conferences that relate to the theme'. Although the material derives from recent academic research, and genealogists are not the target readership, many issues contain items relating to social history that are likely to interest the family historian, and the website reviews for each topic are particularly useful.

For sites relating to non-genealogical publications, see 'Newspapers' on p. 105.

ONLINE NEWSLETTERS

As well as print publications there are, of course, online columns and newsletters for genealogists. Links to these will be found on Cyndi's List at <www.cyndislist.com/magazine.htm>. The majority are US-based, so are not of relevance to UK genealogists where they deal with genealogical records, but many have useful material on general genealogical topics, including the use of the internet.

It is impossible here to give an overview of all the US newsletters, but a good place to start is Ancestry.com, which hosts a number of weekly columns, all accessible from <www.ancestry.com/learn/library/columnists/>. Of these, Drew Smith's 'Digital genealogy' and Elizabeth

Kelley Kersten's 'GC extra' are particularly recommended for material on the use of computers and the internet in genealogy.

Probably the best known of these columns to UK genealogists is Dick Eastman's Online Genealogy Newsletter, which originated on the Genealogy Forum in CompuServe, long before CompuServe was part of the internet. It carries details of new genealogy software and CD-ROMs, genealogical developments on the internet, new websites and more. Although the main focus is on genealogy and IT, it is not exclusively so. Dick has many contacts in the UK, and regularly includes items of genealogy news from Britain.

There are two versions of the newsletter. The Standard Edition is available free of charge and you can read the articles online at <**www.eogn.com/newsletter/**>. The Plus Edition is only available by paying a subscription of $5.95 for three months or $19.95 for a year. It contains all the articles in the Standard Edition with the addition of one or two extra items each week. For the Standard Edition you can sign up to receive an email when it is published; the Plus Edition is emailed to you. There is also a discussion board where you can discuss individual articles and general IT topics with Dick and other readers.

All issues back to the very first in January 1996 can be searched by keyword from <**www.eogn.com/search/**>, while there is also a browsable archive of newsletters up to October 2002 at <**www.ancestry.com/library/view/columns/eastman/eastman.asp**>.

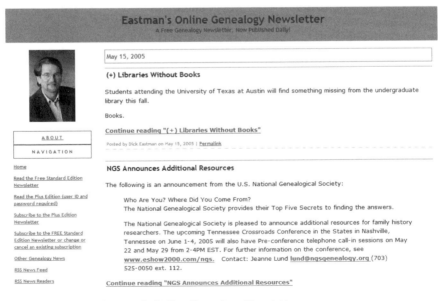

Figure 18-2 Dick Eastman's Online Genealogy Newsletter

There is no general newsletter specific to the British Isles. The 'Genuki UK Family History News' email newsletter, edited by Rob Thompson, ceased at the end of 2004, though back issues can still be consulted at <archiver.rootsweb.com/th/index/UK-FAMILYHISTORYNEWS/>.

There are a few specialist mailing lists which are used to disseminate news. As mentioned on p. 230, John Fuller's NEW-GENLIST mailing list will keep you up to date with new genealogy mailing lists, while NEW-GEN-URL allows people to publicize new genealogy websites. Subscription details for all these lists will be found at <www.rootsweb.com/~jfuller/gen_mail_computing.html>. The Cyndi's List mailing list announces additions to Cyndi's List (see <www.cyndislist.com/maillist.htm>).

Many of the major organizations and data services mentioned in this book have electronic newsletters designed to keep you informed of developments – the National Archives, the FFHS, ScotlandsPeople and Origins, to name just a few. There will normally be a link to information about such newsletters on the home page of a site. There are links to some of the best known on the Genuki mailing lists page at <www.genuki.org.uk/indexes/MailingLists.html>.

A consolidated page of links to recent announcements of genealogy news will be found at <www.rssgenealogy.com>. This includes genealogy blogs (see below), and announcements from genealogy software companies, as well as newsletters.

BLOGS

Over the last couple of years blogs (short for 'web logs') have become very popular as a form of online personal journal. In one sense, they are nothing new – a blog is just a form of online newsletter. Dick Eastman's newsletter at <www.eogn.com>, for example, has recently been recast as a blog without any great upheaval, the blog format allowing it to be updated daily rather than weekly as it had been previously. But one of the things that has made blogging popular is the arrival of sites which making setting up and maintaining a blog very straightforward, without any need to find web space and learn how to create a website from scratch. Blogs also allow visitors to leave comments on each posting. Although reading someone's daily ramblings about how they're getting on with their genealogical research is of limited interest, the blog format is ideal for publishing snippets of information or opinion.

Unfortunately, there do not seem to be any blogs specifically devoted to British family history, though Hugh Watkins's Exploring Ancestry blog (see p. 44) is useful for UK Ancestry subscribers. However, some US-based genealogy blogs such as Genealogy and How at <www.genealogyandhow.com> include items relating to the British Isles or of general interest. A more personal use of blogging can be seen in Kylie Veale's blog at <**www.veale.com.au/phd/html/journal.html**>, which records the progress of her PhD research into online genealogy. Another interesting use is represented by the Genealogical Society Exchange blog at <**genexchange. blogspot.com**>, designed to help genealogical societies share ideas.

For more extensive discussion of blogging for genealogists, see Dick Eastman's piece 'Blogs explained' at <**eogn.typepad.com/eastmans_online_ genealogy/2004/12/blogs_explained.html**>. There is a brief list of genealogy blogs (as of December 2004) at <**www.genealogyandhow.com/2004/ 12/genealogy-blogosphere.htm**>, and a search for 'genealogy blog' in a search engine will turn up many more. Blogger.com at <**www.blogger.com**> is probably the best known site for starting your own blog.

▌ SOFTWARE

The web is an excellent source of information about genealogical software, since all the major software companies, and many individual software authors, have websites providing details of their products. Genealogy shareware can be downloaded from the sites, and even for normal commercial products there will often be a trial or demo version available for download.

It is not possible here to provide a guide to genealogy software, but there are a number of useful resources on the web to point you in the right direction. A very comprehensive listing is the one on Cyndi's List at <**www. cyndislist.com/software.htm**>. George Archer has a listing of 'All Known Genealogy Software Programs in the World' downloadable from <**wdn. com/~garcher/allgen.zip**>. Although now rather out of date, it is still valuable for details of some of the less well known programs.

With so many software packages available, deciding which to buy can be very difficult. There is a useful comparative guide by Bill Mumford at <**www.mumford.ca/reportcard/**> which scores all the main Windows genealogy programs on a dozen criteria, including data recording, reports, source documentation, multimedia and internet features, etc. Richard S. Wilson has a similar page on 'Comparing Genealogy Software Programs' at <**www.rwilson.us/comparison.htm**>. However, such pages do not always have details for the most recent program versions, so it will be worth checking the features either on the website of the software manufacturer – most easily found from Cyndi's List at <**www.cyndislist.com/ software.htm#Software**> – or the software retailers listed in the following section. Dick Eastman's newsletter (see above) is the best way to keep up with new genealogy software releases, and often provides fairly detailed reviews.

If you are just starting to use a computer for genealogy, it is probably worth downloading one of the three major freeware genealogy database programs for Windows:

- **Personal Ancestral File** (currently at version 5.2) is a program developed by the LDS Church for its own members and made available for free download. It can be downloaded from the FamilySearch site at <www.familysearch.org> – click on **Order/Download Products** on the opening screen and then select **Software Downloads – free**. A manual can also be downloaded.
- **Legacy** (currently version 5.0) has been made available as freeware by The Millennia Corporation, and this can be downloaded from <www.legacyfamilytree.com>. This is the Standard Edition, which can be upgraded online to the Deluxe Edition for $19.95.
- **Ancestry Family Tree** is a freeware program from Ancestry.com, downloadable from <www.ancestry.com/aftexec/>. Note that you can only download the program with Internet Explorer and not with other browsers.

Note that these are very substantial downloads (between 5Mb and 13Mb) and could be lengthy if you have a dialup rather than broadband connection.

There are a number of resources for users of handheld computers. The Software page on Cyndi's List has a section devoted to 'Handhelds, Palmtops and PDAs' at <www.cyndislist.com/software.htm#Palm>. Beau Sharborough provides an annual 'roundup' of information about PDAs for genealogists, the latest of which is for 2004 at <www.rootsworks.com/pda2005/>. If you have a handheld computer running the Palm OS, then you will find Palmsource's expert guide to genealogy software at <www.palmsource.com/interests/genealogy/> useful. As well as a list of the software currently available, this page also has a list of relevant discussion forums.

For normal commercial software, some of the online shops discussed in the next section offer a selection, while specialist suppliers have a wider range and can offer more detailed advice. The main suppliers of genealogy software in the UK are:

- Back to Roots <www.backtoroots.co.uk>
- S&N Genealogy <www.genealogysupplies.com>
- TWR Computing <www.twrcomputing.co.uk>.

Most genealogical software companies also have online ordering facilities, and if you can survive without a printed manual, you can often download the software after making a credit card payment.

▌ONLINE SHOPS

There are an increasing number of online shops for genealogy books, data and software. Almost all use secure online ordering, though some are just online lists and orders must be sent by email or post.

The FFHS's online shop, GENfair, is at <**www.genfair.co.uk**> and sells not only the Federation's own publications, both books and data, but also books from many other publishers. In order to make an online purchase your browser needs to download the shopping software, but you can browse the site without doing this. As mentioned on p. 307, the site also includes many 'stands' where the publications of local family history societies can be bought.

Parish Chest at <**www.parishchest.com**> is an 'online family history fair' with products from around 40 different suppliers, each of whom has a separate page on the site listing their products. Unfortunately this means that material relating to a particular county, for example, may be in many different areas of the site, but there is a search facility that lets you search for items of interest.

The IHGS has an online shop at <**www.ihgs.ac.uk/shop/**>. In addition to buying books and software online, you can also use the site to book places on the Institute's courses.

The National Archivist site has an online shop at <**shop.nationalarchivist. com/acatalog/**> offering genealogy software and a wide ranged of scanned books on CD-ROMs.

The Archive CD Books Project has built up a very substantial collection of historical books scanned onto CD-ROM, covering every type of printed material, available from their online shop. The main page is at <**www.archivecdbooks.org**> and there are distinct sites devoted to books from Great Britain, Australia, Canada, the Netherlands and the USA. Sites with scanned books from Ireland, New Zealand, South Africa, Germany and Denmark are promised. The British site at <**www.rod-neep.co.uk**> provides general information about the project.

The National Archives has an online bookshop at <**www.nationalarchives. gov.uk/bookshop/**>, from which you can buy this book at a discount if this isn't your own copy. The Society of Genealogists has an online shop for its own publications at <**www.sog.org.uk/acatalog/**>, which can also be used to book places on the Society's lectures and courses.

The Internet Genealogical Bookshop, run by Stuart Raymond, has a website at <**www.samjraymond.btinternet.co.uk/igb.htm**>. Books must be ordered by email and paid for on receipt of invoice.

Many other bookshops are listed on Cyndi's List at <**www.cyndislist. com/books.htm**>. For a list of genealogy bookshops in the UK, North

America and Australasia, consult Margaret Olson's 'Links to Genealogy Booksellers' at <homepages.rootsweb.com/~socgen/Bookmjo.html>, though be warned that some of the UK links were seriously out of date when I looked at them in mid-2005.

If you are searching for second-hand books you will find many booksellers online. Yahoo UK has a substantial list at <uk.dir.yahoo.com/ Regional/Countries/United_Kingdom/Business_and_Economy/Shopping_ and_Services/Books/Bookstores/Antique_ _Rare_ _and_Used/>. There are also sites, such as UKBookworld at <ukbookworld.com> or Abebooks at <www.abebooks.co.uk>, that will search the catalogues of many individual booksellers. John Townsend has a large stock of second-hand genealogy books, with an online catalogue but offline ordering and payment, at <www.johntownsend.demon.co.uk>.

The online auction site eBay at <www.ebay.co.uk> has a wide selection of genealogy items for sale, mainly books and CD-ROMs. These can be found under **Non-Fiction Books | Genealogy/FamilyHistory**, though searching on "Genealogy" may be quicker. The newsgroup soc.genealogy. marketplace carries postings by those selling genealogical products or individuals trying to find a taker for second-hand material.

SECURE PURCHASING

Concern is often expressed about the security of online payments, and many people are wary of making online purchases, but the reservations are out of all proportion to the actual risks. In fact, online transactions are much more secure than ordering over the phone or allowing a waiter to take the card out of your sight. As long as your browser is using a secure connection, which means that anything you type in is encrypted before being sent across the internet to the supplier, your card details will be infinitely more secure than most of the ways you already use your card.

The clearest indication that the security risks on the internet are low is that the credit card companies themselves are not unduly concerned. Their online leaflet 'Card Fraud, the Facts 2004' at <www.cardwatch.org.uk/ pdf_files/cardfraudfacts2004.pdf> states that most internet fraud 'involves using card details fraudulently obtained in the real world to make card-not-present transactions in the virtual world'. This is certainly bad news for retailers but hardly a cause for concern about e-commerce among card-holders. Contrary to the impression you might have, 'the incidence of computer hackers stealing and using cardholder data from websites is very low'.

The leaflet offers several pieces of advice for safe internet shopping, of which the most important are:

- Only shop at secure websites – ensure that the security icon, the locked padlock or unbroken key symbol, is showing in the bottom right of your browser window before sending your card details. The beginning of the retailer's internet address will change from 'http' to 'https' when a purchase is made using a secure connection. Use sites you can trust, for example sites you know or that have been recommended to you or that carry the TrustUK logo.
- Keep PINs, passwords and personal information safe – always be wary of emails asking you to click on a link or confirm your details. Reputable retailers, banks and the police would never ask you to disclose or confirm sensitive personal or security information, including your PIN. If in doubt, phone the organization first.

The leaflet is summarized on the Government's Crime Reduction site at <**www.crimereduction.gov.uk/fraud16.htm**>.

Official guidance from the Department of Trade and Industry about secure online shopping can be found on the Consumer Direct site, which has a number of fact sheets with consumer advice on using the internet at <**www.consumerdirect.gov.uk/general/internet/**>. There is also basic advice on 'Internet scams' at <**www.consumerdirect.gov.uk/goods-service/scams/ fs_i01.shtml**>.

The only real dangers are that a supplier will subsequently store your credit card details unencrypted on a computer which is then stolen or hacked into (which is just as likely to happen with telephone orders), or that you have bought something from a bogus company. As long as you are dealing with an established supplier, such as those mentioned here, there is no reason to be suspicious of online transactions.

Although individual credit card purchases are the most common way of paying for goods and services over the internet, there is an alternative method you may come across. Web-based payment systems like PayPal (<**www.paypal.com**>) and WorldPay (<**www.worldpay.co.uk**> for the UK site) work by giving you an account from which you can then make online payments. All your financial transactions are with the payment system itself, which pays other sites on your behalf, so you are only giving your financial details to a single site. This sort of system is particularly good for traders who may not qualify to accept credit card payments, and is much used by online auction systems such as eBay, where the participants are private individuals rather than businesses and would not be permitted to accept credit card payments.

SERVICE ONLINE

In fact a more significant problem with online suppliers is getting hold of them to deal with problems relating to your order or the product you have bought, particularly if the website gives no phone number or postal address. However, online traders based in the UK are bound by the same consumer protection legislation as any other trader, and there is a non-profit organization called TrustUK <**www.trustuk.org.uk**>, endorsed by the Government, which has been set up to promote good practice in online trading. The TrustUK website has a page devoted to 'What to look out for when buying online', which offers advice on how to make trouble-free internet purchases.

TrustUK also approves other schemes for guaranteeing good practice and levels of service in online shopping. Any business trading online under a TrustUK-approved scheme undertakes to:

- Protect your privacy
- Ensure that your payments are secure
- Help you to make an informed buying decision
- Let you know what you have agreed to, and how to cancel orders should you need to
- Deliver the goods or services ordered within the agreed time period
- Protect children
- Sort out any complaints, wherever you live.

Before the advent of the internet, purchasing anything abroad from the comfort of the UK was far from straightforward. Online shopping has made this much easier and, of course, those who live outside the UK can now easily order materials from British genealogy suppliers. Some practical difficulties remain: returning wrong or faulty products is not made easier by the internet, though of course it is no more difficult than with traditional catalogue-based home shopping.

Also, you are less likely to be familiar with the reputations of overseas traders, which could be a source of concern in areas where UK consumer legislation does not apply – an impressive website does not guarantee quality of service, let alone financial viability. However, one of the strengths of the internet is that it is a good word-of-mouth medium, and it is very unlikely that there could be an unreliable company whose misdeeds have escaped being reported in the genealogy newsgroups or mailing lists. These are therefore good places to look for reports from other customers on their experiences with companies, or to place a query yourself. For software, the soc.genealogy.computing newsgroup is full of comments, positive and negative, on software products and the companies that supply them. For UK genealogy companies, look at the archives of the soc.genealogy.britain newsgroup for past comments on genealogy suppliers, or post a query yourself.

▋PROFESSIONAL RESEARCHERS

There are many reasons, even with the internet, why you might want to employ a professional genealogist to undertake research for you: if you cannot get to the repository where original records are held, whether for reasons of time or distance; or if the records themselves are difficult for the non-specialist to use or interpret.

The SoG has a leaflet 'Employing a professional researcher: a practical guide' on its website at <**www.sog.org.uk/leaflets/researcher.html**>, while Cyndi's List has a page on 'Professional Researchers, Volunteers & Other Research Services' at <**www.cyndislist.com/profess.htm**>.

The Association of Genealogists and Researchers in Archives (AGRA) is the professional body for genealogical researchers, with a website at <**www.agra.org.uk**>. This provides a list of members, and an index to this by specialism, whether geographical or subject-based. Many but not all of the Association's members can be contacted by email. The Association's code of practice is also available on the site.

The National Archives' website also has a database of Independent Researchers who are prepared to undertake commissions for research in records at the National Archives. The database is accessible from <**www.nationalarchives.gov.uk/irlist/**> and must be searched by subject heading, chosen from a drop-down list.

For Scotland, the Association of Scottish Genealogists and Record Agents (ASGRA) is the professional association for researchers, and its site at <**www.asgra.co.uk**> has details of members and their specialisms.

If you have Irish ancestry, the Irish Family History Foundation's network of genealogy centres may be of use. There is a centre for each county, both in the Republic of Ireland and in Northern Ireland, and these hold copies of local material from many of the main sources for Irish genealogy (census, tithe applotments, etc.) as well as transcripts of many parish registers. The centres provide research services using these records. The Foundation's website at <**www.irishroots.net**> has links to all the local centres as well as details of services available. Individual researchers for Ireland can be found on the National Archives of Ireland website at <**www.nationalarchives.ie/genealogy/researchers.htm**> and the Association of Professional Genealogists in Ireland at <**indigo.ie/~apgi/**>.

▋LOOKUP SERVICES

If all you need is someone to check a particular reference for you, employing a professional researcher will be overkill. The internet makes it easy to find someone with access to particular printed publications, or records on CD-ROM, who will do a simple lookup for you. So-called 'lookup exchanges' give a list of publications and the email address of someone prepared to do searches in each. There is, unfortunately, no central listing of these, but most are county-based and there are links to the relevant exchanges from the individual Genuki county pages. The county forums on RootsChat at <www.rootschat.com> have places for posting lookup offers and requests.

Since lookups are done entirely on a voluntary basis, requests should be as specific as possible, and you may need to use a specific subject line in your message – see the details at the top of each page before sending a request. And, of course, be reasonable in what you expect someone to do for you in their own time.

CHAPTER 19

ISSUES FOR ONLINE GENEALOGISTS

While online genealogy is essentially about finding and making use of information, it is important to be aware of some general issues involved in using internet resources and in using the web as a publishing medium. Also important are the limitations in what is and is not likely to be on the internet. The aim of this chapter is to discuss some of these issues.

GOOD PRACTICE

Needless to say, technophobes, Luddites and other folk of a backward-looking disposition are happy to accuse the internet of dumbing down the noble art of genealogy – anything so easy surely cannot be sound research.

Loath as I am to agree with technophobes, there is actually some truth in this. Though the medium itself can hardly be blamed for its misuse, the internet does give scope to a sort of 'trainspotting' attitude to genealogy, where it is just a matter of filling out your family tree with plausible and preferably interesting ancestors, with little regard for accuracy or traditional standards of proof. Because more can (apparently) be done without consulting original records, it becomes easy to overlook the fact that a family tree constructed solely from online sources, unchecked against *any* original records, is sure to contain many inaccuracies even if it is not entirely unsound. This is far from new, of course; today's is hardly the first generation in which some people have been more concerned for their family tree to be impressive rather than accurate. The internet just makes it easier both to construct and to disseminate pedigrees of doubtful accuracy.

But genealogy is a form of historical research, and you cannot really do it successfully without developing some understanding of the records from which a family history is constructed, and the principles for drawing reliable conclusions from them.

Some of the tutorial materials mentioned in Chapter 2 address these issues, but the most coherent set of principles and standards available online are those developed by the US National Genealogical Society, which can be found at <**www.ngsgenealogy.org/comstandards.htm**>:

- Standards for Sound Genealogical Research
- Standards for Using Records, Repositories, and Libraries
- Standards for Use of Technology in Genealogical Research
- Standards for Sharing Information with Others
- Guidelines for Publishing Web Pages on the Internet.

The first of these is essential reading for anyone new to genealogy. The third is important enough in the context of this book to bear reproducing in full – see the box overleaf.

USING ONLINE INFORMATION

The nature of the primary data online has an important implication for how you use information found on the internet: you need to be very cautious about inferences drawn from it. For a start, *all* transcriptions of any size contain errors – the only question is how many. Where information comes from parish registers, for example, you need to be cautious about identifying an individual ancestor from a single record in an online database. The fact that you have found a baptism with the right name, at about the right date and in about the right place does not mean you have found an ancestor. How do you know this child did not die two weeks later; how do you know there is not a very similar baptism in a neighbouring parish whose records are not online; how do you know there is not an error in the transcription? As more records are put online with images accompanying transcriptions or indexes, the last question may become less important, but no future internet development will allow you to ignore the other questions.

Unfortunately, the very ease of the internet can sometimes make beginners think that constructing a pedigree is easier than it is. It is not enough to find a plausible-looking baptism online. You have to be able to demonstrate that this must be (not just 'could be') the same individual who marries 20 years later or who is the parent of a particular child. The internet does not do this for you. The only thing it can do is provide *some* of the material you need for that proof, and even then you will have to be more careful with online material than you would be with original records.

In particular, negative inferences (for example so and so wasn't born later than such and such a date) can be very important in constructing a family tree, but the original material on the internet will rarely allow you to make such inferences. Not even where a particular set of records has

Standards For Use Of Technology In Genealogical Research
Recommended by the National Genealogical Society

Mindful that computers are tools, genealogists take full responsibility for their work, and therefore they –

- learn the capabilities and limits of their equipment and software, and use them only when they are the most appropriate tools for a purpose.

- refuse to let computer software automatically embellish their work.

- treat compiled information from on-line sources or digital databases like that from other published sources, useful primarily as a guide to locating original records, but not as evidence for a conclusion or assertion.

- accept digital images or enhancements of an original record as a satisfactory substitute for the original only when there is reasonable assurance that the image accurately reproduces the unaltered original.

- cite sources for data obtained on-line or from digital media with the same care that is appropriate for sources on paper and other traditional media, and enter data into a digital database only when its source can remain associated with it.

- always cite the sources for information or data posted online or sent to others, naming the author of a digital file as its immediate source, while crediting original sources cited within the file.

- preserve the integrity of their own databases by evaluating the reliability of downloaded data before incorporating it into their own files.

- provide, whenever they alter data received in digital form, a description of the change that will accompany the altered data whenever it is shared with others.

- actively oppose the proliferation of error, rumor and fraud by personally verifying or correcting information, or noting it as unverified, before passing it on to others.

- treat people online as courteously and civilly as they would treat them face to face, not separated by networks and anonymity.

- accept that technology has not changed the principles of genealogical research, only some of the procedures.

been put online in its entirety could you start to be confident in drawing a negative inference. For example, there is no simple conclusion to be drawn if you fail to find an ancestor in the 1901 census. He or she could have no longer been alive, or was living abroad, or is in the census but has been mistranscribed in the index, or was in the census until the relevant enumeration book went missing. Of course, such problems relate to all indexes, not just those online, but you can never be *more* confident about online records.

Also, you need to be very cautious about drawing conclusions based not on primary sources but on compiled pedigrees put online by other genealogists. Some of these represent careful genealogical work and come with detailed documentation of sources, others may just have a name and possible birth year, perhaps supplied from memory by an ageing relative – insufficient detail to be of great value, with no guarantee of accuracy, and impossible to verify. At best you can regard such materials as helpful pointers to someone who might have useful information, or to sources you have not yet examined yourself. It would be very unwise simply to incorporate the information in your own pedigree simply because it appears to refer to an individual you have already identified as an ancestor.

COPYRIGHT AND PRIVACY

The internet makes it very easy to disseminate information, but just because you *can* disseminate material it does not mean that you *should*. Both websites and email messages are treated by the law as publications. If you include material you did not create, you may be infringing someone's copyright by doing so. Of course, genealogical facts themselves are not subject to copyright, but a modern transcription of an original record will be, and a compilation of facts in a database is also protected, though for more limited duration.

This means you should not put on your own website, upload to a database, or post to a mailing list:

- Material you have extracted from online or CD-ROM databases
- Material scanned from books that are still in copyright
- Genealogical data you have received from others (unless they give their permission of course).

There is an exemption of 'fair use' which allows some copying, but this is only for purposes of criticism or private study, not for republishing or passing on to others. Extracting a single record from a CD-ROM and emailing it to an individual is probably OK, but posting the same information to a mailing list, which means it will be permanently archived, is not. Note that some companies include licence conditions with CD-ROMs stating that you must not supply the information to third parties. Whether or not such a strict condition would stand up in court – a similar ban on look-ups in a reference book would seem to be ridiculous – the supply of genealogy data on CD-ROM would be threatened by significant levels of copyright infringement.

A number of people have been shocked to find their own genealogical databases submitted to an online pedigree database without their knowledge. Mark Howells covers these issues very thoroughly in 'Share and Beware – Sharing Genealogy in the Information Age' at <**www.oz.net/ ~markhow/writing/share.htm**>. Barbara A. Brown discusses the dissemination of 'dishonest research' in 'Restoring Ethics to Genealogy' at <**www. iigs.org/newsletter/9904news/ethics.htm.en**>.

The recently revised Crown Copyright rules, however, mean that you *can* include extracts from unpublished material held by the National Archives as long as the source is acknowledged (see 'Crown Copyright in the Information Age' at <**www.opsi.gov.uk/advice/crown-copyright/ crown-copyright-in-the-information-age.pdf**>). In general, you should have no qualms about the textual content of other historical material over 150 years old if you are transcribing it yourself. But a transcription of a manuscript document is probably to be regarded as an original work, and recently made images of documents are certainly copyright, regardless of the status of the original document. If in doubt, consult the repository concerned.

David Hawgood's 'Copyright for Family Historians' at <**www.genuki. org.uk/org/Copyright.html**> offers some guidance tailored for genealogists, while for more general information, there is the official government-sponsored website on copyright at <**www.intellectual-property.gov.uk**>.

Another important issue is privacy. There may be no legal bar to publishing information about living people without their permission, particularly if it's taken from official and public sources, but most people regard this as discourteous at the very least. In any case, it's difficult to see any need to publish such information in order to further genealogical research, which makes it hard to justify. On the other hand, in the absence of any legal protection, it's not clear what you can do about it if someone publishes personal information about your immediate family online.

Myra Vanderpool Gormley discusses these issues in 'Exposing Our Families To The Internet' at <**www.ancestry.com/columns/myra/Shaking_ Family_Tree06-19-97.htm**>. The privacy policies of some pedigree databases and tools for removing living people from genealogy databases are discussed in Chapter 10, p. 143.

There is a mailing list, LEGAL-ENGWLS, for the discussion of 'legal aspects of genealogical research in England and Wales including copyright, database rights, data protection, and privacy' – details at <**lists.rootsweb. com/index/intl/UK/LEGAL-ENGWLS.html**>.

FUTURE DEVELOPMENTS

ON THE HORIZON

There can be no argument about the wealth of genealogical material that is available on the web, and it will only increase. What is difficult to foresee is whether, and when, some of the less widely used types of record will be put online. It is easy to appreciate the market for census records, and the rationale for funding archival cataloguing projects. But will county record offices, say, be able to fund the digitization of material with a less universal appeal? The limitation on digitization is not technical; it is the amount of manpower required to transcribe or index handwritten documents. Barring a dramatic breakthrough in handwriting recognition, it would be optimistic to expect the technical situation to change, so it will be a matter of funding and potential income.

However, you can get some idea of the sort of thing that might be coming by looking at the Archives Portal's list of most recent projects at <**www. portal.nationalarchives.gov.uk/portal/searches/recentlist.asp**>, while doing a keyword search at <**www.portal.nationalarchives.gov.uk/portal/searches/ searchbykeyword.asp**> will bring up a list of all relevant projects – keywords can be chosen from a drop-down list which includes 'Family History', 'Local History', 'National Library Catalogues', 'Digitisation', 'Directories'. Another hint of what might be on the horizon comes from TNA's document titled 'New Opportunity – Licensed Internet Associateships From the National Archives' at <**www.nationalarchives.gov.uk/ business/pdf/licensed_associateships.pdf**> which lists the classes of record they consider good candidates for digitization, listed on the final page.

It seems that, whatever else happens at a national level, there will be lots of local and specialist projects.

Genealogists make up a very sizeable and growing constituency, and there is no reason why grants should not be forthcoming to fund digitization projects if archives and genealogical organizations can draft the required proposals, and genealogists make it clear which records they regard as the priority.

QUALITY CONCERNS

While the increasing amount and range of genealogical material online, both free and commercial, can only be a good thing, it does not mean that current developments are without their problems and that there are no matters of concern.

The National Audit Office's report on the 1901 census, 'Unlocking the Past: the 1901 census online', at <**www.nao.org.uk/publications/nao_ reports/02-03/02031259.pdf**> does much to address the technical problems of this project, but it offers no analysis of why the transcriptions were immediately perceived as poor. You might think that this is water under the bridge, but the GRO's rejected plans for the digitization of civil registration records suggest otherwise: one of the most worrying things about their proposals was the low quality threshold they envisaged for the indexing and digitization. As the FFHS put it in their submission to parliament, 'the level of accuracy will only be that which is affordable by the company winning the tender'.[19] To call this 'scandalous' hardly does it justice. That anyone, let alone a government agency, should take such a view about the nation's most important set of personal records is truly shocking. After the 1901 census, the least we might expect is that rigorous quality standards, and the procedures to support them, would be required in tenders for genealogical data conversion.

It seems that family historians will need to continue to be vigilant about official proposals for genealogical data services. The advisory panels for the National Archives and ScotlandsPeople are one way of doing this, and no doubt the Society of Genealogists and the Federation of Family History Societies will continue to make collective representations.

With commercial companies, of course there is no possibility of vigilance before the fact, but it may be that it is not so necessary. With civil registration index material and several of the censuses available at more than one site, one hopes that competition, not to mention pride in their own products, will prompt sites to strive for a good reputation. On the other hand, perhaps this is an optimistic view: as there are so many reasons why one might fail to locate an ancestor in a census, only some of which can be put down to poor transcription or indexing, it may be they can afford to be cavalier about quality.

With so many massive datasets where it's impossible to check every entry, one of the problems is that it is extremely difficult to come to firm conclusions about which site has the best quality data and which has the most (and most serious) errors. Also, because of differences in the search facilities, it's not always possible to make direct comparisons – there's no easy way to tell whether Ancestry's 1901 census has more gender errors in relation to particular forenames than TNA's, because the latter doesn't allow a search on forename and gender alone. This means it's not even a straightforward matter to develop diagnostic tests, as a basis for some sort of independent benchmarking.

But it would be a start if we could persuade data providers, commercial or otherwise, to institute some better safeguards to identify obvious errors, as well as inconsistencies that suggest possible error.

---

19 At <www.publications.parliament.uk/pa/cm200405/cmselect/cmdereg/118/4102607. htm>.

FINDING MATERIAL

Information is not much use if you cannot find it. Search engines are able to capture only a fraction of the material on the web. Of course, it is impossible to foresee technological advances, but there is no sign at the moment that the coverage of search engines will improve significantly. Websites of individual genealogists, in particular, will probably become harder to find. In addition, the increasing amount of data held in online databases is not discoverable by search engines, and it becomes more important than ever for gateways and directories (or even books!) to direct people to the sources of online data.

The quality of indexing provided by search engines is limited by the poor facilities currently available for marking up text in HTML with semantic information. Search engines cannot tell that Kent is a surname in 'Clark Kent' but a place name in 'Maidstone, Kent'. This is because web authors have no way of indicating this in HTML markup. As so many British surnames are the names of places or occupations, this is a significant problem for UK genealogists.

The situation could improve when a more sophisticated markup language, XML, starts to be used widely on the web – this allows information to be tagged descriptively, and will enable the development of a special markup language for genealogical information. Such a development (and its retrospective application to material already published on the web) is some way off and will require considerable work, though the LDS Church has made a start by proposing an XML successor to GEDCOM (see the GEDCOM FAQ at <**www.familysearch.org/Eng/Home/FAQ/faq_gedcom. asp**>). But the benefits of such an approach are already apparent in a project like the Old Bailey Proceedings (see p. 157), which can distinguish between the names of the accused, the victim, and witnesses.

Another problem is the increasing number of sites with surname resources, making it impossible to check *everywhere* for others who share your interests. Mercifully, the number of pedigree databases (see Chapter 10) remains manageable for the present, but the number of sites, particularly message boards, with surname-related material makes exhaustive searching impossible.

However, on a more positive note, it's clear that, with so much work being done on making archival catalogues available, it will become easier than ever to track down original documents in record offices and other repositories, and genealogists in general will start to make much more use of records that in the past only the expert might have been able to take advantage of.

OUTLOOK

In spite of the undoubtedly welcome developments that will be taking place online, it's important to keep a sense of perspective. Nothing that happens on the internet in the next decades is going to affect what genealogists need to do: consult records and share information. Nor is there any prospect of basing a family tree solely on digitized records – just consider how long it's taking to get civil registration records online!

The internet is not going to 'automate' family history or modify its principles and methods. Nor does it need to – there is nothing wrong with the traditional methods of genealogy. What the internet has revolutionized is not the process of genealogy, but the ease with which some of the research can be carried out.

The key aspects of this are:

- the number of people with shared interests who have internet access
- the increasing amounts of data available online.

Although microfilm and microfiche are not going to disappear in the immediate future, any more than books are, the internet is now the publishing medium of choice for all large genealogical data projects, whether official, commercial or volunteer-run. Where public records or public funding is concerned, the web, because of its low cost and universal access, is the default publishing medium as a matter of principle.

Both the number of internet users and the amount of data available have now reached a critical mass, with the result that the genealogist without internet access is in a minority and at a relative disadvantage in access to data and contact with other genealogists.

Of course you can still research your family tree without using the internet, but why would you choose to?

INTERNET GLOSSARY

Adobe Acrobat	A file format, popular for documents which need to be made available online with fixed formatting. Files have the extension .pdf, and so the term 'PDF file' is often used. See p. 293.
blog	An online personal journal (short for 'web log').
charter	The description of the aims and coverage of a news-group.
client	A piece of software on a user's computer which connects to a *server* to retrieve or submit data, e.g. your email software is an 'email client' which connects to your provider's email server; your browser is a 'web client' which gets data from a web server.
database	1) A collection of individual items of information ('records') which can be retrieved selectively via a search facility.
	2) A software program for managing data records (short for 'database management system').
directory	1) A collection of links to internet resources, arranged in a hierarchy of subject headings.
	2) On some operating systems, a hierarchical folder containing individual computer files.
domain name	The part of an internet address which is formally registered and owned, and which forms the latter part of a server or host name, e.g. *bbc.co.uk* is the domain name, while <news.bbc.co.uk> and <www.bbc.co.uk> are individual servers within that domain.
download	To transfer a file from another computer to your own computer.

FAQ
Frequently Asked Questions, a document listing common questions in a particular area, along with their answers.

flame
A rude or abusive message.

freeware
Software which can be downloaded and used free of charge (cf. *shareware*).

FTP
File Transfer Protocol, a method of transferring files across the internet (see p. 300).

gateway
1) A subject-specific *directory*.
2) A link which allows messages to pass between two different systems, e.g. newsgroups and mailing lists.

GIF
A graphics file format, mainly used on the web for graphic design elements, less suitable for colour photographs.

hit
A matching item retrieved in response to a search.

host
A computer connected to the internet which allows other internet users access to material stored on its hard disk.

hosting
Providing space on a *host* for someone's web pages.

HTML
HyperText Markup Language, in which web pages are written.

ISP
Internet Service Provider.

JPEG
A graphics file format, mainly used for photographs.

mailing list
A discussion forum which uses email.

meta-search engine
A site which automatically submits a search to a number of different *search engines*.

netiquette
The informal, consensual rules of online communication.

newsgroup
Open discussion forums held on an internet-wide network of 'news servers'.

plug-in
A piece of software used by a web browser to display files it cannot handle on its own.

portal
A collection of internet resources for a particular audience – see the discussion on p. 15.

robot
A piece of software which trawls the internet looking for new resources, used by search engines to create their indexes.

search engine
Commonly, a website which has a searchable index of web pages, though more accurately *any* piece of software which searches an index.

searchbot
A piece of software which searches the web for you (a contraction of 'search robot').

server	A computer, usually with a permanent internet connection, which responds to requests from a *client* for data. There are different types of server according to the service offered, e.g. mail server, web server, list server.
shareware	Software which can be downloaded free of charge, but requires payment for registration after a trial period (cf. *freeware*).
spam	Unsolicited messages sent to multiple recipients.
subscribe	To join a mailing list.
URL	Uniform Resource Locator, a standard way of referring to internet resources so that each resource has a unique name. In the case of a web page, the URL is the same as the web address.
World Wide Web	A collection of linked pages of information retrievable via the internet.
XML	eXtensible Markup Language, a more sophisticated and flexible markup language than *HTML*, likely to be increasingly used for websites.

There are many internet glossaries online:

- The Internet Language Dictionary at <**www.netlingo.com/inframes.cfm**>
- Foldoc (the Free On-line Dictionary of Computing) <**foldoc.doc.ic.ac.uk/foldoc/**>
- Google Groups Usenet Glossary <**groups.google.com/googlegroups/glossary.html**>
- Living Internet <**www.livinginternet.com**>.

For glossaries of genealogy terms see p. 13.

BIBLIOGRAPHY

Anthony Adolph, *Collins Tracing Your Family Tree* (Collins, 2004)

Amanda Bevan, *Tracing Your Ancestors in the Public Record Office*, 6th edn (Public Record Office, 2002)

Peter Christian, *Web Publishing for Genealogy*, 2nd edn (David Hawgood, 1999)

Peter Christian, *Finding Genealogy on the Internet*, 2nd edn (David Hawgood, 2002). Full text online at <**www.spub.co.uk/fgi/**>

Jean Cole & John Titford, *Tracing your Family Tree*, 4th edn (Countryside Books, 2003)

David Hawgood, *FamilySearch on the Internet* (David Hawgood, 1998)

David Hawgood, *Genuki* (Federation of Family History Societies, 2000). Full text online at <**www.hawgood.co.uk/genuki/**>

Mark Herber, *Ancestral Trails*, 2nd edn (Sutton, 2004)

David Hey, *Journeys in Family History: The National Archives' Guide to Exploring your Past, Finding your Ancestors* (The National Archives, 2004)

Cyndi Howells, *Cyndi's List*, 2nd edn (Rutledge Hill, 2004)

Cyndi Howells, *Planting Your Family Tree Online* (Genealogical Publishing Company, 2001)

Chris Pomery, *DNA and Family History* (The National Archives, 2004)

Reader's Digest, *Explore Your Family's Past* (Reader's Digest, 2002)

Virginia Shea, *Netiquette* (Albion Books, 1996). Full text online at <**www.albion.com/netiquette/book/**>

Richard S. Wilson, *Publishing Your Family History on the Internet* (Betterway Books, 1999)

INDEX